*Sunset*

# *ideas for great*
# DECORATING

By Scott Atkinson, Christine Barnes, Barbara J. Braasch,
Susan Lang, and the Editors of Sunset Books

Sunset Books ■ Menlo Park, California

## Sunset Books

Vice President, General Manager:
*Richard A. Smeby*

Vice President, Editorial Director:
*Bob Doyle*

Production Director:
*Lory Day*

Director of Operations:
*Rosann Sutherland*

Retail Sales Development Manager:
*Linda Barker*

Executive Editor:
*Bridget Biscotti Bradley*

Art Director:
*Vasken Guiragossian*

## Staff for this book:

Developmental Editor:
*Linda J. Selden*

Copy Editors:
*Phyllis Elving, Marcia Williamson*

Design:
*Barbara Vick*

Illustrations:
*Beverley Bozarth Colgan, Bill Oetinger,
Mark Pechenik, Sally Shimisu*

Photo Director:
*JoAnn Masaoka Van Atta*

Production Coordinators:
*Eligio Hernandez, Patricia S. Williams*

Computer Production:
*Kathy Avanzino Barone, Linda Bouchard,
Susan Bryant Caron*

Principal Photographers:
*Philip Harvey, E. Andrew McKinney*

Proof reader:
*Mary Roybal*

10 9 8 7 6 5 4 3 2 1
First printing July 2003

Copyright © 2003, Sunset Publishing
Corporation, Menlo Park, CA 94025.
First edition. All rights reserved, including
the right of reproduction in whole or in
part in any form.

ISBN 0-376-01260-9
Library of Congress Control Number:
2003104631

Printed in China

For additional copies of *Ideas
for Great Decorating* or any other
Sunset book, see our web site
at *www.sunsetbooks.com* or call
1-800-526-5111.

## An Instant Decorating Library!

*Ideas for Great Decorating* is a compilation of six previously published books that proved to be particularly popular: *Ideas for Great Kitchens, Ideas for Great Bathrooms, Ideas for Great Great Rooms, Ideas for Great Tile, Ideas for Great Window Treatments,* and *Ideas for Great Patios & Decks.* We hope you will find both value and comprehensiveness in this collection. You'll be able to decorate the home of your dreams—including an outdoor patio or deck—with one book as your guide. From a comfortable armchair you can examine scores of up-to-the-minute rooms in full color or explore the latest in beautiful designs and materials. When you're ready to dig in, you'll also find solid planning information as practiced by the pros.

Many individuals and firms assisted in the planning of these Ideas for Great books. We'd especially like to thank The Plumbery and The Kitchen Source at The Bath & Beyond in San Francisco, and Chugrad McAndrews for *Ideas for Great Kitchens* and *Ideas for Great Bathrooms;* Alchemie Ceramic Studio, ASN Natural Stone, Country Floors, Fireclay Tile, Galleria Tile, Chugrad McAndrews, Oceanside Glasstile, Buddy Rhodes Studio, Lynne B. Roe, ANN SACKS Tile & Stone, Diane Swift, Joseph A. Taylor of the Tile Heritage Foundation, and Tile Visions for *Ideas for Great Tile;* Calico Corners, Juliana Edlund, Kathy Harding of Harding & Raez Interiors, Joan Osburn, Kim Smith of Young's Interiors, and Karen Winger for *Ideas for Great Window Treatments;* and ASN Natural Stone of San Francisco, Eco Timber of Berkeley, California, and Chugrad McAndrews for *Ideas for Great Patios & Decks.*

Design credits for specific photos are listed on pages 670–680.

# contents

*Sunset*

*ideas for great*

# KITCHENS

By the Editors of
Sunset Books

Sunset Books ■ Menlo Park, California

# contents

# what's cooking?

E FFICIENCY, flexibility, and a bit of fun—that's the recipe for today's kitchen. More varied than ever, kitchen design features sophisticated new colors, fresh styles, and innovative components.

Many homeowners appreciate the clean lines and bright colors of the European-style kitchen. Its frameless cabinets, in high-gloss lacquer or laminate, hold a score of efficient aids such as lazy Susans, wire-frame pullouts, and built-in pantry packs. Appliances are built in, from the refrigerator and microwave oven to the toaster. Gleaming gourmet accessories abound. Even sinks and faucets debut in new shapes and finishes.

On the other hand, cheery country and traditional styles are on the rebound. Often the focus of a kitchen is its freestanding range, either a high-output "residential/commercial" model or a reconditioned heirloom. Adding warmth and hospitality are homey accents like pot racks, freestanding furniture, open shelving or plate rails, tiled backsplashes, and hardwood flooring.

In many families, the kitchen is evolving into an all-purpose room, including dining table or breakfast booth, computer desk, entertainment area, fireplace—even laundry center. Popular as ever are kitchen islands and peninsulas, which define the work area yet allow the cook to converse freely with family and friends.

# A PLANNING PRIMER

**S**IT back, close your eyes, and visualize your dream kitchen. Do sleek new cabinets and gleaming appliances float before your eyes? Now come back down to earth. What's the clearance between the dishwasher and that new granite-topped island? If you're not quite sure how to fit the pieces together, this book will help. **USE THIS CHAPTER** as a workbook, a sequential course in basic kitchen planning. Begin by evaluating your existing kitchen; wind your way through layout and design basics; then meet the professionals who can give you a hand. **FOR IDEAS** and inspiration, peruse the color photos in the next two chapters, examining the many views of successful design solutions and getting familiar with the latest in cooktops, downlights, and built-ins. That dream kitchen will reappear, this time on solid ground.

# taking stock

**FIRST THINGS FIRST.** *Before you rush into a shopping spree, take the time to survey what you have now. A clear, accurate base map is your most useful planning tool.*

## Measure the space

To make your kitchen survey, you'll need either a folding wooden rule (shown above) or steel measuring tape. First, sketch out your present layout (don't worry about scale), doodling in windows, doors, islands, and other features. Then measure the elements along each wall at counter height.

After you finish measuring one wall, total the figures; then take an overall measurement from corner to corner. The two figures should match, Measure the height of each wall in the same manner.

## Make a base map

Now draw your kitchen to scale on graph paper—most kitchen designers use ½-inch scale (¹⁄₂₄ actual size). An architect's scale is helpful but isn't really required. Some standard drafting paper with ¼-inch squares and a T square and triangle greatly simplify matters.

The example shown below includes both centerlines to the sink plumbing and electrical symbols—outlets, switches, and fixtures. Add any other features that may affect your plans.

## A SAMPLE BASE MAP

### ARCHITECTURAL SYMBOLS

WALL

WINDOW

DOOR SWING

DUPLEX WALL OUTLET

WALL SWITCH
CEILING FIXTURE

WALL FIXTURE

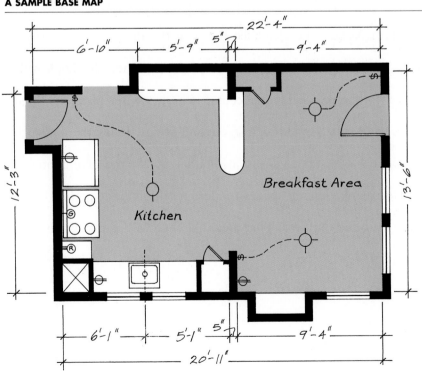

# A KITCHEN QUESTIONNAIRE

This questionnaire will organize your responses to your present kitchen and stimulate your thoughts about exactly what you want in a new one. When used along with your base map, it also provides a starting point for discussing your ideas with architects, designers, or showroom personnel. Note your answers on a separate sheet of paper, adding any important preferences or dislikes. Then gather your notes, any clippings you've collected, and a copy of your base map, and you're ready to begin.

1. What's your main reason for changing your kitchen?

2. How many are in your household? List adults, teens, children, seniors, pets.

3. Will this be a two-cook kitchen?

4. Are users right-handed? Left-handed? How tall?

5. Is the kitchen to be used by a disabled person? Is that person confined to a wheelchair?

6. Do you entertain frequently? Formally? Informally? Do you like compartmentalized work spaces or great-room (open) designs?

7. Would you like an island or peninsula?

8. What secondary activity areas do you want?
☐ Baking center  ☐ Planning desk or office
☐ Breakfast nook  ☐ Entertainment center
☐ Laundry/ironing center  ☐ Wet bar

9. Are you considering any structural modifications?
☐ Skylight  ☐ Greenhouse window or sunroom
☐ Second cook's alcove  ☐ Pass-through  ☐ Other

10. Is the kitchen located on the first or second floor? Is there a full basement, crawl space, or concrete slab below? Is there a second floor, attic, or open ceiling above?

11. Can present doors and windows be moved? Could an interior wall be removed to enlarge the kitchen? Is an addition possible?

12. Can existing plumbing be moved? To where?

13. What type of heating system do you have? Do any walls contain ducting?

14. What's the rating of your electrical service?

15. What flooring do you have? Do you need new flooring?  ☐ Wood  ☐ Resilient  ☐ Ceramic tile  ☐ Stone  ☐ Other

16. What are present wall and ceiling coverings? What wall treatments do you like?  ☐ Paint  ☐ Wallpaper  ☐ Wood  ☐ Tile  ☐ Faux finish  ☐ Plaster  ☐ Glass block

17. List your present appliances. What new appliances are you planning? Will they be built in or freestanding?

18. What overall style (for example, high-tech, country, or regional) do you have in mind for your kitchen?

19. What style is your home's exterior? What style are adjacent interior spaces?

20. What color schemes do you prefer?

21. What storage needs do you have? What items do you use daily? Weekly? Monthly? What don't you need? What will you add in the future?

22. What are your cabinet requirements?
☐ Appliance garage  ☐ Pullout shelves
☐ Lazy Susan  ☐ Tilt-down sink front  ☐ Pantry pack
☐ Storage wall with pullout bins  ☐ Tray divider
☐ Drying rack  ☐ Spice storage  ☐ Flatware drawer
☐ Pullout cutting board  ☐ Knife storage
☐ Wine rack  ☐ Waste container  ☐ Recycling bins
☐ Open shelving  ☐ Other

23. Which cabinet materials do you like—wood, laminate, or other? If wood, should it be painted or stained? Light or dark? If natural, do you want oak, maple, pine, cherry? Do you want flat, raised, or recessed panel doors? Glass doors on wall cabinets?

24. Should the soffit space above wall cabinets be boxed in? Open for decorative articles? Or should cabinets run continuous to the ceiling?

25. What countertop materials do you prefer?
☐ Laminate  ☐ Ceramic tile  ☐ Solid-surface
☐ Wood  ☐ Stone  ☐ Stainless steel
More than one material?

26. Do you want a 4-inch or full backsplash? Should it match or contrast with countertops?

27. Would you prefer a vent hood or downdraft stovetop ventilation system? Do you want a decorative ceiling fan?

28. What lighting type or types would work best?
☐ Incandescent  ☐ Fluorescent  ☐ Halogen
☐ 120-volt or low-voltage?

29. What fixture types will you need?
☐ Surface-mounted  ☐ Recessed downlights
☐ Track lights  ☐ Pendant fixtures
☐ Undercabinet strips  ☐ Indirect soffit lighting
☐ Display lights inside cabinets

30. What time framework do you have for completion?

31. What budget figure do you have in mind?

# layout basics

**NOW COMES** *the fun of really planning your new kitchen. Layout is a three-part process that includes weighing basic options; blocking out storage, countertops, and work centers; and double-checking efficient heights and clearances. There's no perfect sequence—the trick is to work back and forth. In very small or oddly shaped spaces you'll certainly need to compromise.*

### Classic kitchen layouts

While brainstorming, it helps to have some basic layout schemes in mind. The floor plans shown below are practical both for utilizing space well and for employing efficient work triangles (see facing page).

**ONE-WALL KITCHEN.** Small or open kitchens frequently make use of the one-wall design, incorporating a single line of cabinets and appliances. This is not ideal, as there is a lot of moving back and forth—from refrigerator to range to sink. Still, it's the only choice for some small areas or open floor plans.

**CORRIDOR KITCHEN.** A kitchen open at both ends is a candidate for the corridor or galley kitchen; the design works well as long as the distance between opposite walls is not too great. Traffic flow can be a problem—it's tough to divert kitchen cruisers away from the cook.

**L-SHAPED KITCHEN.** This layout utilizes two adjacent walls, spreading out the work centers; typically, the refrigerator is at one end, range or wall ovens are at the other end, and the sink is in the center. The L-shaped kitchen gives a comfortable work triangle. You'll have to decide how to utilize the corner space (see page 17).

### SAMPLE LAYOUTS & WORK TRIANGLES

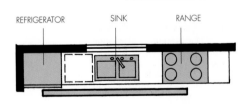

**ONE-WALL KITCHEN**

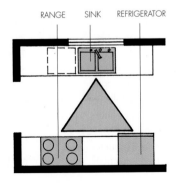

**CORRIDOR KITCHEN**

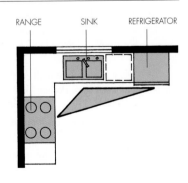

**L-SHAPED KITCHEN**

# CONSIDER THE WORK TRIANGLE

Ever since kitchen layout studies in the 1950s introduced the term, designers have been evaluating kitchen efficiency by means of the work triangle. The three legs of the triangle connect the refrigerator, sink, and range (or cooktop). An efficient work triangle reduces the steps a cook must take during meal preparation. The ideal sum of the three legs is 26 feet or less, with individual legs no shorter than 4 feet and no longer than 9 feet. Whenever possible, the work triangle should be uninvaded by traffic flow.

Today, the reign of the work triangle is being challenged by two-cook layouts, elaborate island and peninsula work centers, and specialized appliances such as modular cooktops, built-in grills, and microwave and convection ovens. Nevertheless, the triangle is still a valuable starting point for planning kitchen efficiency. It may be useful to sketch in multiple triangles to cover different requirements.

**U-SHAPED KITCHEN.** Three adjacent walls make up the efficient U-shaped design (efficient, that is, as long as there is sufficient distance between opposite walls). Often this layout opens up space for auxiliary work areas in addition to the central work triangle—for example, a second sink for washing vegetables, a baking center, a second cooktop and dishwasher, or even a complete work center for a second cook.

**G-SHAPED KITCHEN.** This newly popular shape combines the efficient U-shaped layout with an attached peninsula at one end. The G shape offers plenty of opportunities for specialized work centers and helps shield the cook from distracting traffic; however, it may seem a little claustrophobic to some cooks.

**WHAT ABOUT AN ISLAND?** A kitchen island is a popular addition to many kitchen remodels. The extra cabinets and countertop add storage and work space, block off unwanted traffic flow, and can function as an eating counter.

On the minus side, islands can cramp space and cut into work triangles and traffic flows. And it's usually easier to bring utilities to a "landlocked" peninsula than to a free-floating island.

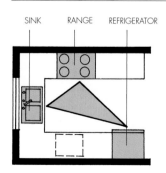

**U-SHAPED KITCHEN**

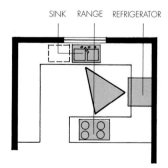

**G-SHAPED KITCHEN**

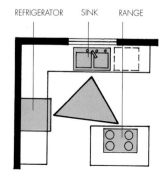

**L-SHAPED WITH ISLAND**

## KITCHEN PLANNING AT A GLANCE

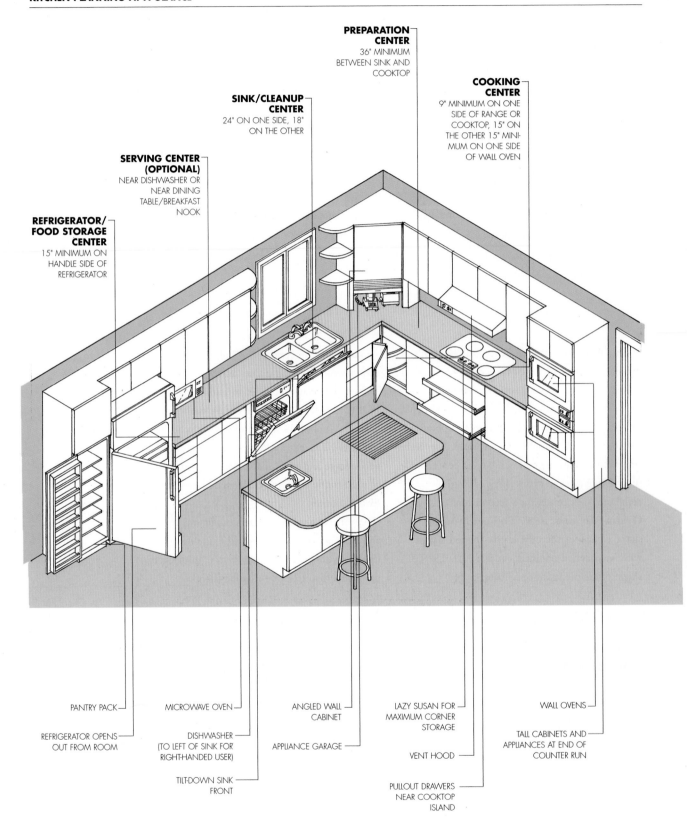

**PREPARATION CENTER**
36" MINIMUM BETWEEN SINK AND COOKTOP

**COOKING CENTER**
9" MINIMUM ON ONE SIDE OF RANGE OR COOKTOP, 15" ON THE OTHER 15" MINIMUM ON ONE SIDE OF WALL OVEN

**SINK/CLEANUP CENTER**
24" ON ONE SIDE, 18" ON THE OTHER

**SERVING CENTER (OPTIONAL)**
NEAR DISHWASHER OR NEAR DINING TABLE/BREAKFAST NOOK

**REFRIGERATOR/ FOOD STORAGE CENTER**
15" MINIMUM ON HANDLE SIDE OF REFRIGERATOR

PANTRY PACK

REFRIGERATOR OPENS OUT FROM ROOM

MICROWAVE OVEN

DISHWASHER (TO LEFT OF SINK FOR RIGHT-HANDED USER)

TILT-DOWN SINK FRONT

ANGLED WALL CABINET

APPLIANCE GARAGE

LAZY SUSAN FOR MAXIMUM CORNER STORAGE

VENT HOOD

PULLOUT DRAWERS NEAR COOKTOP ISLAND

WALL OVENS

TALL CABINETS AND APPLIANCES AT END OF COUNTER RUN

## Mapping the work centers

One key to planning an efficient kitchen layout is to concentrate on the work centers, allowing for both adequate countertop space and storage in each area.

The drawing on the facing page outlines the major points you'll need to consider. The National Kitchen & Bath Association compiled these figures by studying many efficient kitchens, big and small; you may or may not be able to fit in all these features.

When plotting the centers, think through the steps you'd take bringing food into the house, preparing it, serving it, cleaning up, and storing plates and utensils. As a rule, items should be stored in the area of first use. The one exception? Everyday dishes and flatware: you might store them near the point of last use—the dishwasher or sink.

To sketch your evolving ideas, lay tracing paper on top of your new base map. You might make scale outlines of cabinet and appliance shapes, photocopy them, and cut them out. Move the cutouts around on a tracing of your base map, then draw the shapes onto the plan.

**REFRIGERATOR/FOOD STORAGE CENTER.** Allow at least 15 inches of countertop space on the handle side of the refrigerator as a landing area for groceries; if that's impossible, locate this space across from the fridge, no more than 48 inches away. Ideally, the refrigerator is at the end of a cabinet run, near an access door, with the door rotating out. (Need to place the refrigerator inside a cabinet run? Think about a built-in, side-by-side model, or one or more under-counter pullouts, as shown on pages 102–103.)

Also consider an 18- or 21-inch drawer unit. A smaller unit is too narrow to be useful, and drawers 24 inches or larger almost inevitably fill up with junk.

An over-the-refrigerator cabinet is a good storage place for infrequently used items. Custom pullouts or a stock "pantry pack" are an excellent use for the tall, narrow space beside the refrigerator.

**SINK/CLEANUP CENTER.** More time is spent at the sink than anywhere else in the kitchen. So a main sink should be central in your plan, ideally at the center of the cook's work path. It's best to locate the sink and cleanup center between the refrigerator and range or cooktop.

Allow at least 24 inches of counter space on one side of the primary sink and 18 inches on the other. If you're planning a second, smaller sink elsewhere, those clearances can be less—3 inches and 18 inches. (In a corner, these figures may be the sum of two angled countertops.)

Traditionally, designers place the dishwasher for a right-hander to the left of the sink area and to the right for a lefty. But do whatever makes you comfortable. Either way, it should be placed within 36 inches of the sink's edge.

Plan to store cleaning supplies in or near the sink area. Many kinds of bins and pullouts—both built-ins and retrofits—are available for under-sink storage. Tilt-down fronts for sponges and other supplies are available on many sink base cabinets. This is also a prime location for waste and recycling bins; again, pullout and tilt-down options abound.

**PREPARATION CENTER.** It's ideal to locate this center adjacent to a sink and between the sink and cooktop or range. Alternatively, put it opposite the refrigerator on an island or peninsula supplied with a secondary sink and a cooktop.

Plan a minimum of 36 inches of countertop. If two centers are adjacent, add 12 inches to the longest countertop requirement. If two cooks work together, plan a minimum of 36 inches of counter space for each. A second sink can help the second cook immensely.

Although it may not be a good idea to raise and lower countertop heights (if you have an eye toward resale, that is), the preparation center is a good place to customize. A marble counter insert is a boon for the serious pastry chef.

Appliance garages with tambour or paneled doors are still popular for this area, but be sure to leave at least 16 inches of usable counter depth outside such a cupboard. Need a place for

# UNIVERSAL DESIGN

If you are remodeling to accommodate a disabled or elderly person, or if you're simply looking down the road, be aware of the growing trend toward universal or barrier-free design. In many cases, general recommendations for kitchen heights and clearances (see facing page) now reflect universal guidelines; but in addition, it's best to consider some specifics.

For example, does the kitchen have a low counter for sitting to chop vegetables or to cut out cookies? Is there a stool to pull up by the range for stirring food? Are doorways wide enough for a wheelchair? Is the eating area set up for easy access? What about the sink?

Special heights, clearances, and room dimensions may be required. To accommodate a wheelchair, the room's access door must be at least 32 inches wide and traffic patterns 36 inches wide. You'll also need to plan open turnaround areas near the sink and major appliances that are at least 30 by 48 inches.

It's important to leave the spaces below both sink and preparation areas open for seated use. The knee space should be a minimum of 30 inches wide by 27 inches high by 19 inches deep. Plan to enclose plumbing and gas and electric lines, but leave an access door.

Frequently used storage areas should be located between 15 and 48 inches high. Likewise, place door handles, switches, and other controls no higher than 48 inches from the floor.

You should also exchange standard door knobs, faucet handles, and cabinet hardware for levers and pulls that can be operated with one closed hand or a wrist.

Think comfort and safety. Allow extra task lighting for aging users, and strive to provide as many visual aids as possible—such as contrasting countertops and switches, and large, easy-to-read range or cooktop controls placed at the front of appliances. Aim for matte finishes, not glaring, glossy surfaces. Flooring should be slip resistant—carpeting is gaining in popularity. A batch-feed (lid-controlled) garbage disposal is safer than one controlled by a wall switch. Side-by-side refrigerators and side-hinged ovens are simpler to access. Consider electric heat sources instead of open gas flames. Some cooktops have automatic-shutoff features.

Also be on the lookout for the growing number of controls, fixtures, and fittings specifically designed for "universal" use.

spices or staples? An open shelf or backsplash rack will do the job. Knife drawers, pullout cutting boards, and waste or compost bins are other niceties to consider here.

**COOKING CENTER.** Plan at least 9 inches of countertop area on one side of the range or cooktop and 15 inches on the other as a landing area for hot pans and casseroles, and to allow pot handles to be turned to the side (for safety's sake) while pots are in use. If the range or cooktop meets a tall end cabinet, keep 15 inches on the open side and at least 3 inches on the cabinet side. Protect the cabinet with flame-retardant material.

You should also allow 15 inches of countertop beside a wall oven. If the oven does not open into a major traffic area, the 15 inches can be opposite, but no more than 48 inches away. Typically, wall ovens are placed at the end of a cabinet run. As separate wall ovens are used less frequently than the cooktop or range, they're considered outside the primary work triangle.

Although we think of the microwave oven as part of the cooking center, many people prefer to place it near the refrigerator/freezer or in a separate center. Mount the microwave so its bottom is from 24 to 48 inches off the floor. Again, plan to have at least one 15-inch landing zone nearby.

Plan to store frequently used pots and pans in base pullout drawers mounted on heavy-duty, full-extension drawer guides (see page 83). Frequently used utensils should be kept at least 22 inches off the floor.

**SERVING CENTER.** Everyday dishes, glassware, flatware, serving plates, and bowls, as well as napkins and place mats, belong in this optional area. A warming oven (see "A Shopper's Guide," page 98) might be handy here. The dishwasher should be nearby; some models even have integral trays that can be placed right into the flatware drawer.

**SOME AUXILIARY CENTERS.** Several additional kitchen areas have become so popular that they are quickly gaining work-center status. Before solidifying your plans, think about whether or not you wish to include one or more of these features:

- baking center
- breakfast/dining area
- menu-planning/office center
- built-in pantry or wine cellar
- entertainment center
- laundry/ironing center

## Heights & clearances

As shown at top right, there are standard minimum clearances in a well-planned kitchen. These dimensions ensure enough space for a busy cook and some occasional cookie monsters; enough door clearance for free access to cabinets, dish-washer, and refrigerator; and enough traffic lanes for diners to comfortably enter and exit a breakfast nook. No entry doors, cabinet doors, or appliance doors should swing into each other.

Shown at bottom right are standard depths and heights for base and wall cabinets and shelves, plus recommended heights for stools, desktops, and eating counters.

Counter heights are based on kitchen industry standards but may be altered to fit the cook or cooks—provided that base cabinets and appliances can be accommodated. The formula for ideal food-preparation height is 2 to 3 inches below the cook's flexed elbows. For baking tasks, it's 5 inches below the elbows.

## Turning corners

Corners are a problem when planning cabinet runs. Simply butting two cabinets together wastes storage space in the corner: on a base run, this adds up to a 24- by 24-inch waste; above, it's 12 by 12 inches.

Angled cabinets, blind cabinets, and lazy Susans (see pages 84–85) all supply corner solutions. Be sure that drawers and doors of adjacent units will open without banging into each other. Cabinet manufacturers offer so-called "filler strips" to cure this common woe; the strips separate cabinets by an inch or two.

**STANDARD KITCHEN DIMENSIONS**

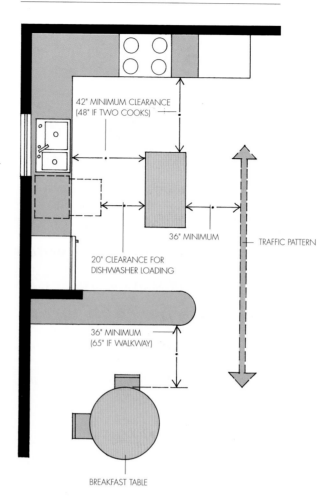

42" MINIMUM CLEARANCE
(48" IF TWO COOKS)

36" MINIMUM

20" CLEARANCE FOR
DISHWASHER LOADING

TRAFFIC PATTERN

36" MINIMUM
(65" IF WALKWAY)

BREAKFAST TABLE

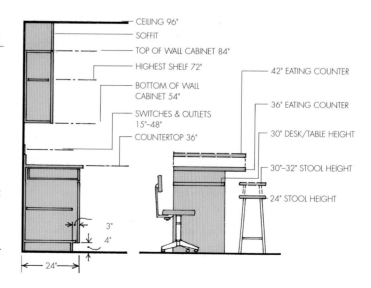

CEILING 96"
SOFFIT
TOP OF WALL CABINET 84"
HIGHEST SHELF 72"
BOTTOM OF WALL CABINET 54"
SWITCHES & OUTLETS 15"–48"
COUNTERTOP 36"

42" EATING COUNTER
36" EATING COUNTER
30" DESK/TABLE HEIGHT
30"–32" STOOL HEIGHT
24" STOOL HEIGHT

3"
4"
24"

# design ideas

**WITH A BASIC** *floor plan now in mind, you can begin to fine-tune your decorating scheme. Wall and ceiling coverings, cabinetry, flooring, hardware, and even appliances are powerful tools for evoking both style and mood. Style effects are directly linked to color, pattern, texture, size, and shape.*

*You'll find scores of design ideas beginning on page 28. Here, we introduce some reliable basic design concepts for you to use as starting points.*

*Do you want your new kitchen streamlined or unfitted? The high-tech design shown at right shows a minimalist's touch, sporting sealed concrete countertops, colorful European-like steel cabinets, floating shelves, and unrimmed sink. By contrast, the kitchen shown on the facing page features a furniture-like center island, a freestanding range, glass pendant fixtures, and earthy surfaces of maple, limestone, and tile.*

## What's your style?

A decorating style has physical characteristics that identify it with a particular region, era, or artistic movement—Colonial, English Victorian, Southwestern, Arts and Crafts, Art Deco, and so on. Because certain colors, materials, and decorative motifs are linked to certain historic decorating styles, they can be used to evoke the character of a period—or simply to personalize and give dignity to a bland modern room.

Representative kitchen styles include the following:

- Period (or traditional)
- Regional
- Country
- Romantic
- Contemporary (also high-tech)
- Eclectic

This said, rarely are styles slavish replicas of historical designs. More typically, designers select among elements that echo the mood of a

period or regional look. What matters is that you choose a style and mood you find sympathetic and comfortable. And if the kitchen is open to adjoining spaces, it should match or at least complement the overall look. Study the photos on pages 28–75—you may find style ideas there that you'd like to adapt to your own setting. Consumer and trade publications also offer helpful information on up-to-date decor.

*Plentiful natural light beams in on this combined kitchen and breakfast area—a study in white and green. A faux finish on open walls and in soffit areas echoes the soft green marble countertops and backsplashes. White cabinets, ceiling, and appliances provide brightness. The floors are bleached oak.*

## Looking at lines

Most kitchens incorporate different types of line—vertical, horizontal, diagonal, curved, and angular. But often one predominates and characterizes the design. Vertical lines give a sense of height, horizontal lines add width, diagonals suggest movement, and curved and angular lines impart grace and dynamism.

Continuity of lines gives a sense of unity to a design. Try an elevation (head-on) sketch of your proposed kitchen. How do the vertical lines created by the base cabinets, windows, doors, wall cabinets, and appliances fit together? It's not necessary for them to align perfectly, but you might consider small changes such as varying the width of a wall cabinet (without sacrificing storage) to line it up with the range, sink, or corresponding base cabinet.

You can follow a similar process to smooth out horizontal lines. Is the top of the window continuous with the top of the wall cabinets? If the window is just a few inches higher, you can either raise the cabinets or add trim and a soffit.

## Weighing the scale

When the scale of kitchen elements is proportionate to the overall scale of the kitchen, the design seems harmonious. A small kitchen seems even smaller if fitted with large appliances and expanses of closed cabinets. Open shelves, large windows, and a simple overall design can visually enlarge such a room. Smaller objects arranged in a group help balance a large item, making it less obtrusive.

## Studying shapes

Take a look at the shapes created by doorways, windows, cabinets, appliances, peninsula, island, and other elements in your kitchen. If these shapes are different, is there a basic sense of harmony? If you have an arch over a cooking niche, for example, you may want to repeat that shape in a doorway, on frame-and-panel cabinet doors, or in the trim of an open shelf. Or you can complement an angled peninsula by adding an angled corner cabinet or cooktop unit on the opposite wall.

## Color concepts

The size and orientation of your kitchen, your personal preferences, and the mood you want to create all affect the selection of your color scheme. Light colors reflect light, making walls appear to recede; thus, decorating a small kitchen in light colors can make it seem more spacious. Dark colors absorb light and can make the ceiling feel lower or visually shorten a narrow room.

When considering colors for a small kitchen, remember that too much contrast has the same effect as a dark color: it reduces the sense of expansiveness. Contrasting colors work well for adding accents or drawing attention to interesting structural elements. But if you need to conceal a problem feature, it's best to use one color throughout the area.

Depending on the orientation of your kitchen, you may want to use warm or cool colors to balance the quality of natural light.

*The earthy textures and soft colors of tumbled marble tiles are interspersed with brighter, random-pattern accent tiles in this backsplash. An eggplant-colored concrete countertop makes a bold, contemporary statement.*

While oranges, yellows, and colors with a red tone impart a feeling of warmth, they also contract space. Blues, greens, and colors with a blue tone make an area seem cooler—and larger.

A light, monochromatic color scheme (using different shades of one color) is restful and serene. Contrasting colors add vibrancy and excitement to a design, though a color scheme with contrasting colors can be overpowering unless the tones of those colors are subdued. Another possibility is to include bright, intense color accents in furnishings and accessories that can be changed without too much trouble or cost.

After you narrow down your selections, make a sample board to see how your choices work together. Color charts for various appliances and fixtures are readily available, as are paint chips, fabric swatches, and wallpaper and flooring samples.

Remember that the color temperature and intensity and the placement of light fixtures will have an effect on overall color rendition. For details, see pages 110–111.

## Texture & pattern

Textures and patterns work like color in defining a room's space and style. The kitchen's surface materials may include many different textures—from a shiny tile backsplash to rough oak cabinets to an appealingly irregular quarry-tile floor.

Rough textures absorb light, make colors look duller, and lend a feeling of informality. Smooth textures reflect light and tend to suggest elegance or modernity. Using similar textures helps unify a design and create a sustained mood.

Pattern choices must harmonize with the predominant style of the room. Although we usually associate pattern with wall coverings or cabinet doors, even natural substances like wood and stone create patterns.

While variety in texture and pattern adds interest, too much variety can be overstimulating. It's best to let a strong feature or dominating pattern be the focus of your design and choose other surfaces to complement rather than compete with it.

# remodeling realities

*IF YOUR KITCHEN requires only a new cooktop, a faucet, and some wallpaper to update it, you probably won't need to find out just what lurks behind those walls. But if you're relocating or adding appliances, installing a vent hood, or removing a wall, you'll have to bone up on some basic remodeling realities, whether or not you're hiring professional help. These next pages offer an overview of kitchen systems.*

## STRUCTURAL FRAMING

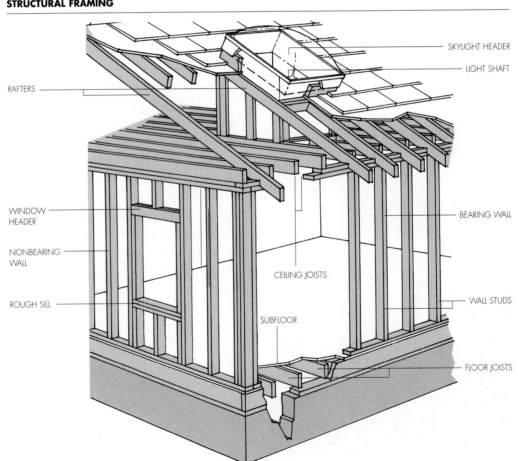

RAFTERS

SKYLIGHT HEADER

LIGHT SHAFT

WINDOW HEADER

NONBEARING WALL

ROUGH SILL

CEILING JOISTS

SUBFLOOR

BEARING WALL

WALL STUDS

FLOOR JOISTS

## Structural changes

If you're planning to open up space, add a sky-light, or lay a heavy stone floor, your kitchen remodel may require some structural modifications.

As shown at left, walls are either bearing (supporting the weight of ceiling joists and/or second-story walls) or nonbearing. If you're removing all or part of a bearing wall, you must bridge the gap with a sturdy beam and posts. Nonbearing (also called partition) walls can usually be removed without too much trouble—unless pipes or wires are routed through them.

Doors and windows require special framing, as shown; the size of the header depends on the width of the opening and your local building codes. Skylights require similar cuts through ceiling joists and/or rafters.

Planning a vaulted or cathedral ceiling instead of ceiling covering and joists? You'll probably need to install a few beams to maintain structural soundness.

Hardwood, ceramic tile, and stone floors require very stiff underlayment. A solution is to beef up the floor joists and/or add additional plywood or particleboard subflooring on top. You may also need stronger floor framing to handle a large commercial range.

## Plumbing restrictions

What if you wish to move the sink to the other side of the room or add a kitchen island with a vegetable sink or wet bar?

Generally, it's an easy job—at least conceptu-ally—to extend existing water-supply pipes to a new sink or appliance. But if you're working on a concrete slab foundation, you'll need to drill through the slab or bring the pipes through the wall from another point above floor level.

Every house has a main soil stack. Below the level of the fixtures, it's your home's primary drainpipe. At its upper end, which protrudes through the roof, the stack becomes a vent. A new fixture located within a few feet of the existing main stack usually can be drained and vented directly by the stack. In some areas, a

**PLUMBING PIPES**

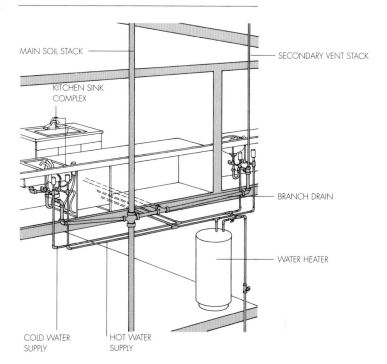

MAIN SOIL STACK

KITCHEN SINK COMPLEX

SECONDARY VENT STACK

BRANCH DRAIN

WATER HEATER

COLD WATER SUPPLY

HOT WATER SUPPLY

new island sink can be wet-vented (using an oversize branch drain as both drain and vent), though this is illegal in other areas. Sometimes a fixture located far from the main stack will require its own branch drain and a secondary vent stack of its own rising to the roof—an expensive proposition. Be sure to check your local codes for exact requirements.

When you convert from electricity to gas or simply relocate a gas appliance, keep in mind some basic guidelines. The plumbing code, or separate gas code, will specify pipe size (figured according to cubic-foot capacity and the length of pipe between the meter or storage tank and the appliance). All gas appliances should have name plates stamped with a numerical rating in BTUs per hour.

Each appliance must have a nearby code-approved shutoff valve with a straight handle so gas can be easily turned off during an emergency.

## Electrical requirements

Electrical capacity is probably the problem most often overlooked by would-be remodelers. All those shiny new appliances take power to operate! In fact, the typical kitchen makeover requires three to five new circuits.

Requirements for electrical circuits serving a modern kitchen and dining area are clearly prescribed by the National Electrical Code (NEC). Plug-in outlets and switches for small appliances and the refrigerator must be served by a minimum of two 20-amp circuits. Light fixtures share one or more 15- or 20-amp circuits, which also run, as a rule, to the dining room, living room, or other adjacent space.

If you're installing a dishwasher and/or disposal, you'll need a separate 20-amp circuit for each. Most electric ranges use an individual 50-amp, 120/240-volt major appliance circuit. Wall ovens and a separate cooktop may share a 50-amp circuit. Kitchen receptacles must be protected by ground fault circuit interrupters (GFCIs) that cut off power immediately if current begins to leak anywhere along the circuit.

Older homes with two-wire service (120 volts only) of less than 100 amps simply can't support many major improvements. To add a new oven or dishwasher, you may well need to increase your service type and rating, which means updating the service entrance equipment.

**ELECTRICAL WIRING**

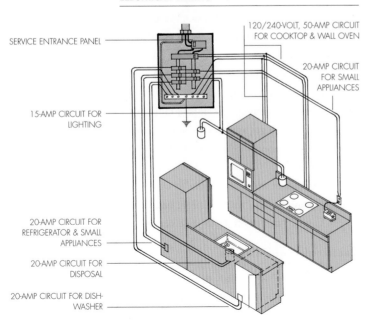

SERVICE ENTRANCE PANEL

120/240-VOLT, 50-AMP CIRCUIT FOR COOKTOP & WALL OVEN

20-AMP CIRCUIT FOR SMALL APPLIANCES

15-AMP CIRCUIT FOR LIGHTING

20-AMP CIRCUIT FOR REFRIGERATOR & SMALL APPLIANCES

20-AMP CIRCUIT FOR DISPOSAL

20-AMP CIRCUIT FOR DISHWASHER

**MECHANICAL SYSTEMS**

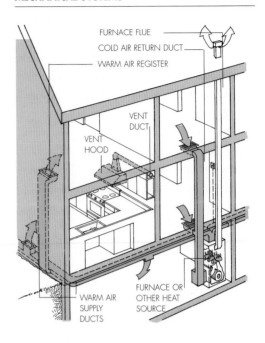

FURNACE FLUE

COLD AIR RETURN DUCT

WARM AIR REGISTER

VENT DUCT

VENT HOOD

WARM AIR SUPPLY DUCTS

FURNACE OR OTHER HEAT SOURCE

## Mechanical (HVAC) systems

Heating, ventilation, and air-conditioning hardware—lumped together as "HVAC" systems—may all be affected by your proposed kitchen remodel. Changes will be governed either by your local plumbing regulations or by a separate mechanical code.

Air-conditioning and heating ducts are relatively easy to reroute, as long as you can gain access from a basement, crawl space, garage wall, or unfinished attic. Radiant-heat pipes or other slab-embedded systems may pose problems; check them out. Registers are usually easy to reposition; the toe space of base cabinets is a favorite spot for retrofits. Don't place any cold air returns in the new kitchen.

Are you planning a new freestanding range, a cooktop, wall ovens, or a built-in barbecue? You'll need to think about ventilation, providing either a hood above or a downdraft system exiting through the floor or an exterior wall. The downdraft system is especially apt for a new kitchen island or peninsula, but vent hoods are more efficient. See pages 100–101 for ventilation principles and options.

## DOLLARS AND CENTS

How much will your new kitchen cost? According to the National Kitchen & Bath Association, the average figure is $22,100. This is, of course, only the sketchiest of estimates. You may simply need to replace countertops, add recessed downlights, reface your cabinets, or exchange a worn-out range to achieve a fresh look. On the other hand, extensive structural changes coupled with ultra-high-end materials and appliances could easily add up to $100,000.

As shown below, kitchen cabinets typically eat up 48 percent of the pie; labor comes in at around 16 percent; countertops add 13 percent; and, on the average, appliances, fixtures, and fittings tally another 12 percent. Structural, plumbing, and electrical changes all affect costs significantly.

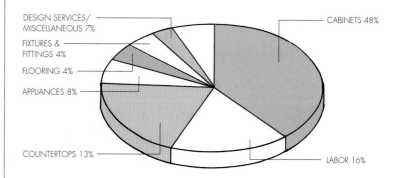

DESIGN SERVICES/ MISCELLANEOUS 7%
FIXTURES & FITTINGS 4%
FLOORING 4%
APPLIANCES 8%
CABINETS 48%
COUNTERTOPS 13%
LABOR 16%

How do you keep the budget under control? For starters, identify whether you're looking at a simple face-lift, a more extensive replacement, or a major structural remodel. Cabinet and appliance prices vary dramatically, depending on whether they're low-, middle-, high-, or ultra-high-end. Obtain ballpark figures in different categories, mull them over, then present your supplier, architect, or designer with a range of options and a bottom line with which you can be comfortable. You can, of course, save substantially by providing labor yourself—but be sure you're up to the task!

If you use the services of a design professional, expect to be charged either a flat fee or a percentage of the total cost of goods purchased (usually 10 to 15 percent). General contractors include their fees in their bids.

Don't make price your only criterion for selection. Quality of work, reliability, rapport, and on-time performance are also important. Ask professionals for the names and telephone numbers of recent clients. Call several and ask them how happy they were with the process and the results. Some may allow you to come and take a look at finished work.

# gearing up

**ONCE YOU'VE** *worked out an efficient layout, planned your storage requirements, and decided on color and design schemes, it's time to draw up a revised floor plan. For help selecting new appliances, cabinets and countertops, flooring, and so on, see "A Shopper's Guide," beginning on page 79. Be sure to think about light fixtures and electrical switches or receptacles. And don't forget such finishing touches as doorknobs and drawer pulls, hinges and moldings, curtains and blinds—details that can really pull a design together.*

*The owners of this urban kitchen wanted more space and a breakfast counter, too, but they had a problem: plumbing pipes ran from floor to ceiling directly through the area. Solution? The pipe run was boxed in and wrapped in classic white woodwork to match the frame-and-panel cabinets.*

## The final plan

Draw your new floor plan, or working drawing, the same way you did the existing plan (see page 10). On the new plan, include existing features you want to preserve and all the changes you're planning to make. If you prefer, you can hire a designer, drafter, or contractor to draw the final plan for you. Elevation sketches aren't usually required, but they'll prove helpful in planning the work.

For more complicated projects, your city or county building department may require additional or more detailed drawings of structural, plumbing, and wiring changes. You may also need to show areas adjacent to the kitchen so officials can determine how the project will affect the rest of your house. To discover just which building codes may govern your remodeling proj-

ect and learn whether a permit is required, check with your local building department.

If you do the ordering of materials, you'll need to compile a detailed master list. This will help you keep track of purchases and deliveries. For each item, specify the following information: name and model or serial number, manufacturer, source of material, date of order, expected delivery date, color, size or dimensions, quantity, price (including tax and delivery charge), and—where possible—a second choice.

## Need help?

The listing below covers professionals in kitchen design and construction and delineates distinctions (although there's overlap) between architects, designers, contractors, and other professionals.

Finding the right help need not be daunting. In choosing a professional, look for someone who is technically and artistically skilled, has a proven track record, and is adequately insured against any mishaps on the job. It's also important to work with someone with whom you and your family feel comfortable. A kitchen remodel is more than just a construction project; it's a personal matter.

**ARCHITECTS.** Architects are state-licensed professionals with degrees in architecture. They're trained to create designs that are structurally sound, functional, and aesthetically pleasing. They also know construction materials, can negotiate bids from contractors, and can supervise the actual work. Many architects are members of the American Institute of Architects (AIA). If structural calculations must be made, architects can make them; other professionals need state-licensed engineers to design structures and sign working drawings.

If your remodel involves major structural changes, an architect should definitely be consulted. But some architects may not be as familiar with the latest in kitchen design and materials as other specialists.

**KITCHEN DESIGNERS.** These people know the latest trends in cabinets and appliances, but may lack the structural knowledge of the architect and the aesthetic skill of a good interior designer (see at right).

If you decide to work with a kitchen designer, look for a member of the National Kitchen & Bath Association (NKBA) or a Certified Kitchen Designer (CKD), a specialist certified by the NKBA. These associations have codes of ethics and sponsor continuing programs to inform members about the latest materials and techniques.

**RETAIL SPECIALISTS.** This category includes showroom personnel, building-center staff, and other retailers. Some are quite qualified and genuinely helpful. But others may be motivated simply to sell you more goods. If your kitchen needs only a minor face-lift, this help may be all you need. If you're tackling a large job, check qualifications carefully.

**INTERIOR DESIGNERS.** Even if you're working with an architect or kitchen designer, you may wish to call on the services of an interior designer for finishing touches. These experts specialize in the decorating and furnishing of rooms and can offer fresh, innovative ideas and advice. And through their contacts, a homeowner has access to materials and products not available at the retail level.

Some interior designers offer complete remodeling services, including the increasingly sophisticated field of lighting design. Many belong to the American Society of Interior Designers (ASID), a professional organization.

**GENERAL CONTRACTORS.** Contractors specialize in construction, although some have design skills and experience as well. General contractors may do all the work themselves, or they may assume responsibility for hiring qualified subcontractors, ordering construction materials, and seeing that the job is completed according to contract. Contractors can also secure building permits and arrange for inspections as work progresses.

When choosing a contractor, ask architects, designers, and friends for recommendations. To compare bids, contact at least three state-licensed contractors.

**SUBCONTRACTORS.** If you act as your own contractor, you will have to hire and supervise subcontractors for specialized jobs such as wiring, plumbing, and tiling. You'll be responsible for permits, insurance, and possibly even payroll taxes, as well as direct supervision of all the aspects of construction. Do you have the time and the knowledge required for the job? Be sure to assess your energy level realistically.

# GREAT KITCHEN IDEAS

**I**N THE OLD DAYS, a picture was worth a thousand words. And regardless of the current exchange rate, photos are still the best way to show what's new in kitchen design. **I**N TERMS OF STYLE, these rooms represent as broad a palette as possible. You'll find European cabinets and components, French country motifs, classic brass, high-tech concrete, and stainless steel. But don't worry too much about sticking to one theme: creative kitchens often combine elements of several. **E**ACH REAL-LIFE situation is different, too. Most of these designs address special problems or requests, and some of these solutions may work for you. Many of the ideas can be combined or scaled up or down, depending on your needs. If it's individual units that catch your fancy, you'll find more details in "A Shopper's Guide," beginning on page 79.

great kitchen ideas

# high style

**W**E **OPEN** our showcase with an overview of kitchen looks and layouts. There are big kitchens and small kitchens here, simple hardworking spaces and expansive rooms with the latest in amenities.

When planning, it's best to explore your space preferences early. Do you want your kitchen open or closed? The popular great room is simply any large space that houses the kitchen, eating area, and living areas, thus viewing the kitchen as an entertainment space and bringing family and friends together during meal preparation.

There are potential drawbacks. The open kitchen can seem "cold," and work areas must be blocked out carefully. Noise can be a problem, and privacy is obviously reduced. In remodeling, a great-room layout almost always means knocking out an existing wall or two. Some serious cooks are appalled by the idea of a space where they can't concentrate in solitude, or where messy pots are on view!

The two main poles of kitchen style are country and contemporary. Beyond that, there are period, geographical, romantic, gourmet, and eclectic styles. Hybrids abound. Many new designs strive to blend traditional looks with modern convenience. As a starting point, do you want things streamlined or unfitted? High-tech or homey? Do you wish to display kitchen goods and collectibles or hide them away? You'll see examples of all these approaches on the following pages.

*The view through the column-flanked opening reveals an Arts-and-Crafts kitchen with dark oak flooring, stained cherry woodwork, and an unstained, furniture-like center island.*

*Cheery morning light pours into this French-bistro-inspired kitchen through both windows and a panel of glass blocks set between two steel pot racks. The compact plan includes a stainless steel-topped island for a food-prep sink and a granite-topped breakfast peninsula (the main sink area lies just beyond). Hanging glass pendants and canary-colored plaster walls complete the picture.*

Blending crisp modern details with a thoroughly traditional style, this open kitchen revolves around its curved, granite-topped island. Additional textural interest is provided by the dark cherry counters, the gleaming hardwood floor, stainless-steel appliances, and a subdued tile backsplash. A white-painted bookcase (right) adds a relaxed feel and makes good use of a potentially awkward corner wall.

This layout really goes with the flow. The kitchen was designed to be an integral part of an open living space that's frequently used for entertaining. Perimeter work areas, housed in furniture-grade cabinets topped with Italian marble, curve gracefully toward a high-ceilinged, skylit living room. The view in the opposite direction (left) shows a serving peninsula with wet bar, ice-maker, and lighted cabinets for glassware.

A house addition formed the shell for this beautifully detailed "colonial" kitchen. The antique range (shown below) was the starting point; its brick-lined surround and the homeowner's period collectibles occupy one wall, along with a built-in refrigerator concealed behind period-style doors. A long, fir-topped center island, equipped with food-prep sink, divides the range area from a window-lined dining alcove (left). Modern amenities (facing page) include a brick-lined pizza oven and a walk-in pantry with copious storage.

Country to the max, this small, U-shaped kitchen features waxed-pine cabinets that were designed as furniture, like the display hutch in the foreground. Diagonally laid 8-inch saltillo floor pavers lead to the main work area. Solid-surface countertops, leaded windows, ceiling timbers, and racks for pans and dried flowers keep the country look. Wall cabinets have novel fabric panels (shown at right) and include a "false front" of apothecary drawers (there are larger, more usable drawers behind).

A vintage 1920s range set the tone for this nostalgic white-on-white design. Hexagonal mosaic floor tiles, like those of a bygone ice-cream parlor, team with subway-style white wall tiles set in a classic running-bond pattern. Off camera are modern wall ovens and other non-'20s conveniences.

Sleek and professional but warm and family-oriented: these are the seemingly opposite qualities reconciled in this makeover of a 1960s kitchen. Hard-edged steel cabinet and appliance surfaces play against the rich, butter-yellow marble of the center island and backsplash. The 15- by 20-foot room is the same size as the original kitchen but looks dramatically more inviting, its sensuously curved ceiling soffit echoing the curve of the new island.

An open, ultramodern, white-on-white kitchen is part of a "zero tolerance" house design—no moldings, no fudging, no extraneous details to interrupt the clarity of the look. The kitchen nestles behind the dining area, concealed by a high white knee wall. Euro-style laminate cabinets fit above custom 24-inch German wall tiles, which also form the countertops. The dark gray sealed-concrete floor has radiant heat underneath. Low-voltage cable lights do a spare but playful dance overhead.

Expressively casual, this remodeled bungalow kitchen is tiny, unfitted, and exuberant at the same time. Natural cherry cabinets are mixed with forest green units, pockets of open shelving, curtain fronts, concrete counters, a solid-surface apron sink, handmade tile, and a quilted-steel backing in the cooking area. The floor is another stylish throwback—real linoleum! The modern range has a downdraft vent, which saves the space of an overhead hood. Another space-saving trick: the refrigerator, out of view to the left, is recessed into the wall of an adjacent utility room.

This was a small, dark kitchen, redone on a budget. Twin greenhouse windows flanking the reconditioned range bring in daylight and make the space seem larger. New surfaces include fruitwood-stained maple cabinets with Italian pulls and counters made from inexpensive machined floor tiles with tight, easy-to-clean grout lines. A granite-topped island on casters adds counter surface but can be pushed aside to open up the space.

One hundred percent
Southwest, down to the mortar
and metate, this design revolves
around a central vent hood clad
in a four-sided mural of hand-
painted tile. The Southwest motif
and the mural's colors continue in
countertops, backsplashes, and a
lighted display niche; hand-hewn
cabinet fronts and timbers complete the look. The bronze-colored
floor pavers get their warm
patina from wax, a traditional
sealer for terra-cotta floors.

Formal as can be, this kitchen
is defined by its long, limestone-
topped island and ceiling-hung
wall cabinets. The cabinets'
two-sided glass doors have
frames that follow the arched
window by the sink; their glass
shelves are accented by small
built-in downlights. Cabinet
wood is lightly pickled and
stippled to support the look of
the heavily fossilized counter
surfaces. A band of gray-green
trim tile along the backsplash
adds a muted note of contrast.
French doors lead to an outdoor entertainment area.

*Here the idea was to create
an open, gracious, great-room
kitchen where guests would feel
as comfortable as family. The
range surround, cast in concrete,
is matched in tone by limestone-
colored concrete countertops and
plastered walls. Cherry cabinetry
and terra-cotta pavers lend
warmth to the decor; so does the
fireplace at far right.*

Electric and eclectic colors tie
together the far-flung areas of
this large studio space, which
revolves around a central
timber pole. Natural woods
meet dye stains, paint, and
a richly hued concrete floor.
The kitchen proper is simple,
open, and airy, featuring
cable-hung shelves that turn
a corner with ease.

# on the surface

**S**URFACES are a major element of kitchen style. In fact, many popular styles are defined, at least in part, by the countertops, floor coverings, and wall and ceiling treatments you choose. Also factor in the finishes on fixtures and appliances.

Surfaces can be hard or soft, bright or subdued, glossy or matte. Light surfaces spread light, dark ones absorb it. Many new kitchen designs lean toward quieter colors but gain impact with more sensational textures.

Just a few years ago, the average countertop, usually laminate, included a 4-inch lip on the back. Today's higher backsplashes, however, often feature materials that are found there alone. Geometric or hand-painted art tiles are popular choices. Stone tiles are an economical alternative to solid granite or marble. Stainless-steel and mirrored surfaces are showing up in high-tech surroundings.

*Faux-finished walls and ceiling, fir floor, plus wall and floor stenciling keep a 1937-vintage range comfortable in its modern surroundings, which include a granite eating counter and stylish, stainless-steel pendant lights.*

*Clean, simple diamond accents are formed from blue glass mosaics embedded in a plastered backsplash above the kitchen range.*

Beyond aesthetic considerations, you should weigh the physical characteristics of surfaces. Most kitchens take a lot of wear and tear. Is your countertop choice water resistant, durable, and easy to maintain? Is the floor hard to walk on, noisy, or slippery underfoot?

Your kitchen will probably include a good bit of wall space. What's the best kind of paint for kitchen walls? Latex is easy to work with, but alkyd paint (often called oil-base paint) provides high gloss and will hang on a little harder. Look for products labeled gloss or semigloss if you want a tough, washable wall finish.

Maximum impact at minimum cost was the challenge. The choice, according to the project designer, was "to go with color, period—to make that work as the detailing." Fir trim and stainless-steel appliances team with vibrant paints, stains, green-laminate countertops, and charcoal vinyl floor tiles.

*A free-form floating island of granite sweeps around twin sinks and a column for a sleek, contemporary effect. The island was designed to function both as a buffet table and as a piece of modern art.*

Outdoor sign-making techniques helped create these cabinet doors. Test negatives were made by putting tree branches and leaves on white paper and spray-painting them black; then the manufacturer was asked to render the favorite composition onto metal in two different shades of green. The inserts fit into the cabinets' cedar door frames just like standard panels. Counters and backsplash are slate-patterned plastic laminate.

This new kitchen, designed to look older, blends concrete countertops and matching textured plaster with colorful slate backsplash tiles, flat-paneled cabinets, and floating, open shelves. Rustic flooring is of hand-hewn pearwood planks. Wall cabinet panels are gleaming wire mesh, matching the metallic accents of the modular cooktop, vent hood, drawer pulls, and pot-filling faucet.

*Reedlike patterns swirl across these cabinet-door panels of stainless steel. The coarse but almost organic appearance was achieved by repeated passes with a hand-held grinder. Because light plays off the multifaceted surface, the doors seem to change as you pass by.*

Cows amble across a
pastoral vista and stare
placidly out at the own-
ers of this hand-painted
backsplash mural. Large
tiles with thin grout lines
keep the composition
unified. The countertop
is granite; cabinets
are maple.

Sealed concrete
makes a handsome,
durable surface for
countertops and floor.

Vibrant colors from an earthy palette
set the tone for this kitchen, where the
floor and the backsplash include
rows of tumbled marble interspersed
with glazed accent tiles. This remodel
balances traditional features—
white-paneled cabinetry and beaded
wainscoting—with contemporary
elements such as concrete counters
and stainless-steel appliances.

great kitchen ideas

# storage solutions

**CONSIDER** the kitchen cabinet. Most often it's either stained brown or painted white. But today's homeowners want more zip, so cabinet manufacturers are developing more venturesome designs to go with a rapidly expanding spectrum of surfacing choices and appliances. Architects and designers are using vivid colors, sculptural shapes, and inventive finishing techniques to turn cabinets into memorable kitchen furniture.

Do you want seamless European-style cabinets or traditional faceframe units? (For further details, see pages 80–87.) Consider the pros and cons of open shelves: on the plus side, they offer readily accessible and pleasantly casual storage and display space. In the minus column, remember that open goods get dusty—and that anything untidy is always in view. Glass-fronted wall cabinets are similarly open to view, especially if you choose clear rather than semiopaque glazing.

*Floating shelves, a coat of rich indigo paint, and a collection of vintage pottery transform a once-bland kitchen wall into a stunning showcase.*

*The deep green of the glass-fronted cabinets, the four-square paint detail on each drawer front, and the golden glow of the maple counters and back-splash turn the corner of this kitchen into a dramatic display area for crockery.*

Pullout drawers and shelves provide handy storage for kitchen goods. Appliance garages, fronted with flip-up or tambour doors, can help corral food processors and other small accessories. Kitchen islands are also great places to add storage. No room? Consider a movable cart with a butcher-block top.

What about a food pantry? Place one inside a cabinet run or look to a more remote location. Are there two cooks and multiple prepping and cooking centers? One solution, though potentially space-consuming, is to store multiple versions of basic utensils and spices.

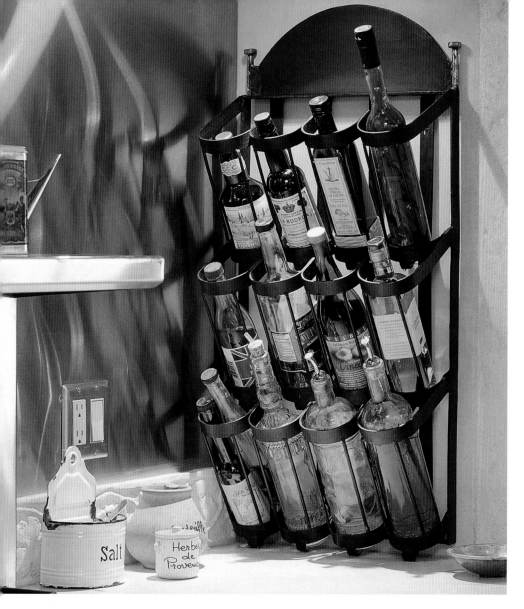

A wrought-iron wine rack, discovered while window-shopping down a wine-country street, takes on new life rangeside as a holster for flavored oils and other chef's accoutrements.

A pine pantry armoire with Shaker-simple lines contrasts with formal cherry cabinetry elsewhere in the kitchen. Behind the upper doors is a battery of pullouts on heavy-duty drawer guides; below are partitioned drawers, including a stainless-steel bread insert. The custom unit has a crown molding at top and sits on furniture-style "legs."

Tight inside corners are always trouble: either you give up the space on one side, or the opposing drawers smack into each other. This two-sided, arrow-shaped custom unit offers a fresh solution.

*It would be hard to find a more stylish set of storage bins than these hand-crafted, slatted creations, housed in an island that faces the main kitchen sink.*

*It looks like a blank cabinet end—but it's really the cabinet "door" that's the dummy. Inside is a compact, orderly pantry with ample, adjustable shelves and wire-fronted door racks.*

*Today's emphasis on recycling brings its challenges. How do you integrate potentially messy holding bins into an otherwise seamless kitchen design? This elegant solution is located at the end of a long kitchen island, facing away from the side most visible. The lipped plastic trash containers sit inside drawer cutouts and slide in and out as needed on sturdy drawer guides.*

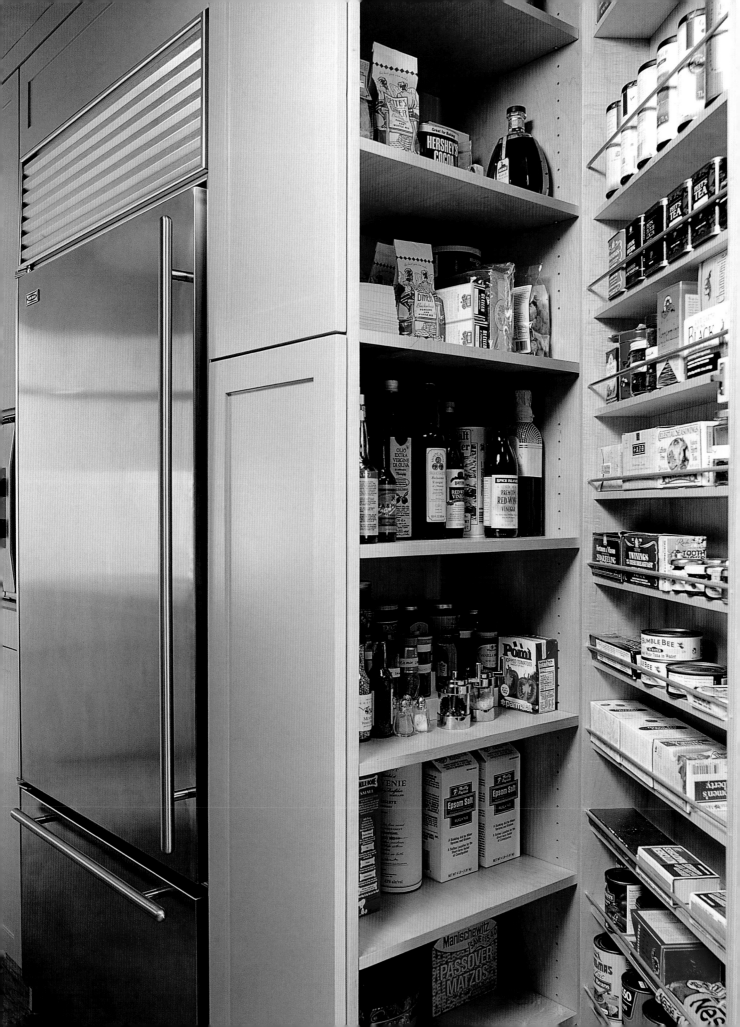

*A brick furnace flue, uncovered during the remodeling of a small country kitchen, becomes an earthy backdrop for a redwood trellis— originally designed for clematis or roses but now sprouting copper pots.*

*The kitchen island is the heart of this study in black and white. The butcher-block top provides plenty of surface for food preparation; pots are close at hand and provide a striking accent. The rack was constructed from two commercial units.*

*In this hardworking remodeled kitchen, there's plenty of storage space for pans near the microwave (near right) and under the cooktop (far right).*

# bright ideas

**N**O MATTER HOW efficient its layout, a kitchen with poor lighting is an unpleasant and tiring place to work. A good lighting plan creates shadowless, glare-free illumination for the entire room as well as bright light for specific tasks.

Daylight can enter a kitchen through windows, skylights, doors, or all three. For more even light, consider using two windows on adjacent walls or adding a skylight. Prefabricated greenhouse units, often placed be-hind sinks and countertops, are attractive space-stretchers and come with shelves for pots and planters; some also have sides or tops that open for ventilation. Similarly, bay and bow windows expand space and add light beside breakfast nooks and dining alcoves. Glass blocks let in soft, diffused light while providing privacy, security, and insulation. When it comes to linking the kitchen with a sunny deck or garden, French or sliding doors are unrivaled.

*A sleek white kitchen is viewed from the entrance hall through an interior "window," which provides discreet display space with curving glass shelves and a halogen downlight.*

*This remodel is organized around a dramatic new pointed dormer window, almost Gothic in feeling, that rises from behind the sink to the very peak of the gable. The new window frames a view of trees and dominates the white-painted kitchen, flooding it with daylight.*

You'll want strong, shadowless artificial light right over each kitchen work area. If your counter-tops, range, cooktop, and work spaces are well-lighted, general illumination need only be bright enough to ensure safe movement about the room. Architectural coves (built-in uplights) above the cabinets are a good way to supply a soft wash of ambient light. With multiple sources and dimmer controls, you can turn up the light full-throttle when working or gently subdue it after hours. When choosing kitchen fixtures, keep in mind that they'll need frequent cleaning.

*This kitchen combines sunlight
and storage in a single glass
cabinet system. Only the cooktop's
hood and venting mechanism
are opaque. The rest of the wall
consists of glass shelves sandwiched
between two translucent vertical
layers: frosted, rimless glass door
panels at the front, and a wall
of translucent panels along the
exterior of the house.*

Factory-made, wood-framed
windows were ganged
to brighten and visually
expand a once-dark kitchen
with potential garden views.
Fixed panes align above
and below tall casement
windows in the 8-foot-
square window wall. The
shapes repeat in an adjacent
3-foot-wide French door.

*A custom-designed greenhouse addition lends an airy, outdoor feel and plenty of light to the adjacent kitchen. Low-voltage cable lights fill in at night— and, occasionally, during high-contrast daylight hours. Their thin wire supports and decorative shades float unobtrusively while adding a touch of fun.*

*The owner of this kitchen (part of a remodeled old winery) wanted lots of light, but the raised ceiling made it a challenging task. Stylish red Italian pendants, each housing tiny but efficient halogen bulbs, solved the problem and defined the space. Electrical conduit, painted white, leads from the roofline down to the fixtures, which were originally designed to be ceiling-mounted.*

*Incandescent bulbs on continuous track strips run through the soffit area above wall cabinets and backlight "etched" arrangements of bundled twigs. The lights provide enough illumination for people to negotiate the kitchen at night when other light sources are off.*

*In this kitchen, available light is maximized by two rows of windows on the north-facing wall. A variety of electric light sources fill in: fluorescent tubes both under and over the cabinets, MR-16 downlights, and 100-watt A-bulbs in decorative Italian glass pendants. Incandescent strip lights add a warm glow to the display niche over the refrigerator.*

# elegant options

As LIFE speeds up, many of us are spending more home time in the kitchen. It's natural that the space is being redefined to include such extras as breakfast banquettes, dining tables, message centers or office desks, and comfortable sitting areas. Correspondingly, such standard living-room features as fireplaces, media centers, and art displays are moving here, too.

Kitchen islands are serving as space dividers, storage lockers, wet bars, eating counters, and repositories for school projects and business reports alike. Islands also figure importantly in multi-cook and specialized work stations. A baking center might benefit from a stone-topped surface that's lower than adjacent countertops. Kitchen entertaining calls for chairs or stools, a serving center, and perhaps a wet bar.

On the office front, is there space for a computer, if needed? Phone and fax? Standard desk height is 30 inches; keyboard surfaces are usually slightly lower. How will you hide the inevitable clutter?

Media centers are entering this room now. Maybe you'd like built-in audio speakers connected to a central home system (it's a good idea to have at least a separate volume control in the kitchen). Or you might plan a large-screen TV or full-blown home theater adjacent to a great room's comfortable sitting area.

Increasingly, kitchen additions are planned with direct access to the garden or patio through a set of glazed patio doors.

*Occupying a curved alcove off this kitchen is an 8-foot-diameter half-round booth, upholstered in green leather, comfortably encircling a pedestal table.*

*A formal espresso bar and serving area makes perfect use of this detached kitchen corner. Dish cabinets are cherry; the countertop and integral sink are patinated copper.*

*Below the espresso machine, which is permanently mounted, is a handy ice-maker for those wanting cold drinks rather than hot.*

*A mother and designer needed a work space that would allow her to keep track of both dinner and her energetic offspring. The answer was a bank of built-ins made from the same maple as the kitchen cabinets and living-room units beyond. A pullout (shown at right) houses a sewing machine and typewriter and extends beyond base cabinets, ready for action.*

*As today's kitchens become central in both daily and entertainment operations, more families want media centers incorporated into their design. Here, a large-screen TV (it can be concealed behind cabinet doors) fills the space above the refrigerator. The view from the island's seating is great.*

The broad, granite-topped peninsula angling out from this kitchen's main wall is a sleek, hardworking room divider. One side functions as an informal breakfast area. The other is all business, because that's where an author creates the elegant pastries that star in her cookbooks. The polished-granite top is 4 feet wide and more than 11 feet long—providing ample room for bowls, mixers, rolled-out dough, and baking sheets. The counter's cool surface, a comfortable 35 inches off the floor, is great for working with dough. An electric oven is built into one end of the peninsula, but the kitchen also contains one gas and one convection oven.

Ingenious storage solutions also help with serious baking. Shown on this page, at top left, a 35-inch-tall, roll-around island neatly stacks as many as 17 baking sheets. A 24-inch-wide, 30-inch-long, 4¼-inch-deep drawer (top right) also pulls its own weight, with com-partments that house a large array of baking supplies. Shown at bottom left is the owner's rolling pin collection. A shallow, egg-wide (1¼ inches) trough (lower right) machined into the granite countertop stops any ovoid wanderers.

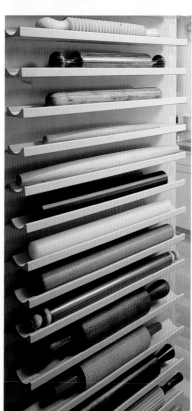

*A handsomely trimmed upholstered banquette fits neatly into one end of this traditional kitchen. The dining area's back wall, divided by plate rails, displays a colorful tableware collection. Angling across the corner is a cabinet with built-in wine storage.*

*Trim new European washer and dryer units blend seamlessly into a floor-to-ceiling cabinet. This laundry area includes a pullout hamper and a recessed ironing board unit, complete with both a task light and an electrical outlet for the iron. The board disappears behind a door when not in use.*

*A benevolent cherub presides over an earthy brick fireplace that's snugged into this kitchen corner. The scrolled acanthus-leaf orna-ment echoes its lines.*

# A SHOPPER'S GUIDE

Frameless laminate cabinets, solid-surface countertops, batch-feed garbage disposals, halogen cooktops, low-voltage wall washers—enough! The inexperienced shopper can be overwhelmed with the latest in gleaming stainless or bright enameled kitchen components. That's where this chapter can help. To keep things simple, we focus on one element at a time: cabinets, countertops, sinks, appliances, flooring, windows, and light fixtures. Color photos show the latest styles; text and comparison charts give you the working knowledge to brave the appliance center, to communicate with an architect or designer, or simply to replace that dingy old-fashioned countertop. Armed with the basics, it's usually easy to go on to the fine points. And you can often borrow literature, samples, or swatches to study at home for color, size, and stylistic compatibility.

# Cabinets

FROM FRAME TO FRAMELESS, THE OPTIONS ARE ENDLESS

Cabinets are the key element in kitchen storage. They set the tone of the room's decorative personality and form the backbone of its organization. For this reason—and because they represent the largest single investment in a new kitchen—it is important to study the many options available before making a decision.

## Traditional or European-style?

The two basic cabinet construction styles are frame and frameless.

Traditional American cabinets mask the raw front edges of each box with a 1-by-2 "faceframe." Doors and drawers then fit in one of three ways: flush; partially offset, with a lip; or completely overlaying the frame.

The outer edges of the faceframe can be planed and shaped (called "scribing") according to individual requirements. Since the faceframe covers up the basic box, thinner or lower-quality wood can be used in its sides—somewhat decreasing the cost. But the frame takes up space and reduces the size of the openings, so drawers or slide-out accessories must be significantly smaller than the full width of the cabinet—somewhat decreasing storage capacity.

Europeans, when faced with postwar lumber shortages, came up with "frameless" cabinets. A simple trim strip covers raw edges, which butt directly against one another. Doors and drawers often fit to within

**CABINET CLOSEUPS**

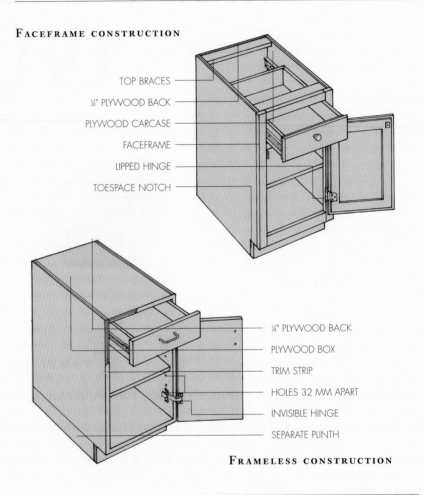

FACEFRAME CONSTRUCTION

TOP BRACES
¼" PLYWOOD BACK
PLYWOOD CARCASE
FACEFRAME
LIPPED HINGE
TOESPACE NOTCH

¼" PLYWOOD BACK
PLYWOOD BOX
TRIM STRIP
HOLES 32 MM APART
INVISIBLE HINGE
SEPARATE PLINTH

FRAMELESS CONSTRUCTION

⅛ inch of each other, revealing a thin sliver of the trim. Interior components, such as drawers, can be sized practically to the full dimensions of the box.

Another big difference: frameless cabinets typically have a separate toe-space pedestal, or plinth. This allows you to set counter heights specifically to your liking, stack base units, or make use of space at floor level.

The terms "system 32" and "32-millimeter" refer to precise columns of holes drilled on the inside faces of many frameless cabinets. These holes are generally in the same places, no matter what cabinets you buy, and interchangeable components such as door hinges, drawer guides, shelf pins, and pullout baskets just plug right into them.

*Cabinet doors and drawers set the look. The styles here include classic raised-panel fronts with bright white lacquer finish (upper left); frameless, overlay-style doors made from ash (upper right); and flat-panel, faceframe construction in vertical-grain fir (lower right).*

## Stock, custom, or semi-custom?

Cabinets are manufactured and sold in three different ways. The type you choose will affect the cost, overall appearance, and workability of your kitchen.

**STOCK CABINETS.** Buy your kitchen "off-the-shelf" and save—if you're careful. Mass-produced, standard-sized cabinets are the least expensive way to go, and they can be a good choice if you clearly understand the cabinetry you need for your kitchen. As the name implies, the range of sizes is limited.

Even so, you can always specify door styles, direction of door swing, and whether side panels are finished. And you can sometimes get options

**COMPARING CABINETS**

| | Stock | Custom | Semi-custom |
|---|---|---|---|
| **Where to buy** | Lumberyards, home centers, appliance stores, some showrooms (most stock is made in this country). | Few cabinetmakers have showrooms; most offer pictures of completed jobs. Be safe: visit some installations. | These cabinets are mainly showroom items, but some are found in home centers and department stores. |
| **Who designs** | You should, because the clerk helping you may know less about cabinets than you do. Don't order if you're at all unsure. | You; your architect, builder, or kitchen designer; or the maker (but be careful: cabinetmakers aren't necessarily designers). | The better (and more expensive) the line, the more help you get. Top-of-the-line suppliers design your whole kitchen. |
| **Cost range** | Less than the two other choices, but you'll still swallow hard when you see the total. Look for heavy discounts at home centers, but pay attention to craftsmanship. | Very wide; depends, as with factory-made boxes, on materials, finishes, craftsmanship, and options you choose. | A basic box can cost about what stock does, but each upgrade in door and drawer style and finish boosts the cost considerably. |
| **Options available** | Only options may be door styles, hardware, and door swing—but check the catalog; some lines offer a surprising range. | You can often—but not always—get the same options and European-made hardware that go in semi-custom cabinets. | Most lines offer choices galore—including variations in basic sizes and cabinets for corners. Check showrooms and study catalogs. |
| **Materials used** | Cheaper lines may use doors of mismatched or lower-quality woods, composite, or thinner laminates that photo-simulate wood. | Anything you specify, but examine samples. Methods vary by cabinetmaker; look at door and drawer hardware in a finished kitchen. | Factory-applied laminates and catalyzed varnishes are usually of high quality and durable. Medium-density fiberboard is the quality alternative for wood in non-showing parts of the basic box. |
| **Delivery time** | You may be able to pick up cabinets at a warehouse the same day you order. Wait is generally shorter than for other types. | Figure five weeks or longer, depending on job complexity, number of drawers, and finishes. Allow extra time. | Five to eight weeks is typical, whether cabinets are American or imported, but delivery can actually take up to six months. Order early. |
| **Installation & service** | Depends on where you buy; supplier may recommend a contractor. Otherwise, you install yourself. Service is virtually nonexistent. | In most cases, the maker installs. Buy from an established shop and you should have no trouble getting service. | Better lines are sold at a price that includes installation and warranty. Some cabinets are virtually guaranteed for life. |
| **Other considerations** | You often pay in full up front, giving you little recourse if cabinets are shipped incorrectly. Be sure order is clear and complete. | Make sure the bid you accept is complete—not just a basic cost-per-foot or cost-per-box charge. | With some manufacturers, if cabinets are wrong, you'll wait as long for the right parts to arrive as you did in the first place. |

and add-ons such as breadboards, sliding shelves, wine racks, and special corner units.

A recent development, the so-called RTA ("ready-to-assemble") cabinet costs even less than other stock units, but requires some basic tools and elbow grease to put together. An RTA cabinet is shown on the facing page.

You may see stock lines heavily discounted at some home centers. But buying such cabinets can be a lot like doing your own taxes: you may find you're lacking the knowledgeable help that could clarify the possibilities and save you money.

**CUSTOM CABINETS.** Many people still have a cabinetmaker come to their house and measure, then return to the cabinet shop and build custom cases, drawers, and doors.

Custom cabinet shops can match old cabinets, size truly oddball configurations, and accommodate complexities that can't be handled with stock or semi-custom cabinets. A skilled craftsperson can create kitchen woodwork that looks like fine furniture. Such jobs, however, may cost

*READY-TO-ASSEMBLE (RTA) CABINET*

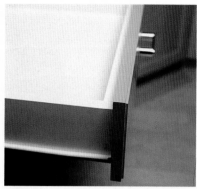

*Be sure to look at drawer components and hardware. Options shown here include (from top to bottom) budget-oriented drawer boxes with self-closing epoxy guides; molded metal sides with integral runners; sturdy, full-extension, ball-bearing guides; and premium hardwood boxes with dovetail joints and invisible, under-mounted guides.*

considerably more than medium-line stock or semi-custom cabinets.

**SEMI-CUSTOM CABINETS.** Between stock and custom cabinets are "semi-custom" or "custom modular" units, which can sometimes combine the best of both worlds. They are manufactured, but they are of a higher grade and offer more design flexibility than stock cabinets. Not surprisingly, they cost more, too.

Semi-custom systems come in a wide range of sizes, with many options within each size. You can change virtually everything on these basic modules: add sliding shelves; replace doors with drawers; set a matching hood unit over the cooktop; add wire baskets, flour bins, appliance garages, and pullout pantries. If necessary, heights, widths, and depths can be modified to fit almost any design.

Be advised, though: because these cabinets are configured to order and because most are imported from abroad, they could take longer to materialize than custom units from a local cabinetmaker. Order as much ahead as possible.

## Judging quality

To determine the quality of a cabinet, first look closely at the drawers. They take more of a beating than any other part. Several designs are shown. You'll pay a premium for such details as solid-wood drawer boxes, dovetail joints, or full-extension, ball-bearing guides.

Door hinges are also critical hardware elements. European or "invisible" hinges are most trouble-free. Choose these unless you want the period look of surface hardware. Check for adjustability; invisible hinges should be able to be reset and fine-tuned with the cabinets in place.

Most cabinet boxes are made from sheet products like plywood, particleboard (plain or laminated), or medium-density fiberboard. Solid lumber is sometimes used, but is usually reserved for doors and drawer faces.

Hardwood plywood is surfaced with attractive wood veneers on face and back. The higher the face grade, the more you'll pay. Particleboard costs less, weighs more, and is both weaker and more prone to warping and moisture damage than plywood. Generally, particleboard cabinets are faced with either high-pressure plastic laminates (see page 88) or a softer material called melamine. Medium-density fiberboard (MDF), a denser, furniture-grade particleboard, is tougher,

**BASE CABINET OPTIONS**

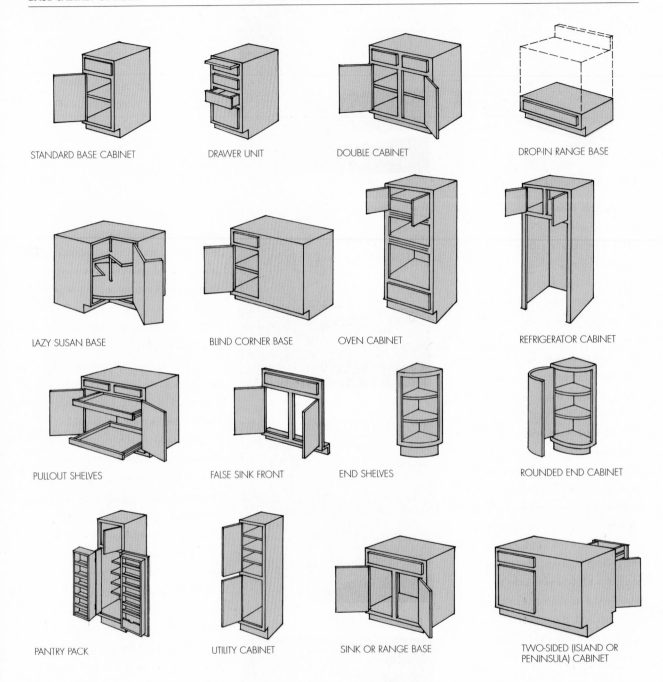

STANDARD BASE CABINET

DRAWER UNIT

DOUBLE CABINET

DROP-IN RANGE BASE

LAZY SUSAN BASE

BLIND CORNER BASE

OVEN CABINET

REFRIGERATOR CABINET

PULLOUT SHELVES

FALSE SINK FRONT

END SHELVES

ROUNDED END CABINET

PANTRY PACK

UTILITY CABINET

SINK OR RANGE BASE

TWO-SIDED (ISLAND OR
PENINSULA) CABINET

smoother, and available with high-quality hardwood veneers.

Make sure laminate and edge banding are thick enough not to peel at the corners and edges. "Once a cheap cabinet starts peeling," one shop warned, "that's it."

## What choices are available?

The illustrations on these two pages show many basic cabinet units. You'll find variations on these in most lines.

The three main cabinet categories are base, wall, and tall or special-use. Because it's more economical to build

with standardized dimensions, sizes tend to be consistent from line to line. Cabinet sizes must also match standard fixtures and appliances.

**BASE CABINETS.** Base cabinets combine storage space with working surface. Though usually equipped with only one top drawer, some base cabinets have three or four drawers, making them particularly useful near the sink, range, or refrigerator. "Sink" units have a false drawer front or a tilt-out drawer at the top.

Standard dimensions are 24 inches deep by 34½ inches high; the addition of a countertop raises them to 36 inches. In width, base cabinets range from about 9 to 48 inches, increasing in increments of 3 inches from 9 to 36 inches and in increments of 6 inches after that.

**WALL CABINETS.** Usually screwed to studs in the walls, these cabinets can also be hung from ceiling joists over peninsula and island installations. Wall cabinets come as single or double units and in various specialty configurations.

Typically 12 inches deep, wall cabinets can vary in width from about 9 to 48 inches. Though the most frequently used heights are 15, 18, and 30 inches, units actually range from 12 to 36 or more inches high. The shorter cabinets are typically mounted above refrigerators, ranges, and sinks. The tallest ones extend to high soffits or ceilings.

**SPECIAL-USE UNITS.** Manufacturers also produce a variety of special-purpose cabinets. You can buy cabinets with cutouts for sinks, built-in ranges, wall ovens, or microwaves. Island and pantry units also fall into this category.

Perhaps more options exist for corners than for any other kitchen cabinet space. These include angled units with larger doors, double-door units that provide full access to the L-shaped space, and lazy Susans or slide-out accessories that bring items forward from the back recesses of the space.

## Getting help

The cabinets are only part of the puzzle. When you buy them, some of what you're paying for is varying degrees of help with the design.

A designer will help you figure out how you'll use the kitchen. Some retailers will give you a questionnaire (much like the one on page 11) to

**WALL CABINET OPTIONS**

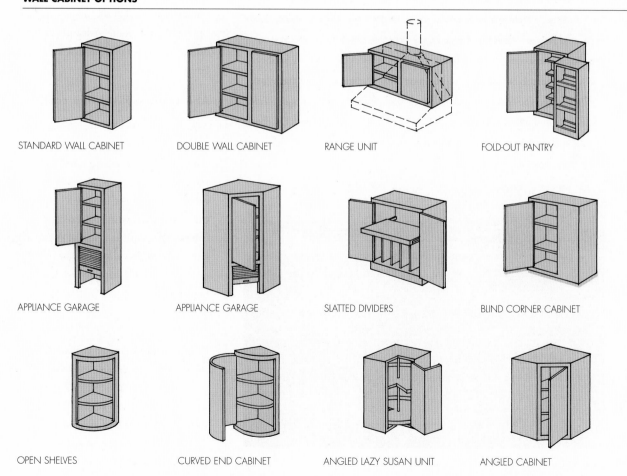

STANDARD WALL CABINET     DOUBLE WALL CABINET     RANGE UNIT     FOLD-OUT PANTRY

APPLIANCE GARAGE     APPLIANCE GARAGE     SLATTED DIVIDERS     BLIND CORNER CABINET

OPEN SHELVES     CURVED END CABINET     ANGLED LAZY SUSAN UNIT     ANGLED CABINET

## WHAT ABOUT REFACING?

If your goal is just to update your present kitchen, and/or if you're on a tight budget, you might consider a speedier, cost-effective alternative to replacing your cabinets: refacing them.

Basically, "refacing" means just that. A specialty company or cabinetmaker removes existing doors and drawer fronts and replaces them with new ones. Visible surfaces like cabinet ends, edge banding, and faceframes are finished to match; the results look as if you'd replaced the entire cabinet system.

When is refacing a good idea? If the basic boxes are in good shape and you're satisfied with your current layout, this could be an attractive possibility. You can usually choose from a broad range of door and drawer styles, hardware, and finishes. Typically, the company's representative will show you samples, take measurements, and return for the installation. Refacers probably won't work on cabinet interiors, so you may wish to clean or paint these first.

Where can you locate refacing firms? Look in the yellow pages under Cabinet Refinishing & Refacing or Kitchen Cabinets & Equipment. Or check large home centers or lumberyards; some offer these services or can steer you in the right direction.

pinpoint what's unsatisfactory about your current kitchen, how often you do any specialty cooking, whether your guests always end up in the kitchen, whether you buy food in bulk, and other clues to a final design that really suits the way you live.

Pick a "look," then shop for it; compare features, craftsmanship, budget, and cost. Some designers represent a particular line, so shop around to get an idea of what's currently available.

Your existing floor plan (see page 10) is the best aid you can offer a designer. Some staff designers in showrooms will do a new cabinet plan for you, applying the charge against the purchase price of the cabinets. Some showrooms use computer renderings to help customers visualize the finished kitchen—with prices for different cabinet options just a keystroke away.

## And what will all this cost?

There are no figures after "Cost range" in the chart on page 82. Why? The wide and changing range of styles—and prices—makes buying cabinets much like buying a car. Like car makers, every manufacturer or cabinetmaker picks a slot of the market, then offers various styles and options that build upward from a base price.

*Dark-stained cabinets visually shrank the kitchen (above left). After the original doors were removed, the installer covered the existing shells with white plastic laminate, then routed out the openings. The final, room-brightening transformation was adding the new white doors and drawers (below left).*

*A CORNUCOPIA OF CABINET PULLS*

Know your budget. You'll quickly find out what kinds of cabinets you can afford; with your plan in hand, you can get a basic price for standard cabinets relatively easily. But extras will drastically alter the quote—so the same basic cabinet can end up costing a number of different prices. Bids should be full quotes based on a fully specified room sketch listing the options desired in each cabinet. Is installation to be included? If so, spell it out.

Within each line, costs are largely determined by the nature of the doors and drawers you choose. The simplest, least expensive option is often a flat or "slab" door, popular in seamless European designs. Frame-and-panel designs are more traditional and come in many versions, including raised panel (both real and false), arched panel, beaded panel, and recessed or flat panel.

Are cabinet pulls included? If not, you'll pay more for them, but you can choose exactly what you want (for a sampling, see the photo above).

# Countertops

THINK STYLE, DURABILITY, AND EASY MAINTENANCE

Chop on it, knead on it, serve from it: you ask a lot, every day, of your kitchen countertop. No one material is best for all purposes, but each of those described below and on the facing page looks distinctive and has specific merits.

## What are the choices?

Plastic laminate, ceramic tile, solid-surface acrylics, wood, stainless steel, and stone are the six major countertop materials in current use. We discuss each of these options here. Cast concrete and soapstone are both showing up, too—most often in modernistic and traditional designs, respectively.

## Shopping around

The problem is that you probably won't find all these materials in the same place. Some dealers are listed in the yellow pages under Countertops or Kitchen Cabinets & Equipment; they'll probably have tile, plastic laminate, solid-surface products, and—maybe—wood. Large home centers and lumberyards usually carry plastic laminate and wood. For other dealers or fabricators, check listings under Concrete Products, Marble—Natural, Plastics, Restaurant Equipment, Sheet Metal Work, and Tile. Designers and architects can also supply samples of materials.

---

## COMPARING COUNTERTOPS

### Plastic laminate

**Advantages.** You can choose from a wide range of colors, textures, and patterns. Laminate is durable, easy to clean, water resistant, and relatively inexpensive. Ready-made molded versions are called post-formed; custom or self-rimmed countertops are built from scratch atop particleboard or plywood substrates. There are many more laminates available for the latter tops, and edging options abound. With the right tools, you can install laminate yourself.

**Disadvantages.** It can scratch, chip, and burn, and it's hard to repair. Ready-made postformed tops can look cheap; other edgings may collect water and grime. Conventional laminate has a dark backing that shows at its seams; new solid-color laminates, designed to avoid this, are more expensive and somewhat brittle. High-gloss laminates show every smudge.

---

### Ceramic tile

**Advantages.** It's good-looking and comes in many colors, textures, and patterns. It is heat resistant and, if installed correctly, water resistant. Price depends on how many tiles are used and whether they're formed by machine or by hand. Buy a tile that's rated for countertop use. Grout is also available in numerous colors. Patient do-it-yourselfers are likely to have good results.

**Disadvantages.** Some tile glazes can react adversely to foods, acids, or household chemicals; be sure to ask. Unglazed tiles can be sealed, but some sealers are unsafe around food. Many people find it hard to keep grout satisfactorily clean (using epoxy grout and thin, uniform grout spaces can help). The hard, irregular surface can chip china and glassware.

# COMPARING COUNTERTOPS

### Solid-surface

**Advantages**. Durable, water resistant, heat resistant, nonporous, and easy to clean, this marble-like material can be shaped and joined with virtually invisible seams. Many different edge treatments are possible. It allows for a variety of sink installations, including integral units like the one shown on page 91, Blemishes and scratches can be sanded out.

**Disadvantages.** It's expensive, requiring professional fabrication and installation for best results. It also requires very firm support below. Until recently, color selection was limited to white, beige, and almond; now stone patterns and pastels are common. Costs climb quickly for wood inlays and other fancy edge details.

### Wood

**Advantages**. Wood is handsome, natural, easily installed, and easy on glassware. If given a good surface finish, it can resist water damage. Maple butcher-block, the most popular, is moderately priced; it's sold in 24-, 30-, and 36-inch widths and with either long, edge-grain strips or blockish, end-grain squares. Other hardwoods are sometimes used in wider, edge-joined form.

**Disadvantages.** It's harder to keep clean than nonporous materials. It can scorch and scratch, and it may blacken or discolor when near a source of moisture. You can seal it with traditional mineral oil or with a longer-lasting, nontoxic penetrating sealer (though cutting might mar this finish). Or use a permanent surface finish, such as polyurethane (but then you definitely can't cut on it).

### Stainless steel

**Advantages**. Stainless steel is waterproof, heat resistant, easy to clean (if matte-finish), and durable. You can get a counter with a sink molded right in. It's great for a part of the kitchen where you'll be using water a lot.

**Disadvantages.** Don't cut on it, or you risk damaging both countertop and knife. While 16-gauge stainless itself is inexpensive, the cost of fabrication—sink cutouts, faucet holes, and bends and welds for edges and backsplashes—can be quite high. Custom detailing and high-chromium stainless up the price even more. You can, however, reduce the cost by using flat sheeting and a wood edge, as shown at left.

### Stone

**Advantages.** Granite, marble, and limestone all popular for countertops, are beautiful natural materials. Their cool surface is very useful when you're working with dough or making candy. They're heat-proof, water resistant, easy to clean, and very durable.

**Disadvantages.** Oil, alcohol, and any acid (such as that from lemons or wine) will stain marble and limestone or damage their finish; granite can stand up to all of these. Solid slabs are very expensive, and decorative details add more cost. Recently, some homeowners and designers have turned to stone tiles—including slate—as less expensive alternatives. When considering a stone other than granite, be sure to study the latest sealers.

# Waterworks

SINKS, FAUCETS, FILTERS, AND ACCESSORIES ABOUND

The cleanup center sees lots of active duty in every busy kitchen; in fact, studies claim that up to 50 percent of kitchen time is spent there. So doesn't it make sense to pay special attention to sinks, faucets, dishwashers, and related accessories when you're planning your new kitchen?

## The new world of sinks

Recently, sinks and faucets have become prime design accents—a place to add a bit of dash to an otherwise restrained scheme.

When it comes to the primary kitchen sink, the traditional single-bowl version has some serious competition. Today's sink is a multitask center, and double-, even triple-bowl designs are now the norm. They come detailed with many custom-fitted accessories, such as cutting boards, colanders, rinsing baskets, and dish racks.

The one exception is the so-called apron sink, an unabashedly old-fashioned single sink that sits atop a lowered base cabinet (one is shown above right).

**MATERIALS.** Common sink materials include stainless steel, enameled cast iron or steel, composites, and solid-surface acrylics. Vitreous china is also making a comeback. For smaller auxiliary sinks or "bar" sinks, you can use more decorative surfaces like copper or brass. All of these materials are outlined on the facing page.

In addition, you may see new sinks made from ceramic fireclay, concrete, or soapstone. Color-consistent fireclay seems especially promising, since scratches or dings can be scrubbed or buffed out.

**SINK SIZES.** The traditional one-piece sink measures about 22 inches deep and 24 inches wide. Double- or one-and-a-half-bowl sinks average 33 inches wide; triple-bowl versions, or those with integral drain boards, can stretch to 42 inches. Sinks are getting deeper, a boon for those washing big pots and baking sheets.

**RIM OR NO RIM?** You also have a choice of mounting methods with vari-

*A country kitchen's apron sink sits atop a lowered base cabinet. They're joined by an old-fashioned wall faucet and a pine-paneled dishwasher.*

ous sink models. Self-rimming sinks with molded overlaps are supported by the edge of the countertop cutout; they work well with any countertop material. Undermounted sinks are positioned under the countertop and held in place by metal clips; they have a modern look that works well with stone and solid-surface edges. Flush-mounted sinks are set into the counter substrate to align with the surface material—usually tile.

# COMPARING SINKS

### Stainless steel

Stainless steel sinks come in 18- to 22-gauge (18-gauge is best, 22-gauge is flimsy) and either matte or mirror finish. Chromium/nickel blends are the only true "stainless" sinks; cheaper grades will stain. Matte finishes are much easier to keep looking clean than mirrored, and they mask scratches better. You'll find a large selection of double- and triple-bowl designs; integral drain boards are available, too. Stainless is relatively noisy, so look for a sink with an undercoating.

### Enameled cast iron/steel

Here's where the colors come in. Enameled cast-iron sinks have a heavier layer of baked-on enamel than steel, making them quieter and less likely to chip, but also more expensive. These sinks have become quite popular, especially with the advent of new European designs. White, black, gray, and a palette of other colors and flecked patterns are available in many double- and triple-bowl models. The cast edges of self-rimming versions are prone to warping; be sure to check when you take delivery.

### Composite

This durable, resilient newcomer comes with either a smooth or textured finish; it's lighter than cast iron. Composite can be fairly expensive. Some complain about limited style and color options (usually white or off-whites); some dislike the "plastic" look. Quartz sinks, or composites with high quartz content, are toughest; they resemble enamel but are easier to maintain.

### Integral solid-surface

Today's solid-surface countertop (see page 89) can be coupled with a molded, integral sink for a sleek, sculpted look. Sink color can either match the countertop exactly or complement it. Edge-banding and other border options abound, including decorative grooving and adjacent drain boards. Although they're not indestructible, solid-surface sinks can be repaired if nicked or scratched. These sinks come in single-bowl versions only. Check the depth—they may not be as deep as you'd like.

### Vitreous china

Vitreous china sinks, a common bathroom component, are starting to show up in the kitchen. The material (made with clay that's poured into molds, fired in a kiln, and glazed) is heavy and is easy to clean; it also resists scratches and stains. These are highly ornamental, sculpted sinks, often with handpainted accents. On the down side, they can be very expensive and are subject to chipping.

### Brass and copper

These elegant surfaces are outstanding as accents. However, they require considerable maintenance—especially if highly polished—so you may wish to reserve them for wet-bar or other occasional uses. Bar or hospitality sinks come with either a 2- or 3½-inch drain opening; if you're planning to add a disposal (see page 93) you'll want the larger opening. An 18-inch diameter is typical.

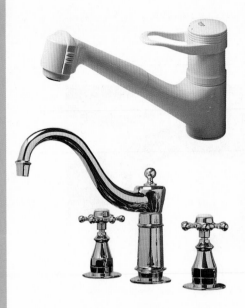

*Sink faucets run a gamut from old-fashioned to high-tech, from soft pewter-finish to jazzy epoxy, and from single-lever to spread-fit.*

## Faucets

Today's kitchen faucets fall into one of two camps: European-style or traditional. Enameled single-lever fixtures with pullout sprayers and interchangeable attachments are fashionable, but traditional gooseneck styles with individual handles remain popular, too.

Finishes include polished chrome, brushed chrome, nickel, polished and antiqued brass, soft pewter, elegant gold, and jazzy enameled epoxy. For sheer durability and low maintenance, a polished chrome surface with high nickel content is still the best bet.

Sink faucets are available with single-, center-set, or spread-fit controls. A single-lever fitting has a combined faucet and lever or knob controlling water flow and temperature. A center-set control has separate hot and cold water controls and a faucet, all mounted on a base or escutcheon. A spread-fit control has separate hot and cold water controls and a faucet, independently mounted. While most faucets are sink-mounted, certain installations call for either deck-mounted or wall-mounted fittings. When you select your sink, be sure the holes in it will accept the type of faucet you plan to buy as well as any additional accessories, such as hot water dispenser, soap dispenser, water purifier, and a dishwasher's air gap.

Ask yourself three questions when you're attracted to clever, streamlined designs. How well could you work the controls with greasy hands? Can the spout fit over a large pan? And how easy would it be to clean or maintain the installation?

Whatever style you choose, you get pretty much what you pay for. Solid-brass workings, though pricey, are most durable. Ceramic- or plastic-disk valve designs are easier to maintain than older washer schemes.

If you'd like to give yourself a little treat, take a cue from restaurant kitchens. Instead of lugging heavy pots of water from sink to stovetop, consider installing a so-called pot filler (like the one shown at bottom left on the facing page) near the range or cooktop.

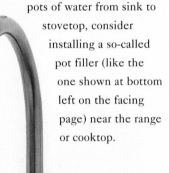

## Hot & cold water dispensers

Half-gallon-capacity instant hot water dispensers have been around for some time now. The heater fits underneath the sink; connected to the cold water supply, it delivers 190°F to 200°F water. Most units plug into a 120-volt grounded outlet installed inside the sink cabinet. Mount the dispenser either on a sink knockout or nearby on the countertop.

Cold water spouts operate in a similar manner, but a below-counter chiller is substituted for the heater. Some units combine both hot and cold water levers in one unit.

New compact water purifiers look just like hot water or soap dispensers on the sink; the main unit fits compactly below the sink like other water appliances. Filtration systems vary widely. Reverse-osmosis filters are considered most effective, but their output is limited. If you have questions about your water's composition, first have it tested, then choose the right system for the job.

## Garbage disposals

Today's garbage disposals handle almost all types of food waste. They come in two types: batch-feed and continuous. Batch-feed disposals kick into gear when you engage the lid; continuous-feed models are activated by an adjacent wall switch or sink-mounted air switch. Batch-feed types are considered safer, but come with fewer options.

Look for sturdy motors (½ horsepower or more), noise insulation, and efficient antijam features. Generally, the fatter the disposal, the more the insulation—and the quieter it's likely to run.

The disposal links with the sink drain below the countertop. It may require its own 120-volt electrical circuit; the connection may be either plug-in or hard-wired.

Some building codes prohibit the use of disposals, while others require them. Be sure to check!

## Dishwashers

Whether portable or built-in, most dishwashers are a standard size: roughly 24 inches wide, 24 inches deep, and 34 inches high. A few compact units and European imports come as narrow as 18 inches. Standard finishes include enameled steel (usually white, black, or almond), stainless steel, and black glass. You can also choose replaceable panels to match base cabinet runs.

Quiet is a blessing in a dishwasher—especially when the kitchen is open to adjacent spaces. Improved insulation has led to operating levels as low as 50 decibels.

First, examine the racks. They should be adjustable and able to accommodate your cooking equipment and dishes. Then consider such energy-saving devices as a booster heater that raises the water temperature for the dishwasher only, separate cycles for lightly or heavily soiled dishes, and air-drying choices. Other features include a delay start that allows you to wash dishes at a preset time (during the night instead of at peak-energy hours), prerinse and pot-scrubbing cycles, and a strainer filtering system (actually like a small disposal).

Like a garbage disposal, the dishwasher connects to the sink drain (in fact, it frequently empties directly through the disposal). You'll also need to tap into the hot water supply pipe and provide a separate 120-volt circuit for power. Many local codes require you to install an air gap along with the dishwasher; this device, which mounts atop the sink or countertop, keeps waste water from backing up if there's a drop in water-supply pressure.

*POT FILLER*

*REVERSE-OSMOSIS WATER FILTER*

*ULTRA-QUIET DISHWASHER*

# Ranges, Cooktops, and Ovens

## GAS OR ELECTRIC, THEY OFFER RED-HOT LOOKS AND EFFICIENCY

**W**hat's best, the flexibility of separate cooktops and ovens or the traditional integrated range? On one level, the choice is one of function. But in addition to that, it's a question of style: the range creates a focal point, invoking the traditional image of "hearth and home." Separates, on the other hand, look right in clean, contemporary surroundings.

### Ranges

Most ranges have a cooktop with oven below; a few models offer an additional upper microwave oven with a built-in ventilator or downventing cooktop. Standard range width is 30 inches, but sizes go as narrow as 21 inches and, in commercial designs, as wide as 48 inches or more.

**FREESTANDING, SLIDE-IN, OR DROP-IN?** Take your choice of three range types: freestanding, slide-in, or drop-in. Freestanding ranges sit anywhere; slide-ins are similar, but come without side panels to fit between cabinets. Drop-in models rest on a wood platform within adjacent base cabinets; their integral rims seal any food-collecting gaps.

**WHICH STYLE IS FOR YOU?** Choose from standard models—gas or electric; reconditioned "heirloom" ranges; dual-fuel designs; shiny commercial units; or safer residential/ commercial versions. For a discussion of burner options, see pages 96–97; for oven specifics, turn to pages 98–99.

*EUROPEAN "HEIRLOOM" RANGE*

- **ELECTRIC RANGES** may have standard coils, solid-element burners, or a smooth ceramic top, plus radiant-heat or combination convection/radiant ovens.

- **GAS RANGES** have either radiant-heat or convection ovens; lower ovens may be self-cleaning or continuous-cleaning. Some offer interchangeable cooktop modules.

- **DUAL-FUEL RANGES** combine the responsiveness of a gas cooktop with the even heating of one or two electric ovens—producing, in theory, the best of both worlds.

- **HEIRLOOM RANGES** are refurbished oldsters that lend an ambiance of comfortable permanence to both country and period design schemes. They're usually freestanding gas models with few modern amenities; some have integral griddles and/or warming trays. New ranges with an "old" look are also available, but these can be very expensive.

- **COMMERCIAL GAS UNITS** have been much in demand in recent years—partly due to their increased BTU output and partly because of their look of serious culinary business. Their performance is excellent, but they create many problems for home use: they're not as well-insulated as residential units; they may be too heavy for your floor; they're tough to clean; and they're potentially dangerous for children.

- **RESIDENTIAL/COMMERCIAL UNITS**, a recent response to the commercial craze, were designed specifically for the home. These have the commercial look and the high BTU output but are better insulated; they also offer additional niceties such as pilotless ignition and self- or continuous-cleaning ovens.

DROP-IN RANGE

RESIDENTIAL/COMMERCIAL RANGE

## Cooktops

For flexibility, specialized cooking, or simply a trim, modern look, separate cooktops make good sense. Their rapidly increasing use in island and peninsula designs is part of this trend.

Before confronting the bewildering array of cooktops on the market, you'll need to make some basic decisions. First, what type of energy do you prefer? Gas units heat and cool quickly, and the flame is visible and easy to control. Electric units provide low, even heat. Unless you buy a downventing

MODULAR COOKTOP

## COMPARING COOKTOPS

### Smoothtop (ceramic glass)

Electric smoothtop cooktops have burners similar to traditional coil designs but with ceramic glass on top, which disperses heat and makes the cooktop much easier to clean. In the past, these tops have received thumbs down for slow heating, but newer designs have coils closer to the surface; some models also include fast-starting coils. Warning lights on some new models stay on until the top is cool enough to touch.

Early smoothtops also scratched or cracked. Newer formulations are more durable. Popular finishes include classic black and flecked patterns (the latter hide abrasions). Look for independent sizing controls for smaller or larger pans. Smoothtop surfaces require flat-bottom pans for best heat dispersal.

### Solid-element electric

These trim-looking burner units are basically cast-iron disks with resistance coils below. Because of the continuous surface, the disks produce more even heat than standard coils; and because they're sealed, they're easier to clean. Better models have thermostats or on-off cycles to keep heat even and to protect the unit. With some, central "button" sections glow when the power is on.

Owner complaints? Solid-element burners may not produce enough heat for certain types of cooking. The disks may discolor over time with overzealous scrubbing. Like smoothtop surfaces, solid-element disks require flat-bottom pans for best results.

### Induction

This is cooking with magnetism, and the response is as instant as gas. Once you set an appropriate pan in place and turn on the unit, a sensor triggers an induction coil that sets up an electromagnetic field reaching about an inch above the cooking surface. Remove the pan and there's no live heat source. Chefs love induction's ability to slow-simmer.

Are there minuses? Induction is expensive and not widely available. You must use pans of a ferrous metal—cast iron, magnetic stainless steel, or porcelain steel. Some cooks complain that it won't produce enough heat.

model, the cooktop will require an overhead hood. (For venting specifics, see pages 100–101).

- **STANDARD** gas and electric cooktops are built into counters like self-rimming sinks, with connections below. Most units have four burners, though some have five, six, or even more. The majority of cooktops come in 30- or 36-inch widths; they're all at least 2 to 3 inches shallower than the standard 24-inch cabinet depth. Drop-in cooktops with no venting included run from about 2½ to 8 inches

high; figure about 16½ inches for downventing models.

- **CONVERTIBLE** gas and electric cooktops are similar to conventional models but offer interchangeable and reversible modules that let you replace burners with grills, griddles, and other specialized accessories.

- **COMMERCIAL** or residential/commercial (see page 95) gas units house up to eight burners; many styles offer hot plates or griddles. Typically, burners are 6 to 7 inches high with short legs for installing on a base of tile, brick, or

other noncombustible material.

- **MIX-AND-MATCH MODULES** or "hobs," typically 12 inches wide, may be grouped together with connecting hardware or embedded separately, if you choose. Modules consist of standard gas, halogen, smoothtop electric, solid-element electric, barbecue, griddle, electric wok, or deep fryer (sometimes also serving as steamer) units. Some of these fit in as little as 2 inches of vertical space, freeing up the cabinet below for drawers or a complementary oven.

## COMPARING COOKTOPS

### Halogen

The latest technological kitchen marvel, halogen rivals magnetic induction as the most "now" of heat sources. Still more expensive to operate than gas, halogen is nonetheless the most efficient electric source; and, unlike most electric burners, halogen offers rapid on-off and infinite adjustment controls.

Halogen burners come as one of a pair of burners in 12-inch modules, or in standard four-burner setups combining one halogen with three standard smoothtop burners. Halogen's weakness? It's still quite expensive. The light can burn out, but is expected to last approximately eight years before needing replacement.

### Gas

Gas cooktops are the choice of most gourmet cooks; they respond instantly when turned on or off, or when settings are changed. Gas is also more economical to operate than any electric alternative. Smaller modular units house two standard burners, or one standard (8,000 BTU) and one "commercial" (12,000 BTU). Stylish sealed gas burners are fused to the cooktop; they're easier to clean than conventional burners and just as efficient. All standard units have pilotless ignition now, and some manufacturers offer an instant reignition feature.

Drawbacks? Some people dislike the odor. Gas may be harder to maintain than an electrical heat source. Simmering can be difficult. White grates may discolor over time.

### Commercial gas

Commercial gas units are made of heavy-duty cast iron or fabricated metal finished in stainless steel, black enamel, or silver gray. Commercial gas cooktops are usually 6 to 7 inches high with short legs for installing on a base of tile, brick, or other noncombustible material. They often come with hot plates or griddles. Simmering can be difficult; a cast-iron simmer top may be available.

Commercial/residential gas units combine the commercial output with features such as integral top grates, designer colors, and self-insulation (so installing requires no additional insulation).

## Wall ovens

Built-in ovens save counter space by fitting inside base cabinets or special vertical storage units. With separate ovens, as with cooktops, you have several choices: conventional radiant heat, convection, or microwave.

Teaming a conventional oven with a microwave or energy-saving convection oven is a popular choice. Double ovens can be installed one above the other or side by side below the countertop (some cooks find this a convenient use of space, while others find it frustrating). You can also purchase combination or multi-mode units that allow you to switch between functions, but they're pricey.

Your oven's interior may be "you-clean" (old-fashioned elbow grease required), continuous cleaning (a steady, slow process with a result that may never look clean), or self-cleaning (pyrolytic)—the most effective method.

RADIANT-HEAT OVENS. Conventional radiant-heat ovens are available as single or double units. Built-in ovens are sized to fit standard, 24-inch-deep cabinet cavities; deeper units are also available. The most common width is 27 inches, though many space-efficient European imports are 24 inches; recently, the 30-inch-wide oven has caught on. So-called "built-under" ovens provide a range effect without interrupting the countertop; add the low-clearance cooktop of your choice.

You can choose to include built-in warmer shelves, rotisseries, attached meat thermometers, variable-speed broilers, multiple-rack systems, pizza inserts, and digital timing devices.

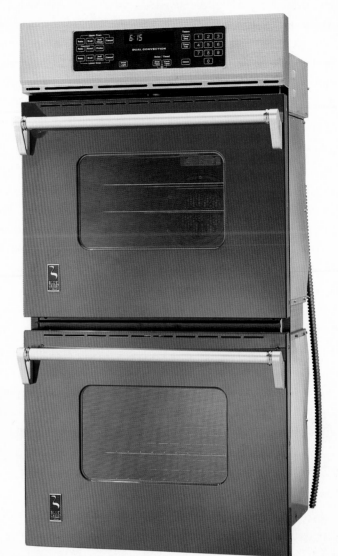

*STACKED WALL OVENS*

*WARMING OVENS*

**CONVECTION OVENS.** Both gas and electric convection ovens use a fan to circulate hot air around the oven cavity. More energy-efficient than radiant-heat ovens, they can cut cooking time by 30 percent and use reduced temperatures. So-called "true-convection" models have isolated heating elements and fans to provide more even results.

Convection is excellent for roasting and baking (it first caught on in commercial bakeries) but is less effective for foods cooked in deep or covered dishes (cakes, stews, casseroles). Some cooks complain that convection heat dries out certain foods.

**MICROWAVE OVENS.** Foods cook quickly with high-frequency microwaves, but they don't brown. Some models offer a separate browning element; other built-ins combine microwave with radiant and/or convection cooking. Microwave models range from subcompacts (about .5 cubic foot) up to full size (1 cubic foot or bigger). Most units are hinged on the left.

*BUILT-UNDER OVEN*

*OVER-COUNTER MICROWAVE*

Microwaves can be placed on a counter, built into cabinetry, or purchased as part of a double wall oven or double oven range. You might even consider two microwaves—one small, portable unit near the refrigerator or breakfast nook for quick warming, the second in a bank of wall ovens. When possible, mount the microwave so its bottom is 24 to 48 inches off the floor.

Some models, specially designed to be installed above a range (underneath wall cabinets), incorporate a vent and cooking lights; these are wider (30 inches) and shallower (13 to 17 inches deep). Some designers frown on over-the-cooktop placement because it's potentially hazardous when burners below are in use.

Microwave features include memory bank, programmable cooking, timers, temperature probe, rotisserie, and electronic sensors (these automatically calculate cooking time and power levels). However, if you use a microwave primarily to heat coffee or convenience foods, you can probably bypass these bells and whistles.

# Ventilation

CLEAN THE AIR—AND DO IT WITH STYLE

Installing a kitchen without planning for proper ventilation is akin to lighting a fire in the fireplace without opening the flue. The system you choose must tackle smoke, heat, grease, moisture, and odors, while remaining as quiet as possible (8 sones or less). Vent units range from totally discreet to bold and flashy.

Your main choice is between hoods and downdraft systems.

## Vent hoods

Unless your range is downvented, you'll need a hood above the cooktop. Ducted hoods channel air outside; roof- or wall-mounted exterior blowers are the best blend of quiet operation and efficiency. There are two basic types: freestanding and cabinet- or wall-mounted. In addition, the cabinet-mounted hood comes in a sleek, low-profile version that pulls out from under a wall-hung cabinet for use. Whichever type you prefer, look beyond style for convenient, variable speed controls and built-in lighting.

If exterior venting is impossible, cabinet-mounted ductless hoods can draw out some smoke and grease through charcoal filters—but they return air and heat to the room.

A hood should cover the entire cooking area and extend 3 to 6 inches over on each side. If the hood is 16 to 21 inches deep, place its bottom edge 24 inches above cooktop. Position a 24-inch-deep hood up to 30 inches away.

*FREESTANDING VENT HOOD*

CABINET-MOUNTED HOOD

## Downdraft systems

If your kitchen style is open and orderly, you may wish to put a downdraft system in the range or cooktop instead of a hood overhead—especially if the unit is housed in an island or peninsula. Standard, convertible, and modular cooktops all come with downventing options. Some have grillwork between cooktop modules; others run along the back and may be raised electronically for use. The downdraft unit sets up air currents that draw smoke, heat, and moisture down; grease is trapped below.

Are there drawbacks? Downvents don't work as well on a tall stockpot as on a skillet at cooktop level. However, recent systems are more efficient than those available just a few years ago. There have also been problems with long, twisted duct runs. Always route a downdraft system to the closest outside wall.

## What size do you need?

The power of a fan or blower is rated in cubic feet per minute (CFM).

To find the number of CFM for your wall- or cabinet-mounted hood, the basic formula is: 50 to 70 CFM times the square footage (length times width) of the hood opening. The minimum rating is 300 CFM.

To determine the rating for a freestanding hood, the formula is: 100 CFM times the hood's square footage.

The minimum rating is 600 CFM. The shorter and straighter the duct run, the more efficient your hood will be.

Commercial ranges and cooktops can really crank out the heat; you may need to make extra provisions for these. In addition, if you live in a super-insulated modern house and are planning a powerful vent system, you could require an intake fan or window to replace the air that's being sucked out. If you have questions, consult an experienced HVAC professional.

LOW-PROFILE, PULLOUT HOOD

DOWNDRAFT VENT

# Refrigerators

COOL NEW ALTERNATIVES TO THE OLD ICEBOX

*BUILT-IN, SIDE-BY-SIDE REFRIGERATOR, OPEN AND CLOSED*

Refrigerators come in three basic versions: freestanding, built-in, and under-counter. Which you choose depends on space, aesthetics, and budget. You'll want to take a close look at available features. Think energy, too: every refrigerator should come with an energy guide label that tells you just how that model rates.

## Freestanding models

Standard refrigerators measure from 27 to 32 inches deep, so they stand out from 24-inch-deep base cabinets.

Consider these features: number of shelves, humidity drawers, meat storage compartments, temperature controls, defrosting method, ice-maker and water dispenser, convenience

*UNDER-COUNTER WINE COOLER*

*MODULAR PULLOUT DRAWER*

door, and energy-saving devices such as a power-saver switch.

Popular two- or three-door, side-by-side refrigerator/freezers permit easy visibility and access to food, but their relatively narrow shelves make it difficult to store bulky items. Their opposing door swings can block countertop access on both sides.

Other double-door models have the freezer positioned at the unit's bottom or top. The bottom-mount design has a handy freezer pullout drawer and makes it easier to reach the more often used refrigerator section. The top-mount style comes in the greatest number of sizes and options.

Though single-door refrigerators are smaller and more economical, they typically offer little freezer space, and that space may not get cold enough. Many of these units must be defrosted manually.

As a rule of thumb, figure 8 cubic feet of refrigerator space for two people; add 1 cubic foot for each additional family member and 2 extra cubic feet if you entertain frequently. A refrigerator runs best when it isn't stuffed to the gills.

Two cubic feet per person is the rule for a freezer compartment.

## Built-ins

Gaining in popularity are relatively expensive 24-inch-deep built-ins, which fit right into a standard run of cabinets. Most models offer interchangeable door panels to match surrounding cabinet doors. Others flaunt the "commercial" look, matching stainless steel with glass doors.

Because these units have compressor and condenser units mounted on top, they don't require dust-gathering gaps for ventilation; they also can be

cleaned and serviced in place. One minus (besides the high price) is the relatively shallow interior.

## Under-counter models

Standard under-counter refrigerators, traditional choices for very small kitchens or separate entertainment areas, are 33 to 34 inches high, 18 to 57 inches wide, and 25 to 32 inches deep, with a 2.5- to 6-cubic-foot capacity.

Now there's also a new generation of trim built-ins that slide into 24-inch-deep base cabinet runs, offering interchangeable refrigerator, freezer, and even wine-cooling compartments. Some models feature handy pullout drawers for easy low-level access. Not only do these "modular" units blend into sleek modern kitchens, they can be positioned just where they're needed in multitask, several-cook layouts.

# Trash Talk

## PUT GRIME AND GARBAGE IN THEIR PLACES

Frequently, today's cleanup centers include both a dishwasher (see page 93) and a trash compactor—one on either side of the sink. In addition, you'll find a broad selection of built-in bins, baskets, and pullouts for organizing trash, recyclables, and composting scraps. Here are some shopping tips.

### Trash compactors

Compactors reduce bulky trash such as cartons, cans, and bottles to a fourth of the original size. A typical compacted load—a week's worth of trash from a family of four—will weigh 20 to 28 pounds. Remember that a compactor is for dry, clean trash only—you'll still have to do some work.

Once considered an unequivocal boon, the trash compactor is currently viewed with disdain by many. Opponents state that recycling programs in urban areas have made compactors unnecessary; others argue that compressed trash takes longer to break down in landfills. But in remote locales, or in spots where recycling is nonexistent or impractical, a compactor might at least reduce the volume of trash that's thrown away.

If you're considering one, look for such features as a separate top-bin door for loading small items (even while the unit is operating), drop-down or tilt-out drawers for easy bag removal, and a charcoal-activated filter or deodorizer to control odor. Also

*RECYCLING BINS*

look for a toe-operated door latch and a key-activated safety switch.

Standard appliance colors are available; finish options include custom wood panels with or without trim kits. Sizes vary from 12 to 18 inches wide (15 inches is standard), 18 to 24½ inches deep, and 34 to 36 inches high.

### Bins & baskets

Trudging to the garage with every recyclable can or compost scrap can get old quickly. But where in the kitchen can you temporarily store potato peelings, aluminum and tin cans, glass bottles and jars, plastic milk jugs, newspapers, or paper bags?

If you're lucky enough to have a walk-in pantry, you might find space there for standard recycling bins or baskets. Otherwise, base cabinet drawers and pullouts or tall utility cabinets are the place to start.

Some bins and baskets sit behind standard doors; some pivot into place when the door opens; others slide out on pullout guides or from their own stackable frames. You can also buy special-use base cabinets with built-in dividers and tilt-down bins or retrofit standard two-drawer cabinets. Of course, if you're planning custom cabinets, you can also design your own system.

# CLOSING THE DOOR ON LAUNDRY

It's a dirty world, and often all that stands between you and the mess outside is your washer and dryer. They usually do their grime fighting in remote (and inconvenient) recesses of the house—a laundry room, garage, or hallway closet. But increasingly, the dynamic duo is being put to work in the handier, more accessible kitchen.

Here the goal is to hide both machines behind seamless doors when not in use. A standard, side-by-side pair can be housed in a recessed alcove or a popout that borrows from an adjacent space. Add shelves or wall cabinets for laundry goods, and perhaps a utility sink alongside. Cover it all up with easy-to-open bifold, sliding, or pocket doors—or with seamless cabinet doors that offer access to each area independently.

Or nestle a compact washer and dryer—either side-by-sides or stackables—into a continuous cabinet run, masking them with standard cabinet doors to match surroundings. Adjacent cabinets or drawers might house an ironing board, a pullout sorting table, and a tilt-down clothes bin.

Remember that you'll need to wire and plumb these appliances as required; also, a gas dryer will require a vent duct to the outside.

*A stackable washer and dryer (top left) saves floor space; a built-in ironing board (top right) folds behind its closed door. Side-by-side unit (above) slides below counter height.*

# Flooring

ADD A FIRM—OR EVEN A RESILIENT—FOUNDATION

Two primary requirements for a kitchen floor are moisture resistance and durability. Resilient flooring, ceramic tile, and properly sealed hardwood or masonry are all good candidates. Resilient flooring is the simplest (and usually the least expensive) of the four to install; the other three are trickier. Tinted concrete is also catching on in high-tech surroundings. And don't rule out carpeting, especially the newer stain-resistant industrial versions.

## Planning checkpoints

Confused by the array of flooring types available today? For help, study the guide on the facing page. It's also a good idea to visit flooring suppliers and home centers; most dealers are happy to provide samples.

Beyond aesthetic considerations, you need to weigh the physical characteristics of flooring materials. Kitchen floors take a lot of wear and tear. Is your choice water resistant, durable, and easy to maintain? Is it hard to walk on, noisy, or slippery?

## What about subflooring?

Don't make any final flooring decision until you know the kind of subfloor your new flooring will require.

With proper preparation, a concrete slab can serve as a base for almost any type of flooring. Other subfloors are more flexible and not suitable for rigid materials such as masonry and ceramic tile unless they are built up with extra underlayment or floor framing. But too many layers underfoot can make the new kitchen floor awkwardly higher than surrounding rooms. If in doubt, check with a building professional or a flooring dealer.

*Cork tiles make a cushy kitchen floor that blends with many styles.*

# COMPARING FLOORS

## Resilient

**Advantages**. Generally made from solid vinyl or polyurethane, resilients are flexible, moisture and stain resistant, easy to install, and simple to maintain. Another advantage is the seemingly endless variety of colors, textures, patterns, and styles available. Tiles can be mixed to form custom patterns or provide color accents. Old-fashioned linoleum and cork are back as premium-grade materials.

Sheets run up to 12 feet wide, eliminating the need for seaming in many kitchens; tiles are

generally 12 inches square. Vinyl and rubber are comfortable to walk on. Prices are generally modest, but you'll pay more for custom tiles or imported products. A polyurethane finish may eliminate the need for waxing.

**Disadvantages.** Resilients are relatively soft, making them vulnerable to dents and tears, though such damage can often be repaired. Tiles may collect moisture between seams if improperly installed. Some vinyl still comes with a photographically applied pattern, but most is inlaid; the latter is more expensive but wears much better.

## Ceramic tile

**Advantages.** Made from hard-fired slabs of clay, ceramic tile is available in hundreds of patterns, colors, shapes, and finishes. Its durability and easy upkeep are definite advantages.

Tiles are usually classified as *quarry tile,* commonly unglazed (unfinished) red-clay tiles that are rough and water resistant; *terra-cotta,* unglazed tiles in earth-tone shades; *porcelain pavers,* rugged tiles in stone-like shades and textures; and *glazed floor tile,* available in glossy, matte, or textured finishes and in many colors.

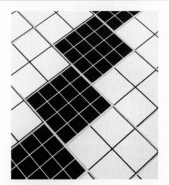

Floor tiles run the gamut of widths, lengths, and thicknesses—8-inch and 12-inch squares are most plentiful. Costs range from inexpensive to moderate; in general, porcelain is most expensive. Purer clays fired at higher temperature are generally costlier but better wearing.

**Disadvantages.** Tile can be cold, noisy, and, if glazed, slippery underfoot. Porous tiles will stain and harbor bacteria unless properly sealed. Grout spaces can be tough to keep clean, though mildew-resistant or epoxy grout definitely helps.

## Hardwood

**Advantages.** A classic hardwood floor creates a warm decor, feels good underfoot, and can be refinished. Oak is most common, with maple, birch, and other species also available.

The three basic types are narrow *strips* in random lengths; *planks* in various widths and random lengths; and wood *tiles,* laid in blocks or squares. Wood flooring may be factory-prefinished or unfinished, to be sanded and finished in place. "Floating" floor systems have several veneered strips atop each backing board. In

addition, you'll now find "planks" and "tiles" of high-pressure plastic laminate that look surprisingly like the real thing.

**Disadvantages.** Moisture damage and inadequate floor substructure are two bugaboos. Maintenance is another issue; some surfaces can be mopped or waxed, some cannot. Bleaching and some staining processes may wear unevenly and are difficult to repair. Cost is moderate to high, depending on wood species, grade, and finish.

## Stone

**Advantages.** Natural stone (such as slate, flagstone, marble, granite, and limestone) has been used as flooring for centuries. Today, its use is even more practical, thanks to the development of efficient sealers and surfacing techniques. Stone can be used in its natural shape—known as flagstone—or cut into rectangular blocks or more formal tiles. Generally, pieces are butted tightly together; irregular flagstones require wider grout joints.

**Disadvantages.** The cost of masonry flooring can be quite high, though recent diamond-saw technology has lowered it considerably. Moreover, the weight of the materials requires a very strong, well-supported subfloor. Some stone is cold and slippery underfoot, though new honed and etched surfaces are safer, subtler alternatives to polished surfaces. Certain stones, such as marble and limestone, absorb stains and dirt readily. Careful sealing is a must.

# Windows and Skylights

HELP YOUR NEW DESIGN SEE THE LIGHT OF DAY

Whether you'd like a sunny breakfast nook, a green-house unit for culinary plants, or simply a row of glass block sparkling in a backsplash area, you have an impressive collection of both ready-made and custom products to choose from. You can also combine glass in different forms (windows, skylights, blocks) and finishes (clear, translucent) to bring in more light and view while still protecting privacy.

## Windows

Windows are available with frames made of wood, clad wood, aluminum, vinyl, steel, or fiberglass (a newcomer). Generally, aluminum windows are the least expensive, wood and clad wood the most costly. Vinyl- or aluminum-clad wood windows and all-vinyl windows require little maintenance.

Operable windows for kitchens include double-hung, casement, sliding, hopper, and awning types. Which you choose depends partly on your home's style and partly on your ventilation needs. In addition, there are such specialty units as bays and bows—both popular for "stretching" breakfast areas—and greenhouse units, which can add space behind the sink or countertop.

Many of the greatest strides in window technology are taking place in glazing. Insulating glass is made of two or more panes of glass sealed together, with a space between the

panes to trap air. Low-e (low-emissivity) glass usually consists of two sealed panes separated by an air space and a transparent coating. Some manufacturers use argon gas between panes of low-e glass to add extra insulation.

Window shopping can require at least a passing acquaintance with

*Among the myriad of window styles are (1) primed wood casement with simulated divided lights, (2) wood slider with aluminum cladding and snap-on grille, (3) prefinished wood casement, (4) anodized aluminum slider, (5) vinyl double-hung, (6) wood circle with aluminum cladding, and (7) aluminum octagon.*

some specialized jargon. For a quick gloss, see "Window Words," at right.

## Skylights

You can pay as little as $100 for a fixed acrylic skylight, about $500 for a pivoting model that you crank open with a pole, or several thousand dollars for a motorized unit that automatically closes when a moisture sensor detects rain. The most energy-efficient designs feature double glazing and "thermal-break" construction.

Fixed skylights vary in shape from square to circular; they may be flat, domed, or pyramidal in profile. Most skylight manufacturers also offer at least one or two ventilating models that open to allow fresh air in and steam and heat out. Think of rotary roof windows as a cross between windows and skylights. They have sashes that rotate on pivots on each side of the frame, which permits easy cleaning. Unlike openable roof skylights, they are typically installed on sloping walls.

If there's space between the ceiling and roof,

*GLASS BLOCK*

you'll need a light shaft to direct light to the room below. It may be straight, angled, or splayed (wider at the bottom).

## Glass block

If you'd like to have some ambient daylight but don't want to lose your privacy, check out another glazing option, glass block. It provides an even, filtered light that com-plements many kitchen designs.

You can buy 3- or 4-inch-thick glass blocks in many sizes; rectangular and curved corner blocks are also available in a more limited selection. Textures can be smooth, wavy, rippled, bubbly, or crosshatched. Some blocks are clear, others softly translucent.

To locate glass block, look in the yellow pages under Glass—Block Structural, Etc. You may be able to special-order blocks through a regular glass or tile dealer.

---

## WINDOW WORDS

Strange, intimidating words seem to orbit the subject of windows and their components, construction, and installation. Here's a crash course in standard window jargon, enough to help you brave a showroom, building center, or product brochure.

**Apron.** An applied interior trim piece that runs beneath the unit, below the sill.

**Casement.** A window with a frame that hinges on the side, like a door.

**Casing.** Wooden window trim, especially interior, added by owner or contractor. Head casing runs at the top, side casings flank the unit.

**Cladding.** A protective sheath of aluminum or vinyl covering a window's exterior wood surfaces.

**Flashing.** Thin sheets, usually metal, that protect the wall or roof from leaks near the edges of windows or skylights.

**Glazing.** The window pane itself—glass, acrylic plastic, or other clear or translucent material. It may be one, two, or even three layers thick.

**Grille.** A decorative, removable grating that makes an expanse of glass look as though it were made up of many smaller panes.

**Jamb.** The frame that surrounds the sash or glazing. An extension jamb thickens a window to match a thick wall.

**Lights.** Separately framed panes of glass in a multipane window; each light is held by muntins.

**Low emissivity.** A high-tech treatment that sharply improves the thermal performance of glass, especially in double-glazed windows, at little added cost.

**Mullion.** A vertical dividing piece; whereas muntins separate small panes of glass, mullions separate larger expanses or whole windows.

**Muntin.** A slender strip of wood or metal framing a pane of glass in a multipane window.

**R-value.** Measure of a material's ability to insulate; the higher the number, the lower your heating or cooling bills should be.

**Sash.** A window frame surrounding glass. It may be fixed or operable.

**Sill.** An interior or exterior shelf below a window unit. An interior sill may be called a stool.

**U-value.** Measure of the energy efficiency of all the materials in the window; the lower the U-value, the less the waste.

# Light Fixtures

SPOTLIGHTING THE LATEST IN ARTIFICIAL LIGHT SOURCES

*WALL SCONCES*

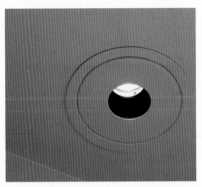

*RECESSED DOWNLIGHT*

*TRACK FIXTURES*

*LOW-VOLTAGE CABLE LIGHT*

*UNDER-CABINET STRIP LIGHTS*

Designers separate lighting into three categories: task, ambient, and accent. Task lighting illuminates a particular area where a visual activity—such as measuring baking ingredients—takes place. Ambient, or general, lighting fills in the undefined areas of a room with a soft level of light—enough, say, to munch a midnight snack by. Accent lighting, which is primarily decorative, is used to highlight architectural features, to set a mood, or to provide drama.

## Which fixtures are best?

Generally speaking, small and discreet are the bywords in kitchen light fixtures; consequently, recessed downlights are the most popular choice in today's kitchens. Though these fixtures, fitted with the right baffles or shields, can handle ambient, task, and accent needs by themselves, you'll probably want other sources, too, at least to fill in shadows. Typically, downlights follow countertops or shine on the sink or island. Track lights or mono-spots also offer pinpoint task lighting and can be aimed at a wall to provide a wash of ambient light.

In addition, designers frequently tuck task lighting behind a valance under wall cabinets and over countertops. For a whimsical touch, you might run decorative strip lights in a toe-space area or soffit.

Surface-mounted fixtures, once a kitchen mainstay, are now used specifically to draw attention. Hanging pendants are attractive in a breakfast nook or over an island—or anywhere where they won't present a hazard. Low-voltage cable lights combine the flexibility of standard track fixtures with a dash of high-tech style.

Dimmers (also called rheostats) enable you to set a fixture at any level from a soft glow to a radiant brightness. They also save energy.

## Light bulbs and tubes

Light sources can be grouped according to the way they produce light. INCANDESCENT LIGHT. This light, the kind used most frequently in our homes, is produced by a tungsten thread that burns slowly inside a glass bulb. A-bulbs are the old standbys; R- and PAR- bulbs produce a more controlled beam; and silvered-bowl types diffuse light. A number of decorative bulbs are also available.

Low-voltage incandescent lighting is especially useful for accent lighting. Operating on 12 or 24 volts, these lights require transformers, which are sometimes built into the fixtures, to step down the voltage from 120-volt household circuits.

Low-voltage fixtures are relatively expensive to buy. But in the long run, low-voltage lighting can be energy- and cost-efficient if carefully planned.

**FLUORESCENT LIGHT.** Fluorescent tubes are unrivaled for energy efficiency and last far longer than incandescent bulbs. In some areas, general lighting for new kitchens must be fluorescent.

Older fluorescent tubes have been criticized for noise, flicker, and poor color rendition. Electronic ballasts and better fixture shielding have remedied the first two problems; as for the last one, manufacturers have developed fluorescents in a wide spectrum of colors, from very warm to very cool.

**QUARTZ HALOGEN.** These bright, white sources are excellent for task lighting, pinpoint accenting, and other dramatic accents. Halogen is usually low-voltage but may use standard line current. The popular MR-16 bulb creates the tightest beam; for a longer reach and wider coverage, choose a PAR-bulb.

Halogen has two disadvantages: its high initial cost and its very high heat production. Be sure to choose a fixture specifically intended for halogen bulbs, and shop for UL-approved fixtures.

## COMPARING LIGHT BULBS AND TUBES

### INCANDESCENT

**A-Bulb**
**Description.** Familiar pear shape; frosted or clear.
**Uses.** Everyday household use.

**T—Tubular**
**Description.** Tube-shaped, from 5" long. Frosted or clear.
**Uses.** Cabinets, decorative fixtures.

**R—Reflector**
**Description.** White or silvered coating directs light out end of funnel-shaped bulb.
**Uses.** Directional fixtures; focuses light where needed.

**PAR—Parabolic aluminized reflector**
**Description.** Similar to auto headlamps; special shape and coating project light and control beam.
**Uses.** Recessed downlights and track fixtures.

**Silvered bowl**
**Description.** A-bulb, with silvered cap to cut glare and produce indirect light.
**Uses.** Track fixtures and pendants.

**Low-voltage strip**
**Description.** Like Christmas tree lights; in strips or tracks, or encased in flexible, waterproof plastic.
**Uses.** Task lighting and decoration.

### FLUORESCENT

**Tube**
**Description.** Tube-shaped, 5" to 96" long. Needs special fixture and ballast.
**Uses.** Shadowless work light; also indirect lighting.

**PL—Compact tube**
**Description.** U-shaped with base; 5¼" to 7½" long.
**Uses.** In recessed downlights; some PL tubes include ballasts to replace A-bulbs.

### QUARTZ HALOGEN

**High intensity**
**Description.** Small, clear bulb with consistently high light output; used in halogen fixtures only.
**Uses.** Specialized task lamps, torchères, and pendants.

**Low-voltage MR-16— (mini-reflector)**
**Description.** Tiny (2"-diameter) projector bulb; gives small circle of light from a distance.
**Uses.** Low-voltage track fixtures, mono-spots, and recessed downlights.

**Low-voltage PAR**
**Description.** Similar to auto headlight; tiny filament, shape, and coating give precise direction.
**Uses.** To project a small spot of light a long distance.

*Sunset*

*ideas for great*

# BATHROOMS

By the Editors of
Sunset Books

Sunset Books ■ Menlo Park, California

# contents

# Make a
# big splash

**T**HE WORD is out: people today want bathrooms to be bold, beautiful, and—especially—comfortable.

It wasn't always that way. The first wooden bathtubs, scenes of the painfully elaborate Saturday-night scrubs immortalized by Western movies, appeared in the mid-1800s. Soon these leaky vessels were replaced by cast-iron tubs—essentially horse troughs with legs. The bathroom as we know it came indoors only in the 1920s, and with no great fanfare. Health and privacy concerns, not aesthetics, prompted the move.

A new but mandatory 5- by 7-foot space—a "terra incognita"—now appeared on architects' and tract-builders' plans.

Today, whether due to the development of two-earner families, to greater stress in the outside world, or simply to the whims of the "me" generation, homeowners are asking their architects and designers to give new thought to the use of this space. The bathroom is no longer an out-of-sight, out-of-mind proposition; it's a rewarding part of the good life.

Now bathrooms tend to be bigger. They tend to be compartmentalized for multiple uses. And many are geared for relaxation as well as efficiency. The whirlpool tub—a trimmed-down version of the outdoor spa—has become a focal point in many designs. The "master suite"—a formal integration of bedroom, bath, and auxiliary spaces—is perhaps the crowning expression of the bathroom's newly expanded identity. Exercise equipment, saunas, steam showers, grooming alcoves, walk-in dressing wings, even indoor atriums are all options in the new master suite.

As with contemporary kitchen design, there's a freer mixing of materials and styles; an emphasis on artificial lighting and an appreciation of natural light expressed in the use of windows, skylights, and glass block; an interest in raised ceilings and fine detailing; and a new creativity in approaches to cabinetry.

Antique fixtures and fittings are being treated with fresh respect, but teamed with a huge assortment of new styles and finishes.

There's a growing attention to water conservation—in fact, it's mandated in some communities. Manufacturers are offering ultra-low-flush toilets, low-flow shower heads, and sink faucets that save water or shut off when the user's hand is withdrawn.

Safety is a concern. It's now much easier to find sturdy grab bars, nonskid fixtures, and shatterproof materials. You can buy pressure-balancing or temper-ature-limiting plumbing fittings to prevent scalds.

As the population ages and we gain new awareness of the needs of the phys-ically challenged, the "universal" or barrier-free bath is receiving deserved attention. Besides providing easy access, a major goal for today's barrier-free bath is aesthetic: it shouldn't look like a barrier-free bath.

Brainstorming a new bathroom is a threefold process—planning the space, defining a style, and choosing components. That's the sequence this book follows. You can tackle these steps in order or browse at will, either using the book as a detailed planning resource or simply choosing images and ideas to help your architect or designer understand more clearly what you want.

Ready to begin transforming that old bath? Simply turn the page.

# A PLANNING PRIMER

**W**ARM and traditional, high-tech, or colorfully whimsical: the individual styles may look different, but successful bathrooms have a lot in common. When a bathroom looks great and functions well, you can be sure that hours of planning went into its realization. Behind those shiny new fixtures and tiles are codes and clearances, critical dimensions, and effective design principles. **USE THIS CHAPTER** as a workbook for basic planning. We help you evaluate your existing bathroom first. Then we guide you through layout and design basics, and finish up by explaining how design and construction professionals can help you. **FOR INSPIRATION**, peruse the photos of successful bathrooms in the next two chapters. You'll see the latest in tubs and tiles, sinks and skylights, lighting and laminates. Soon you'll be on your way to creating the bathroom of your dreams.

# taking stock

**BEFORE YOU BEGIN** *a bathroom shopping spree, take time to assess what you already have. A clear, accurate base map—such as the one shown below—is your best planning tool.*

## Measure the space

To make your bathroom survey, you'll need either a folding wooden rule (shown above) or a steel measuring tape. First, sketch out your present layout (don't worry about scale), doodling in windows, doors, fixtures, and other features. Then measure each wall at counter height.

After you finish measuring, total the figures. Then take an overall measurement from corner to corner. The two figures should match. Measure each wall in the same manner.

## Make a base map

Now draw your bathroom to scale on graph paper (most bathroom designers use ½-inch scale—¼₄ actual size). An architect's scale is helpful but not really necessary. A T-square and triangle are all you need—plus some standard drafting paper with ¼-inch squares.

The example shown below includes a center-line to the sink plumbing and electrical symbols—for outlets, switches, and fixtures. Sketch in other features that might affect your plans.

**A SAMPLE BASE MAP**

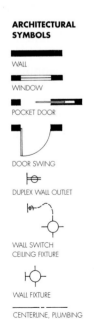

**ARCHITECTURAL SYMBOLS**

WALL

WINDOW

POCKET DOOR

DOOR SWING

DUPLEX WALL OUTLET

WALL SWITCH
CEILING FIXTURE

WALL FIXTURE

CENTERLINE, PLUMBING

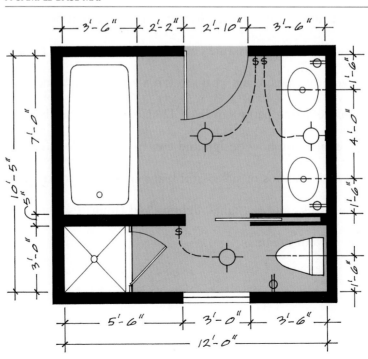

# A BATHROOM QUESTIONNAIRE

This questionnaire can help you analyze conditions in your present bathroom as you begin to think about remodeling or adding another bath. When used with your base map, it also provides a good starting point for discussing your ideas with architects, designers, or showroom personnel. Note your answers on a separate sheet of paper, adding any important preferences or dislikes that come to mind. Then gather your notes, any clippings you've collected, and a copy of your base map, and you're ready to begin.

1. What's your main reason for changing your bathroom?

2. How many people will be using the room? List adults, children, and their ages.

3. Are users left-handed? Right-handed? How tall is each one?

4. Is the bath to be used by an elderly or disabled person? Is that individual confined to a wheelchair?

5. How many other bathrooms do you have?

6. Are you planning any structural changes?

   ☐ Addition to existing house
   ☐ Greenhouse window or sunroom
   ☐ Skylight  ☐ Other

7. Is the bath located on the first or second floor? Is there a full basement, crawl space, or concrete slab beneath it? Is there a second floor, attic, or open ceiling above it?

8. If necessary, can present doors and windows be relocated?

9. What's the rating of your electrical service?

10. What type of heating system do you have? Does any ducting run through a bathroom wall?

11. What is the style of your home's exterior?

12. What style (for example, high-tech, country, romantic) would you like for your new bathroom?

13. Do you favor compartmentalized layouts or a more open look?

14. List your present fixtures. What new fixtures are you planning?

    ☐ Bathtub  ☐ Shower  ☐ Tub/shower combination
    ☐ Vanity  ☐ Sink or multiple sinks  ☐ Toilet
    ☐ Bidet

15. What secondary activity areas would you like to include?

    ☐ Dressing area  ☐ Makeup area
    ☐ Steam shower or sauna  ☐ Exercise facilities
    ☐ Desk  ☐ Entertainment center  ☐ Garden
    ☐ Laundry facilities

16. What color combinations do you like? And what fixture finish do you prefer: white, pastel, full color?

17. What cabinet material do you prefer: wood, laminate, or other? If wood, should it be painted or stained? Light or dark? If natural, do you want oak, maple, pine, cherry?

18. What countertop and backsplash materials do you prefer?

    ☐ Laminate  ☐ Ceramic tile  ☐ Solid surface
    ☐ Wood  ☐ Stone  ☐ Other

19. What are your storage requirements?

    ☐ Medicine cabinet  ☐ Drawers  ☐ Vanity
    ☐ Tall cabinet
    ☐ Linen closet  ☐ Laundry hamper or chute
    ☐ Rollout baskets
    ☐ Open shelving  ☐ Other

20. What flooring do you have? Do you need new flooring?

    ☐ Wood  ☐ Resilient  ☐ Ceramic tile  ☐ Stone
    ☐ Other

21. What are present wall and ceiling coverings? What wall treatments do you like?

    ☐ Paint  ☐ Wallpaper  ☐ Washable vinyl paper
    ☐ Wood  ☐ Faux finish  ☐ Ceramic tile  ☐ Other

22. Would you prefer natural or mechanical ventilation?

23. What natural light sources are possible?

    ☐ Skylight  ☐ Window  ☐ Clerestory
    ☐ Glass block

24. Which forms of artificial lighting will you want?

    ☐ Incandescent  ☐ Fluorescent  ☐ Halogen
    ☐ 120-volt or low-voltage?

25. What lighting fixture types will you need?

    ☐ Recessed downlights  ☐ Track lights
    ☐ Wall-mounted fixtures  ☐ Ceiling-mounted fixtures
    ☐ Makeup lights  ☐ Indirect soffit lighting
    ☐ Display lighting

26. What time framework do you have for completion?

27. What budget figure do you have in mind?

# layout
# basics

**NOW COMES** *the fun of planning your new bathroom. Layout is a three-part process that includes weighing basic options; blocking out placement of fixtures, cabinets, and amenities; and double-checking efficient heights and clearances. There's no perfect sequence—the trick is to work back and forth. These rules are not absolute, and in very small or oddly shaped spaces you'll certainly need to compromise.*

## Classic layouts

While brainstorming, it helps to have some basic layout schemes in mind. The floor plans shown on the facing page are both practical and efficient. Keep in mind that these layouts can be combined, adapted, and expanded to meet your needs. For installation examples, see "Great Bathroom Ideas," beginning on page 137.

**POWDER ROOM.** This two-fixture room, also known as a guest bath or a half-bath, contains a toilet and a sink and perhaps some limited storage space. Fixtures can be placed side by side or on opposite walls, depending on the shape of the room. Very small sinks are available for extra-tight spaces.

Because the guest bath has high visibility but only sporadic use, it's a good place to enjoy more decorative but perhaps less practical finishes such as copper, glass, or upholstery. The door should swing open against a wall clear of any fixtures. Since space may be tight, a pocket door may be the solution.

Consideration should be given to privacy, ventilation, and soundproofing. A powder room should preferably open off a hallway—not off a living, family, or dining space.

**FAMILY BATH.** The family bath usually contains three fixtures—a toilet, a sink, and a bathtub or shower or combination tub/shower. The fixture arrangement varies, depending on the size and shape of the room. Family baths often have cluster, or corridor, layouts; these should be at least 5 by 7 feet.

Compartmentalizing fixture areas enables several family members to use the bathroom at the same time. A common arrangement is to isolate the toilet and shower (often including a small secondary sink in this area) from the basin and grooming area. This configuration can work well when adding a new bathroom isn't feasible.

The family bath is one of the most frequently used rooms in the house. Therefore, you'll want to choose durable, easy-to-clean fixtures and finishes.

**CHILDREN'S BATH.** Ideally, this bathroom is located so that each child has easy access.

When several children are involved, consider a single bath with two doors, or shared bathing and toilet facilities and an individual sink and

**SAMPLE LAYOUTS**

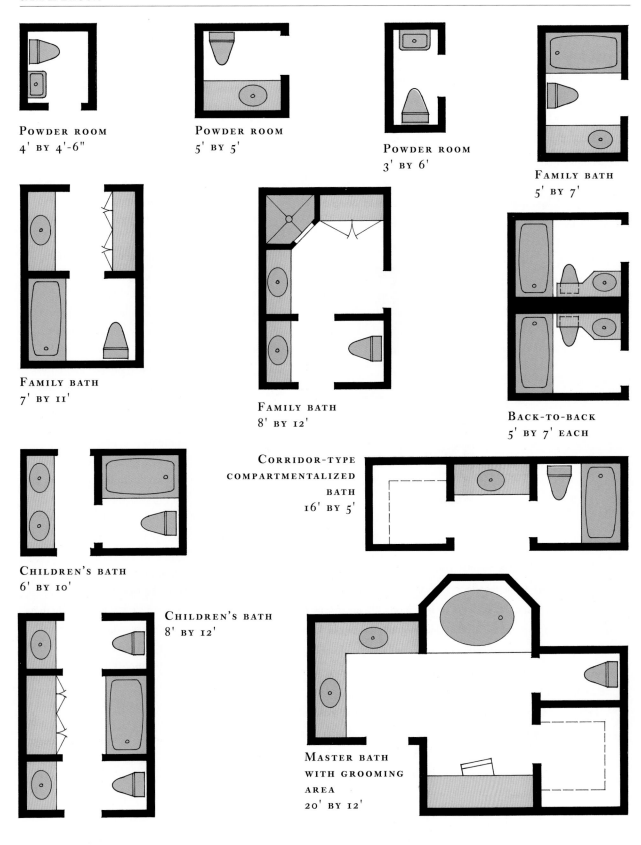

POWDER ROOM
4' BY 4'-6"

POWDER ROOM
5' BY 5'

POWDER ROOM
3' BY 6'

FAMILY BATH
5' BY 7'

FAMILY BATH
7' BY 11'

FAMILY BATH
8' BY 12'

BACK-TO-BACK
5' BY 7' EACH

CHILDREN'S BATH
6' BY 10'

CORRIDOR-TYPE
COMPARTMENTALIZED
BATH
16' BY 5'

CHILDREN'S BATH
8' BY 12'

MASTER BATH
WITH GROOMING
AREA
20' BY 12'

## UNIVERSAL DESIGN

If you are remodeling a bath for a disabled or elderly person, or if you're simply looking down the road, be aware of the growing trend toward "universal" or barrier-free design.

Special heights, clearances, and room dimensions may be required. For instance, to accommodate a wheelchair, the room's openings—from door to shower to toilet enclosure—should be at least 34 inches wide. You'll also need to plan turnaround areas near fixtures; a 5-foot diameter is ideal. The door should swing out to allow easy movement in and out of the room. The shower should be curbless so a wheelchair can roll in unobstructed.

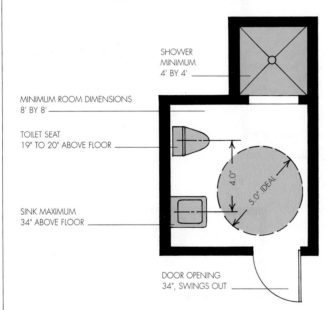

SHOWER
MINIMUM
4' BY 4'

MINIMUM ROOM DIMENSIONS
8' BY 8'

TOILET SEAT
19" TO 20" ABOVE FLOOR

4.0'

5.0' IDEAL

SINK MAXIMUM
34" ABOVE FLOOR

DOOR OPENING
34", SWINGS OUT

User-friendly heights are also critical. A sink must be no more than 34 inches from the floor and important storage areas should be between 15 and 48 inches high. It's important to leave an open space below the sink that allows ample knee room for a seated user; plan to cover under-sink plumbing. No handles, switches, or other controls should be more than 48 inches off the floor.

Exchange standard doorknobs, faucet handles, and cabinet hardware for levers and pulls that can be operated with one closed hand or a wrist. Grab bars are a boon in shower, tub, and toilet areas. Plan a seat inside the shower or tub. Extra lighting may also be required.

dressing area for each child. Color coding of drawers, towel hooks, and other storage areas can prevent territorial squabbles.

Children's baths require special attention to safety and maintenance. Single-control faucets minimize the possibility of a hot-water burn. Slip-resistant surfaces can help avoid accidents. Plastic-laminate counters and cabinets are durable and simplest to clean.

**MASTER BATH/SUITE.** This room has become more than just a place to grab a quick shower and run a comb through your hair. No longer merely a utilitarian space, today's master bath reflects the personality and interests of its owners. Besides toilet and bathing facilities and dressing and grooming areas, it can include amenities such as fireplaces, whirlpool baths, oversize tubs, saunas, and bidets. Outside such a bath is a natural place for a spa, sunbathing deck, or private garden.

Here are some "extras" you can plan into your master bath. Make sure that you provide adequate ventilation to prevent water damage (from splashes and condensation) to delicate objects and equipment.

■ **EXERCISE ROOM.** Depending on space, you can set up everything from a space-efficient "ballet barre" to a fully equipped in-house gym.

■ **MAKEUP CENTER.** A well-lit area for makeup application and storage is an asset in almost any bath. The area could include an adjustable makeup mirror with magnification and its own light source (see page 218).

■ **ENTERTAINMENT CENTER.** Whether built in or housed in a freestanding furniture piece, entertainment amenities like a TV, VCR, and sound system can amplify a master suite's sense of luxury and relaxation.

■ **ART GALLERY.** You can showcase works of art or build craft pieces, such as handmade tiles or a stained-glass window, right into the design.

■ **GREENHOUSE.** Because of the high moisture and humidity level, plants often thrive in a bathroom. It's an ideal place to bring a touch of nature into the house.

## Arranging fixtures

The more facts you have available, the easier it will be to work with your layouts. You'll keep costs down if you select a layout that uses the existing water supply, drain lines, and vent stack. If you're adding on to your house, try to locate the new bathroom near an existing bathroom or the kitchen. It's also more economical to arrange fixtures against one or two walls, eliminating the need for additional plumbing lines.

To begin, position the largest unit—the bathtub or shower—within the floor plan, allowing space for convenient access, for cleaning, and (if needed) for bathing a child.

Next, place the sink (or sinks). The most frequently used fixture in the bathroom, the sink should ideally be out of the traffic pattern. Allow ample room in front for reaching below the sink, and give plenty of elbow room at the sides.

Locate the toilet (and bidet, if you have one) away from the door; often the toilet is placed beside the tub or shower. A toilet and bidet should be positioned next to each other. Don't forget the swing radius for windows and doors.

There are standard minimum clearances in a well-planned bathroom (see "Heights and clearances," below). If an elderly or disabled person will use the space, you'll need to increase these clearances as much as possible (see "Universal Design," on the facing page).

To visualize possible layouts, first draw scale outlines of fixtures and cabinets you're considering, then photocopy these and cut them out. Move the cutouts around on a tracing of your base map. Then draw the shapes onto the plan.

## Heights and clearances

Building codes and bath industry guidelines specify certain clearances between, beside, and in front of bathroom fixtures to allow adequate room for use, cleaning, and repair. To help in your initial planning, check the minimum clearances shown at right.

Generally, you can locate side-by-side fixtures closer together than fixtures positioned opposite

## MINIMUM FIXTURE CLEARANCES

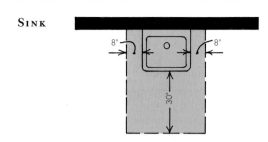

SINK

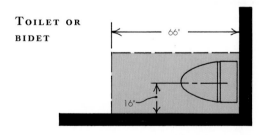

DOUBLE SINK

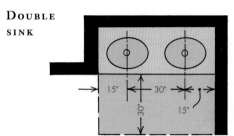

BATHTUB

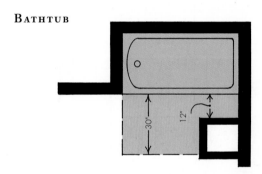

TOILET OR BIDET

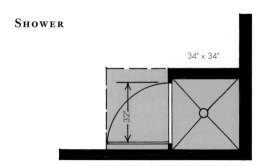

SHOWER

**STANDARD HEIGHTS**

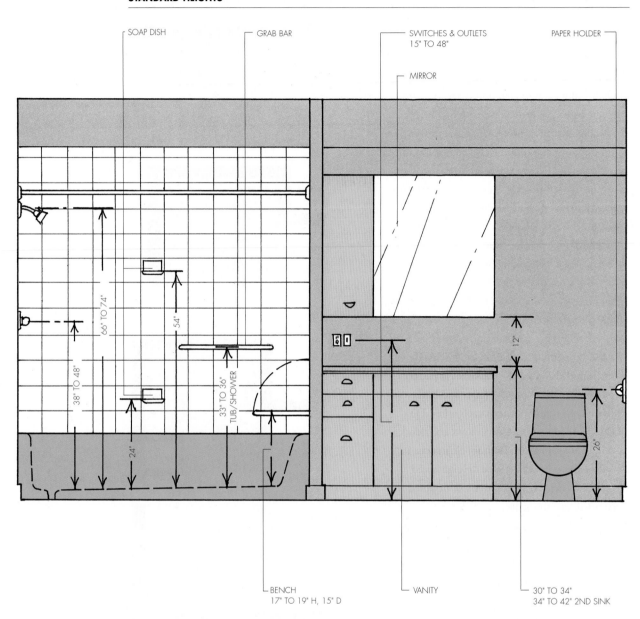

SOAP DISH

GRAB BAR

SWITCHES & OUTLETS
15" TO 48"

PAPER HOLDER

MIRROR

66" TO 74"

54"

38" TO 48"

33" TO 36"
TUB/SHOWER

24"

12"

26"

BENCH
17" TO 19" H, 15" D

VANITY

30" TO 34"
34" TO 42" 2ND SINK

each other. If a sink is opposite a bathtub or toilet, keep a minimum of 30 inches between them, preferably more.

Shown above are standard heights for cabinets, countertops, shower heads, and accessories. If you're planning multiple sinks, the first should be no higher than 34 inches off the floor; if desired, the second may be between 34 and 42 inches above the floor, depending on the height of the user.

## Playing it safe

About 25 percent of all home accidents occur in the bathroom. Through precautionary planning, however, you can greatly reduce the risk of injury.

First, select nonslip fixtures and surface materials. Anchor carpeting and buy rugs or bath mats with nonskid backing. Large tubs, especially those mounted in tall platforms or recessed with steps, are dangerous for children and adults with physical problems. Choose tempered glass, plastic, or other shatterproof materials for construction and accessories. Avoid mounting objects such as towel bars with sharp corners at eye level, and plan to clip or round countertop edges.

If children live in or visit your house, plan to store medicines and household cleansers in cabinets with safety latches or locks. Make sure that you can access the bathroom from the outside during an emergency.

Also be sure electrical receptacles are grounded and protected by ground fault circuit interrupters (GFCIs), which cut off power immediately if current begins leaking anywhere along the circuit. Outlets should be out of reach from the shower or bathtub. Keep portable heaters out of the bathroom. Install sufficient lighting, including a night light.

To avoid scalding, lower the setting on your water heater (see "Water and Energy Conservation," at right), install a temperature-limiting mixing valve, or use a pressure-balanced valve to avoid having sudden temperature drops.

Install L-shaped or horizontal grab bars, each capable of supporting 300 pounds, in tub and shower areas. Installation must be done properly—plywood reinforcing and bracing between wall studs may be required. Plaster-mounted bars don't provide reliable support.

## What about storage?

While a powder room has minimal storage requirements, a family bath should include individual storage space for each family member, as well as places to keep cleaning supplies, paper products, soap, and incidentals. Vanities and other cabinets come with a variety of racks, shelves, pullouts, and lazy Susans, making limited storage space more efficient.

Today's bathrooms may also double as dressing and grooming areas as well; take time to consider these requirements. And how about a compact washer and dryer team, or a built-in ironing board?

# WATER AND ENERGY CONSERVATION

There are several simple conservation measures you can take in the bathroom. If you intend to replace fixtures and fittings, look at those specifically designed to save water and energy. Many manufacturers offer water-saving toilets, faucets, shower heads, and hand-held shower attachments at prices comparable to those of their conventional counterparts. Such fixtures and fittings can reduce both the amount of water used and the amount of energy needed to heat water for bathing.

New ultra-low-flush (ULF) toilets use only 1.6 gallons or less per flush, compared with 5 to 7 gallons used by conventional toilets. These water-savers are often required in new construction. How much do ULFs really save over conventional toilets? Conservative estimates are 20 percent of total indoor water consumption for a family of four. Water-saving devices can be installed on old toilets.

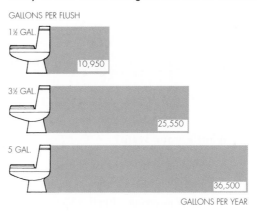

GALLONS PER FLUSH

1½ GAL.    10,950

3½ GAL.    25,550

5 GAL.    36,500

GALLONS PER YEAR

New shower heads should be low-flow types, rated at no more than 2.5 gallons per minute. Some faucet and shower fittings include control devices that reduce flow while maintaining spray force. Others have aerators or fine mesh screens that break the water into droplets and disperse it over a wider area.

To save energy used for heating the bathroom and heating the water, make sure that the water heater, pipes, and walls are appropriately insulated. You can also save energy by reducing the water heater's temperature setting from the average 140°F to 110° or 120° (some older dishwashers, though, require water that's hotter).

For more details on water- and energy-saving products, see "A Shopper's Guide," beginning on page 189.

# design
# ideas

**WITH A** *basic floor plan now in mind, you can begin to fine-tune your decorating scheme. Wall and ceiling coverings, flooring, woodwork, hardware, and even fixtures and fittings are powerful tools for evoking both style and mood. Style effects are directly linked to color, pattern, texture, size, and shape.*

*You'll find scores of successful designs beginning on page 137. Here, we introduce some reliable design concepts—for you to use as starting points, not as strict rules.*

### What's your style?

A decorating style has physical characteristics that identify it with a particular region, era, or artistic movement—English Victorian, Southwestern, Arts and Crafts, Art Deco, and so on. Because certain colors, materials, and decorative motifs are linked to certain historic decorating styles, they can be used to evoke the character of a period—or simply to personalize and give dignity to a bland modern room.

Representative styles include the following:
- Period (or traditional)
- Regional
- Country
- Romantic
- Contemporary (also high-tech, modernistic)
- Eclectic

This said, rarely are styles slavish replicas of historical designs. More typically, designers

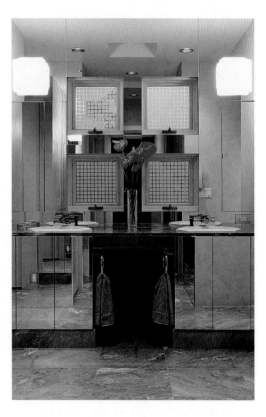

select among elements that echo the mood of a particular period or look. What matters is that you choose a style and mood you find sympathetic and comfortable. And if the bathroom is linked to adjoining spaces, its look should match or at least complement the overall style.

Do you prefer quiet
tradition or high-
impact modernism?
The elegant bath shown
at left is dressed with
classic stone surfaces,
frame-and-panel
cabinets, an arched
window, and other
traditional accessories.
On the facing page,
a bold, contemporary
design continues step
and square motifs
found throughout the
house; mirrored
surfaces increase
the impact.

*Color or no color? The monochromatic, white-on-white scheme shown at right features artfully varied tile shapes and sizes for subtle visual interest. In contrast, the bath on the facing page playfully mixes warm red-stained woodwork, variegated pink concrete counter-tops, and yellow walls with cool-colored stone on floor and shower.*

### Line, shape, and scale

Three visual keys to planning a balanced, pleasing bathroom design are line, shape, and scale. You'll need to think about each of these elements—as well as color, texture, and pattern—to achieve the look you want.

**LINE.** Most bathrooms incorporate many different types of lines—vertical, horizontal, diagonal, curved, and angular. But often one predominates, and can characterize the design. Vertical lines give a sense of height, horizontals impart width, diagonals suggest movement, and curved and angular lines contribute a feeling of grace and dynamism.

Continuity of line unifies a design. Try an elevation (head-on) sketch of your proposed bathroom. How do the vertical lines created by the shower or tub unit, cabinets, vanity, windows, doors, and mirrors fit together? Does the horizontal line marking the top of the window align with those created by the tops of the shower surround, door, and mirror?

**SHAPE.** Continuity and compatibility in shape also contribute to a unified design. Of course, you needn't repeat the same shape throughout the room—carried too far, that becomes monotonous.

Study the shapes created by doorways, windows, countertops, fixtures, and other elements.

Look at patterns in your flooring, wall coverings, shower curtain, and towels. Are they different or similar? If similar, are they boringly repetitive? Think of ways to complement existing shapes or add compatible new ones; for example, you might echo an arch over a recessed bathtub in the shape of a doorway, or in shelf trim.

SCALE. When the scale of bathroom elements is in proportion to the overall size of the room, the design feels harmonious. A small bath seems even smaller if equipped with large fixtures and a large vanity. But the same bath can look larger or at least in scale if fitted with space-saving fixtures, a petite vanity, and open shelves.

## Color

The size and orientation of your bathroom, your personal preferences, and the mood you want to create all affect color selection. Light colors reflect light, making walls appear to recede; thus, a small bath decorated in light colors feels more spacious. Dark colors absorb light and can make a ceiling seem lower or shorten a narrow room.

When considering colors for a small bathroom, remember that too much contrast has the same effect as dark color: it reduces the sense of expansiveness. Contrasting colors work well for adding accents or drawing attention to interesting structural elements. But if you need to conceal a problem feature, it's best to use one color throughout the area.

Depending on the orientation of your bathroom, you may want to use warm or cool colors to balance the quality of the light. While oranges, yellows, and colors with a red tone impart a feeling of warmth, they also contract space. Blues, greens, and colors with a blue tone make an area seem cooler—and larger.

A light, monochromatic color scheme (using different shades of one color) is restful and serene. Contrasting colors add vibrancy and excitement to a design. But a color scheme with contrasting colors can be overpowering unless you choose subdued tones of those colors.

## Texture and pattern

Textures and patterns work like color in influencing a room's style and sense of space. The bathroom's surface materials may include many different textures—from glossy countertops to sturdy but soft-looking wood cabinets to rustically irregular terra-cotta tile flooring.

Rough textures absorb light, make colors look duller, and lend a feeling of informality. Smooth textures reflect light and tend to suggest elegance or modernity. Using similar textures helps unify a design and create a mood.

Pattern choices must harmonize with the predominant style of the room. Although we usually associate pattern with wall coverings or tile, even natural substances such as wood and stone create patterns.

While variety in texture and pattern adds interest, too much variety can be overstimulating. It's best to let a strong feature or dominant pattern be the focus of your design and choose other surfaces to complement rather than compete with it.

# remodeling
# realities

**IF YOUR** *bathroom needs only a new vanity, a faucet, and some wallpaper to update it, you probably won't need to find out just what lurks behind those walls. But if you're shifting or adding fixtures, installing a vent fan, or removing a wall, you'll have to bone up on some basic remodeling realities. These next pages offer an overview of bathroom systems.*

## STRUCTURAL FRAMING

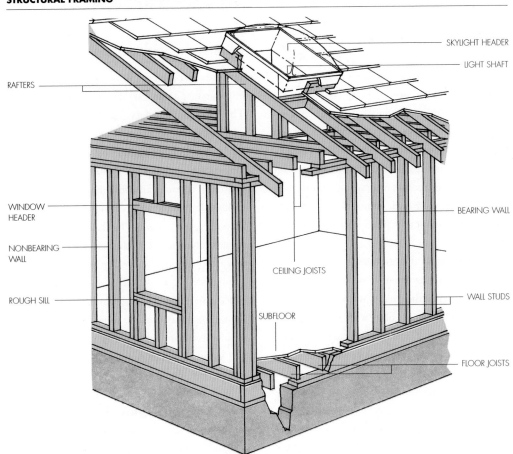

SKYLIGHT HEADER

LIGHT SHAFT

RAFTERS

WINDOW HEADER

NONBEARING WALL

ROUGH SILL

CEILING JOISTS

SUBFLOOR

BEARING WALL

WALL STUDS

FLOOR JOISTS

## Structural changes

If you're planning to open up a space, add a skylight, or recess a shower or tub into the floor, your remodel may require some structural modifications.

As shown on the facing page, walls are either bearing (supporting the weight of ceiling joists and/or second-story walls) or nonbearing. If you're removing all or part of a bearing wall, you must bridge the gap with a sturdy beam and posts. Nonbearing (also called partition) walls can usually be removed without too much trouble—unless pipes or wires run through them.

Doors and windows require special framing, as shown; the size of the header depends on the width of the opening and your local building codes. Skylights require similar cuts through ceiling joists and/or rafters.

A standard doorway may not be large enough to accommodate a new tub or whirlpool. If you're remodeling, make sure you can get such a fixture into the room.

Hardwood, ceramic, or stone floors require very stiff underlayment. You may need to beef up the floor joists and/or add additional plywood or backerboard on top. For a large new tub, you may also need to supply stronger floor framing.

## Plumbing restrictions

Your plumbing system is composed of two parts: a water-supply system, which brings water to the house and distributes it, and a drain-waste-ventilation (DWV) system, which removes water and waste.

Every house has a main soil stack. Below the level of the fixtures, it's the primary drainpipe. At its upper end, which protrudes through the roof, the stack becomes a vent. To minimize costs and keep the work simple, arrange a fixture or group of fixtures so they are as close to the present pipes as possible.

A proposed fixture located within a few feet of the main stack usually can be vented directly by the stack. Sometimes a fixture located far from the main stack requires its own branch

**PLUMBING**

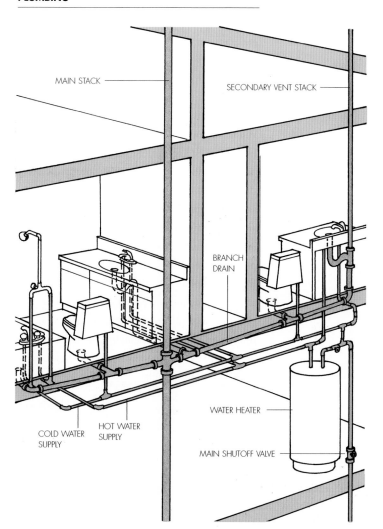

MAIN STACK

SECONDARY VENT STACK

BRANCH DRAIN

WATER HEATER

COLD WATER SUPPLY

HOT WATER SUPPLY

MAIN SHUTOFF VALVE

drain and a secondary vent stack (a big job). Be sure to check your local plumbing codes for exact requirements.

Generally, it's an easy matter—at least conceptually—to extend existing water-supply pipes to a new sink or tub. But if you're working on a concrete slab foundation, you'll need to drill through the slab or bring the pipes through the wall from another point above floor level.

## Electrical requirements

When planning your new bathroom, take a good look at the existing electrical system. Most houses today have both 120-volt and 240-volt capabilities. But older homes with two-wire (120 volts only) service of less than 100 amps might not be able to supply the electricity needed to operate a new whirlpool tub, sauna, steam generator, or electric heater. You may need to upgrade your electrical system.

The National Electrical Code (NEC) requires that all bathroom receptacles be protected by ground fault circuit interrupters (GFCIs). If you're adding a new wall, you may be required by code to add an outlet every 12 feet or one per wall. In addition, codes may strictly dictate the placement of outlets, appliance switches, and even light fixtures in wet areas.

While it's possible to locate electrical wiring inside conduit that is surface-mounted, it is preferable to enclose all wires within the walls. Before completing your plan, try to track down any plumbing pipes, heating ducts, or other electrical wires already concealed there; sleuth from open areas (the basement, the attic, an unfinished garage) to identify spots where such utilities enter the walls.

### ELECTRICAL WIRING

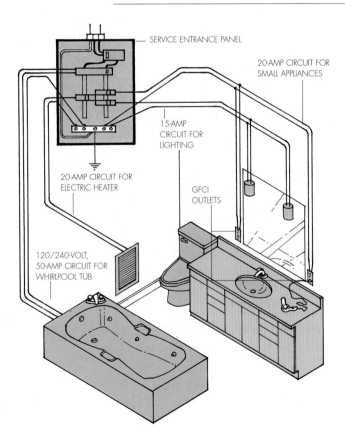

## MECHANICAL SYSTEMS

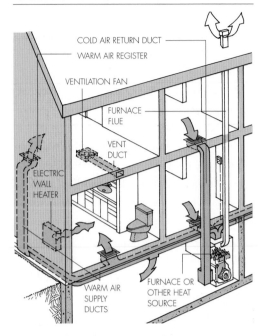

## Mechanical (HVAC) systems

Unless the bath contains a heating duct and register, you'll need to determine how to extend the supply and return air ducts (a major undertaking) to connect with the rest of your central system. Since you'll be using the bathroom only intermittently, you may wish to provide an auxiliary heat source rather than link to your central system. A small wall- or ceiling-mounted heater can provide all the warmth you need. If you're working on an addition, consider installing a radiant-heat floor.

All gas heaters require a gas-supply line and must be vented to the outside, so you'll probably want to locate a gas heater on an exterior wall. Otherwise, you'll have to run the vent through the attic or crawl space and the roof.

Ventilation is critical. Even if you have good natural ventilation, you may want to add some forced ventilation. In a windowless bathroom, a fan is required by code. It's important that your exhaust fan have adequate capacity, rated in cubic feet per minute (CFM). The fan should be capable of exchanging the air at least eight times per hour. (For vent fan particulars, see page 209.)

## DOLLARS AND CENTS

How much will your new bathroom cost? According to the National Kitchen & Bath Association, the average figure is $9,300. This is, of course, only the sketchiest of estimates. You may simply need to replace a countertop, add light fixtures, or exchange a worn-out bathtub to achieve a satisfying change. On the other hand, extensive structural changes coupled with ultra-high-end materials and fixtures can easily add up to $40,000 or more.

As shown below, labor typically eats up 21 percent of the pie; cabinets come in at around 33 percent; and, on the average, fixtures and fittings represent another 16 percent. Structural, plumbing, and electrical changes all affect the final figure significantly.

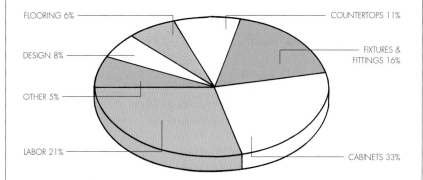

FLOORING 6%
COUNTERTOPS 11%
DESIGN 8%
FIXTURES & FITTINGS 16%
OTHER 5%
LABOR 21%
CABINETS 33%

How do you keep the budget under control? For starters, identify whether you're looking at a simple face-lift, a more extensive replacement, or a major structural remodel. Fixture, fitting, and material prices vary greatly. Obtain ballpark figures in different categories, mull them over, then present your architect, designer, or retailer with a range of options and a bottom line with which you can be comfortable. You can, of course, save a substantial piece of the pie by providing labor yourself—but be sure you're up to the task.

If you use a design professional, expect to be charged either a flat fee or a percentage (usually 10 to 15 percent) of the total cost of goods purchased. General contractors include the fee in their bids.

Don't make price your only criterion for selection. Quality of work, reliability, rapport, and on-time performance are also important. Ask professionals for the names and telephone numbers of recent clients. Call several and ask them how happy they were with the process and the results. Some may allow you to come and take a look at the finished work.

# gearing
# up

**ONCE YOU'VE** *worked out an efficient layout, decided on storage requirements, and planned color and design schemes, it's time to draw up a revised floor plan. For help choosing new fixtures, cabinets, countertops, flooring, and so on, see "A Shopper's Guide," beginning on page 189. Be sure also to think about light fixtures and electrical switches and receptacles. And don't forget such finishing touches as doorknobs and drawer pulls, towel bars and moldings, curtains and blinds—details that can really pull a design together.*

### The final plan

Draw your new floor plan, or working drawing, the same way you did the existing plan (see page 118). On the new plan, include existing features you want to preserve and all the changes you want to make. If you prefer, you can hire a designer, drafter, or contractor to draw the final plan for you. Elevation sketches usually aren't required, but they'll prove helpful in planning the work.

For more complicated projects, your local building department may require additional detailed drawings of structural, plumbing, and wiring changes. You may also need to show areas adjacent to the bathroom so officials can determine how the project will affect the rest of your house. To discover just which codes may affect your project and whether a permit is required, check with your city or county building department.

If you do the ordering of materials for your project, you'll need to compile a detailed master list. Not only will this launch your work, but it will also help you keep track of purchases and deliveries. For each item, specify the following information: name and model or serial number, manufacturer, source of material, date of order, expected delivery date, color, size or dimensions, quantity, price (including tax and delivery charge), and—where possible—a second choice.

*Formal as can be, this bath includes lightly pickled frame-and-panel cabinets with crown moldings and furniture-like bases; elegant limestone on both floors and countertops; and a classic pewter finish on faucets, cabinet pulls, and wall sconces.*

## Need help?

The listing below covers professionals in bathroom design and construction and delineates some of the distinctions (although there's overlap) between architects, designers, contractors, and other specialists.

**ARCHITECTS.** Architects are state-licensed professionals with degrees in architecture. They're trained to create designs that are structurally sound, functional, and aesthetically pleasing. They know construction materials, can negotiate bids from contractors, and can supervise the actual work. Many architects are members of the American Institute of Architects (AIA). If structural calculations must be made, architects can make them; other professionals need state-licensed engineers to design structures and sign working drawings.

If your bathroom remodel involves major structural changes, an architect should be consulted. But some architects may not be as familiar with the latest in bathroom design and materials as other specialists.

**BATHROOM DESIGNERS.** These planners know the latest trends in bathroom fixtures and furnishings, but may lack the structural knowledge of the architect and the aesthetic skill of a good interior designer.

If you decide to work with a bathroom designer, look for a member of the National Kitchen & Bath Association (NKBA) or a Certified Bathroom Designer (CBD), a specialist certified by the NKBA. These associations have codes and sponsor continuing programs to inform members about the latest building materials and techniques.

**INTERIOR DESIGNERS.** Even if you're working with an architect or bathroom designer, you may wish to call on the services of an interior designer for finishing touches. These experts specialize in the decorating and furnishing of rooms and can offer fresh, innovative ideas and advice. And through their contacts, a homeowner has access to materials and products not available at the retail level.

Some interior designers offer complete remodeling services. Many belong to the American Society of Interior Designers (ASID), a professional organization.

**GENERAL CONTRACTORS.** Contractors specialize in construction, although some have design skills and experience as well. General contractors may do all the work themselves, or they may assume responsibility for hiring qualified subcontractors, ordering construction materials, and seeing that the job is completed according to contract. Contractors can also secure building permits and arrange for inspections as work progresses.

When choosing a contractor, ask architects, designers, and friends for recommendations. To compare bids, contact at least three state-licensed contractors. Give each bidder either an exact description of the proposed changes and a copy of your floor plan or plans and specifications prepared by an architect or designer. Be precise about who will be responsible for what work.

**SUBCONTRACTORS.** If you act as your own contractor, you will have to hire and supervise subcontractors for specialized jobs such as wiring, plumbing, and tiling. You'll be responsible for permits, insurance, and possibly even payroll taxes, as well as direct supervision of all the aspects of construction. Do you have the time and the knowledge required for the job? Be sure to assess your energy level realistically.

*A traditional Japanese soaking tub is the focal point of this tile-lined open bath.*

# GREAT BATHROOM IDEAS

**T**HERE'S NOTHING LIKE a picture book when you're looking for inspiration. With this in mind, we offer the following gallery of bathroom designs. **THE PHOTOGRAPHS** included here represent as broad a range of styles as possible. You'll find small guest baths, larger family baths, and luxurious master baths. Some homeowners preferred restful, traditional rooms; others opted for open, contemporary expressions in glass and steel. All sought to make the space as pleasingly useful as possible. As one new master-suite owner commented, "All we need now is a hot plate." **ONE OF THESE** solutions may seem just right for your situation. Many of the approaches can be scaled up or down. Or you may simply wish to incorporate one or more of the design elements or fixture installations you see here into your own bath plan. In that case, consult "A Shopper's Guide," beginning on page 189.

# high style

**W**E **OPEN** our pictorial showcase with an overview of bathroom looks and layouts. We present big rooms and small ones—powder rooms, family baths, children's baths, and luxurious master suites. Some of these projects were make-overs of existing rooms. Others borrowed space from adjoining rooms or pushed out into back gardens or side yards. A few were completely new additions or in new homes built from scratch. In your own planning, it's advisable to establish your space options early.

Do you want your bathroom strictly functional or outfitted with the latest amenities? The popular master suite is simply any large space that includes the bathroom, bedroom, and dressing room in one integrated layout. Satellite areas might house an exercise room, a whirlpool tub and sauna, a home office, a library, or a comfy couch and media center.

*Even a small bathroom can evoke a sense of serenity. This design in a tall, skinny space illustrates what you might call a luxurious minimalism, with industrial-looking plumbing fixtures and fittings providing their own spare form of ornament.*

*Wildly colorful tile brings a blast of fun to this shared children's space—and is easy to clean, too.*

The two main poles of bathroom style are traditional and contemporary. Beyond that, there are period, regional, country, romantic, European-style, and eclectic looks. Hybrids abound. Many new designs strive to blend traditional looks with modern amenities such as whirlpool tubs and steam showers. As a starting point, do you want things stream-lined or unfitted? High-tech or homey? Do you want one large area or separate compartments for different uses? You'll see all these approaches in the following pages.

*Exuding confident retro style, this formerly drab master bath is now splashed with intensely green Venetian-glass mosaic tiles. A walk-in, sealed steam shower (facing page) is the focal point; roomy, resin-coated wardrobe cabinets (upper left) and a credenza-style vanity lie beyond. These spaces gain light and some separation from the nearby bedroom through translucent wall panels (lower left) set behind the vanity's floating gilt mirror.*

*Glass block, a blue glass countertop, and white laminate Euro-style cabinets with stainless-steel detailing all contribute to a cleanly modern, minimalist look (right). Flooring is concrete with radiant heat. The cylindrical walk-in shower (top) features more curved glass block, with a strip in blue, plus carefully crafted tilework.*

*A tiny jewel, this small bath is the only one in the house, so every inch counts. The space-saving curved counter-top (left) eases traffic flow and, along with the mirror's curved top, stretches the eye toward the tile-lined pedestal tub. A small built-in dressing bench (top) tucks into a corner between door and shower.*

*A small single bath is stretched by a clever space-expanding trick: the granite countertop and cherry cabinets are stylishly narrow except where they bow out to accommodate the perfectly round sink. Black diamond accent tiles and the shower's etched-glass door lend an Art Nouveau air.*

*A luxurious marble-lined whirlpool tub and walk-in shower (right) hold down one wall of this classic master-suite wing. Glass block and a skylight provide plenty of daylight while ensuring privacy. As the camera pans right, we walk through a door into the spacious dressing area (below), with floor-to ceiling storage cabinets on the left and a built-in makeup center at right. Beyond, through another door, lies a well-appointed exercise room, complete with its own auxiliary air-conditioning system.*

This Asian-inspired master bath is in
dressy black—from the rich slate of its
floor, wainscoting, and walk-in corner
shower to the glossy fixtures. Wall surfaces
are hand-painted gilt for a soft but
striking contrast.

*Barrier-free baths can also be beautiful, as these two designs demonstrate. As shown at left, a marble-lined bathroom's accessible shower not only looks great but comes outfitted with an adjustable shower head, a padded bench, and a padded curb so the bather can ease right in. The design shown above uses a barrier-free pedestal sink, an angled mirror, and a cantilevered counter. Even the tub's grab bars and sinkside shower controls are good-looking.*

*Modern as can be, this guest bath's marble-trimmed walk-in shower (right) features a stainless-steel European-style "column" in its corner. In the opposite corner of the room, a techy steel pedestal sink (below) is reflected in floor-to-ceiling mirrors broken only by a vertical strip of makeup lights.*

Here's another layout option: a free-floating vanity and makeup center that serves as a room divider (left). This partition wall, with cloudy lavender sponge paint making it seem to float upward from the limestone floor, conceals the bathing area. Turn the corner (below), and there are a curbless shower and pedestal-mounted tub wrapped with louvered windows.

In keeping with this home's Arts and Crafts styling, the bath is outfitted with a classic freestanding tub and twin pedestal sinks. White frame-and-panel wainscoting and window trim carry out the look, as do the period-style wall sconces. Marble floor tiles add a rich contrast.

This bathroom has a luxurious classicism. Arches spring from crisp white pilasters, and marble is everywhere—in muted beige on the walls and in multihued mosaic bands on the floor. The imposing, twin-basin console sink is topped by a gilt mirror; fittings and accessories are also coated in gold.

Why not dress a bathroom like any other room? In this unfitted traditional design, what looks like an antique country table is a new custom-built vanity with turned wooden legs and a limestone top scooped for double sinks. The fir-framed medicine cabinet is 6 inches deep—twice the standard size—to make up for losing covered storage underneath the sinks. Tiled wainscoting, a sisal rug, creamy wall sconces, and classic crown moldings round out the look.

Clean white woodwork, hand-painted tile, and subtle pink wallpaper distinguish this fastidiously detailed, romantic-style bath. Looking past the shower and one grooming area, you see the wood- and tile-lined pedestal tub and a garden view.

Every detail of this expanded master bath is richly inventive. A built-in, stair-stepped cabinet divides the bathroom from the bedroom beyond. Combining openness with privacy, the shower stall's interior glass wall is sandblasted to chest height. Sliding glass doors open to a deck, helping to dissolve the distinction between indoors and out.

Attic spaces are naturals for bathroom additions, but all those roof angles can present a puzzle. This small guest bath gains daylight from a custom angle-topped window. An old-fashioned claw-foot tub and freestanding vanity open up floor space, revealing more of the homey fir planks.

*Wrapped in comfortable carpeting, this high-ceilinged master suite extends past twin vanities to the bath area beyond. The back-to-back sink areas are identical; they're separated by large grooming mirrors housed in clear glass frames, through which both light and views may enter. The marble-lined pedestal tub is backed by large greenhouse windows; the wall of a patio beyond protects the bather's privacy.*

# on the surface

**M**ANY STYLES are established, at least in part, by the materials you choose for countertops, floor coverings, and wall and ceiling treatments. Also factor in the finishes on cabinets, fixtures, fittings, and accessories.

Just a few years ago, the average vanity top, usually laminate, included a 4-inch lip on the back. Today's higher backsplashes, however, often feature materials that are found there alone. Geometric or handpainted art tiles are popular choices. Seamless backsplash mirrors are popular, too—but can be tough to keep clean.

Floor choices are increasing. Besides time-tested tile and vinyl, we're seeing more stone used in baths—the result of newly affordable stone-tile offerings and the sealers that protect them. Wood and carpeting are also showing up, especially in detached areas away from direct-splash zones.

For painting walls, both standard treatments and faux finishes are familiar. Other wall options include tile, stone, terrazzo, wood, plaster, wallpaper, upholstery, and glass block.

Beyond aesthetic considerations, you should weigh the physical characteristics of surface materials. Most bathrooms take a lot of wear. Is your countertop choice water resistant, durable, and easy to maintain? Is the floor hard to walk on, noisy, or slippery? Are walls easy to clean? A powder room or master suite might be the place to try delicate materials that would be impractical in a family bath.

*Intricate North African-derived tile designs fill both walls and floor, but somehow look all of a piece. The two dominant patterns, on walls and floor, are separated by contrasting borders.*

*Guest baths are a place to try a new wall treatment. Here, colored joint compound was knife-applied over a lighter base tint; a top glaze accents both.*

This master bath, designed to coexist with existing bathrooms from the 1920s, is a striking example of balanced tile design. Floor diagonals of earthy quarry tile are echoed by diagonals on the countertops and backsplash; green trim tile fronts the cabinets. Matching Malibu designs are used on floor borders and backsplash, and the tub surround is marked by a complementary pattern.

A tropical fish peers imperturbably from the oceanic backdrop of a tubside wall. This custom work artfully blends both mural and mosaic techniques, as painted pieces follow natural contours instead of a rigid grid.

In this colorful bathing space, a stainless-steel soaking tub occupies an outside corner below windows with partially sandblasted glass panels. The nearby surfaces are clad with marble and slate tiles and terra-cotta-colored plaster.

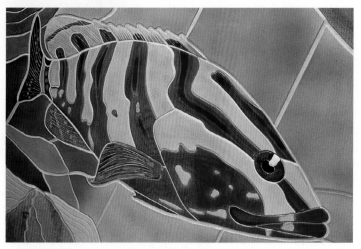

Bright and cheery, this country bath carries white-painted beaded wainscoting along the walls, around the tub, and even inside the tubside display niche.

Stylishly traditional, this bathroom showcases formal frame-and-panel walls throughout. The sink area has classic wood frames surrounding the green marble panels, but in the adjacent shower area the panel framing switches subtly from painted wood to white, watertight marble.

Clean white woodwork and Carrara marble set the tone, but the unusual floor strikes a pleasingly contrasting note. The stained fir floor's central "rug" is made from bamboo; it's set off by a painted black inlay.

Here's a study in black, white, and chrome. The white is Carrara marble. Cabinets are black lacquer below and, flanking the mirror, stainless steel with frosted-glass door panels. Walls and ceiling are coated with rough-textured plaster—in a water-proof formulation designed to survive humid spaces.

*Wallpaper, whether used overall, above wainscoting, or simply for an ornate border, is showing new flair. This powder room wears a hand-painted, hand-embossed pattern.*

*Don't rule out upholstery: its benefits include elegant color, soft texture, and good soundproofing. The upholstered walls shown here create a romantic-style backdrop for a makeup center.*

Textured-looking faux-finished walls, baseboards, and ceiling trim form a visual partnership with the freestanding vanity's carved front. A hand-painted concrete floor completes the picture.

Stone-textured concrete tiles are wrapped in square-within-square fashion by contrasting concrete rectangles and small square accents. The glass-tile baseboard shows just how well mosaic tiles can handle curves.

# waterworks

**YOUR CHOICES** of sink, tub, and shower do a lot to determine how your bathroom will be used, the way its traffic will flow, and what its general ambience will be like. In the following pages, we honor these often unsung heroes. You'll find more on fixtures in "A Shopper's Guide," beginning on page 189.

Sink designs have become wildly varied in the last few years. You'll see both pedestal and wall-hung sinks, in a rainbow of colors and finishes and in classic, retro, and contemporary styles. Both deck-mounted and integral sinks are sporting new looks. And what about a sculptural sinktop basin? Faucets and fittings also come in many new shapes and finishes.

Tubs form another focal point—a symbol of luxury and repose. You can choose a basic bathtub or a classic, freestanding claw-foot model. Pedestal tubs present a seamless, built-in look to the world. Whirlpool tubs abound. Or consider a traditional soaking tub in acrylic or wood.

Tub/shower units save space, but if the room is available, most users prefer to have a separate shower. Though market offerings include a plethora of prefabricated stalls, the larger, custom walk-in shower—perhaps with a built-in bench—is worth a careful look. Or examine the sleek new European modules, some with multiple shower heads, computerized temperature controls, even built-in audio systems. You'll find myriad options in shower fittings. When planning a shower, remember to think about ventilation, lighting, and privacy.

*Like an art installation, this elegant terra-cotta sink and its freestanding, hand pump-inspired faucet give washing your hands a theatrical quality.*

*Try to find the faucet downspout: it's hidden under the raised section of the stainless-steel counter behind the integral sink. Only the faucet handles—minimalist curves of steel—are visible.*

*A crystal sink bowl
sits atop a transparent
shelf in a small
powder room. Drain
fittings run through
the glass countertop,
making a design
statement of their own.*

*An elliptical console sink
with sculptural legs
strikes a traditional tone
in this bathroom. It's
stylistically at home with
classic tile work on the
walls and floor.*

*Gracefully blending the old and the new, a modern whirlpool tub meets turn-of-the-century wood wainscoting and marble; chrome accessories glow with soft filtered light from etched-glass windows.*

A combination of a Japanese-style soaking tub and a modern shower, this granite-surfaced fixture runs the full width of a narrow bathroom wall. The over-scaled window adds light and visually stretches the space while allowing bathers to contemplate the landscape beyond.

A wooden soaking tub sits atop a commanding corner pedestal, surrounded by curved marble steps and counters. The floor is mosaic tile, and walls gleam with alternating bands and patches of wall tile and trim. The tub is centered below an airy skylight well.

*Like a futuristic
monolith, this striking
cylindrical shower
"pod" is the sculp-
tural heart of an
ultramodern master
bath. For privacy's
sake in the multiuse
room, the shower's
lower sections are
translucent rather
than transparent.*

*Pale green glass
mosaic tiles line
a spacious tub/shower
corner, complete with
Roman tub spout,
whirlpool jets, hand-
held shower, and stan-
dard wall-mounted
shower head. An oper-
able porthole window
provides light and
ventilation.*

# bright ideas

**A** GOOD LIGHTING PLAN provides shadowless, glare-free illumination for the entire bath as well as bright, uniform light for specific tasks. And as you'll see, openings and light fixtures can also create dramatic visual effects.

Daylight can enter a bathroom through windows, skylights, doors, or all three. When a bathroom faces the street or the neighbors, it may be best to trade a little light for privacy. Glass block, translucent glazing, and decorative glass—stained, sandblasted, or beveled—all can provide decorative flair while maintaining a reserved exterior.

Besides natural light, you'll need good artificial lighting. The trick is to provide task light that's gently flattering and yet strong enough for grooming (for details, see pages 216–217). Be sure to choose warm fluorescent tubes or bulbs with good color-rendering properties for accurate makeup light and reliable skin tones.

*A lone, low-voltage pendant with a beaded-glass shade is reflected in the sinkside mirror. The mirror also shows a black track fixture that lights the bath space beyond.*

*Black tiles drink up lots of light, but this room's glazing is up to the balancing act. Steel-framed windows back both the sink area and a short return wall; they're met by glass block, which follows the sinuous curves of the tub while yielding both light and privacy. A small awning window opens off the tub for ventilation.*

Other use areas such as the tub, shower, and toilet compartments, may need their own light fixtures. Fluorescent sources can give good general lighting, and are required in some energy-conscious areas. Indirect fixtures work well: consider cove lighting, soffit lighting, translucent diffusers, and other bounce sources that spread a soft, even light.

Multiple sources and multiple controls allow you to alternate between morning efficiency and nighttime repose. Consider dimmers here. Also plan to provide low-energy night lighting for safety and convenience.

*A rustic bathroom's hinged wooden windows surround a granite-wrapped pedestal tub, opening the room directly to the deck and landscape beyond.*

*Like a lovely green wind, these elegant stained-glass windows atmospherically enhance a luxurious pedestal tub. The leaded glass makes a bright focal point while ensuring privacy.*

*This bath opened right onto a neighbor's view, so the architect used some nontraditional glazing in the sinkside window frames. Most of the lower "window" sections are mirrored; besides aiding grooming, they reflect light and views from another source. The sculptural ripple inserts do admit light, but their translucent nature masks views in and out.*

*This master bath's task light comes from a diffused inset fixture (shown at left) that puts makeup light right where it's needed. Additional ambient light glows from a translucent panel housed in the display niche; its source is a bank of fluorescent tubes concealed in a storage cabinet beyond. Continuing the subtle illumination scheme, the shower (above) has a panel in its ceiling that evenly diffuses light from a bright tungsten fixture.*

*Small baths can gain a semblance of extra space with window pop-outs. In this case, the shower/tub area has been stretched with a greenhouse window unit, which adds daylight, views, display space, and—thanks to its translucent, tempered wall panels—a measure of seclusion.*

*This comfortable master bath has a long, open fir vanity with a*

*hand-tooled marble top. The corresponding mirror-faced cabinet is*

*broken by flush-mounted incandescent vertical tubes for makeup light,*

*and the backsplash and counter areas are washed by additional light*

*from beneath the cabinet. A double-hung wooden window further*

*brightens the room.*

*At either side of the sink, stylish wall sconces are mounted directly to the seamless mirrored surface, giving the area balanced, effective grooming light. A skylight well above brings welcome daylight to the windowless space.*

# elegant options

**A**s life speeds up, many of us treasure our quiet time. So it's understandable that for some people the bathroom is becoming a down-time retreat including such extras as a soaking tub, exercise area, and comfortable sitting space. Even such standard living-room features as fireplaces, media centers, wet bars, and art displays are moving in. Master suites blur the distinctions between bed and bath, organizing separate zones for bathing, grooming, dressing, working, and relaxing in a private part of the house. The desire for repose may tempt you to provide a comfortable couch, built-in bookcases, and perhaps a corner wet bar or espresso counter. Maybe you'd like built-in audio speakers connected to a central home system (it's a good idea to have at least a separate volume control in the bathroom). Or indulge yourself in a large-screen TV or full-blown home theater serving both bed and bath areas.

*Situated just off the main bath, this dressing room uses pine built-ins and a cushion-topped dressing bench to frame a decorative leaded-glass window.*

If you'd like a traditional dressing table, you'll need to find a spot for it out of the main flow. Where will you store cosmetics, jewelry, and accessories? What mirrors and lighting will you need? Do you want an auxiliary sink?

A walk-in closet can neatly combine clothes storage with a dressing area. Or opt for built-in drawers, pullouts, and a freestanding closet or armoire. If space permits, this area can serve as a bridge between bedroom and bath. Good ventilation, especially for areas adjacent to a shower or tub, is crucial.

*The view from tubside shows two additional wings in a classic master-suite layout. At back left, a fitness room is equipped with an exercise bike, a treadmill, a dumbbell set, and a wall-mounted TV. At back right, a grooming center fits alongside a built-in dresser; a walk-in dressing room lies just beyond.*

*A comfortable bedroom, a cheery two-sided fireplace, and a whirlpool tub all team up in this spacious master suite. The bath continues around the corner. Elegant granite and cozy carpeting help tie the areas together.*

*When it's windy, cold, and dark outside, what could be more relaxing than slipping into a warm tub and taking a long soak in front of a blazing fire? This bathroom revolves around a 5- by 8-foot platform with a whirlpool bath; the two-way fireplace sits in a wall shared by the adjacent bedroom.*

*A cedar-and-granite grooming area (above), complete with twin sinks and expansive mirrors, occupies one wall of a comfortable master suite. A striking cedar storage wall (right) divides bedroom from bath and also works, on the bedroom side, as a headboard.*

*This white laminate built-in presents a seamless European-style face of flush-front doors and drawers; mirrors add space-stretching flash to an otherwise blank wall.*

*As today's bath serves more functions, it may incorporate traditional closet and bureau units. This dressing room links a master bedroom with the bath proper and features maple built-ins with lots of nooks and crannies. There's also a comfort-able shoelace-tying sitting spot.*

*A tiled sink counter steps down smoothly to a cushy, built-in window seat, perfect for a quiet, private read. Leaded-glass windows behind supply lots of natural light.*

*This bedroom/bath transition zone combines*

*an antique vanity and a large framed*

*mirror to create a stylish makeup area.*

*The window bay beyond, trimmed with*

*traditional frame-and-panel woodwork,*

*becomes a light-filled sitting spot.*

# A SHOPPER'S GUIDE

**N**OT TOO long ago, you simply purchased a white pedestal sink, a mirrored medicine cabinet, a 30- by 60-inch tub, and a toilet and called it a bathroom. But much has changed. Today, there are integral solid-surface sinks; contoured acrylic whirlpool tubs; one-piece, ultra-low-flush toilets. And that's just the beginning of what's new. Who has the time and energy to sort it all out? **THIS CHAPTER** will help. Our color photographs present the latest in fixtures and materials. And text and comparison charts give you the working knowledge to brave the showrooms, to communicate with an architect or designer, or simply to replace that dingy, old-fashioned wall covering with something both more stylish and more practical. **ARMED WITH THE BASICS**, it's much easier to go on to the fine points. Most bathroom professionals are knowledgeable and ready to assist. Often you can borrow literature, samples, and swatches to bring home to check for color, size, and stylistic compatibility.

# Cabinets

STYLISH STORAGE BOXES HELP SET THE TONE

In earlier days, "bathroom storage" meant a clunky medicine cabinet mounted above the pedestal or wall-hung lavatory sink. Then along came boxy vanities, and the bathroom acquired a bank of drawers to one side of the plumbing compartment.

As changing life-styles demand expression and bathrooms become grooming centers, exercise gyms, and spas, storage needs and configurations are also changing. One or more base cabinets may still form the backbone of the contemporary storage scheme, but bath storage areas have become more stylish, their design integrated with that of mirrors, sink, lighting, and backsplash treatments. Perhaps you'll wish to curve a custom unit around a corner, let built-ins form knee walls between use areas, or plan a floor-to-ceiling storage column.

## Traditional or European-style?

First, you'll need to choose between two basic cabinet styles, frame and frameless.

Traditional American cabinets mask the raw front edges of each box with a 1-by-2 "faceframe." Doors and drawers then fit in one of three ways: flush; partially offset, with a lip; or completely overlaying the frame. The outer edges of the faceframe can be planed and shaped (called "scribing") to fit the contours of an adjacent wall or ceiling. But the frame takes up space and reduces the size of the openings, so

**CABINET CLOSE-UPS**

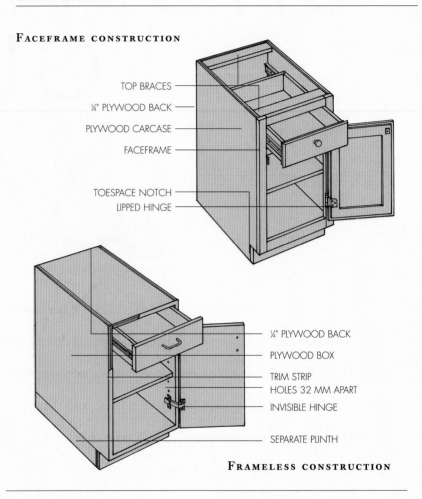

FACEFRAME CONSTRUCTION

TOP BRACES
¼" PLYWOOD BACK
PLYWOOD CARCASE
FACEFRAME

TOESPACE NOTCH
LIPPED HINGE

¼" PLYWOOD BACK
PLYWOOD BOX
TRIM STRIP
HOLES 32 MM APART
INVISIBLE HINGE

SEPARATE PLINTH

FRAMELESS CONSTRUCTION

drawers or slide-out accessories must be significantly smaller than the full width of the cabinet.

Europeans, when faced with post-war lumber shortages, came up with "frameless" cabinets. A simple trim strip covers raw edges, which butt directly against one another. Doors and drawers often fit to within ⅛ inch of each other, revealing a thin sliver of the trim. Interior components—such

as drawers—can be sized larger, practically to the full dimensions of the box.

The terms "system 32" and "32-millimeter" refer to precise columns of holes drilled on the inside faces of many frameless cabinets. These holes are generally in the same place no matter what cabinets you buy, and interchangeable components such as shelf pins and pullout bins just fit right into them.

Bathroom cabinets are sporting
new looks—and some old ones,
too.  The styles
shown here include a furniture-
like, frame-and-panel
piece with built-in valance
lighting (above); a space-saving
corner pedestal in traditional
cherry (left); and a
modern update of the tried-
and-true medicine cabinet that
includes strip lights and other
amenities (right).

## Stock, custom, or modular?

Cabinets are manufactured and sold in three different ways. The type you choose may affect the cost, appearance, and workability of your bathroom.

**STOCK CABINETS.** Mass-produced, standard-size cabinets are the least expensive option, and they can be an excellent choice if you clearly understand what cabinetry you need. You may find stock lines heavily discounted at some home centers. A recent development, the so-called RTA ("ready-to-assemble") cabinet, costs even less but requires some basic tools and elbow grease to put together. An RTA vanity is shown on the facing page.

As the name implies, the range of stock sizes is limited. Even so, you can always specify door styles, direction of door swing, and finish of side panels.

**CUSTOM CABINETS.** Many people still have a cabinetmaker come to their house and measure, then return to the cabinet shop and build custom cabinet boxes, drawers, and doors.

Custom shops can match old cabinets, size oddball configurations, and accommodate complexities that can't be handled with stock or modular units. But such work can cost considerably more than medium-line stock or modular cabinets.

**MODULAR SYSTEMS.** Between stock and custom cabinetry are "custom modular cabinets" or "custom systems," which can sometimes offer the best of both worlds. They are manufactured, but they are of a higher grade and offer more design flexibility than stock cabinets. Not surprisingly, they cost more, too.

*A CORNUCOPIA OF CABINET PULLS*

You can change virtually everything on these basic modules: add sliding shelves; replace doors with drawers; add wire bins, hampers, and pullouts. If necessary, heights, widths, and depths can be modified to fit almost any design. Be advised, though: these cabinets could take a long time to show up at your doorstep.

## What about dimensions?

The classic bathroom vanity measured about 32 inches high (with countertop) by 21 inches deep and about 30 inches wide. But bath cabinets are growing— new offerings may be up to 36 inches high by 24 inches deep and 48 inches wide. You can make longer cabinet runs by joining units together.

Some bath cabinet lines include wall cabinets and tall storage units; otherwise, look to kitchen cabinet manufacturers for ideas.

## Judging quality

Within each line, costs are largely determined by the style of the doors and drawers you choose. The simplest, least expensive option is often a flat or "slab" door, popular for seamless European designs. Frame-and-panel designs are more traditional and come in many versions, including raised panel (both real and false), arched panel, beaded panel, and recessed or flat panel.

To determine the quality of a cabinet, first look closely at the drawers. They take more of a beating than any other part of your cabinets. Several drawer designs are shown at far right. You'll pay a premium for such features as solid-wood drawer boxes, sturdy dovetail joints, and full-extension, ball-bearing guides.

*READY-TO-ASSEMBLE (RTA) CABINET*

Are cabinet pulls included? If not, you'll pay more for them, but you'll be able to choose exactly what you want. For a sampling, see the photo on the facing page.

Door hinges are critical hardware elements. European or "invisible" hinges are most trouble-free; consider these unless you need the period look of surface hardware. Check for adjustability; hinges should be able to be reset with the cabinets in place.

Most cabinet boxes are made from sheet products like plywood, particleboard (plain or laminated), or medium-density fiberboard. Though solid lumber is sometimes used, it is usually saved for doors and drawers.

Hardwood plywood is surfaced with attractive wood veneers on both face and back. The higher the face grade, the more you'll pay. Particleboard costs less, weighs more, and is both weaker and more prone to warping and moisture damage than plywood. Generally, particleboard vanities are faced with high-pressure plastic laminate or with a softer material called melamine. Medium-density fiberboard (MDF), a denser, furniture-grade particleboard, is available with high-quality hardwood veneers.

*Be sure to examine drawer components and hardware. Options shown here, top to bottom, include budget-oriented melamine drawer boxes with self-closing epoxy guides; sturdy, full-extension, ball-bearing guides; and premium hardwood boxes with dovetail joints and invisible, under-mounted guides.*

# Countertops

MODERN ALTERNATIVES FOR CLASSIC SURFACES

**E**ven after being steamed or splashed, good countertops still come up shining because they're moisture resistant—or better yet, waterproof. The best materials look great under stress and are less likely to scratch or chip.

## What are your choices?

Plastic laminate, ceramic tile, solid-surface acrylics, and stone are the four major countertop materials in current use. Synthetic marble, while still common, is losing some ground to solid-surface materials. Custom glass and cast concrete are gaining in popularity, especially in stylish master suites and powder rooms. Wood is sometimes used for countertops, too; but to prevent water damage, the surface of wood countertops must be treated (perhaps repeatedly) with a durable finish.

## Shopping around

When shopping, you probably won't be able to compare all the materials in one place. Some dealers with showrooms are listed in the yellow pages under Countertops or Kitchen Cabinets & Equipment; they'll probably have tile, plastic laminate, solid-surface products, and—maybe—wood. Large building-supply centers carry plastic laminate, synthetic marble, and

---

## COMPARING COUNTERTOPS

### Plastic laminate

**Advantages.** You can choose from a wide range of colors, textures, and patterns. Laminate is durable, easy to clean, water resistant, and relatively inexpensive. Ready-made molded versions are called postformed; custom or self-rimmed countertops are built from scratch atop particleboard or plywood substrates. There are many laminates available for these tops, and edging options abound. With the right tools, you can install laminate yourself.

**Disadvantages.** It can scratch, chip, and stain, and it's hard to repair. Ready-made postformed tops can look cheap, and other edgings may collect water and grime. Conventional laminate has a dark backing that shows at its seams; new solid-color laminates, designed to avoid this, are somewhat brittle and more expensive. High-gloss laminates show every smudge.

### Ceramic tile

**Advantages.** It's good-looking; comes in many colors, textures, and patterns; and is heat resistant and water resistant if installed correctly. Cost runs from inexpensive to pricey, depending on whether the tile is formed by machine or by hand and how many units are needed. Buy a tile that's rated for countertop use. Grout is also available in numerous colors. Patient do-it-yourselfers are likely to have good results.

**Disadvantages.** Some tile glazes can react adversely to acids or cleaning chemicals; be sure to ask. Many people find it hard to keep grout satisfactorily clean. Using epoxy grouts and thin, uniform grout lines can help. The hard, irregular surface can chip china and glassware.

wood. For other dealers or fabricators, check the categories Marble—Natural; Plastics; Glass—Plate; Concrete Products; and Tile. Designers and architects can also supply samples.

## Backsplash fever

These days, bathroom designers are using the backsplash— the wall surface surrounding the countertop proper—to make an aesthetic statement. A good backsplash also has practical advantages: if properly installed, it seals the area from moisture, and it makes the wall a lot easier to clean.

## COMPARING COUNTERTOPS

### Solid-surface

**Advantages.** Durable, water resistant, heat resistant, nonporous, and easy to clean, this marble-like material can be shaped and joined with virtually invisible seams. Different edge treatments are available. It allows for a variety of sink installations, including integral units that combine both basin and countertop (see page 196). Blemishes and scratches can be sanded out.

**Disadvantages.** It's expensive, requiring professional fabrication and installation for best results. It needs very firm support below. Until recently, color selection was limited to white, beige, and almond; now stone patterns and pastels are common. Costs climb quickly for wood inlays and other fancy edge details.

### Synthetic marble

**Advantages.** This group of man-made products, collectively known as "cast polymers," includes cultured marble, cultured onyx, and cultured granite. All three are relatively easy to clean. Cultured onyx is more translucent than cultured marble. These products are often sold with an integral sink. Prices range from inexpensive to moderate. You can color-coordinate a synthetic marble top with tub, shower, and wall panels.

**Disadvantages.** Synthetic marble is not very durable, and scratches and dings are hard to mend (the surface finish is usually only a thin veneer). Backings, typically, are porous. Quality varies widely; look for Cultured Marble Institute or IAPMO certification.

### Stone

**Advantages.** Granite, marble, and limestone, all popular for countertops, are beautiful natural materials. In most areas, you'll find a great selection of colors and figures. Stone is water resistant, heatproof, and very durable. Surface finishes range from polished to honed (matte) and even rougher textures. A number of thicknesses are available, and edges can be shaped in numerous ways.

**Disadvantages.** Oil, alcohol, and any acid (even chemicals in some water supplies) can stain marble or limestone and damage its finish; granite can stand up to all of these. Solid slabs are very expensive. Some designers suggest stone tiles—including slate—as less expensive choices. When shopping, take time to study the latest sealer options.

# Sinks and Faucets

WASHING UP IN STYLE—ANY STYLE

No longer just a basin and a mirror, the sink area has become a thoughtfully planned environment for grooming and personal care. Layouts with two sinks—housed in one continuous vanity, in side-by-side alcoves, or in matching configurations on opposite walls—are popular. Some bathrooms also include a separate, smaller wash basin in the toilet compartment or makeup area.

Sinks and faucets have become design accents in their own right—a comparatively low-commitment way to try adding a bit of dash to an otherwise restrained design scheme. (If you later decide you don't like the boldness, it's a lot simpler to change a faucet than a shower or tub surround.)

## Sink options, new and old

Sinks are available in a huge array of styles, shapes, and materials. You can make the sink stand out—or blend its look with that of a period-style tub, shower, or toilet fixture. Whether for an antique or ultramodern design, some sink manufacturers can provide custom colors on special orders.

**DECK-MOUNTED SINKS.** The vanity-bound basin is still the most common arrangement. You'll find a wide selection of materials in deck mounts, including vitreous china, fiberglass-reinforced plastic, enameled steel, and enameled cast iron. Vitreous china (made with clay that's poured into molds, fired in a kiln, and glazed) is heavy, comes in many colors, and is easy to clean; it also resists scratches, chips, and stains. Fiberglass is lightweight and moderately priced, but tends to scratch and dull. An enameled steel surface is easy to clean and lighter and less expensive than vitreous china or enameled cast iron—but also much less durable. Enameled cast iron is more expensive and durable than vitreous china or enameled steel, but is very heavy.

Other sink materials include translucent glass, hand-painted ceramics, stainless steel, brass, copper, and even wood. These materials are strikingly elegant as accents but can require zealous maintenance.

You have a choice of mounting methods with various deck-mounted models. Self-rimming sinks with molded overlaps are supported by the edge of the countertop cutout; flush deck-mounted sinks have surrounding metal strips to hold the basin to the countertop; unrimmed sinks are recessed under the countertop and held in place by metal clips. Some deck-mounted sinks are designed as seemingly "freestanding" fixtures, where the entire basin sits sculpturally atop the counter and drains down through it.

**INTEGRAL-BOWL SINKS.** A solid-surface countertop (see page 195) can be coupled with a molded, integral sink for a sleek, sculpted look. The one-piece molded unit sits on top of a vanity or cabinet; predrilled holes are often part of the package. A countertop with an integral bowl has no joints, so installation and cleaning are easy.

Sink color can either match the countertop or complement it; for example, you might choose a cream-colored sink below a granite-patterned counter. Edge-banding and other border options abound. Other integral sinks come in cast polymers, vitreous china, and fiberglass.

Check the sink's depth before buying: some versions may be shallower than you'd like.

**PEDESTAL SINKS.** Pedestal sinks are making a big comeback, in a wide range of traditional and modern

*New sink models include a wide range of both deck-mounted designs and above-counter versions. You'll also find a growing number of eclectic, almost sculptural sinks, like the one shown below right.*

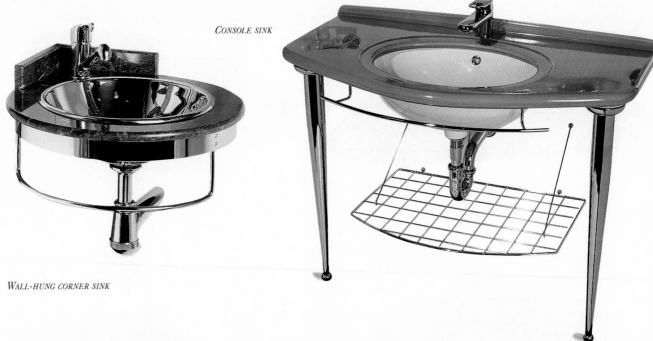

*CONSOLE SINK*

*WALL-HUNG CORNER SINK*

designs. Typically of vitreous china, these elegant towers are usually easy to install and clean around. The pedestal often, but not always, hides the plumbing.

Pedestal sinks are typically among the highest-priced basins. Another disadvantage: they provide no storage space below the basin.

**WALL-HUNG SINKS.** Like pedestals, wall-hung sinks are enjoying a contemporary revival. Materials and styling are along the same lines; in fact, some designs are available in either version.

Wall-hung sinks come with hangers or angle brackets for support. Generally speaking, they are among the least expensive and most compact sink options and are relatively easy to install. If you're putting in a wall-hung model for the first time, plan to tear out a strip of the wall to add a support ledger.

**CONSOLE SINKS.** If you like the look of pedestal or wall sinks, but yearn for a bit more elbow room, take a look at so-called console sinks. These "stretch models" join a wider rectangular deck with either two or four furniture-like vanity legs. Some versions include storage space below.

## Faucets

The world of sink faucets is constantly changing, presenting new colors, shapes, styles, and accessories.

Popular finishes include polished chrome, brushed chrome, nickel, polished or antiqued brass, soft pewter, elegant gold plate, and jazzy enameled epoxy. For durability and low maintenance, polished chrome with a high nickel content is still the best bet. You can choose a showstopper in boldest

*PEDESTAL SINKS*

modern or most quaintly antique styling, coordinate with tub fittings, or pick the same handles for all fixtures in the room.

You can buy faucets with digital temperature readouts, scaldproof models, and spouts that stop the flow when your hand is removed. How about a swiveling European faucet with an adjustable spray, a drinking spout, and a gum-massage attachment?

Sink faucets are available with single, center-set, or spread-fit controls. A single-control fitting has a combined faucet and lever or knob controlling water flow and temperature. A center-set control has separate hot and cold water controls and a faucet, all mounted on a base or escutcheon. A spread-fit control has separate hot and cold water controls and an independently mounted faucet. Pop-up or plug stoppers are sold separately or with the faucet and water controls.

When you're attracted to clever, streamlined designs, ask yourself two questions. How well could you work the controls with soaped-up hands and sleep-bleared eyes? And how easy would it be to clean or maintain the installation?

Whatever style you choose, most bathroom professionals agree that you get what you pay for. Solid-brass workings, though pricey, are considered most durable. Ceramic-disk and plastic-disk valve designs are generally easier to maintain than older washer schemes.

While most faucets are sink-mounted, other installations call for either deck-mounted or wall-mounted fittings. When you select your sink, be sure any holes in it will match the type of faucet you plan to buy, as well as any additional accessories.

*Sink faucets run the gamut from antiquelike to high-tech, from soft pewter-finish to jazzy epoxy, and from single-control to spread-fit.*

# Tubs and Showers

LUXURIOUS OPTIONS FOR QUIET SOAKS, BOLD SPRAYS

In many modern baths, the tub is the focus of the room, a gratifying symbol of luxury and relaxation. In new installations, whirlpool tubs—now available in more traditional tub styles and sizes—are in high demand.

But for on-the-go workday bathing, a separate shower, unless space prohibits, is a nearly universal request. A well-designed shower is also safer to use than many tub/showers, which may lack both firm footing and adequate grab bars.

## Tub choices

The market overflows with bathtub styles. The 30- by 60-inch tub, which often controlled the dimensions of the 5- by 7-foot bathroom of the past, no longer rules the buyer. Tubs come in new and more comfortable shapes and

MOLDED WHIRLPOOL TUB

sizes and in a wide range of styles and colors.

**THE BASIC BATHTUB.** The boxy, familiar tub is enameled steel, relatively inexpensive, and lightweight— but noisy, cold, and prone to chipping. Built-to-last enameled cast-iron tubs are more durable and warmer to the touch, but very heavy (they may require structural reinforcement).

Traditional tubs come in two basic styles: recessed and corner. Recessed tubs fit between two side walls and against a back wall; they have a finished front or "apron." Corner models have one finished side and end and may be right- or left-handed. Some more stylish tubs are finished on three sides, allowing placement along an open wall.

A 72-inch-long tub is better than the standard 60-inch model, if space allows; a depth of 16 inches is more comfortable than the standard 14.

*PEDESTAL TUB*

hot-water connection; once your soak is over, the water is drained.

Most models resemble standard acrylic platform tubs; a pump and venturi jets are what create the whirlpool effect. Jet designs vary. Generally, you can opt for high pressure and low volume (a few strong jets) or low pressure and high volume (lots of softer jets). Typically, the more jets, the easier it is to access an aching body part—though some users find these setups less soothing and prefer the massage effect of the stronger jets.

Though some professionals build custom whirlpool tubs from scratch and even retrofit old bathtubs, it's simplest and safest to buy a complete whirlpool kit. Look for a unit that's UL-approved. Want extras? Consider adding a digital temperature control, a timer, a built-in fill spout, or a cushy neck roll.

**THE AGE OF PLASTICS.** The most innovative tubs these days are usually plastic—either vacuum-formed acrylic or injection-molded thermoplastics like ABS. These lightweight shells are easy to transport and retain heat well. But best of all is their range of contours and sizes. Plastic tubs are available in neutrals and in the latest colors. The one drawback: dark, shiny surfaces tend to scratch or dull easily.

These tubs are usually designed for platform or sunken installation. Some models sit atop the surrounding deck, like a self-rimmed sink; others are undermounted. Though warmer to the touch than cast iron, plastic tubs lack iron's structural integrity—be sure to provide solid support beneath one.

**FREESTANDING TUBS.** An old-fashioned freestanding tub, such as the enduring claw-foot model, makes a nice focal point for a traditional or country design. You can buy either new reproductions or a reconditioned original. Such tubs can double as showers with the addition of Victorian-inspired shower-head/diverter/curtain rod hardware.

Looking for traditional fixtures and fittings? Recently, many new sources for renovators' supplies have sprung up; check specialty shops and antique plumbing catalogs.

**WHIRLPOOL TUBS.** Think of these hydromassage units simply as bathtubs with air jets. Unlike an outdoor spa, the whirlpool uses a standard

*SOAKING TUB*

*CURBLESS BUILT-IN SHOWER*

laminate, and synthetic marble. Some have ceilings. For comfort, choose a shower that's at least 36 inches square.

The term "shower stall" needn't mean something boxy and boring—or even, for that matter, economical. Circular, corner, and angular wraparounds are available with enough spray heads and accessories to please the most demanding shower connoisseur. Circular showers often have clear or tinted acrylic doors that double as walls.

**BUILD YOUR OWN.** You can also mix and match base, surround, and doors to create the shower of your choice.

A shower base or "pan" can be purchased separately or in a kit that includes the shower surround. Most bases are made of plastic, terrazzo (a concrete/stone mix), cast polymer, or solid-surface materials and come in standard sizes in rectangular, square, or corner configurations with a predrilled

Because of their extra weight when filled, deep whirlpool tubs may need special floor framing. Your unit may also require a dedicated 120- or 240-volt circuit to power the pump and controls.

**SOAKING TUBS.** These tubs, like Japanese furos (made of wood), have deep interiors. They come in recessed, platform, and corner models, with rectangular or round interiors of fiberglass or acrylic.

Hot tubs, which use a wooden-barrel design and continuous water supply, can present moisture problems in all but the best-ventilated spaces. They are probably best confined to a deck or private garden.

## Shower styles

You can select a prefabricated shower stall, match separate manufactured components, or build completely from scratch. Think about amenities such as a comfortable bench or fold-down seat, adjustable or hand-held shower heads, a place for shampoos and shaving equipment, and sturdy grab bars.

**PREFABRICATED SHOWER STALLS.** If your remodel calls for moving walls or doors, you may be able to fit a one-piece molded shower or tub/shower surround through the opening—though these units are really designed for new houses or additions. One-piece showers are available in fiberglass-reinforced plastic, plastic

*PREFABRICATED CORNER SHOWER*

hole for the drain. It's easy to find a base that works with another maker's tub since many manufacturers produce both—and in many colors. Of course, you can also have a tile professional float a traditional mortar base and line it with the tile of your choice.

Shower surrounds require solid framing for support. You can add prefabricated wall panels or use a custom wall treatment such as ceramic tile, stone, or a solid-surface material over a waterproof backing. Molded wall panels of fiberglass or synthetic marble may include integral soap dishes, ledges, grab bars, and other accessories. These manufactured panels are sized for easy transport, then assembled and seamed on-site.

Doors for showers come in a variety of styles: swinging, sliding, folding, and pivoting. For tub/showers, choose sliding or folding doors. Doors and enclosures are commonly made of tempered safety glass with aluminum frames. These frames come in many finishes; you can select one to match your fittings. The glazing itself can be clear, hammered, pebbled, tinted, or striped. The seamless look is popular, though expensive.

Swinging, folding, and pivoting doors can be installed with right or left openings. Folding doors are constructed of rigid plastic panels or flexible plastic sheeting. Glass requires more maintenance; some bathers keep a squeegee nearby for daily cleaning.

*Multitier cedar benches (right) help turn a space into a comfortable, burn-free sauna room. Trim wall controls (top) drive a built-in steam shower.*

## SAUNAS AND STEAM SHOWERS

These luxurious features, once found mainly in gyms and health clubs, have recently been invited to enter the residential bathroom as well.

A sauna is a small wood-lined room (often sold prefabricated) that heats itself to around 200°F. Traditionally, sauna walls, ceilings, floor slats, and benches are built from wood such as aspen, redwood, or cedar. Besides insulated walls, a solid-core door, and double-paned glass (if any), you'll also need an electric or gas sauna heater, a thermostat and timer, some lighting, and both inlet and outlet vents for cross-ventilation. Minimum size for a sauna is about 65 cubic feet per person.

Steam hardware for residential use is compact enough to be housed in any number of locations—inside a storage cabinet, in an adjacent closet or alcove, or in a nearby crawl space. The generator is sized according to the number of cubic feet in your enclosure and, to a lesser extent, the material the enclosure is made from. Besides the steam box, outlets, and control pad, all you need is an airtight shower door, a comfortable bench, and a waterproof, steam-resistant surround. Your new shower may already meet these requirements.

Of course, people with known cardiovascular problems should be cautious about using a sauna or steam.

## Tub and shower fittings

These days you'll find nearly as many styles and finishes for tub and shower fittings as for bathroom sinks. In addition, you can choose a line of integrated fittings, or at least use the same handles and finish from sink to tub to shower.

**TUB FITTINGS.** For tub/showers, you can opt for either single or separate controls. Tubs require a spout and drain. Tub/showers need a spout, shower head (see facing page), diverter valve, and drain. These can be deck- or wall-mounted; some installations use a combination. The best fittings have solid brass workings and come in many finishes, including chrome, brass, nickel, pewter, gold plate, and enameled epoxy. You'll also find color-coordinated pop-up drains and over-flow plates.

Ever had a tub spout poke you while you were trying to relax? Mount it along the back wall or deck. Position handles where you can get to them easily. Roman or waterfall spouts are striking-looking and can fill tubs much faster than standard fittings—assuming that supply pipes (see page 131) are large enough for the task.

Unfortunately, tubs, especially whirlpools, aren't great for really getting clean. For that, add a separate hand shower controlled by a nearby diverter valve.

**SHOWER FITTINGS.** Multiple, adjustable, and low-flow are the bywords for today's shower fittings. Large walk-in showers often have two or more shower heads: fixed heads at different levels, or hand units on adjustable vertical bars. Massage units and overhead "shampoo" heads often supplement the basic head or heads.

*ROMAN TUB SPOUT*

*WALL SPOUT*

*DECK-MOUNT FITTINGS WITH HAND SHOWER*

*"Shampoo" shower heads*

*Temperature-limiting valve*

*Adjustable bar with hand shower*

*Spray-bar jets*

"Surround" designs combine one or more fixed heads with wall-mounted auxiliary jets or adjustable multijet vertical bars. How do you control all these jets? Diverters may have three or more settings for orchestrating multiple water sources. It's smart to consult a bathroom professional for complex shower schemes—otherwise, you may experience unequal pressures and water temperatures.

Safety plays a part in new designs, too. If you've ever suffered a pressure drop when someone flushes a toilet or starts the washer, you'll appreciate single-control shower fittings with pressure balancing to prevent scalding rises in temperature. Several companies make designs that incorporate adjustable temperature limiters. You can also buy quick-reacting thermostatic valves, with or without zoomy digital readouts.

Low-flow shower heads, rated at 2.5 gallons per minute or less, are required in much new construction, and many cities are demanding that less efficient heads be replaced in bathroom remodels.

You'll probably find that low-flow retrofits splash more and are slightly noisier than standard heads. Less expensive models deliver fine droplets that won't wet your body as quickly—and might even feel a little cool by the time they get down to your knees. On/off valves are built into many low-flow heads. Make sure levers are shut-offs, not just spray adjustments.

For safety and convenience, it's best to place shower controls to the front and/or side of the enclosure—not directly below the shower head.

# Toilets and Bidets

FRONT-PAGE NEWS ABOUT TWO HO-HUM FIXTURES

*TRADITIONAL TWO-PIECE TOILET*

New styling, new colors, and new efficiency have all but replaced the tried-and-true water closet. In addition to standard and antique models, vitreous china toilets now come in sleek-looking European designs, standard or low-profile heights, and rounded or elongated bowls. Do you want classic white, shiny black, or a soft pastel? Ultra-low-flush or pressure-assisted mechanics?

The bidet is a European standby that's gaining popularity on this side of the Atlantic. It's used primarily for personal hygiene. Like toilets, bidets are made of vitreous china, in a number of styles, colors, and finishes to match toilets and other fixtures.

## Toilets

As water shortages drive home the fact that water is a finite resource, the new word in toilets is ultra-low-flush (ULF). Why change? Older toilets use 5 to 7 gallons or more per flush. In 1994, codes were changed to require 1.6-gallon-per-flush toilets for new construction. Some water districts even offer a rebate if you install a ULF fixture in your present home.

Some homeowners complain that ultra-low-flush toilets don't really save water in the long run because they may require several flushings. One reply to this problem is the pressure-assisted design, which uses a strong air vacuum to power a quick, intensive flush. Pressure-assisted models are noisier than other low-flush toilets, but the disturbance is very brief.

The basic choice in toilets is between traditional two-piece and European-style one-piece designs. Two-piece toilets have a separate tank that's either bolted directly to the bowl or, in the case of some period reproductions, mounted on the wall above. One-piece toilets are also known as "low-boy" or "low-profile" models. Some toilets come with seats, some don't. If you're splurging, you might consider an electronic seat that's heated and/or programmed with a bidet-like spray jet.

Before installing a new toilet in an older house, check the offset—the distance between the back wall and the center of the drain hub (measured to the hold-down nuts). Most newer models are designed for a 12-inch offset.

How about retrofits? Variable-buoyancy flappers, flap actuators that ride on the overflow tube, and dual-handle mechanisms will greatly increase the efficiency of your existing water-guzzler. Some water districts will send you parts free. With the new devices, you still have the pressure of the original volume, but the flap will close while several gallons still remain in the tank.

## Bidets

A bidet, best installed next to the toilet, is floor-mounted and plumbed with hot and cold water. Available in styles and finishes to match new toilets, it comes with either a horizontal spray mount or a vertical spray in the center of the bowl. Some models include rim jets to maintain bowl cleanliness. Most versions have a pop-up stopper that allows the unit to serve also as a foot-bath or laundry basin.

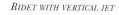

*BIDET WITH VERTICAL JET*

*In the past, "ultra-low-flush" sometimes meant very little flush. A pressure-assisted toilet tank uses water-compressed air to add a power boost. It's noisier than some flushing actions, but just for a moment.*

*LOW-PROFILE, ONE-PIECE TOILET (LEFT) AND BIDET*

# Heating and Ventilation

CLEAR THE AIR WHILE TAKING THE CHILL OFF

Certain elements of your bathroom's clmate—steam, excess heat, early morning chill—can be annoying and unpleasant. When you remodel, consider adding an exhaust fan to freshen the air and draw out mold-producing moisture and a heater to warm you on cool days. Installing such climate controllers may be simple, and could make a big difference.

## Heating the bathroom

Nothing spoils the soothing effects of a long, hot soak or shower faster than stepping out into a cool room—or even one of average house temperature. A small auxiliary heater in the wall or ceiling may be just what you need to stay warm while toweling off. Add a timer, and you can wake up to a toasty bathing space.

Bathroom heaters warm rooms by either of two methods—convection or radiation. Convection heaters warm the air in a room; radiant heaters emit infrared or electromagnetic waves that warm objects and surfaces.

**ELECTRIC HEATERS.** Because electric heaters are easy to install and clean to operate, they're the most familiar choice. Besides the standard wall- and ceiling-mounted units, you'll find heaters combined with exhaust fans, lights, or both.

Wall- or ceiling-mounted convection heaters usually have an electrically heated resistance coil and a

small fan to move the heated air. A toe-space heater—recessed into a vanity below the sink—helps warm (and dry) the floor more quickly. Options include thermostats, timer switches, and safety cutoffs.

Radiant heaters using infrared light bulbs ("heat lamps") can be surface-mounted on the ceiling or recessed between joists.

**GAS HEATERS.** You'll find heaters available for either propane or natural gas. Though most are convection heaters, there is one radiant type—a catalytic heater. Regardless of how they heat, all gas models require a gas supply line (see page 132) and must be vented to the outside.

**HEATED TOWEL BARS.** Besides gas and electricity, another heat source has reappeared on the bathroom scene: hot water. The original idea was to warm and dry bath towels, but now these hydronic units—wall- or floor-mounted—are being billed as "radiators" as well. In addition to water-powered towel warmers, you can also find sleek electric versions (see below right).

## Ventilating the bathroom

Even if you have good natural ventilation, an exhaust fan can exchange the air in a bathroom faster, and in bad weather it can keep the elements out and still remove stale air. Some fans include lights or heaters or both.

It's important that your exhaust fan have adequate capacity. The Home Ventilating Institute (HVI) recommends that the fan be capable of exchanging the air at least eight times every hour. To determine the required fan capacity in cubic feet per minute (CFM) for a bathroom with an 8-foot ceiling, multiply the room's length and width in feet by 1.1. For example, if your bathroom is 6 by 9 feet, you would calculate the required fan capacity as follows:

6 x 9 x 1.1 = 59.4 CFM

Rounding off, you would need fan capacity of at least 60 CFM. If your fan must exhaust through a long duct or several elbows, you'll need greater capacity to overcome the increased resistance. Follow the manufacturer's recommendations.

Most fans have a noise rating measured in sones: the lower the number, the quieter the fan.

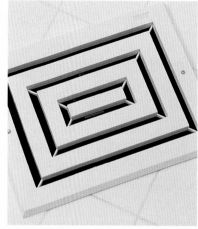

*Most modern vents and heaters are trim, discreet built-ins. A ceiling fan (above right) blends with white field tiles and draws heat and moisture from shower steam. An electric toe-space heater (above left), centered below the sink area, emits welcome warmth on chilly mornings.*

*Heated towel bars keep bath linens toasty while doubling as radiators. Brass rack (facing page) harnesses old-fashioned hydronic heat; modern slat design (right) comes in many colors—and in both hydronic and electric versions.*

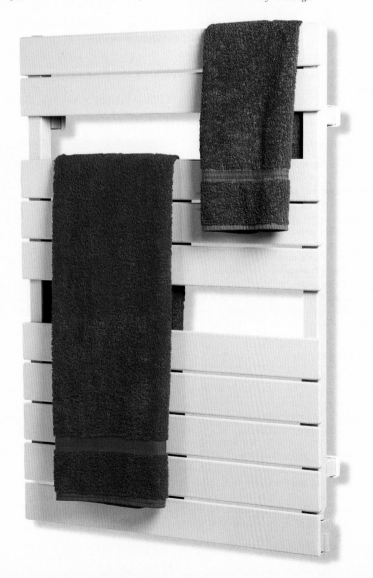

# Flooring

HARD-WORKING FOUNDATIONS DANCE NEW STEPS

The primary requirements for a bathroom floor are moisture resistance and durability. Resilient tiles and sheets, ceramic tile, and properly sealed masonry or hardwood are all good candidates. Resilient flooring is the simplest (and usually the least expensive) to install; the others are a little trickier. For a touch of comfort, don't rule out carpeting, especially the newer stain-resistant industrial versions.

## Planning checkpoints

Confused by the array of flooring types available? For help, study the guide below. It's a good idea to visit flooring suppliers and home centers. Most dealers are happy to give or lend samples to study.

For safety's sake, a bathroom floor must be slip resistant, especially in wet areas. Tiles, either ceramic or resilient, are safest in matte-finish or textured versions. Smaller ceramic tiles, with the increased number of grout surfaces they require, offer extra traction. A rubberized mat or throw rug (if it will stay put) can provide firm footing—and a warm landing zone—near the tub or shower.

Don't be afraid to mix and match flooring materials. Today's layouts often use different materials in the wet and dry areas of the bath. Cozy carpeting is showing up in dressing

---

## COMPARING FLOORING

### Resilient

**Advantages.** Generally made from solid vinyl or polyurethane, resilients are flexible, moisture and stain resistant, easy to install, and simple to maintain. Another advantage is the seemingly endless variety of colors, textures, patterns, and styles available. Tiles can be mixed to form custom patterns or provide color accents.

Sheets run up to 12 feet wide, eliminating the need for seaming in many bathrooms; tiles are generally 12 inches square. Vinyl and rubber are comfortable to walk

on. A polyurethane finish may eliminate the need for waxing. Prices are generally modest, but expect to pay a premium for custom tiles and imported products.
**Disadvantages.** Resilients are relatively soft, making them vulnerable to dents and tears; often, though, such damage can be repaired. Tiles may collect moisture between seams if improperly installed. Some vinyl still comes with a photographically applied pattern, but most is inlaid; the latter is more expensive but wears much better.

### Ceramic tile

**Advantages.** Made from hard-fired slabs of clay, ceramic tile is available in hundreds of patterns, colors, shapes, and finishes. Its durability, easy upkeep, and attractiveness are definite advantages.

Tiles are usually classified as quarry tiles, commonly unglazed (unfinished) red-clay tiles that are rough and water resistant; terracotta, unglazed tiles in earth-tone shades; porcelain pavers, rugged tiles in stonelike shades and textures; and glazed floor tiles, available in glossy, matte, or textured finishes.

Floor tiles run the gamut of widths, lengths, and thicknesses—8-inch and 12-inch squares are most plentiful. Costs range from inexpensive to moderate; in general, porcelain is most expensive. Purer clays fired at higher temperature generally make costlier but better-wearing tiles.
**Disadvantages.** Tile can be cold, noisy, and, if glazed, slippery underfoot. Porous tiles will stain and harbor bacteria unless properly sealed. Grout spaces can be tough to keep clean, though mildew-resistant or epoxy grout definitely helps.

areas, grooming centers, and even exercise rooms. Hardwood strips or planks can play a similar role in period or country designs.

If you're on a tight budget, save the honed marble or fine ceramic tile for a focal point, such as around a platform tub or walk-in shower.

## What about subflooring?

Don't make any final decision until you know what kind of subfloor your new flooring will require.

With proper preparation, a concrete slab can serve as a base for almost any type of flooring. Wood subfloors are not suitable for rigid materials such as

masonry and ceramic tile unless they are built up with extra underlayment or floor framing. But adding too many layers underneath can make the bathroom awkwardly higher than surrounding rooms. Be sure to check with a building professional or a flooring dealer for specifics.

---

## COMPARING FLOORING

### Hardwood

**Advantages.** A classic hardwood floor creates a warm decor, feels good underfoot, and can be refinished. Oak is most common, with maple, birch, and other species also available.

The three basic types are narrow strips in random lengths; planks in various widths and random lengths; and wood tiles, laid in blocks or squares. Wood flooring may be factory-prefinished or unfinished, to be sanded and finished in place. "Floating" floor systems have several veneered strips

atop each backing board. In addition, you'll now find "planks" and "tiles" of high-pressure laminate that look surprisingly like the real thing.

**Disadvantages.** Moisture damage and inadequate floor substructure are two bugaboos. Maintenance is another issue; some surfaces can be mopped or waxed, some cannot. Bleaching and some staining processes may wear unevenly and are difficult to repair. Cost is moderate to high, depending on wood species, grade, and finish.

### Stone

**Advantages.** Natural stone (such as slate, marble, granite, and limestone) has been used as flooring for centuries. Today, its use is even more practical, thanks to the development of efficient sealers and surfacing techniques. Stone can be used in its natural shape—known as flagstone—or cut into rectangular blocks or tiles. Generally, pieces are butted tightly together; irregular flagstones require wider grout joints.

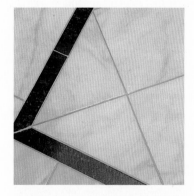

**Disadvantages.** The cost of masonry flooring can be quite high, though recent diamond-saw technology has lowered it considerably. Moreover, the weight of the materials requires a very strong, well-supported subfloor. Some stone is cold and slippery underfoot, though new honed and etched surfaces are safer, subtler alternatives to polished surfaces. Certain stones, such as marble and limestone, absorb stains and dirt readily. Careful sealing is essential.

### Carpeting

**Advantages.** Carpeting cushions feet, provides firm traction, and helps deaden sound. It's especially useful to define subareas within multiuse layouts or master suites. New tightly woven commercial products are making carpeting more practical. Like resilient flooring, carpeting is available in an array of styles and materials, with prices that vary widely.

**Disadvantages.** Generally, the more elaborate the material and weave, the greater the problems from moisture absorption, staining, and mildew. Carpeting used in bathrooms should be short-pile and unsculptured. Woven or loop-pile wool should be confined to dressing areas. Nylon and other synthetic carpets are a wiser choice for splash zones; these are washable and hold up better in moist conditions.

# Wall Coverings

BOLD, BEAUTIFUL BACKDROPS FOR YOUR DREAM BATH

In addition to the shower and tub-surround areas, your bathroom will probably include a good bit of wall space. These surfaces must be able to withstand moisture, heat, and high usage. They also go a long way toward defining the impact of your room.

Here are four popular wall treatments. You might also choose to use stone (see page 195), solid-surface materials, or other countertop choices. Glass block (page 215), whether serving as window or wall, can admit soft natural light while maintaining privacy. And fabric-upholstered walls, though they probably don't leap to mind right away, can add a dash of style and a measure of soundproofing in powder rooms or master bath areas where there's no shower or tub.

## Paint

Everybody thinks of paint first. But what's best for the bathroom?

The suitable choices are latex or alkyd paint.

Latex is easy to work with, and you can clean up wet paint with soap and water. Alkyd paint (often called oil-base paint) provides high gloss and will hang on a little harder than latex; however, alkyds are trickier to apply and require cleanup with mineral spirits. Usually, the higher the resin content, the higher the gloss; so look for products labeled gloss, semigloss, or satin if you want a tough, washable finish.

Faux (literally, false) finishes produce the patterns or textures of materials other than plain paint. In one version, many closely related pastels are built up in subtle layers with brush strokes, by stippling, or with a sponge. Other faux treatments might layer paint textures and/or multiple colors to mimic anything from stenciled wallpaper to ancient stone.

## Ceramic tile

Tough, water-resistant tile is always a good choice for a bathroom, and the range of colors, textures, shapes, and sizes opens up many creative possibilities.

Wall tiles are typically glazed and offer great variety in color and design. Generally less heavy than floor tiles, their relatively light weight is a plus for vertical installation. Made by machine, these tiles have crisp, precise shapes—they're usually set closely together, with thin ($\frac{1}{16}$-inch) grout lines. Common sizes include 3 by 3, 4¼ by 4¼, and 6 by 6 inches; larger squares and rectangles may also be available.

Prices range from as little as 50 cents per commercial tile to $20 or more per square foot for custom colors or one-of-a-kind creations. Decorative art tiles can make striking accents in a field of less expensive wall tiles, especially in low-impact areas such as backsplashes and tub surrounds.

*GLOSS WALL TILES*

*MATTE WALL TILES*

*STONE-TEXTURED WALL TILES*

Many wall tile lines feature coordinated border and trim pieces. Some integrated lines include matching floor tiles, countertop tiles, and coordinated bathroom fixtures and accessories.

Remember that neither glazed wall tiles nor art tiles are waterproof on their own. Water-resistant backing, adhesive, and grout can improve performance; but for vulnerable locations like showers, it's best to choose vitreous or impervious tiles.

## Wallpapers

A wallpaper for the bathroom should be scrubbable, durable, and stain resistant. Vinyl wallpapers, which come in a wide variety of colors and textures, fill the bill. New patterns, including some that replicate other surfaces (such as linen), are generally subtle. A wallpaper border can add visual punch to ceiling lines and openings.

Textile wall coverings come in many colors and textures, from casual to formal. They're usually made of cotton, linen, or other natural plant fibers or of polyester, often bonded to a paper-type backing. Grass cloth is a favorite among textile wall coverings; hemp is similar but has thinner fibers. Keep in mind that most textiles fray easily and are not washable, though most will accept a spray-on stain repellent.

## Wood

Solid wood paneling—natural, stained, bleached, or painted—provides a warm ambience in country schemes. Wainscoting is traditional, with a chair rail separating wood paneling below it from the painted or papered wall above it.

Generally, solid boards have edges specially milled to overlap or inter-

lock. Hardwood boards are milled from such species as oak, maple, birch, and mahogany. Common softwoods include cedar, pine, fir, and redwood.

Moldings are also back in vogue. You'll find basic profiles at lumberyards and home centers. Specialty millwork shops are likely to have a wide selection and will often custom-match an old favorite to order.

When shopping, you'll encounter words like clear, stain-grade, and paint-grade. The molding you want depends on the finish you plan: clear finishes require the best lumber; moldings that are to be painted can be of lesser grades.

*Wallpapers and borders like those shown above add soft, traditional charm. But before you choose a paper, consider the territory: hard-use areas such as family baths and kids' baths might require tougher, washable vinyl products.*

*WOOD WAINSCOTING*

# Windows and Skylights

THESE OPENINGS SHED DAYLIGHT ON YOUR NEW DESIGN

After years of timidly guarding their users' privacy, bathrooms are now taking advantage, in earnest, of available light and views.

You can use glass in different structures (windows, skylights, blocks) and finishes (clear or translucent) to bring in more daylight and views while still protecting the bathroom enclosure from the world outside.

## Windows

Windows are available with frames made of wood, clad wood, aluminum, vinyl, steel, or fiberglass (a newcomer). Generally, aluminum windows are the least expensive, wood and clad wood the most costly. Vinyl- or aluminum-clad wood windows and all-vinyl windows require little maintenance.

Operable windows for bathrooms include double-hung, casement, sliding, and awning types. Which you choose depends partly on your home's style and partly on ventilation needs. Also, consider such specialty units as bays, bows, and greenhouse windows—all attractive as tub surrounds.

Many of the greatest strides in window technology are taking place in glazing. Insulating glass is made of two or more panes of glass sealed together, with a space between the panes to trap air. Low-e (low-emissivity) glass usually consists of two sealed panes separated by an air space and a transparent coating. Some manufacturers use argon gas between panes of low-e glass

to add extra insulation. Look for quality and a guarantee when choosing insulating glass: with low-quality installations, a streaky look can develop between panes.

Window shopping can require at least a passing acquaintance with some specialized jargon. For a quick glossary, see "Window Words," opposite.

## Skylights

You can pay as little as $100 for a fixed acrylic skylight, about $500 for a pivot-

*Among the many window styles are primed wood casement with simulated divided lights (1), wood slider with aluminum cladding and snap-on grille (2), prefinished wood casement (3), anodized aluminum slider (4), vinyl double-hung (5), wood circle with aluminum cladding (6), and aluminum octagon (7).*

ing model that you crank open with a pole, or several thousand dollars for a motorized unit that automatically closes when a moisture sensor detects rain.

The most energy-efficient designs feature double glazing and "thermal-break" construction.

Fixed skylights vary in shape from square to circular; they may be flat, domed, or pyramidal in profile. Most skylight manufacturers also offer at least one or two ventilating models that open to allow fresh air in and steam and heat out. Think of rotary roof windows as a cross between windows and skylights. They have sashes that rotate on pivots on two sides of the frame, which permits easy cleaning. Unlike openable roof skylights, these are typically installed on sloping walls.

If there's space between the ceiling and roof, you'll need a light shaft to direct light to the room below. It may be straight, angled, or splayed (wider at the bottom).

## Glass block

If you'd like to have some ambient daylight but don't want to lose your privacy, consider another glazing option—glass block. It provides an even, filtered light that complements many bath designs.

You can buy 3- or 4-inch-thick glass blocks in many sizes; rectangular and curved corner blocks are also available in a more limited selection. Textures can be smooth, wavy, rippled, bubbly, or crosshatched. Most block is clear, though Italian block also comes in blue, rose, and green tones, and German block comes in gold tone.

To locate glass block, look in the yellow pages under Glass—Block Structural, Etc. You may be able to special-order blocks through a regular glass or tile dealer.

---

# WINDOW WORDS

Strange, intimidating words seem to orbit the subject of windows and their components, construction, and installation. Here's a crash course in standard window jargon, enough to help you brave a showroom, building center, or product brochure.

**Apron.** An applied interior trim piece that runs beneath the unit, below the sill.

**Casement.** A window with a frame that hinges on the side, like a door.

**Casing.** Wooden window trim, especially interior, added by owner or contractor. Head casing runs at the top, side casings flank the unit.

**Cladding.** A protective sheath of aluminum or vinyl covering a window's exterior wood surfaces.

**Flashing.** Thin sheets, usually metal, that protect the wall or roof from leaks near the edges of windows or skylights.

**Glazing.** The window pane itself—glass, acrylic plastic, or other clear or translucent material. It may be one, two, or even three layers thick.

**Grille.** A decorative, removable grating that makes an expanse of glass look as though it were made up of many smaller panes.

**Jamb.** The frame that surrounds the sash or glazing. An extension jamb thickens a window to match a thick wall.

**Lights.** Separately framed panes of glass in a multipane window; each light is held by muntins.

**Low emissivity.** A high-tech treatment that sharply improves the thermal performance of glass, especially in double-glazed windows, at little added cost.

**Mullion.** A vertical dividing piece; whereas muntins separate small panes of glass, mullions separate larger expanses or whole windows.

**Muntin.** A slender strip of wood or metal framing a pane of glass in a multipane window.

**R-value.** Measure of a material's ability to insulate; the higher the number, the lower your heating or cooling bills should be.

**Sash.** A window frame surrounding glass. It may be fixed or operable.

**Sill.** An interior or exterior shelf below a window unit. An interior sill may be called a stool.

**U-value.** Measure of the energy efficiency of all the materials in the window; the lower the U-value, the less the waste.

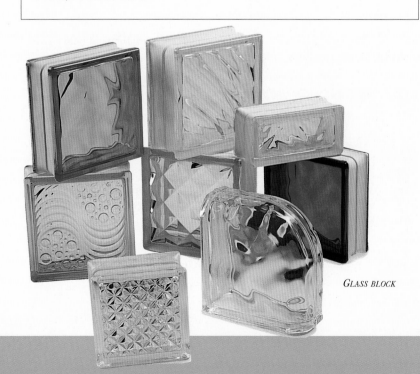

*GLASS BLOCK*

# Light Fixtures

LIGHT UP THE NIGHT WITH THESE ARTIFICIAL SOURCES

*WALL SCONCES*

Designers separate lighting into three categories: task, ambient, and accent. Task lighting illuminates a particular area where a visual activity—such as shaving or applying makeup—takes place. Ambient (or general) lighting fills in the undefined areas of a room with a soft level of light—enough, say, for a relaxing soak in a whirlpool tub. Accent lighting, which is primarily decorative, is used to highlight architectural features or

*UNDER-COUNTER ACCENT LIGHT*

attractive plants, to set a mood, or to provide drama.

## Which fixtures are best?

Generally speaking, small and discreet are watchwords in bathroom lighting; consequently, recessed downlights are very popular. Though these fixtures, fitted with the right baffle or shield, can handle ambient, task, and accent needs alone, it's almost always better to add additional fill light.

In a larger bathroom, a separate fixture to light the shower or bath area—or any other distinct part in a compartmentalized design—and perhaps another for reading may be appreciated. Shower fixtures should be waterproof units with neoprene seals.

Fixtures around a makeup or shaving mirror should spread light over a person's face rather than onto the mirror surface. To avoid heavy shadows, it's best to place mirror lights at the sides, rather than only above the mirror. Wall sconces flanking the mirror not only provide effective light, but offer an opportunity for a stylish design statement.

And just for fun, why not consider decorative strip lights in a toe-space area or a row of hidden uplights atop wall cabinets? These low-key accents help provide a wash of ambient light and can also serve as safe, pleasant night lights.

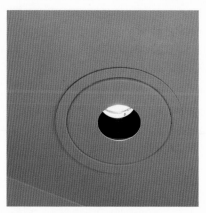

*DOWNLIGHT WITH PINHOLE APERTURE*

## Light bulbs and tubes

Light sources can be grouped in general categories according to the way they produce light.

INCANDESCENT LIGHT. This light, the kind used most frequently in our homes, is produced by a tungsten thread that burns slowly inside a glass bulb. A-bulbs are the old standbys; R and PAR bulbs produce a more controlled beam; silvered-bowl types diffuse light. A number of decorative bulbs are also available.

*INCANDESCENT/FLUORESCENT MIRROR LIGHTS*

Low-voltage incandescent lighting is especially useful for accent lighting. Operating on 12 or 24 volts, these lights require transformers, which are sometimes built into the fixtures, to step down the voltage from standard 120-volt household circuits.

Low-voltage fixtures are relatively expensive to buy. But in the long run, low-voltage lighting can be energy- and cost-efficient if carefully planned.

**FLUORESCENT LIGHT.** Fluorescent tubes are unrivaled for energy efficiency. They also last far longer than incandescent bulbs. In some energy-conscious areas, general lighting for new bathrooms must be fluorescent.

Older fluorescent tubes have been criticized for noise, flicker, and poor color rendition. Electronic ballasts and better fixture shielding against glare have remedied the first two problems; as for the last one, manufacturers have developed fluorescents in a wide spectrum of colors, from very warm (about 2,700 degrees K) to very cool (about 6,300 degrees K).

**QUARTZ HALOGEN.** These bright, white sources are excellent for task lighting, pinpoint accenting, and other dramatic accents. Halogen is usually low-voltage but may use standard line current. The popular MR-16 bulb creates the tightest beam; for a longer reach and wider coverage, choose a PAR bulb. There's an abundance of smaller bulb shapes and sizes to fit pendant fixtures and strip lights.

Halogen has two disadvantages: its high initial cost and its very high heat production (halogen bulbs must be used in fixtures appropriate for them). Be sure to shop carefully. Some fixtures are not UL-approved.

## COMPARING LIGHT BULBS AND TUBES

### INCANDESCENT

**A-Bulb**
**Description.** Familiar pear shape; frosted or clear.
**Uses.** Everyday household use.

**T—Tubular**
**Description.** Tube-shaped, from 5" long. Frosted or clear.
**Uses.** Cabinets, decorative fixtures.

**R—Reflector**
**Description.** White or silvered coating directs light out end of funnel-shaped bulb.
**Uses.** Directional fixtures; focuses light where needed.

**PAR—Parabolic aluminized reflector**
**Description.** Similar to auto headlamps; special shape and coating project light and control beam.
**Uses.** Recessed downlights and track fixtures.

**Silvered bowl**
**Description.** A-bulb, with silvered cap to cut glare and produce indirect light.
**Uses.** Track fixtures and pendants.

**Low-voltage strip**
**Description.** Like Christmas tree lights; in strips or tracks, or encased in flexible, waterproof plastic.
**Uses.** Task lighting and decoration.

### FLUORESCENT

**Tube**
**Description.** Tube-shaped, 5" to 96" long. Needs special fixture and ballast.
**Uses.** Shadowless work light; also indirect lighting.

**PL—Compact tube**
**Description.** U-shaped with base; 5¼" to 7½" long.
**Uses.** In recessed downlights; some PL tubes include ballasts to replace A-bulbs.

### QUARTZ HALOGEN

**High intensity**
**Description.** Small, clear bulb with consistently high light output; used in halogen fixtures only.
**Uses.** Specialized task lamps, torchères, and pendants.

**Low-voltage MR-16— (mini-reflector)**
**Description.** Tiny (2"-diameter) projector bulb; gives small circle of light from a distance.
**Uses.** Low-voltage track fixtures, mono-spots, and recessed downlights.

**Low-voltage PAR**
**Description.** Similar to auto headlight; tiny filament, shape, and coating give precise direction.
**Uses.** To project a small spot of light a long distance.

# Finishing Touches

ACCENTS AND ACCESSORIES COMPLETE THE PICTURE

In bathroom design, as in life in general, it's sometimes the little things that count. Don't forget to plan in those subtle amenities that can furnish delightful finishing touches.

Accessory lines are more complete than ever; some towel bars, hooks, and tissue holders even correspond with faucet handles on sinks, tubs, and showers. Additional matchables may include soap dishes, toothbrush holders, cup holders, cabinet pulls (see page 192), switch plates, mirrors, light fixtures, and wall tiles. And how about

*OPTICAL MAKEUP MIRROR*

a pedestal sink or bathtub that's part of the same collection?

Other popular amenities include adjustable makeup mirrors (typically 3x or 5x power), with or without optical glass and internal illumination; shaving mirrors for the shower; heated towel-bar warmers or "radiators" (see pages 208–209); and home-entertainment components (TVs, built-in speakers, control panels wired to remote audio systems).

*A well-stocked bath showroom displays a dazzling array of accessories.*

*BARRIER-FREE GRAB BARS*

*In addition to
fine design and
craftsmanship, this
bathroom gains
visual coherence
from an integrated
product line.
Coordinated compo-
nents extend from
fixtures—tub, toilet,
and sink—to wall
lights, mirror,
shelves, and
wall tiles.*

*Sunset*

*ideas for great*

# GREAT ROOMS

By Barbara J. Braasch and
the Editors of Sunset Books

Sunset Books ■ Menlo Park, California

# contents

# ROOMS FOR ALL REASONS

GREAT ROOMS, FAMILY ROOMS, and even family kitchens are variations on the same theme: they are all gathering spaces designed to be used for more than one purpose. Whether folks get together here for cooking and eating, socializing with family and friends, watching television, listening to music, or playing games, these rooms shine when the gang's all here. UNIFYING AREAS where so many disparate activities take place can be a real challenge, but in the pages of this book we'll show you how other people have altered their houses to do just that. THE FRESH IDEAS presented here can help you transform a not-so-fulfilling space in your own home into the one special place where your family truly lives.

### Great rooms

What is a great room? Ask people who have one and they'll tell you it's the most lived-in part of a modern home. Designed to be shared by family and friends, a great room often includes kitchen, dining, and living functions in areas that are physically and visually open to each other. Activity zones flow together rather than being completely separated by walls.

The idea dates back to colonial days, when a family lived, slept, cooked, ate, and entertained in one large space—often sharing the area with their livestock. Though sleeping now takes place in another part of the home and livestock is relegated elsewhere, today's great room is very much in keeping with the old tradition.

This open and airy space not only serves family members, but it also provides an ideal entertaining area. Often the great room boasts a broad expanse of windows offering panoramic views or glass doors opening onto a deck or terrace.

Comfortable seating areas foster conversation, and when it's time for hors d'oeuvres, a nearby dining table means they may be enjoyed without moving to another room.

Great rooms should be welcoming day and night, with sunlight streaming in through windows or skylights and interior lighting setting a mood as well as defining separate areas within the room. In a space where so much activity takes place, storage is very important, too. A great room benefits from built-in or freestanding cabinets, bookshelves, and drawers.

Opening up smaller rooms to make one large open space usually involves removing walls and defining separate activity areas instead by means of arches, columns, alcoves, or varied floor or ceiling levels. But sometimes just changing floor coverings or adding rugs is enough to mark where one activity area ends and the next one begins.

*Varying widely in design and decor, these two great rooms share such important features as comfort and convenience. And both make the most of their space with plenty of built-in storage.*

*This high-beamed family room offers plenty of space to play or curl up and read. Built-in shelves at both ends of the window seat hold books.*

## Family rooms and family kitchens

The great room's more modest cousin is the family room. Though it is often situated off the kitchen, no cooking takes place in the family room itself. This is probably a home's most comfortable spot, the place where family members gather to watch television or share other forms of entertainment. Guests may be entertained more formally in a separate living room.

The kitchen is a popular gathering space in its own right. To allow more room for chatting and eating, many of today's family kitchens have been expanded to include a dining area—an island with stools, a kitchen table, or perhaps both—that provides limited space for informal meals and socializing. If there's room for a small seating area as well, guests can converse in comfort without getting in the cook's way.

## Private spaces

Just as families differ, the way they use their homes differs, too. Sometimes the very openness of a great room may make it desirable to dedicate part of your layout as a quiet place to read, watch television, listen to music, or just talk with a friend. Let another space handle crowds—private places are the perfect spots for a favorite chair, a good reading lamp, some books, and perhaps a desk for sorting through mail.

As modern life becomes ever more complicated, many families find the need for an office space set apart from the main gathering area of their home. Connected to the open area with screens, pocket doors, or French doors, this work area can be separate and private when closed off; when the doors or screens are opened, it's part of the loop of family activity.

Built-ins are particularly well suited to such private retreats. Not only do they allow you to tailor space to your specific needs, but they also lend a more formal, businesslike appearance to an area that is to be used as a home office, either occasionally or on a full-time basis.

*Tucked into a nook of a multipurpose room, an inviting personal space allows you to welcome a friend for coffee and a little private conversation.*

# DEFINING YOUR SPACE

**I**T'S OFFICIAL. Surveys by the National Association of Home Builders confirm that the formal living room, like the little-used Victorian parlor, is nearing extinction. Today's families are looking for a more casual, do-everything gathering place, where they can chat with the cook, entertain guests, pay bills, go online, screen movies, do homework, or just relax. Great room, family room, or fusion space—no matter what you call it, it's the heart of the home, the place where we really live.

**USE THIS CHAPTER** of practical ideas as a starting point to help you come up with a fresh, open plan that suits your family's lifestyle. We'll help you evaluate your existing home, guide you through layout and design basics, show you what's involved in the art of the remodel, and explain how designers and contractors can help you realize your dreams.

# a family profile

LIKE TO KEEP AN EYE *on the kids while cooking? Want to curl up on a window seat with a good book or bask in a sunroom? Before you start tearing down walls and rearranging rooms to fulfill those dreams, you'll want to take stock of what you have—and determine how you will reconcile your dreams and your budget.*

### Dreams versus reality

An analysis of how your existing rooms are used will probably surprise you. It will certainly offer a new look at your family's lifestyle.

Begin by listing each room in your house, along with its approximate square footage. List the activities that take place in each room, how often they occur, and who does them. Then organize your list from most-used to least-used rooms. You probably will notice that some large rooms receive little use, a clear indication that you may want to rework that space.

Another helpful tool—and one that's fun to make—is a wish list of all the ideas you have for a new gathering place. Even if many items appear to be way beyond your budget, include everything that family members feel would give them pleasure, from a playroom to a movie theater. Be as specific as possible, adding any illustrations you may have collected.

When your wish list is complete, identify which "wants" are definite "musts," which would be nice but could be omitted if cost prohibits, and which are completely in the realm of fantasy. Then make a second list, describing the "musts" in more detail. Add whatever would be necessary to make your gathering space work the way you want it to, such as new storage, lighting, or furniture. You have now created a reality list, a framework for setting goals to create the home you envision.

### Budgeting for size and style

Before you hire a designer or pick up a sledge-hammer, consider your budget. Altering living

*Replacing a load-bearing wall with a structural beam unites a small sitting area (left) and the kitchen (below) in a single airy space that lets the chef keep an eye on both the meal and family or guests. On the facing page, a kitchen gains built-in seating and generous storage space with the addition of a simple bay.*

space often pits dreams against realities. To reconcile the two, you need to consider three variables—cost, quantity, and quality. In any design change, two of the three factors can remain constant, but the third has to be adjustable.

Allowing cost to be a variable, if you have that luxury, offers the greatest flexibility in terms of dream fulfillment. By increasing the size of your project (quantity) or the level of detailing (quality), you increase cost. But how big does your new space really have to be? Many people opt for as large a space as possible; after all, that's probably what prompted a redesign in the first place. If your vision has little to do with size, however, the quality of the space might be improved by reducing square footage. By using a simpler, not-so-large plan, you can enrich the quality of your space, adding higher-grade materials and special detailing.

# exploring your options

**AS WE ALL KNOW,** *homes were different a century ago, with structured rooms that reflected a more formal way of life. The concept of open living spaces didn't emerge until the 1950s. First, living rooms and dining rooms were blended. Then a separate room was introduced to house that epoch's new marvel, the television.*

Many of us still live in houses with poorly configured floor plans and no all-purpose room where the family can get together. Even if your house was once a perfect fit for your family, your present lifestyle is probably fundamentally different from what it used to be. As a family grows and changes through the years, its home needs to keep pace.

Tailoring your space so that it's more in sync with the way you live today may be easier than you imagine, thanks to new materials, simpler installation techniques, and creative open-space planning.

When thinking of changing or adding space, it's wise to consider both what you need today and what you will need in the future. A desire for more space is often the paramount reason for altering a residence. But new interests, new occupations, and new technology may also act as spurs for conversions. Maybe you would like a place to screen movies or listen to audio equipment. If you work out of your home, configuring space to add office equipment may make good sense.

Fortunate is the family who can transform its home by simple redecoration. Most people need to at least rework space. Often, minor adjustments can solve problems. Adding more light by enlarging existing windows, for example, can make a room seem larger and more inviting. Building a window seat with drawers underneath increases both storage space and seating capacity.

Look around your home for space you might not have thought of before. If your dining room is used only on holidays, you might be able to convert it into a family room and connect it to the kitchen by knocking out a wall or two. Perhaps a rarely used breakfast room can be converted into a combination greenhouse/sunroom. Add window walls, bring in plants, and replace kitchen table and chairs with comfortable wicker furniture and you've turned your underutilized space into a charming spot to entertain family and guests.

Converting an existing space requires fewer structural changes than building an addition. Sometimes you can make rooms flow into one another simply by widening arches between them. Often the way to unify space is to rearrange rooms, remove walls, or raise ceilings. Knocking down walls between kitchen, dining room, and living room can create an all-purpose great room. Transforming a back porch into a sunroom or converting an attached garage into a family room are relatively easy and inexpensive ways to access space.

*French doors connect a remodeled kitchen and breakfast room with the home's new rear terrace, visually "stretching" the interior space into the outdoors and offering diners an alfresco experience.*

# a room redux

**MANY HOMES** *are veritable gold mines of underutilized space that can be drafted into service or, as in the case of a garage or porch, changed from one use to another. Whether you do it yourself or hire professional help, changing your home's structure will require extensive work. Check with your local building department for applicable codes and permits.*

## Structural changes

If you're planning to open up space, add a skylight or window wall, or lay a heavy stone floor, your house may require structural modifications. As shown below, walls are either bearing (supporting the weight of the ceiling joists and/or second-story walls) or nonbearing. If you're removing all or part of a bearing wall, you must

bridge the gap with a sturdy beam and posts. Nonbearing ("partition") walls usually can be removed without too much trouble, unless pipes or wires are routed through them.

Doors and windows require special framing, as illustrated; the required header size depends on the width of the opening and your local building codes. Skylights require similar cuts through ceiling joists and/or rafters. Planning a vaulted or cathedral ceiling instead of your present ceiling? You'll probably need to install a few beams to maintain structural soundness.

Hardwood, ceramic tile, and stone floors require very stiff underlayment. You can solve the problem by beefing up the floor joists and/or adding plywood or particleboard subflooring on top of the existing floor.

## Expanding into the garage

Converting an adjoining garage into a family room—or into a quiet media room or home office off a gathering room—is a relatively easy task. The garage is easily accessible, it's located at ground level, and it offers a large, unobstructed space. Electricity is probably already available, with water and heat not far away, although insulation may be needed.

**STRUCTURAL FRAMING**

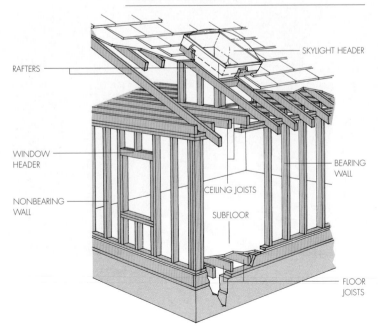

RAFTERS

SKYLIGHT HEADER

WINDOW HEADER

NONBEARING WALL

CEILING JOISTS

SUBFLOOR

BEARING WALL

FLOOR JOISTS

*Annexing an adjacent two-car garage created a spacious gathering place (left) off the kitchen. Columns, a low wall, and a modest change in floor level define cooking, dining, and seating areas. The breakfast table (below) shares views of the television and the fireplace with the seating area.*

A major concern is what to do with the garage door. You will probably want to remove it and frame in the wall, taking advantage of this opportunity to introduce windows or glass doors. For more information, consult the Sunset book *Converting Garages, Attics & Basements.*

With landscaping and a little carpentry, you can re-create an exterior that looks more like an extension of the house than a storage depot for mowers and Mazdas. Check local building codes before banishing the car, though; in many areas, covered spaces must be provided for cars.

## Converting a porch or patio

Turning a framed porch into an extra room may be as simple as adding windows and, if not already installed, lighting and heat. Patio conversion is much more difficult; if the foundation does not meet building codes, you'll virtually be starting from scratch. This may turn out to be as much work as adding an entirely new room.

# HOME THEATER BASICS

A home sound system can range from a traditional stereo with built-in speakers to a complete surround-sound system tied to a big-screen television. What your family needs depends on its musical and viewing interests, the size and arrangement of your house, and your budget. You can install a multiroom sound system that controls music from several locations around the house. Some sophisticated sound systems include telephone and security functions.

What transforms television, VCR, sound system, and other black boxes into a formal home theater is the relationship between these devices, all tied together with low-voltage wires and cables. So if your family gathers around the electronic hearth to watch television, or if you plan a separate media room, you have to consider how to place and wire your audio and video equipment.

You'll need a special A/V receiver to drive the five or more speakers in your viewing room. If you have an existing stereo receiver, you can add a separate surround-sound processor to handle extra speakers. Speakers must be carefully selected and positioned for best sound. What you need will depend on the size and sound-absorbing qualities of your room. For an unobtrusive look, speakers can be recessed into the wall or ceiling.

Televisions are available with a choice of features: direct-view, rear-projection, front-projection, flat-screen, and high-definition. Ask for some showroom help in unraveling your options. Just as important are compatible cable and wiring connections. If you choose to install your own home theater system, see Sunset's *Complete Home Wiring* book for details on components, placement, and wiring.

*This seamless makeover from garage to cozy media room required much attention to detail. Floor coverings, paint, and cabinets were matched to those in the adjoining kitchen, and window size and style were coordinated.*

*The graceful transition between the remodeled kitchen/family room and a wide deck creates a feeling of spaciousness. Transom windows above the French doors brighten the kitchen's once-gloomy high ceilings.*

## Need help?

Depending on the scope of the job and your time and abilities, you may want to call on professional assistance. Finding the right help need not be daunting. Look for someone who is technically and artistically skilled, has a proven track record, and is adequately insured against any mishaps on the job. It is also important to work with someone with whom you and your family feel comfortable. A remodel is more than just a construction project; it's a personal matter.

**ARCHITECTS.** Architects are state-licensed professionals with degrees in architecture. Many are members of the American Institute of Architects (AIA). Trained to create designs that are structurally sound, functional, and aesthetically pleasing, they also know construction materials, can negotiate bids from contractors, and can supervise the actual work. If structural calculations must be made, architects can make them; other professionals need state-licensed engineers to design structures and sign working drawings. If your remodel involves major structural changes, an architect should definitely be consulted.

**INTERIOR DESIGNERS.** Even if you are working with an architect, you may wish to call on an interior designer for the finishing touches. A designer's services can be as simple as editing and arranging what you already have or as complex as creating a complete redesign. Designers can offer fresh, innovative ideas and advice, including updates on the increasingly sophisticated field of lighting design. Many belong to the American Society of Interior Designers (ASID).

**GENERAL CONTRACTORS.** Contractors specialize in construction, although some have design skills as well. General contractors may do all the work themselves, or they may hire qualified subcontractors, order construction materials, and see that the job is completed to contract. Contractors can also secure building permits and arrange for inspections.

**SUBCONTRACTORS.** If you act as your own contractor, you will have to hire and supervise subcontractors for specialized jobs such as wiring, plumbing, and tiling. You'll be responsible for permits, insurance, and possibly even payroll taxes.

# making
# your plans

**MEASURING ALL OF THE PERIMETERS** *and elements of the area you plan to renovate will increase your awareness of the existing space. Scale drawings serve as a good foundation for design and also may satisfy your local building department's permit requirements. If you decide to consult a professional about your project, you may save money by providing measurements and drawings.*

### Drawing your plan

Use your drawings to bring your ideas to life, to check fit, to experiment, and to revise and revise and revise. Good plans, drawn to scale on paper, will save much labor down the road and will ensure the most efficient use of materials.

**ARCHITECTURAL SYMBOLS**

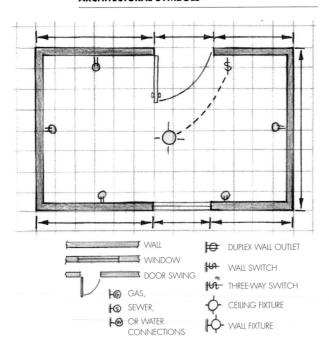

WALL
WINDOW
DOOR SWING
GAS,
SEWER,
OR WATER
CONNECTIONS
DUPLEX WALL OUTLET
WALL SWITCH
THREE-WAY SWITCH
CEILING FIXTURE
WALL FIXTURE

Several computer software programs can help you create floor plans with elevations easily and quickly. Computer-aided design (CAD) software shows you how a room looks in three dimensions and allows you to move walls and windows and drag furniture and fixtures in and out at will. Or you can purchase design and layout kits that contain graph paper and scaled-to-size appliance and cabinet templates.

Take all measurements accurately, since even a fraction of an inch counts in fitting together the elements of a layout. To record your measurements, draw a rough sketch of the perimeter (including doors, windows, recesses, and projections) and any relevant adjacent areas. Don't worry about scale at this point, but make your sketch large enough to write all dimensions directly on it, exact to ⅛ inch.

### Making it fit

A floor plan drawn to scale gives you a bird's-eye view of how your space is laid out. For neat, readable floor plans, start by attaching graph paper (four squares per inch) to a smooth surface with masking tape. Use a ruler or T-square to

*Stone walls, beamed ceiling, and antique maple chopping block add warmth and character to a design that also easily incorporates the latest high-tech appliances.*

draw horizontal lines with a pencil, a triangle to draw vertical lines, and a template or compass to show which way each door swings.

Using a scale of ¼" or ½" = 1' (or whatever is convenient for you), map the outer dimensions of the room, noting doors (and their direction of swing), windows, and any fixed architectural features, such as built-in bookcases or a fireplace. Be accurate in converting your measurements to scale.

Indicate the placement of outlets, light fixtures, wall switches, heaters, and vents. Note window dimensions and height from the floor, plus the measurements of any door frames, window trim, and baseboards that might affect furniture placement, window treatments, or wall coverings.

To identify the various elements in your floor plan, use the architectural symbols shown under the basic floor plan on the facing page.

*Vaulted to 14 feet, this glass-walled 20- by 20-foot addition opens a once-small seating area off the kitchen to views of an azalea garden and a wooded hillside.*

# spatial illusions

**NO ONE KNOWS WHY,** *but when you enter a room that is 1.618 times longer than it is wide, that space appears harmonious and inviting. This was the formula used by the Greeks when they created the Parthenon. But don't despair if your space doesn't match these ideal dimensions. Various strategies can make an area appear larger or smaller.*

## A matter of dimension

Because a floor plan encourages us to think in terms of only two dimensions, many people feel a layout is complete after they have measured the length and width of a space and positioned windows and doors. Not so: the height of the space must also be considered.

We tend to think high ceilings make spaces appear bigger than low ceilings do, but a visual perception may work against that theory. If the distance to the ceiling is the largest dimension, our attention is naturally drawn upward to marvel at the height instead of appreciating what the space offers at eye level. If length and width are greater than height, that is where our attention is focused, and the room feels more spacious.

A room's height needs to be compatible with its length and width. A 10-foot ceiling might feel right in a 25-foot-wide great room, but it could

*Varied ceiling heights, a low stone wall, and different patterns of Saltillo floor tiles create distinct living and dining areas and direct the flow of traffic.*

*Color helps define a well-organized multipurpose space. Sunny yellow walls give the kitchen and breakfast area (left) a warm glow, while a comfortable blue sofa beckons from the sitting area (below).*

make a smaller space resemble an elevator shaft. People need to feel physically comfortable with a room's height, too. If you're tall, a 7-foot ceiling will make you feel like bending your head every time you enter the room.

## Enlarging space

Choreographers know that a theater stage "comes alive" when an imaginary diagonal line is used to create more dynamic space. It's a simple matter of mathematics: just as the hypotenuse of a triangle is the longest line, the diagonal view in a square room—from corner to corner—is the longest dimension. Create views to direct the eye along this long diagonal—to a window or other focal point—and the space will be perceived as larger than it actually is. An unobstructed sight line also makes the entire room appear more welcoming, inviting people in and making a gathering space seem more usable than a tucked-away living room does.

Maximizing the view of a patio or garden with windows or glass doors blurs the lines between the interior and exterior of the house, giving a room a feeling of additional space.

Hanging a mirror adjacent to a window wall reflects the view and further amplifies space.

Color can be used to trick the eye, too. Light colors reflect light, making a room feel larger. Cool hues, such as blues and greens, are considered "receding," appearing more distant than they really are and making a room feel calm and spacious. A standard approach is to paint walls white, but light-value colors like chamois, fawn, or celadon can be just as space-enhancing.

Texture works like color in influencing a room's sense of space. Using similar textures throughout an area helps unify a design, visually enlarging the space as well as creating a mood.

Place large furnishings against walls to keep from breaking up any open space. Sofas and chairs with open arms and exposed legs will allow light to spill around and under them, creating an airier effect. Because glass-topped tables don't interrupt space, they also make rooms seem larger.

Maximize precious floor space with open vertical storage: floor-to-ceiling bookcases or a tall hutch. Choose modest-size furnishings to create a sense of spaciousness. But to keep a room from feeling like a dollhouse, include a larger piece or two to visually anchor the space.

## Subdividing large spaces

Open floor plans and spacious great rooms are the norm in contemporary home design, but they can lack a cozy, intimate feeling and present certain design challenges. Various strategies can be used to tame the space, subtly carving it up without adding walls.

If you are remodeling or building an extension to your house, your options for defining areas within a gathering place are multiplied. Because uniform ceiling heights lend a homogeneous feel to a space, simply raising or lowering part of a ceiling will add interest and establish distinct activity areas. A dining area becomes more dramatic when the ceiling over the space is lowered. Remodeling also makes it possible to change floor levels between areas. A few steps down will handily divide a seating space from the kitchen and dining areas.

To avoid a "ballroom" effect in your great room, with furniture lined up against the walls, you can create inner "rooms" by dividing the larger confines into activity areas. In the seating area, start by creating a conversation grouping around a prominent focal point, such as a fireplace or other strong architectural element. The backs of the seating can form spatial boundaries. A secondary seating area might consist of two club chairs, a table, and a reading lamp near a built-in bookcase wall.

Arrange furniture compactly to hold subarea seating together. Link different areas of the seating space with common flooring, such as hardwood or carpet; delineate and anchor inner rooms with area rugs. Simply changing the direction of an area rug can redefine the imaginary perimeter of an inner room. Placing a low chest or other piece of furniture between distinct areas not only creates an air of separation without blocking a view, but also adds storage space.

Work out a plan that guides foot traffic around, rather than through, inner rooms. Allow

---

## FURNITURE DIMENSIONS

To outfit your room, play around with furniture on the floor plan you have prepared. One initially time-consuming but worthwhile way to do this is to cut out pieces of paper scaled to represent the size and shape of the furniture you will be using. Below are some standard dimensions for basic dining and living room furniture.

|  | WIDTH | DEPTH |
|---|---|---|
| SOFA | 78"–90" | 34"–38" |
| LOVE SEAT | 60"–70" | 34"–38" |
| CHAIR | 28"–36" | 28"–36" |
| ARMLESS CHAIR | 22"–28" | 22"–28" |
| COFFEE TABLE (SQUARE) | 24"–48" | 24"–48" |
| COFFEE TABLE (RECTANGLE) | 24"–48" | 16"–28" |
| COFFEE TABLE (ROUND) | 18"–32" | |
| END TABLE | 14"–24" | 14"–24" |
| SOFA TABLE/CONSOLE | 48"–72" | 15"–20" |
| DINING TABLE (SQUARE) | 36"–48" | 26"–48" |
| DINING TABLE (RECTANGLE) | 60"–84" | 34"–42" |
| DINING TABLE (ROUND) | 36"–60" | |
| DROP-LEAF TABLE | 36"–72" | 21"–63" |
| DINING CHAIR (ARMS) | 22"–24" | 16"–24" |
| DINING CHAIR (ARMLESS) | 18"–22" | 16"–24" |
| BUFFET/LOW CABINET | 48"–72" | 16"–26" |

*A gentle arch and stock columns visually divide the sitting and dining areas of this gathering room (left). Angling the granite-topped island in the kitchen (below) gained space for the owners and helped divert traffic around the food preparation area.*

30 to 36 inches of clearance between major furnishings for easy passage, 18 inches between a coffee table and sofa or between chairs.

Color is another easy way to define different areas. If you can clearly see one part of the great room from another, you'll need to relate their colors. This is a perfect situation for using color complements (hues that work well together) or varying tones of the same color. However, using a constant color for trim—baseboards, cornices, and doors—will give the gathering space a more unified look.

As well as giving people a chance to be together, a gathering space should offer them the chance to be alone, in ones and twos. A small alcove at the edge of any room, created either as an architectural feature or simply by arranging furniture, gives one or two people the opportunity to sit in comfort off by themselves. The set-apart space might have a different style to mark its distinction. In a light and airy gathering place, an alcove can become a sheltering, book-lined alternative. Or a corner of a dark room might be turned into a sunroom, filled with light and flowers.

# bringing in light

**LIGHT CAN LITERALLY TRANSFIGURE** *an area. Welcome daylight into a room by means of carefully placed windows, skylights, a window wall, or glass doors. When planning interior lighting, first consider how people will use the room. Lighting separate areas discretely can divide a room into several activity spaces—without a remodel.*

*Ringing the walls with soffits for low-voltage lighting, washing the fireplace with light, and illuminating a built-in display area transformed a once-bland family room.*

## Blurring boundaries

Consider windows to be see-through walls, a way to extend the inside to the outside. Windows connect us to the outer world and, if carefully positioned, can fill our houses with light and views. Think of a window also as an interior composition, a painting that is part of the wall.

If you want clear views of the outside from a seating area, position windows not more than 2'6" off the floor. Windows higher than that will limit the view; you won't be able to see anything below the horizon line. A window in the middle of a flat surface defines a view in a single direction; a corner window (two windows that meet at the corner of a room) presents no boundaries to the view.

Clerestory windows and frameless windows at the edge of a ceiling make spaces feel bigger because they become part of both the wall and the ceiling. The ceiling is painted with light, making it almost appear to float.

Glass patio doors are unrivaled when it comes to bringing in the outdoors. French doors and

A 20-foot-high ceiling gives this casual gathering place a spacious feeling and brings in additional daylight. Three west-facing windows (above) set into the gable augment a pair of casement windows over the kitchen sink. The high windows were kept small to avoid excess heat gain. The light look is carried throughout the inviting space (left), in furnishings as well as surface materials. Varied textures enliven the room's soothing neutral color scheme.

Hope shimmers and fades, it washes the present in a flattering light and shapes the future into something that won't give you the heebie-jeebies.

*This study's low-voltage lighting was designed to look "soft," in contrast to the hard, industrial appearance of concrete and stone. Light grazing the stone wall provides ambient fill; it's created by a string of reflector lamps hidden inside a light well.*

sliding patio doors are the traditional choices for bridging exterior and interior living spaces. Both types double as windows, offering views, light, and ventilation.

Interior doors can affect the light in a room, too. Glazed panels, bifolds, pockets, French doors, and Japanese shoji panels all let light pass from space to space. You can close off a home office or media room from the rest of a gathering space for privacy or energy efficiency, then open it up when sunny weather—or mood—dictates. Bifolds, pockets, shoji panels, and folding doors succeed when there is no space for a swinging door; accordion, or folding, doors can temporarily close off one area from another.

## Artificial light

Light is the primary tool at your disposal for changing the mood of a room, making a single area perform double duty. Use bright lighting in an eating area, and the space is illuminated for

family dining; subdue the lighting to turn this dining area into an elegant place to entertain.

Light can also be used to differentiate one part of a room from another. By lighting different areas with different intensities, you can distinguish spaces within the larger room.

Designers separate artificial lighting into five categories: ambient, task, accent, portable, and kinetic.

**AMBIENT,** or general, lighting creates a bright, pleasant level of illumination—enough, say, for watching television or navigating safely through a room. Incandescent lighting is the preferred choice because of its warm, flattering tone. Ceiling-mounted fixtures usually are used to provide diffuse illumination.

**TASK** lighting floods a specific area where a visual activity, such as reading or sewing, takes place. This is often achieved with individual glare-free fixtures directed onto work surfaces, such as under-cabinet lights. Ceiling-mounted

*The lighting plan in this family-friendly room is simple, in keeping with the home's classic Georgian style. The chandelier offers ambient light, portable lamps provide task lighting, and the fireplace adds a kinetic glow.*

lights can also be used for task lighting over kitchen islands.

**ACCENT** lighting, primarily decorative, is often used to highlight architectural and design elements, set a mood, and provide drama. Like task lighting, it consists largely of directional light. Wall-washing is a broad, evenly dispersed form of accent lighting that can add drama to an entire wall. Use it to show off an architectural feature, an art collection, or another distinctive part of your room.

**PORTABLE** lighting provides dramatic accents throughout the room. Examples include table lamps, picture lights, and uplighting for plants. This easy-to-add form of lighting is a great way to evoke mood without the expense of recessed installations.

**KINETIC** lighting is a moving force—flickering, leaping, darting—that is used to create an exciting, romantic, or hypnotic atmosphere. Firelight and candlelight are two intriguing forms.

## The right light

Dull or dark surfaces absorb light; glossier surfaces reflect it. A white ceiling can reflect as much as 90 percent of all light aimed at it, while dark flooring can absorb 90 percent of the light.

You have several options for toning down too much light: installing diffusers or lowering the wattage of bulbs, repositioning light sources, or making surfaces less reflective. Consider adding darker colors and eliminating highly polished furnishings, such as brass.

To add brightness, on the other hand, you might paint your walls a lighter color or bounce light around the room by means of refractive surfaces like mirrors and crystal chandeliers.

If you have a corner where light doesn't seem to penetrate, you can brighten it with portable lighting. Make sure lampshades are translucent, not opaque. For an evening party, you might add a collection of candles or cone-shaped uplights.

# storage
# solutions

**WILLIAM MORRIS,** *one of the founders of the Arts and Crafts Movement of furniture design, proclaimed more than a century ago: "Do not keep anything in your house that you do not know to be useful or believe to be beautiful." This is a good organizing principle for storage. In a home redesign, consider every space as a potential storage spot for useful items; plan special places to display beautiful objects.*

## Corralling the clutter

In most homes, bits and pieces of daily living are scattered throughout rooms. But getting organized can start with placing storage space where an object is used—from a drawer in a window seat to a broom closet set into a fireplace area.

The best way to create a workable, lasting solution to your organization needs is to introduce the correct storage system. Wall units range from simple, inexpensive shelving to extensive component systems that include cabinets with doors, adjustable shelves, stacks of drawers, and even desks. Whether you choose custom-built units or modular components, these flexible storage systems can help you make space work harder and smarter to control the chaos of clutter.

Many systems can be reconfigured as your needs change—shelves can be raised or lowered, drawers refitted, and cabinets moved from one location to another. Built-ins, for the most part,

*This hard-working wall contains niches, bookshelves, storage drawers, and a desk. A television slides out of a cabinet at left and pivots for easy viewing.*

are tailored precisely to specific locations in your room and are usually constructed and installed by a woodworking professional.

Individual furniture pieces designed especially for storage, free-standing or custom-fitted, are another option. Furniture has obvious advantages—it's movable, you can see exactly what you're getting, and it can be chosen to match your decor precisely. But you may not be able to find the perfect size or piece you want, and you'll need to consider the placement of storage furniture when you plan seating areas.

## Matching storage to space

Different activity areas within a great room call for different storage solutions. Where family members congregate to play games, read, do homework, and listen to music, versatile modular wall systems are especially popular. With their adjustable shelving, cabinets, drawers, and television bays, these units can organize the myriad paraphernalia that tends to clutter family living spaces. Such storage units also serve as display settings for the family's prized collectibles and art objects.

In the dining area, a wall unit featuring deep cabinets, drawers, and shelves can hold dishes, glassware, serving pieces, and even tablecloths. Combined with a countertop, such a unit also provides a place for buffet-style serving.

A phone/mail center in a nook between the kitchen and dining area or an alcove off the living area might serve as a kind of command post for the house, hiding the controls for temperature, air quality, and lighting. Here, too, could be space to put up the family calendar and bulletin board and to store phone books and address books.

*New cabinets along one wall of the dining area (above right) double the kitchen's counter space and offer a place to display some handsome collectibles. The rear wall of this family room (right) contains a built-in media center, book and display shelves, and storage cabinets.*

# GREAT GATHERING PLACES

**F**OR SHEER INSPIRATION, there's nothing like a showcase home tour to see how other people design interior spaces to match today's lifestyles. The following gallery of innovative fusion rooms is just that. The first two sections demonstrate how different activity areas can be connected for maximum efficiency and aesthetic appeal. Subsequent sections present ways of handling special situations: home offices and other private places, entertainment areas, and rooms planned to take advantage of views. The final part of your gallery tour is reserved for some particularly successful room designs with lasting appeal. **STUDY THESE PAGES** for ideas to use in your own home. Don't let room sizes or decor deter you from noticing how cleverly space has been used. Whether your own project is large or small, you'll pick up some good design ideas.

# kitchen connections

M ANY GREAT ROOMS and family rooms revolve around the kitchen, the place where everyone seems to end up eventually. It's the center of a home, the spot where we gather for morning coffee, pay our bills, make phone calls, check children's homework, and talk over the day's events. Guests naturally congregate here to chat with the cook.

Modern home design reflects the importance of this truly multipurpose room, making it the fastest-growing room in the house in terms of space. Kitchens are being designed with more room than ever before for food preparation, eating, and storage. They include space for the new appliances and amenities we desire, from built-in espresso machines to meal-planning centers.

Opening the kitchen area to the living area of your home—or redesigning the kitchen as a gathering room by adding dining and seating space— almost always means knocking out a wall or two. You may want to add an

island to divert traffic, provide extra seating and counter space, and hide messy pots and pans from view. Keep in mind that when your kitchen is on display from other parts of an open room, it will need to match the style of the rest of the space. Fortunately, kitchen manufacturers produce cabinets that resemble furniture and surfacing materials that blend with all design styles, from high-tech contemporary to comfortable country. You'll see examples of fresh approaches on these pages.

*Pillars replace walls in this light and airy great room. Rugs anchor furniture on the honey maple wood floor and help define seating and dining spaces. The circular glass coffee table mirrors the dining table and reflects the glass cabinet doors. Even the kitchen back-splash (photo at left) is made of glass tiles. Cool colors throughout contribute to a serene and spacious look.*

A spinning wheel lends country charm to this inviting family room. Built-in shelving surrounds the windows, offering ample space for books, collectibles, plants, and a television.

A well-planned lighting scheme gives the kitchen a warm glow. Under-cabinet track lights make it easy to reach for hanging utensils; hood downlights keep spices on display. The open dining area (below) lets guests enjoy the fire in the family room.

*Both the bank of kitchen cabinets and the cooktop hood echo the gleam of the family room's handsome hardwood floor. Upholstered stools front an island divider, giving some guests places to sit and chat with the chef while others sink into the casual living area's comfy furniture.*

*A low sectional couch and fold-up blinds assure that the cozy living area (above) receives unobstructed natural light and views of the patio beyond. Resting on an area rug, furniture is arranged for easy television viewing. Recessed lights in the built-in wall unit show off favorite art objects.*

*When not serving as seating for the dining table, a padded window seat makes an ideal spot for writing letters, paying bills, planning menus, phoning friends, or simply curling up with a good book. Shelves fitted neatly into the alcove keep papers and books organized.*

Light and space first attract the eye in the kitchen and dining area of this multilevel contemporary. But it's the carefully crafted design elements that make it so special—a curved kitchen island capped with concrete and stained to resemble faded leather, custom cabinetry finished like furniture, and stained concrete-block flooring with aluminum strips replacing traditional grout. High overhead, fanciful halogen fixtures direct light over cooking and dining areas.

*In the soaring living room (above), flooring changes to Douglas fir, stained to match the concrete of the kitchen level. Removable backs and arms allow sofas to be separated into chairs or made into a sectional. Along with sleek metal side chairs, they are placed for viewing the side-by-side fireplace and television (left). Wheels make it easy to roll the glass coffee table out of the way.*

*Making a bold architectural statement, this kitchen's custom-crafted, four-sided island is truly a center of attention. Layered with colors and then stained red, cabinets were washed to reveal undertones. In a light-filled bay off the kitchen, the dining area gains fine views without being visually separate from the rest of the great room.*

Tumbled marble countertops (left) complement the glazed porcelain floor tiles that extend throughout much of the house. Beyond a sweeping arch is the seating area (below), where attention focuses on a stone fireplace with handcrafted mantel. The television hides discreetly behind the doors of the corner armoire.

*Graceful arches replace walls to open up a farm-style kitchen to the sitting room and dining room. Dark wood flooring ties the entire space together, while area rugs help create distinct sitting and dining zones.*

*In the dining area, a curved raised fireplace lends a romantic touch to an evening meal, while a chandelier supplies soft light. The kitchen (below), 1900s facade notwith-standing, provides 21st-century amenities: granite-topped counters, tiled backsplashes, and the latest appliances.*

*In an alcove just off the cooking area, a computer looks right at home in the contemporary setting it shares with the dining table and a window seat. All benefit from plenty of natural light. The home office doubles as a center for planning family activities.*

*From the glass-topped dining table, your view is directed toward the seating area, where an intricately crafted entertainment unit serves as a focal point. Through the doorway beyond, bookshelves line a library that can be closed off for privacy.*

One wall of the conversation area (also shown at top on facing page) features a fireplace and artwork illuminated by wall sconces. From the sofa, guests can watch meal preparations, while others may prefer to step through the French doors onto the patio. The console table behind the sofa acts as both room divider and lamp table.

When television and general conversation pall, two comfortable chairs (left) invite people to put up their feet and indulge in a little private talk or peaceful contemplation in a Zen-inspired setting. Glass panels offer framed views of the landscape outside.

great gathering places

# modern math

FINDING SPACE for a multifunctional room without adding on to your home calls for creative thinking. But if you study how your existing rooms are currently being used, you may find that space is hiding just a wall away. Is your formal living room open only for guests, while the family crowds around a kitchen table? Removing the walls that separate the living room from the kitchen or dining area could give you a more usable, family-friendly space. Or perhaps there's a laundry room, back porch, or mud room that you can open up as a dining or seating area off the kitchen. A terrace or porch would extend living space if transformed into a sunroom with places for plants and people.

Areas not originally designed as living spaces often present attractive opportunities for expansion. As photos on the following pages show, attached garages are popular choices for converting into family rooms. An attic may offer space for a combination home office and media center. With good light-ing, climate control, and the right equipment, you can turn a base-ment into a recreation room.

As its name implies, a great room accommodates a range of activities. With careful planning, you may be able to divide an exist-ing room into separate activity areas simply by making minor changes. For example, low book-cases can be positioned as room dividers, and cushions can be fit-ted on a fireplace hearth to create a secondary seating area—without adding an inch of floor space.

*An exterior wall once rose where a handsome wood divider now stands, and the former garage has been beautifully transformed. A brick walkway between house and garage was integrated into the new decorating scheme. A custom-designed double couch (photo at left) lets people choose between television and conversation.*

*The furnishings in this comfortably welcoming gathering space were placed for maximum exposure to the fireplace, a built-in media center, and the view outdoors. The peaked ceiling and artfully bare windows are strong architectural elements; access to the backyard is through the French doors at right. On the other side of the room (below), a large archway was carved through an exterior wall to create a similarly light-filled dining room.*

When all elements of a great room are open to view, dividing the space into separate activity areas requires thoughtful planning. The long great room pictured above and at lower right is an example of how it can be done. Though the hardwood flooring was left bare in the kitchen and dining area, a rug was added to define the conversational grouping. Some of the large pieces of furniture were positioned perpendicular to the walls to break up the linear look.

A fish-filled focal point, this handsome aquarium
subdivides a great room into dining and seating areas
without blocking the view. The cabinet on which the tank
rests also provides storage space.

With a little creativity, even a small space can be transformed into an open plan. Here, arched openings in partial walls link the kitchen with an intimate seating space (right) and a dining area (below), which doubles as an extension of the conversation grouping. The padded bench in front of the fireplace adds seating yet is not a visual barrier. The deft choices of fabric color and patterns and the modest scale of the furniture serve to unify and enhance space.

*Providing space for everything from artwork and well-read*

*classics to audio and visual units, the generous bookcases are,*

*surprisingly, not attached to the wall. Decorative molding was*

*added to the movable shelves to give them a look of perma-*

*nence. The floral ottoman acts as both footstool and coffee table.*

*"Stretching" interior space visually by linking it with a patio or deck is a favorite remodeling strategy. Flanking this handsome fireplace, matching sets of windows above a pair of window seats add light and garden views.*

When both spouses enjoy cooking and entertaining, there's a definite incentive to remodel. This family annexed space on both sides of their existing kitchen and added another 10 feet at the back of the house to create a spacious gathering place. The one-of-a-kind chandelier (lower photo) was made from collected silverware; recessed lighting, on rheostats, gives balanced illumination. Carrying out the cutlery motif, spoon and fork door pulls accent painted floor-to-ceiling cabinets. Open shelving holds cookbooks, magazines, and recipe files.

Finding extra space can be as simple as looking up; at least that was the case for the family who turned their 1913 attic into a combination office (above) and media room (right). As a bonus, they discovered that the original walls and ceiling, though blackened with age, were fitted with fir; all it took was a little soap, water, and oil to restore them to their original good looks.

*Adding a media center to your exercise area might be just the motivation you need for more frequent workouts. "Sink-into-them" chairs in the room below are slipcovered with ultra-suede fabric, which can be cleaned easily.*

# public and
# private places

**I** SLANDS ARE POPULAR vacation destinations because they provide a sense of isolation, an escape from the busy world. The same type of retreat is equally important in a home. Where rooms flow into each other with few, if any, interior walls, we need private spaces that are acoustically or visually separate from the open areas.

Such a quiet retreat might be a book-lined getaway for solitary reading or conversation with one or two friends, or it might be a space equipped with desk and computer where family members can work or study. Add movie, television, or stereo equipment and you can transform this private place into a home entertainment center whenever you wish.

It's surprising how little space an "away room" requires. But if there's just no space for a completely separate private place in your layout, you can still carve out an effective retreat within a great room by arranging furniture to create a small seating area apart from the main conversational grouping. And when your only option for a home office is to incorporate it into a living area, you can use a folding screen to block visual distraction. Carpeting will help muffle noise, or a tall bookcase can be positioned to help deflect sound. Minimize the visual impact of home office equipment by blending it into a wall of cabinets, preferably with doors that can be closed to hide the clutter. These pages showcase some family hideaways.

*Life is not all work, a fact that the owner of this paneled, well-appointed "away space" realizes. Serious business may be conducted from the corner office (right), but in the sitting area (photo at left) a laptop may be no competition for enjoying a movie or football game with friends.*

When a setting calls for warmth, red reigns. Bold and
brazen, the great room above pulsates with energy and
excitement. In contrast, the more intimate seating area up the
brick stairs (right), although tied to the larger space by the
fabric of the window treatment, projects a quieter mood.

*Interior doors can help connect rooms as well as seal them off; these elegant French doors link a seating area with an adjacent retreat. The spacious library and home office invites people to leaf through a book or just enjoy a few quiet moments. Glass door panels and transom bring light into both rooms.*

*With soaring ceilings and no interior walls, open plans for contemporary houses often forgo getaway rooms; the modern showpiece pictured on these pages is a happy exception. On the upper level, owners share their large work space (above) with a media room. From the curved balcony, they have a bird's-eye view of the seating area below. The dining area, set apart from the rest of the gathering space with columns and a low wall as well as a two-step rise, is given a more compact feel by the scalloped lowered ceiling.*

*Just off the kitchen and dining area, the home office in the photo at left can be closed off for total privacy, but its wide doorway keeps the space well connected at other times. Chairs at the kitchen island (below left) add seating space for an intimate living area. Notice how the fireplace mantel extends to crown the room divider, which also holds the television.*

*Wisely, the workspace in this den is oriented so that anyone seated here receives abundant light without glare from the windows. To keep wandering eyes from the distracting view outside, a wall of photographs provides a place to focus inside.*

*The lower level of this home was transformed into a multipurpose room that accommodates adults and children, family and friends. It's a great place for a few people to get together for coffee and heart-to-heart talks, for kids to hang out with pals, or for an entire family to gather for a holiday meal. With a pull-out sofa near the dining table, the entire level can become spacious private quarters for houseguests.*

*Well-planned activity areas have furniture positioned so that several pastimes can take place at once. The couch and chairs (above) offer front-row seating for the latest show. Shelves and cabinets can store books, videos, games, and extra bedding for guests. Completely equipped and color-coordinated, the compact kitchen (left) stands ready to serve drinks, snacks, or even meals.*

*great gathering places*

# that's entertainment

**W**HETHER YOU CALL it a great room, a family room, or a media room, the space in which family and friends gather informally tends to be oriented toward entertainment and recreation.

In today's home, that one large entertaining and family area often contains a big-screen television, a VCR, and speakers. For Hollywood-style glamour, some rooms even have a movie screen and overhead projector. If a room in your home is to be used primarily to watch television, you might as well acknowledge that fact and come up with a way to accommodate this ever-bigger-and-better electronic toy in a manner that's flexible, functional, and attractive, too. Often televisions are placed as afterthoughts when, in reality, they may be the room's main feature. If space is limited, a corner wall unit for video and audio equipment can visually anchor it, gearing the area for both entertainment and conversation. While seating must face a screen for best viewing, chairs should be positioned so that family and friends also can comfortably listen to music, play games, or chat.

Games are popular at any age, so pool tables, chess sets, and card tables—and perhaps electronic games as well—are likely to be a high priority. And many families want space for their small children to play with friends (real or stuffed), create magic shows, and build castles of their own. The children-only layout on page 298 may make you wish you were a kid again.

*This ornately appointed media room, open to the kitchen and dining nook, is designed for entertaining. From the handsome bar to the damask-covered sofa, the room makes a grand setting in which to enjoy music and conversation over cocktails or to watch an event on the wide-screen television (photo at left).*

*Elegant yet relaxed, this airy space adapts equally well to family life and to entertaining. Comfortable leather sofas and a variety of woods and textures lend casual appeal. For support when the television is swiveled or being worked on, a sturdy wood bench (right) was built to fit.*

*Recessed into a wall of custom cabinets, the wide-screen television can be seen easily from each sofa, but it shares star billing with a fireplace and a cherished painting on another wall. The room's clean contemporary decor is an effective foil for treasures from around the world.*

At one end of a rustic-
style retreat (left), a
billiards table invites
a game. In the center of
the room, furniture has
been pulled away from
the walls and allowed
to "float" before the
hearth of the massive
stone fireplace, focal
point for the great
room. The dining table
at the other end of the
room (out of view)
also receives the flicker
of flames.

The epitome of an
electronic entertaining
center, this media room
boasts screen, projector,
and surround-sound
equipment. Movie-
goers here are
cushioned in comfort—
with their feet up. The
projector is suspended
unobtrusively from
the ceiling, and stereo
equipment is concealed
in a closet.

*Knocking out walls maximized gathering space and enhanced the overall flow of the light-filled conversational setting above and at right. Chairs are on casters for easy rearrangement. Changes in ceiling levels add architectural interest and intimacy.*

Tucked into a corner of the great room, a library doubles as a retreat for playing cards or board games. The brass game table has a brushed nickel finish and a vinyl top, with the look and feel of leather without the price. The seats of the rattan chairs are faux leopard skin. French doors extend this quiet corner into the outdoors on fine days.

For the height of convenience, individual trays (left) at each corner of the game table slide out to hold drinks.

*One section of a
colorful multiuse
cabinet folds down to
form a desk (right),
handy for schoolwork,
a board game, or even
a spread of snacks.
On one side, doors
swing open to reveal
a bar; on the other
side, a television
cabinet is built into
the unit (below).*

*This recreation room lives up to its name. The game table stands ready for players to take their places, and comfortable chairs*

*offer relaxed seating for readers, music lovers, and television fans. When closed, the graphically designed wall unit gives little*

*hint of what lies behind its colorful facade; only books, videos, and audio equipment share its open shelves.*

*Under a fabric-draped "big top," the circus has come
to town! Hand-painted clowns and jugglers adorn the walls
of a color-filled kids' retreat (right), while a tightrope
walker balances precariously over a wall sconce (below).
Even a theater awaits an audience. In this sunny space,
all the props are ready for the show to start.*

*An upholstered throne
stands ready for
royalty. Behind the
seat of power, the duck
has all the balls in the
air, but the hang
glider's chute appears
to have been snagged
on the "tent pole."*

great gathering places

# rooms with views

HOMES WITH enviable locations have long been built to be oriented toward their best views. But it took architecture's Modern Movement to call to our attention the idea of bringing the landscape indoors through window walls and glass doors. Whether your great room looks out on a sunny deck or a range of mountains, nothing will stretch its space more or provide greater visual satisfaction than placing the outdoors on display from within.

According to architect and design theorist Christopher Alexander, a view that is framed—or even limited—is more satisfying than an unframed panorama. Grouping windows also creates constant light changes and subtle shadow patterns inside, giving a room an elusive appeal. In multilevel homes, like some of those shown in this section, windows not only permit light to flow throughout the house but offer even more expansive views of the ever-changing landscape.

Whether it's better to dress a window or leave it bare depends on the type of window, its location, and the view it frames. If the view is the star, undressed windows may be the best choice. You'll notice that the families represented on the following pages preferred to forgo window treatments as visual barriers, feeling that their sites offered sufficient privacy and sun control. What your window will wear may depend on how your house is situated on your property and how close it is to the neighbors.

*Grand in scale and site, the great room pictured at left takes full advantage of its location, offering long-range views from dining-area windows and a more personal look at patio and pool (right) from the conversation space. Extending the pavers blurs the distinction between interior and exterior.*

*Bathed in light, this glass-walled sunroom opens up the living area and affords expansive hillside views. A contemporary interpretation of a Victorian solarium, the airy, informal space uses brick flooring, rattan furniture, container plants, and floral art to carry out a garden room decor.*

With its beautiful wood flooring, informal furnishings, and palette of country-side colors, this great room looks perfectly at ease in its vineyard setting. A combination of fixed windows and French doors offers nonstop views and access to the veranda; the overhang provides shade, eliminating the need for shutters or shades. Recessed lighting brightens the evening scene.

Only the window washer knows for sure where the glass begins and ends in this multi-level hillside home. Decor was kept deceptively spare and light in visual weight to avoid competing with the home's strong structural lines and impressive views.

*Windows often act like picture frames, offering tantalizing glimpses of the landscape without revealing its entirety. The muntins on these windows multiply the effect, enhancing the sense of enclosure in the cozy sitting area while showcasing the view.*

*The view is the focal point at one end of a stylish great room. From the kitchen island (to right of photo) to the wicker chairs at left, there are no walls, high furnishings, light fixtures, or window treatments to spoil the scenic effect. On the other side of this room (shown on page 250), seating and dining areas focus on a handsome entertainment unit and a stone fireplace wall.*

Under a dramatic
angular wood ceiling,
the seating area at right
is the center of attention
inside this ultramodern
multilevel. A Bokara
rug grounds furnishings
in front of the fireplace;
a collection of colorful
glass, displayed on
recessed shelving, adds
another focal point.
When work calls, a
shelf-lined retreat on an
upper level houses a
home office (bottom
photo) open to the
gathering space below.
Railings throughout
the house are standard
4-inch "hogwire"
fencing with a
powder coat.

From the raised dining area and the music corner (above),
walls of windows offer inspiring valley views. Glass doors
from the dining level (and the seating area, facing page) lead
out to a hillside deck. Flooring in the dining area is stained
concrete tiles with a design imprint. The exposed wood
beams (left) that support the house make an important design
statement.

*Opening up the dining, seating, and recreation areas of the rustic-style great room at right, a battery of different window shapes and sizes highlight a 180-degree coastal view. For even more expansive vistas, French doors lead onto a deck.*

*"Dramatic" and "grand" are terms that leap to mind for the scene from the windows below—and for the interior space as well. If desired, light pours into the room during the day, or blinds can be lowered to moderate its intensity. In the evening, soft recessed ceiling lighting adds intimacy.*

*All the public spaces of this home are oriented to the scenery outside. Guests who perch on stools in front of the kitchen island (left) get the same grand outlook as those seated in the living and dining areas (above).*

# lasting impressions

**W**E ALL HAVE IDEAS about what makes up the perfect space and how we would like our family to live. The list grows every time we visit a showcase house or run into another problem with our own home's layout. Is the kitchen so poorly laid out that the designated cook has to labor away in solitude? How long has it been since we have eaten dinner around a table? Where can a quiet conversation with a friend be carried on while the children are watching television? Where can we find space for a home office?

We all need gathering places for our family and friends, and as a counterpoint we need private spaces for relaxation, exercise, or homework. To see how some families have achieved a balance, take a look at the following collection of beautifully designed and decorated rooms. Decors differ dramatically, as do room sizes and styles. But all these rooms are alike in the thoughtful planning and the attention to detail that went into creating them.

Combination cooking-dining-living spaces are what today's families frequently choose to reflect their lifestyles. These are often the rooms that best display their owners' personalities. Entertainment areas and private spaces provide clues as to family interests, too. We invite you to take a peek at the rooms on the next several pages for glimpses of how some families live. Your sense of space and style may differ dramatically from these examples, but they should offer inspiration and ideas that you can use.

*When space is at a premium, it takes careful planning to arrive at the best design. Placing an entertainment armoire (right) in the corner between two windows and topping it with plants and accessories fills in what could be a "problem" area. Striped and floral fabrics lend a garden feel (photo at left).*

*Walk right in and sit down—that's the message you get from the comfortable and casual gathering place pictured below. The seating area, located off the kitchen (out of view to the left), offers a pair of roomy chairs and a spacious sectional sofa for taking it easy in front of the hearth. Only a boat model, a telescope, and a long window seat hint at the special appeal of the outside view.*

*Arches, columns, walls of glass, and a dramatic beamed ceiling—these architectural details tie together and add interest to the meal-planning, dining, and seating areas of the great room shown above and at right. The conversational grouping is arranged to ensure front-row seating for entertainment or cozying up to the fire. Audio-visual equipment hides behind the storage unit's closed doors.*

*Only columns separate the seating area (above) from the rest of this great room. Keeping the furniture light and low and the fabric muted allows the home's open design to become the focus of attention. A nook shelters a small bar. Tropical plantings lend a sylvan look to the koi pond off the entry (right).*

With its beige marble flooring, subtle level changes, open
design, and dramatic koi pond centerpiece, this home is
a popular candidate for neighborhood tours. Through the
columns at the right of the photo lies the dining area; the
breakfast room and kitchen are directly behind the pond.
Material for the faux boulders lining the pond was poured
over a chicken-wire base.

At first glance, the dining area on the facing page, with its gilded chandelier and imposing painting, might make you think you're in a European country manor house. But as you walk through the great room (above), you'll soon notice just how comfortable the elegant setting feels; though formal, the decor exudes warmth, inviting you to pull up a chair to the kitchen island divider and join the party. The diagonal placement of the rug in the conversational grouping adds depth to the room.

A fruit-gathering cherub, ornate molding, and a colorful swag (left) set the decorating theme for this Provençal-inspired kitchen. Learning how to drape and gather swags takes time; "swag holders" that secure fabric at the top of the window will help.

The spare elegance of
well-edited space
imparts a feeling of
sophisticated serenity to
this generously scaled
gathering place. Only
a natural woven mat
connects dining and
seating areas. High
fixed windows flanking
the fireplace bring in
light while preserving
streetside privacy.

From the low table and chairs, diners view the home's inner
courtyard in rectangular sections. By day, the artfully bare
window wall takes an architectural stand; by night, the
courtyard gains added appeal through the use of carefully
positioned exterior lights.

*Mahogany gives a rich look to the coffered ceiling and paneled walls of this great room's entertainment zone. Seating is directed toward the stone-clad fireplace and a bar fitted into the corner. Impressive French doors admit light and permit access to the patio and pool beyond.*

*Past the railing, through the arch, and up two steps lie the kitchen and eating areas (above). Though the stone tile flooring matches the fireplace facade (facing page), lighter colors and patterned wallpaper help set these spaces apart. In the seating area, blinds were added to an arched window (left) to control sun and prevent glare on the television screen, hidden behind cabinet doors.*

*It's the fine touches
that define a room's
character and attract
us to the space. Here,
decorative molding
and trim emphasize
windows and doors
(above); a well-crafted
stairway (right)
invites ascent.*

*Think quality when you consider the beautiful detailing in this Mission-style great room. The polished wood couch, chairs, and coffee table, drawn into an intimate grouping, echo gleaming wood floors. The chandelier over the dining table and the lights hanging above the kitchen island are Arts and Crafts–inspired. Recessed cabinets flanking the windows and a storage unit underneath are among the room's useful and decorative built-ins.*

# DESIGN ELEMENTS

Comfort, convenience, and charm — these are the goals of creating a gathering space that warmly welcomes family and friends. But where do you start? To keep things simple, we focus first on your room's envelope: the walls, ceiling, and floor. Then we let in light with windows, skylights, and doors. Armed with the basics, it's easier to progress to such fine points as layering color, planning artificial lighting, selecting hard-working furnishings, and bringing in the personal touches that express your individuality. Consider your choices from both practical and aesthetic viewpoints, using this chapter as a resource.

# Wall Finishes

BOLD, BEAUTIFUL BACKDROPS

Walls and ceiling account for most of your room's square footage, offering large, often blank canvases on which to make an artistic statement about how you live and how you perceive your space. Your wall and ceiling treatments can hide problems, enhance strong points, and pull together a design scheme better than any other element.

Assess your room's basics before making decisions on wall treatment. Start with the quality of light (both natural and artificial), the proportions of the room, and architectural features you may want to downplay or highlight. Soaring ceilings can be "lowered" by painting them a deep, warm color, low ceilings "raised" with a color much lighter than that on the walls. If a room is small and dark, light colors lend a spacious, airy quality. Or the same space can be enlivened with warm, rich colors and textures to give it a cozy feel.

## Paint

Paint is what everybody thinks of first when considering the numerous options for wall treatments. Even with paint, your choices are myriad, from a neutral palette to quiet colors or strong ones. Many paint shops and home improvement centers now offer designer-chosen palettes that allow you to mix wall, ceiling, and trim colors from room to room with confidence. The hand-sponged and marbleized paint effects that were popular in recent decades have given way to quieter decorative applications, such as combing and color washing, that add depth and texture without calling undue attention to themselves. Some designer paints add fibers that transfer denim, suede, flannel, or other feel-good textures directly onto the wall.

Paint finish affects its color and determines its durability. Flat or matte paints absorb the most light, creating an opaque color, and are usually the best choice for ceilings or living areas. Semigloss and gloss finishes reflect a lot of light and can take vigorous scrubbing, making them ideal for trim as well as food preparation areas, but they do highlight any texture or imperfections in walls.

Water-based latex paint is today's preferred choice over alkyd (oil-based) paint. It is nearly odorless, dries in hours rather than days, and cleans up with soap and water. Alkyd paint has

*A dramatic color treatment for an attractive fireplace plays up its architectural style, drawing the eye away from less interesting elements.*

excellent durability but takes longer to dry, requires a paint-thinner cleanup, and may make you choose to vacate your house until the odor dissipates.

## Wallpaper

Textured or patterned wallpaper can add warmth and dimension to a room as well as soften living spaces. Unsurpassed for hiding imperfections and creating detail in a space that lacks it, wallpaper can produce optical illusions suggesting better proportions in rooms that are too long or too boxy, or whose ceilings are too low or too high. Most papers are relatively simple to install.

Traditional styles are available in updated hues, and coverings such as linen look-alikes and grass cloth can add subtle texture while providing a muted backdrop for furnishings. Embossed wall coverings designed to look like stucco, pressed tin, or plaster fresco can impart a sense of history to a contemporary home.

Wall coverings containing or coated with some sort of vinyl will be the sturdiest and easiest to install. But alternatives abound, including silk and other natural fibers that provide a neutral backdrop. Uncoated choices such as

hand-screened papers are gorgeous but may be difficult to hang. The same is true of foils, which can brighten up a dark space, and brown craft paper, at once simple and sophisticated. You will probably want to seek professional help if you decide to use one of these.

## Architectural treatments

From the most elaborate crown molding to the simplest baseboard, millwork can lend architectural interest to almost any space. You can even use it as you would furniture arrangements, to divide a large space into smaller areas—with chair rails to define the dining area, for example. When selecting the style and scale of millwork at your lumberyard, consider your home's architecture as well as its proportions. An elaborate cornice molding would enhance a room of grand, classical proportions, yet look out of place in a smaller, low-ceilinged room.

Solid wood paneling—natural, stained, bleached, or painted—provides a warm ambience in country decorating schemes. Wainscoting is traditional, with a chair rail separating the wood paneling below it from the painted or papered wall above. Installing wood paneling is not a difficult undertaking,

since paneling boards generally have edges specially milled to overlap or interlock. Hardwood boards are most often milled from oak, maple, birch, and mahogany. Common softwoods include cedar, pine, and fir.

Moldings are back in vogue. You'll find basic profiles at lumberyards and home centers. Specialty millwork shops are likely to offer a wider selection and will often custom-match an old favorite. Prefinished pine or hardwood is fine if you want a stained look, but if you plan to paint your molding, medium-density fiberboard (MDF) is less prone to warping and takes paint better.

Also consider architectural accents such as pediments, pilasters, decorative friezes, and ceiling medallions. New pieces are stocked at home improvement centers, vintage originals at architectural salvage yards and specialty stores.

# Flooring

THE LOWDOWN ON THE GROUND LEVEL

Although it accounts for only 30 percent of the surface space, flooring is the hardest-working design element in a room. It has a significant impact not only on the overall look of the room but on your budget as well. Whatever flooring you select, don't forget to factor in the cost of installation. However, even high-end looks can be achieved within reasonable means. Ceramic tiles, concrete tiles, and even vinyl can now simulate many beautiful stone materials. Old wood floors can be refinished.

The major categories of floor coverings are resilient, including vinyl, linoleum, cork, and rubber; hard flooring, including tile, stone, and concrete; wood, in all manner of finishes and styles; and soft flooring, in the form of carpeting, matting, and area rugs. As you look at the comparison chart on the facing page, keep the following design considerations in mind.

If you will be mixing floor coverings, it's important to harmonize tone, texture, and scale, and to plan how you'll make the transition from one type of flooring to another. A wood floor can be a versatile backdrop for a large area, while an area rug placed over one section may become a dramatic focal point that pulls together the room's palette.

Whereas the dining area can sustain a floor high in aesthetic value, such as mahogany with an inlay border, the kitchen end of your open plan may call for a water-resistant covering, such as tile. Vinyl is another practical choice in the kitchen because it cleans up readily and is comfortable to stand on for long periods.

Flooring in seating areas may depend on climate, the need for noise control, and environmental sensitivities. Hot climates suggest cool flooring, such as tile pavers; carpets and rugs are better for colder climes. Tightly looped carpeting also muffles sound. But remember that carpets harbor mites and may be treated with products that aggravate allergies or chemical sensitivities. Whatever soft flooring you buy, be sure it is stain resistant.

*Laminate floor, with a photograph of wood under resin, is hard to distinguish from wood. At top, slate tiles dressed up with limestone strips and glass mosaics give an outdoor look.*

# COMPARING FLOORING

## Resilient

**Advantages.** Softer and quieter underfoot than many other surfaces, resilient floors are flexible, moisture and stain resistant, easy to install, and simple to maintain. A seemingly endless variety of colors, textures, patterns, and styles is available. A relatively new choice is plastic laminate, covering a photo of wood with melamine resin.

Sheet vinyl runs up to 12 feet wide; tiles are generally 12 inches square. Vinyl, cork,

*CORK*

rubber, and leather are all comfortable to walk on. A polyurethane finish may eliminate the need to wax a vinyl floor.

**Disadvantages.** Resilients are relatively soft, making them vulnerable to dents and tears, but often these can be repaired. Moisture can collect in poorly jointed seams if resilient flooring isn't properly installed.

**Cost.** As a category, resilient flooring is modestly priced, though you'll pay a premium for custom and imported products.

## Hard tile

**Advantages.** Durable, attractive, and natural—it's hard to beat clay and stone tile. And with today's sealers, tile is virtually impervious to spills, water, and mud. Clay tiles, from terra-cotta to porcelain, come in every color and design imaginable. Stone tiles range from white marble to black granite, with greens, browns, and grays in between. Economical concrete tiles come in many colors and textures, some mimicking marble and limestone.

*CONCRETE TILE*

Floor tiles run the gamut of sizes; 8- and 12-inch squares are most common.

**Disadvantages.** Tile can be cold, noisy, and, if glazed, slippery underfoot; anything that falls on it will take a beating. Porous tile will stain and harbor bacteria if not properly sealed. Grout spaces can be tough to keep clean, though mildew-resistant or epoxy grout definitely helps. Most hard flooring is heavy, so the subfloor must be strong enough to support it.

**Cost.** Prices range from modest to expensive, depending on the material and finish.

## Wood

**Advantages.** A classic hardwood ages beautifully, feels good underfoot, is relatively easy to care for, and can be refinished when needed rather than having to be replaced. Red and white oak are most commonly used, with maple, birch, and other species also available. Softwoods such as fir and pine provide a rustic look but are more likely to dent and scratch. Environmentally sustainable timber like bamboo is now available as an alternative for eco-conscious consumers. Surface treatments—from bleaching to stain-

*WOOD STENCIL*

ing to painting—can protect wood floors and increase design options.

**Disadvantages.** Moisture damage and inadequate floor substructure are two bugaboos. Maintenance is another issue; while some surfaces can be mopped or waxed, some cannot. Bleaching and some staining processes may wear unevenly, a difficult problem to correct.

**Cost.** Depending on wood species, grade, and finish, cost is moderate to high; wood free of knots and of consistent color and grain will be more expensive.

## Soft coverings

**Advantages.** Carpets, matting, and area rugs can disguise damaged flooring, provide warmth and softness underfoot, reduce noise, conserve energy, function as a focal point, and define a room's subareas. Carpeting is available in an array of materials—synthetic fibers (nylon, acrylic, Olefin, rayon), natural fibers (wool, cotton), or a blend. Wool is the most durable, care-free nylon the most popu-

*SEA GRASS MATTING*

lar. Tightly woven commercial products offer durability and trim appearance.

**Disadvantages.** Generally, the more elaborate the material and weave, the greater the potential for problems from moisture absorption, staining, and mildew. Area rugs need nonslip pads beneath them to extend their life and protect the floor. Matting, while economical, is not as soft underfoot and may be difficult to clean.

**Cost.** Price varies considerably, with wool being the most expensive.

# Windows

## SHEDDING LIGHT ON NEW DESIGNS

**W**hether you'd like to build a sunroom, add on an old-fashioned bay, or light up a dark corner, you're in luck. Manufacturers, home improvement centers, and window stores showcase literally thousands of window styles, including arched casements and fixed windows in semicircles, ovals, trapezoids, and other shapes, all with a dizzying assortment of framing and glazing options. If the window you want isn't standard, many manufacturers will make one to your specifications.

### Window options

If you're switching to a different window style or size, check local building codes before buying; codes specify ventilation requirements and often insist on enough window space for access by firefighters. Also, energy codes govern the allowable ratio of glass to floor area.

Operable windows include double-hung, casement, sliding, and awning types. Which you choose depends partly on your home's style and partly on your ventilation needs. Frames come in wood, clad wood (encased in aluminum or vinyl), aluminum, vinyl, steel, or fiberglass. Generally, aluminum windows are the least expensive, wood and clad wood the most costly. Vinyl- or aluminum-clad wood windows and all-vinyl windows require little maintenance.

Many of the greatest strides in window technology are taking place in glazing. Ordinary flat glass can be strengthened, coated, and tinted to block solar heat yet offer pleasant light inside and a clear view outside. Insulating glass is made of two or more panes of glass sealed together with space between the panes to trap air. Low-emissivity (low-e) glass adds a transparent metallic coating that deflects heat—outward in warm weather, inward in cold weather—and blocks the sun's ultraviolet rays. Low-e glass is nearly as clear as untreated glass. Some manufacturers use argon gas between the panes of insulating glass to increase energy efficiency even more.

*Thanks to insulating glass, wintry weather is kept at bay beyond the graceful, arched windows of this cozy sunroom. At top, blackout blinds hidden behind the door valances and the cornice of the arched window above offer the possibility of total darkness.*

## WINDOW WORDS

Strange, intimidating words seem to orbit the subject of windows. Here's a crash course in standard window jargon, enough to help you brave a showroom or building center.

**Apron.** An applied interior trim piece that runs beneath the unit, below the sill.

**Casement.** A window with a frame that hinges on the side, like a door.

**Casing.** Wooden window trim, especially interior, added by owner or contractor. Head casing runs at the top; side casings flank the unit.

**Cladding.** A protective sheath of aluminum or vinyl covering a window's exterior wood surfaces.

**Flashing.** Thin sheets, usually metal, that protect the wall or roof from leaks near the edges of windows or skylights.

**Glazing.** The window pane itself—glass, acrylic plastic, or other clear or translucent material. It may be one, two, or even three layers thick.

**Grille.** A decorative, removable grating that makes an expanse of glass look as though it is made up of many smaller panes.

**Jamb.** The frame that surrounds the sash or glazing. An extension jamb thickens a window to match a thick wall.

**Lights.** Separately framed panes of glass in a multipane window; each light is held by muntins.

**Low emissivity (low-e).** Denoting a high-tech surface coating treatment that sharply improves the thermal performance of glass, especially in double-glazed windows, at little added cost.

**Mullion.** A vertical dividing piece; whereas muntins separate small panes of glass, mullions separate larger expanses of glass or whole windows.

**Muntin.** A slender strip of wood or metal framing a pane of glass in a multipane window.

**R-value.** Measure of a material's ability to insulate; the higher the number, the lower your heating or cooling bills should be.

**Sash.** A window frame surrounding glass. It may be fixed or operable.

**Sill.** An interior or exterior shelf below a window unit. An interior sill may be called a stool.

**U-value.** Measure of the energy efficiency of all the materials in the window; the lower the U-value, the less the energy waste.

---

If you live in a cold climate, consider another advancement, warm-edge windows. Instead of an aluminum spacer between panes of insulating glass, these windows have a less conductive spacer that doesn't transfer heat as readily. The result is less buildup of condensation around the edge of the window.

### Overhead styles

Skylights can bring light deep into a room and create a sense of drama where there was merely a blank ceiling before. Early versions gained a nagging reputation for leaks, condensation, or heat loss, but if you buy a quality skylight today and have it properly installed, you should find these concerns unfounded.

Fixed skylights vary from square to circular; they may be flat, domed, or pyramidal in profile. Most manufacturers offer several ventilating models.

If there's space between the ceiling and roof, you'll need a light shaft to direct light to the room below. It may be straight, angled, or splayed (wider at the bottom).

Think of roof windows as a cross between windows and skylights. Typically installed on sloping walls, they have sashes that rotate on pivots on two sides, which permits easy cleaning.

### Window dressing

If you opt for an architecturally elegant window, a decorative bay or bow, or a picture window framing a magnificent view, you may choose to leave it bare. Otherwise, a variety of coverings can dress up openings that are not architecturally noteworthy or where privacy and light control are paramount concerns. You'll find blinds, shades, and shutters in many colors and finishes.

*These translucent shades provide a neutral background for the room's decor while softening the light coming in from outside. The view through to the terrace visually extends the room's dimensions.*

# Doors

WINDOWS TO WALK THROUGH

One favorite remodeling strategy is to "stretch" interior space by bridging it to the outdoors with a sunny patio or deck. Hinged French doors or sliding doors help link living space and garden while doubling as view walls. Glazed interior doors are also light catchers. Open or closed, they let sunlight pass from room to room; when shut, they seal off noise and drafts.

## Patio doors

The typical French door is hinged wood with a large tempered-glass panel (sometimes overlaid with a decorative grille) or smaller glass panes separated by muntins. French doors usually come in pairs, with an inactive door held stationary by slide bolts at the top and bottom and an active door closing and locking against it.

Sliding doors take up less room than French doors. They consist of two-door panels of tempered glass in wood, vinyl, or aluminum frames. A sliding door may be purchased with one large glass panel (with or without grille) or multiple panels with muntins.

Like windows, patio doors come with a variety of glazing options. Because of the expanse of glass, it's critical to choose wisely. Low-e glazing (see page 331) can prevent heat absorption, trap existing heat, and prevent fabrics from fading. Double glazing not only adds energy efficiency but also allows shades or blinds to be installed between the

glass panes. Patio door glazing must be tempered or laminated.

Window showrooms and home centers usually stock wood, clad wood, and vinyl doors as well as traditional aluminum sliding doors. Clad wood is a popular choice, combining the traditional wood feel and look inside with a tough, maintenance-free exterior. Vinyl doors are tight, smooth, and nearly maintenance free and won't swell and contract with changing weather as wood can. Today's aluminum sliding doors, outfitted with energy-efficient glazing, effective weather-stripping,

and thermal breaks, have been greatly improved over earlier models.

Patio doors are available in a variety of widths; 80 inches is the standard height, 6 feet the standard width. When sizing up your choices, you'll need to determine door swing or slide direction (both specified when you are facing the unit from outside), plus wall thickness. Designers and architects love French doors to open outward, though installers feel these models are tougher to weatherproof.

To give patio doors added emphasis, think about ganging transoms above

them or installing matching sidelights or tall casement windows alongside them.

If you live in a mild climate, there's another option: tall, movable door panels that slide on tracks from the ceiling. On sunny days, these panels can open a living space or sunroom to the elements.

## Interior doors

Adding glass panels to interior doors keeps them from becoming impenetrable barriers. Glazed interior doors can be found at home centers and door specialty suppliers. You can buy most of them as separates or as kits—with or without the hardware.

For personal space such as an office area, consider fitting doors with privacy locks that have a locking button on the inside but can be easily opened with a key, screwdriver, or paper clip in an emergency.

Other options for dividing interior spaces of a multipurpose room are bifold and pocket doors and track-mounted screens that can be closed for solitude, opened for entertaining—without loss of floor space.

*Similar to French doors, two sets of multifold glass-paned doors (facing page) open the great room to a jasmine-wreathed patio. At right, a pocket door and track-mounted sliding screens offer uncluttered solutions to door-clearance problems. Though the pocket door (top) is rectangular, the curved door rail creates the illusion that it is arched. Traditional shoji screens (bottom) function as both interior doors and movable wall sections. For television-viewing privacy, they can just be pulled shut.*

# Editing with Color

### A CHOICE OF PERSONAL PALETTE

As Martha Stewart says, "A house is not a home until it is full of color—it's the inspiration for decorating." Certainly color does more to set the mood and style of a room than any other design element. To help you develop the skill and confidence to create a color scheme from scratch, we unravel color vocabulary and interpret a color ring.

## Color talk

Hue is just another name for color. Turquoise and fuchsia are hues; so are softer colors like lilac and sage. Both terms are used in art and design. Three characteristics provide the key to combining colors successfully.

VALUE means the lightness or darkness of a color. Robin's egg blue is a light value of blue, washed denim a medium value, and navy a dark value.

TEMPERATURE refers to a color's warmth or coolness. Take a look at the color ring on the facing page. If you draw an imaginary line across it from yellow-green to red-violet, the colors to the left—yellows, oranges, and reds— are warm. These colors tend to make a room feel cozy. Cooler hues—those to the right of your imaginary line—can make a room feel calm and spacious.

INTENSITY describes a color's brightness. The colors on the color ring are fully intense, or "saturated." Low-intensity colors, on the other hand, are more muted. Lime, for example, is an intense yellow-green, willow a less intense version of the same hue.

Designers consider intensity to be color's great unifier. That is, you can combine any colors if they are similar in intensity; they just seem to belong together. If you take a look at color palette cards from paint manufacturers, you'll see that disparate colors with the same intensity are naturally harmonious. For example, bright red and soft sage might clash, but a less intense brick color would be compatible with the sage.

## Color and space

Using color to define or alter space is really about creating illusions. The rule of thumb is that light and cool colors visually expand space, whereas dark and warm colors make it seem smaller. Similarly, low-intensity colors are thought to make a room seem more spacious, intense ones to contract it.

In reality, these optical effects are modified by many factors, such as the

*Bright fabrics and table mats and vibrant wall art add rich layers of color, texture, and pattern to a charming great room.*

*A common color, lemon yellow, is the tie that binds a delightful mix of florals, plaids, and solids in this sunny bay.*

quantity and quality of light a room receives. Painting walls a light color will not transform a naturally dark room into an open, airy space. A rich color will not necessarily add intimacy to a large room. Sometimes it's best to go with what you have rather than try to work against it.

But do consider putting color to use when you want to change the apparent proportions of a room. Painting the end wall of a long, narrow room a warmer, darker color than the others can create the illusion of a better-proportioned room. In a square room, painting one wall a more intense color can diminish a boxy look.

Color can also affect our sense of adjoining space. Carrying the same paint color and flooring throughout makes a smooth visual transition, opening up the space. If you prefer distinctly separate areas, on the other hand, use different colors or intensities of color.

# USING A COLOR RING

**M**ost of us don't think of consulting a color ring when we choose colors for our homes. The colors shown on the ring appeal to a relatively narrow audience, while the sophisticated nuances of color found in home furnishings—celadon, aubergine, cinnabar—never appear. Yet the pure hues on the color ring are the source of all colors used in decorating.

Most decorator colors also contain some black, white, or gray. But spice, pumpkin, and peach, for example, come from pure orange on the color ring; olive is just a dark yellow-green; and iris is really a light blue-violet.

Once you realize that all hues have a place on the color ring, you can make it work well for planning your decorating scheme.

**Primary colors**—red, blue, and yellow—are so named because they cannot be created from other colors. Instead, they make up all other colors, in different combinations and proportions. Intense primaries in large quantities can be harsh; lower-intensity versions of these colors—such as cranberry, navy, and gold—are easier to live with.

**Secondary colors** result from mixing two primaries. Red mixed with yellow makes orange, blue mixed with yellow makes green, and blue mixed with red makes violet.

**Intermediate colors** are created when a primary color is combined with an adjacent secondary color. For example, red (primary) and violet (secondary) combine to make red-violet. Starting with yellow and moving clockwise around the color ring, the intermediate colors are yellow-green, blue-green, blue-violet, red-violet, red-orange, and yellow-orange. More complex than primary or secondary colors, intermediates are among the most versatile of decorating hues.

The relationship of colors on the ring indicates their affinities and contrasts. Adjacent colors (blue, blue-violet, and violet, for example) are called *analogous*. These three share a common color—in this case, blue. Opposing colors, such as blue and orange, are *complementary* colors, meaning that they balance one another in visual temperature. Colors that are approximately opposite are also well balanced; they're known as *near complements*. Lavender blue (a version of blue-violet) is the near complement of yellow.

# Lighting

A good lighting design creates the atmosphere you want for your multipurpose room. The most successful designs accomplish this task in an energy-efficient fashion, with careful consideration given to selecting each type of fixture and bulb.

## Fixtures

Recessed ceiling lights (ideally placed about 4 to 6 feet apart) are the most popular choice for today's general lighting needs. You can also use the traditional central ceiling fixture or indirect light sources such as uplights, wall fixtures, table lamps, or fluorescent-tube lighting concealed in a cove near the ceiling.

Task lighting to illuminate specific activity areas can come from built-in fixtures (such as an under-cabinet light illuminating a countertop), from track fixtures that offer pinpoint lighting, or from portable, free-standing fixtures that direct light where needed. Low-voltage cable lights combine the flexibility of standard track fixtures with a dash of high-tech style.

Accent lighting is often concealed behind a valance or soffit (strip lighting, rope lighting, or small, plug-in lights) or designed to blend into the background (adjustable track lighting or recessed mono-spotlights). About five times brighter than the general lighting in an area, accent lighting should be positioned at an angle that minimizes glare on the featured object.

Decorative lighting draws attention to itself. Plan fixtures like chandeliers, table lamps, wall sconces, or hanging pendants as part of the overall lighting scheme, as they can also provide ambient or even task lighting.

Because more than one type of activity takes place in a great room, a range of light sources is needed. Ideally, each should have a separate control (or a dimmer on a master control) so that a variety of lighting levels can be selected, from soft glow to radiant brightness.

## Bulbs

As the chart on the facing page illustrates, there are three types of light bulbs: incandescent, fluorescent, and quartz halogen.

INCANDESCENT bulbs are the most familiar in households; they come in dozens of shapes and sizes and provide a flattering, natural-looking light. Low-voltage incandescent lighting is especially useful for accent lighting. Operating on 12 or 24 volts, these lights require transformers (sometimes built into the fixtures) to step down the voltage from 120-volt household circuits. Low-voltage fixtures are relatively expensive to buy but can be energy- and cost-efficient in the long run.

FLUORESCENT tubes are unrivaled for energy efficiency. They use only one-fifth to one-third the electricity of a standard incandescent bulb and last

*A successful design for a gathering place, like the serene room shown above, incorporates a lighting plan that features energy- and cost-efficient fixtures and bulbs.*

*Little high-tech fixtures specially designed for halogen bulbs balance artistic form with bright light output.*

10 to 20 times longer. Even though fluorescents cost more initially, they're the least expensive lights to operate and the most earth-friendly choices available. In some places, general lighting for new kitchens must be fluorescent.

While older fluorescents offered poor color rendition, today's versions are available in a range of color-corrected tubes. A compact fluorescent tube can be substituted for an incandescent bulb in many traditional fixtures and also fits specially designed built-ins and free-standing torchères. Overhead fluorescent fixtures come in a wide range of decor-friendly styles and are lauded for their soft, shadowless general lighting. **HALOGEN** bulbs are incandescents' high-tech, energy-efficient cousins, producing a whiter, brighter light. Halogen bulbs are much smaller, making them great candidates for task and accent lighting and for the tiny, sleek, artistic fixtures being designed today. The popular MR-16 bulb creates the tightest beam; for a longer reach and wider coverage, choose a PAR bulb. These hot-burning bulbs can be used safely only in fixtures designed specifically for them; shop for UL-approved fixtures.

# COMPARING LIGHT BULBS AND TUBES

## INCANDESCENT

**A-bulb**
**Description.** Familiar pear shape; frosted or clear.
**Uses.** Everyday household use.

**T—Tubular**
**Description.** Tube-shaped, from 5" long. Frosted or clear.
**Uses.** Cabinets, decorative fixtures.

**R—Reflector**
**Description.** White or silvered coating directs light out end of funnel-shaped bulb.
**Uses.** Directional fixtures; focuses light where needed.

**PAR—Parabolic aluminized reflector**
**Description.** Similar to auto headlamps; special shape and coating project light and control beam.
**Uses.** Recessed downlights and track fixtures.

**Silvered bowl**
**Description.** A-bulb, with silvered cap to cut glare and produce indirect light.
**Uses.** Track fixtures and pendants.

**Low-voltage strip**
**Description.** Like Christmas tree lights; in strips or tracks, or encased in flexible, waterproof plastic.
**Uses.** Task lighting and decoration.

## FLUORESCENT

**Tube**
**Description.** Tube-shaped, 5" to 96" long. Needs special fixture and ballast.
**Uses.** Shadowless work light; also indirect lighting.

**PL—Compact tube**
**Description.** U-shaped with base; 5¼" to 7½" long.
**Uses.** In recessed downlights; some PL tubes include ballasts to replace A-bulbs.

**Compact bulb**
**Description.** Many shapes and sizes, replacing incandescent bulbs without needing special sockets.
**Uses.** Everyday household use in traditional fixtures.

## QUARTZ HALOGEN

**High intensity**
**Description.** Small, clear bulb with consistently high light output; used in halogen fixtures only.
**Uses.** Specialized task lamps, torchères, and pendants.

**Low-voltage MR-16 (mini-reflector)**
**Description.** Tiny (2"-diameter) projector bulb; gives small circle of light from a distance.
**Uses.** Low-voltage track fixtures, mono-spots, and recessed downlights.

**Low-voltage PAR**
**Description.** Similar to auto headlight; tiny filament, shape, and coating give precise direction.
**Uses.** To project a small spot of light a long distance.

# Storage

SHELF-CONSCIOUS CONTROLS TO END CONFUSION

A place for everything and everything in its place—it's an admirable adage that's a bit easier to remember than follow. But a variety of storage systems in a range of styles can help you corral clutter and display prized possessions. You can choose anything from simple shelves to storage walls tailored exactly to fit your needs.

Though expensive, built-ins allow you to customize your storage while maximizing available space. For instance, when you design a custom wall unit you can build all the way up to the ceiling. Painted the color of your walls and finished with matching trim, wall units blend in and take up mini-mal visual space. If you prefer something less permanent, shop for modular units that can be assembled in different ways to accommodate varied storage needs and spaces.

## Book storage

Books are useless unless they are easily accessible. A successful design brings as many volumes as is practical into the mainstream of daily life. If you have books languishing in boxes in a basement, attic, or closet, you may want to convert part of a multipurpose room into a library. If space is at a premium, spread books throughout the area in a number of small collections—cookbooks in or near the kitchen and classics and current best-sellers in the seating area, for example.

One way to incorporate books as well as photos and other display items is with a built-in wall unit that has drawers and cupboards up to counter height for closed storage, then shallower, open shelves up to the ceiling. A sliding ladder affording access to top shelves lends an authentic library look.

*Storage units can be both pretty and practical. This double-duty island separates the kitchen and dining areas from the great room's seating space while offering a convenient spot to store cookbooks and display both cooking utensils and decorative pottery.*

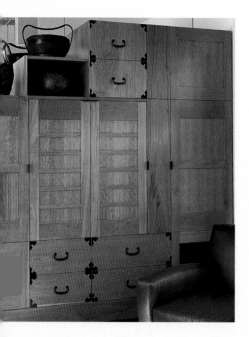

## Computer storage

As technology continues to introduce new tools, we must think creatively about spaces in which to house them. A computer needs a permanent home; it may be fairly new in our lives, but it is most definitely—in one form or another—here to stay.

When you're creating computer storage, remember to include space for printers, modems, external drives, manuals, disk files, and software boxes. Dedicating a separate space within your great room as a home office allows you to incorporate computer paraphernalia into built-in or modular units with drawers for files, shelves for books and manuals, and cabinets for office supplies. But if no separate space exists, even adding a telephone jack near a handy table, desk, or countertop makes it easy for a laptop user to plug into the Internet.

## Media storage

Increasingly complex entertainment systems—including televisions, VCRs,

*An Asian-inspired, multilevel modular system provides display space plus cabinets and drawers to keep miscellany tucked away.*

stereo equipment, CDs, DVDs, videotapes, movie screens, projectors, and remotes—require substantial, well-planned storage. If a television or monitor is to be concealed in a cabinet or enclosure, make sure the enclosure is well ventilated; heat buildup eventually kills transistors and printed circuits.

Remote-controlled, wide-screen, flat-panel televisions (some as thin as 2 inches) can hang on walls, under kitchen cabinets, or virtually anywhere. But any television can be removed from the traffic pattern if you place it near the ceiling, either on a shelf or suspended from a special bracket (available where sets are sold).

Requirements for a large-screen projection television depend on which type you have. The projecting equipment for a front-projection television

needs to be positioned directly in front of the screen, near the base or near the ceiling. The gear required for rear-projection models is concealed in the cabinet containing the screen.

Movie screens are typically installed from the ceiling to roll down as needed. Projectors can be hidden in a cabinet or installed on a shelf across the room.

Stereo components can be stacked, in or out of sight, in a custom audio tower, on a stereo rack, or in a piece of furniture adapted for the task, such as a desk or bookshelf. If you tackle the furniture conversion yourself, arrange components and peripherals according to their serial connection, then drill holes as necessary to lead cables and wires out the back to a heavy-duty outlet strip that's equipped with a surge protector. Use the ganglia model to organize wires and cables: play out just enough wire or cable to reach the required distance to a connection and then wrap the rest in on itself with a twist-tie or rubber band.

*Freestanding shelf supports made of copper pipe create a vivid contemporary display wall with a whimsical space for the television set right in the middle.*

# Double-duty Furnishings

A MARRIAGE OF FORM AND FUNCTION

Sofas, chairs, tables, and storage cabinets can help organize activity areas and traffic patterns within a gathering place merely by their placement. Some of this versatile furniture, built-in or freestanding, serves several purposes. For example, a window seat tucked into an alcove off the kitchen lets people chat with the chef or curl up with a cookbook. Pullout drawers underneath the seat can store books, games, or even table linens.

## Multifunctional furnishings

In an open-plan great room, a kitchen island performs many roles: work surface, casual dining spot, storage unit, and display area. Guests can convene around it without disturbing work in the kitchen. A properly designed island also effectively separates the kitchen from other areas.

Another hard-working paragon of versatility is a dining table. It's the gathering spot for eating, conversation, playing games, and doing homework. Depending on how it is positioned, the dining table can separate kitchen and eating areas from the seating area of a great room.

A sideboard's traditional use is for extra storage and display space in a dining room or kitchen; some styles even include a buffet surface. Depending on its height, it might also be tucked behind a sofa.

Occasional tables, such as long, narrow consoles, often are placed behind a sofa to hold a table lamp, books and magazines, drinks, or objets d'art. When the sofa cannot face the room's entrance, this arrangement makes an effective visual divider that appears more welcoming than the back of the sofa. A library table placed parallel to and out from a wall can subdivide a room as well as doing double duty as a console table and desk, with lamps for both ambient and task lighting. Low bookcases do double duty as space dividers, with a combination of open and closed shelves to provide display room on each side. Glass doors will keep books on open shelves free from dust and valuables safe from small hands.

Coffee tables are usually placed in front of sofas to provide a convenient space to rest books and magazines, drinks and snacks—and even feet. If you wouldn't dream of putting your feet up on a table, you might try an ottoman. This multipurpose piece also can be used for extra seating or, with a large tray on top, be transformed into a coffee table. Some ottomans open up to provide storage space for blankets, games, and toys, and some even convert into an extra bed for guests.

Similar in function and form, coffee tables and ottomans come in many shapes, from long and narrow to square

*To make a seating area in a multipurpose room, pull furniture away from the walls and "float" it around a focal point, such as this fireplace. The oversize ottoman takes the place of a coffee table.*

or round. If an ottoman is to be used primarily as a coffee table, it should be an inch or two higher than the seating. You can more easily enjoy its versatility by adding casters to the legs.

Armoires, having migrated from the bedroom, are now employed as handsome, useful storage for family rooms and other gathering places. These popular options can hold everything from books to video and audio equipment, providing maximum storage space while taking up minimal floor space. Some furniture companies manufacture an office-in-an-armoire suitable for a multifunctional room; you can conceal the contents simply by closing the doors.

## Floating furnishings

Lining the walls of a seating area with furnishings is a conventional decorating approach. But this arrangement tends to

put an uncomfortable distance between people when they're seated and makes it difficult to divide an open plan into activity areas. "Floating" furnishings in the room (pulling them away from the walls) makes for a more intimate, convivial grouping; it also buys valuable space for bookcases and traffic.

The typical floating arrangement consists of a sofa and chairs positioned as a focal point to create an inner room. Furnishings that float need not be parallel to the walls. A sofa placed on the diagonal, across a corner, opens up a room. An area rug that's also on the diagonal strengthens and anchors the arrangement, but you can float seating diagonally even if the rug is parallel to the walls. Adding casters to chairs offers flexible seating possibilities, making it easy to change from one configuration to another.

*Subtly blending home office elements into a family room makes the area perform dual duty. The computer and printer occupy space that once functioned as a wet bar (top left). Discreetly positioned under the skirts of the country French accent table (top right) is a two-drawer filing cabinet.*

# Personal Expressions

FINAL TOUCHES FOR INTEREST AND IDENTITY

A glance at the hub of your home, that informal place where your family comes together, shows not only how you live, but also who you are. Your family's identity and interests are revealed here more than in any other room in the house. The heirlooms, collectibles, paintings, favorite books, and other objects gathered in this comfortable space are meant not to impress but to express the owners' personalities.

## Display guidelines

A casual approach usually reigns when it comes to displaying objects that the family truly enjoys. Wherever the eye falls when you enter a room or look from one room to another, on a table behind a sofa, on top of an armoire—these are all natural placements. Or accessories can be positioned where you want guests to look—by displaying a sculpture on a console table in the line of vision to a window wall, for example.

Designers have a few more formal guidelines, such as the "odd number rule," which recommends grouping an uneven number of pieces together; three to five is typical. Or try their formula "shiny, matte, tall, and fat." This means that, when combining accessories, you might include items that fit all these categories, such as tall shiny candlesticks, a favorite round vase, and grandmother's matte-finish plate.

## Collections

What you choose to collect in life, whether it's cartoon lunch boxes, model cars, or antique teddy bears, reveals much about you—your passions, your experiences, even your sense of humor.

*Anyone who loves literature will admire this Mission-style gathering place. Glass cabinet doors allow easy examination of book titles; a well-positioned table offers ample space for a snack or a story.*

Because collections have such a personal significance, it's important to arrange them in ways that enhance their beauty or meaning.

The most successful arrangements look as though they were effortlessly composed. For maximum impact, consider clustering items. If they vary in size, layer them by placing shorter, smaller objects in front and taller, larger objects in back for a sense of depth. Show off small objects against a wall, on a shelf or tabletop, or on a windowsill. Large objects such as urns or wooden rocking horses can go on the floor, flanking a fireplace or grouped in a corner.

To achieve harmony within a grouping, choose pieces of different shapes and sizes but stick to a common color (verdigris pottery, for example) or material (such as pewter pieces).

Draw attention to three-dimensional works of art, such as a collection of bowls, by silhouetting them against a plain background. If bowls are decorated inside, display them down low, perhaps on a coffee table.

Effective display always involves experimentation. Fortunately, collectibles are easy to rearrange, unlike major furnishings. To start afresh, remove the collection and study your room. Audition your favorite piece in different locations, then add others one by one. You'll quickly appreciate that objects can be used effectively in several spots.

*You reveal who you are by the collections you display. Objets d'art (top left) are colorful indicators of the owner's interests. Chinese porcelains and orchids (top right) complement a library and music room. Seashells, books, glass, and pewter (right center) adorn bar shelves. False-front volumes (bottom right) hide a media room's videotapes.*

# Sunset
BOOKS

# *ideas for great*
# TILE

By the Editors of
Sunset Books

Sunset Books Inc. ■ Menlo Park, California

# contents

# miles and miles of tiles

**M**ADE FROM earth, water, fire—and, to stretch a point, some air, too—no building material is more elemental than ceramic tile. The earliest versions were simply hand-formed slabs of clay left to bake in the sun. Then, someone must have noticed that clay—perhaps some used to line a primitive oven—was tougher and more water-resistant if baked, or fired, at higher temperatures. And adding wet pigment to the surface of the clay before firing opened up an immense world of ornamental possibilities.

The history of decorative tile goes back at least 6,000 years, to the Egyptians, who used glazed bricks to adorn their houses and temples. Aspects of today's tile designs began with the emergence of metallic glazes in the Islamic world during the eighth and ninth centuries, and develop through Mesopotamia and Persia, Byzantium, and on to the encaustic tiles used in English cathedrals in the 1200s. The trail leads to Moorish architectural and garden ornament in Spain, and to Italy, where in the 16th century the tradition of painted majolica tiles was born. In the 18th century, the Dutch city of Delft innovated the production—much exported—of quaint blue-and-white-glazed earthenware, still popular today. Tile experimentation doubled back to England during the Victorian period, with the development of nature-inspired transfer patterns.

The early 20th century produced an American tile zenith, with a cornucopia of Arts and Crafts, Art Deco, Hispanic, and other vibrant design statements. Sadly, during the Depression most of these tile makers folded up shop—but, as we'll see, not for good.

What a long way to today's renaissance, abounding in new decorative wall and floor tiles, borders, relief trim, and hand-painted pieces. The proliferation of art tiles—both new designs and period reproductions—is especially inspiring. Some artisans have dedicated themselves to the styles and glazes of the early 1900s heyday; other firms, both large and small, offer fresh, original creations. Imported tiles from Europe and South America are plentiful. Mosaics are making a definite comeback, both custom art pieces and factory-mounted versions. Classics from the past are inspiring a growing interest in tiles as collectibles.

At the same time, new cutting techniques and sealers have made natural stone tiles affordable as well as elegant. The tile market is also welcoming newcomers in glass and concrete. With all these options, you can use tile to decorate any house or garden area in practically any style you can imagine.

The book before you takes a three-phase tour of today's tile choices. We begin with planning, surveying those places where tile can flourish, and examining basic design principles, including consideration of style, color, pattern, and size. Next, we present an extensive, room-by-room gallery of up-to-the-minute tile ideas illustrated in brilliant color photos. We finish with a glossary of representative tile types and terms, giving you a leg up when you visit the showroom or home center. Read straight through the book for a complete survey, or detour as your fancy dictates.

If you're ready to join our tour, simply turn the page.

# A PLANNING PRIMER

Given the vast range of beautiful tiles available today, it's safe to say that you'll have no problem finding one that pleases your eye. But when visiting showrooms, it's also important to think about use-appropriateness, overall style, and, of course, your budget. THIS CHAPTER is your design workbook. We begin by surveying the many options, review style and design principles, and finish up with some shopping tips. It's both fun and free to brainstorm, and that's an integral part of the planning process. Then consider the details like color, pattern, and scale, juggling them with weightier concerns like maintenance and cost. Thinking of tiling it yourself? For an overview of materials and techniques, see page 371. If you need additional help with planning or installation, we point you toward the professionals who can lend a hand. FOR FURTHER inspiration, you'll find plenty of colorful photos of successful installations in "Great Tile Ideas," beginning on page 373. And for a closer look at tile types, see "A Shopper's Guide" on pages 433–453.

# exploring your options

**TILE LEADS** *a double life: on the one hand, it's an amazingly versatile design tool; on the other, it provides hard-working surfaces that give watertight protection where needed. In planning, you explore both of these aspects, then bring them together. Have fun with the colorful, creative design possibilities, but choose the tile type that's most practical for your purpose.*

## Where does tile go?

Once upon a time, the use of ceramic tile in the typical American home was reserved for bathrooms and, occasionally, formal entry halls. Now, however, tile has spread into kitchens, living spaces, and outdoor areas, too. No wonder its surge in popularity. Aside from its visual appeal, it is durable, colorfast, easy to maintain, and non-allergenic. And recent diamond-saw technology has made stone tiles nearly as available and affordable as ceramic.

**FLOORS.** Tile is a natural for floors, as long as it's slip resistant. In entryways, halls, and other heavy-traffic corridors, tile remains rigid and colorfast. An onslaught of wet galoshes or the muddy paws of a family pet will do it no harm. In the kitchen or bathroom, tile provides excellent protection against drips and spills. Cleaning requires merely a damp mop with a soapless detergent.

Tiled flooring makes a strong decorative statement. Depending on the style you choose,

DESIGN: TAYLOR WOODROW

you can create any atmosphere—from formal elegance to rustic earthiness. You can link and visually expand spaces by extending a tile floor from entry to living room, and then right out onto the patio.

**WALLS.** Any wall that might be sprayed or splashed with water is an obvious candidate for glazed ceramic tile. But don't limit tile to areas that get wet. A wainscot or accent of tile in a living room, dining room, or home office makes a neatly tailored backdrop for furnishings, plants, or a freestanding fireplace.

**TUBS AND SHOWERS.** Around bathroom fixtures, tiled surfaces are waterproof and easy to keep clean of splashes and soap film. Glazed

wall tiles are most familiar, but mosaics shine here, too: they're tough, handsome, and shed water.

**COUNTERTOPS.** Ideal as a working surface near the kitchen sink and stove, most tile is unaffected by a sharp knife or hot pan. And if you use an appropriate grout (see page 371), grease and food spots wipe right off. Tile makes a decorative but functional surface for any bathroom vanity, eating counter, or wet bar.

**BACKSPLASHES.** The part of the wall exposed above kitchen and bathroom counters, this eye-level surface is a great place to focus decorative tile effects. Glazing brings water protection and easy cleanup to these spaces, too.

*Classic kitchen countertop and backsplash* (above) *are lined with handpainted Portuguese tiles. A modernistic version* (left) *teams staggered wall tiles with candy-colored glass dots. Slate floor tiles* (facing page) *are framed by limestone strips and tiny glass mosaics.*

*An outdoor wall niche is lined with colorful, Moroccan-style tile; note how artfully the curved wall planes come together at the top.*

**FIREPLACES.** Because most ceramic tile is baked at a high temperature, it is unaffected by heat. Consider using tile on the outside face, mantel, or hearth of a fireplace. Even a single row of blue-and-white Delft or earth-toned Arts and Crafts tiles can add character.

**STAIRS.** Constant traffic wears down the treads of stairs and steps. Surfacing them with tile will protect them for years. For stair treads, be sure to use slip-resistant tiles or tiles with raised edges. For a simple brightening effect, trim the risers with colorful accent tiles. This will also make steps more visible in dim light.

*Marble tiles, custom-cut and arranged in bold black-and-white geometrics, face this living-room fireplace.*

**DECORATIVE BORDERS.** Whether set edge-to-edge or spaced apart, tiles make beautiful frames for doors or windows. Consider tiled crown and base moldings, too.

**FURNISHINGS.** Adding a tile top can give new life to an old table. And why not tile the bases of window seats and built-in benches?

**SHELVES AND NICHES.** Not only do built-in display shelves, sills, jambs, and greenhouse windows provide many handy horizontal surfaces to decorate, they're also easier to clean when tiled.

**SOLARIUMS.** Both stone and ceramic tiles are naturals for sunrooms. The clay body's thermal mass retains solar heat in winter, and its firm face is undamaged by plant waterings.

**OUTDOORS.** Patios and pools are tried-and-true locations for tile. But what about decorative wall fountains, built-in benches, fireplace surrounds, garden walls, and outdoor kitchens?

**COLLECTIBLES.** Art tiles, especially antiques, are currently in vogue as collectibles. Show off their charm by setting some above a picture rail. Or hang them like paintings.

*Outdoor trim tile adorns both an entry gate* (top) *and on a poolside fountain* (above right). *The gate insert features jigsaw-shaped tiles and a cast center medallion; the pool edging shimmers with iridescent glass. Stair risers* (right) *are dressed up with Spanish relief tiles, which also wrap around the outside wall. Note the unique, curved trim tiles.*

## Tile types

Not all tile is created equal. Instead, tiles are characterized according to how they're made and what they're for.

Ceramic tile is either glazed or unglazed. A glaze is a hard finish, usually incorporating a color, that is applied to the surface of the hardened clay body and then, most often, refired one or more additional times. (For more tile-making details, see page 357.) A glaze can have a high gloss, a matte finish, or a dull, pebbly texture.

Unglazed tiles do not have a baked-on finish. The colors you see—commonly earth tones, ranging from yellow-beige to dark red to deep brown—are either from the natural clay itself or from pigments added prior to forming and baking. This color is consistent throughout the body of the tile, whereas glazed tile has color only on the surface.

- **GLAZED WALL TILES** are available in a tremendous variety of colors and designs. Applied to vertical surfaces, these tiles are lighter and thinner than floor tiles. Because they don't need to be particularly strong or slip resistant, they offer many decorative options.

*Clean, simple diamond accents are formed from blue glass mosaics; they're embedded in a plastered backsplash above the kitchen range.*

DESIGN: TAYLOR WOODROW

- **FLOOR TILES** are larger, thicker, and more durable than wall tiles. They come as squares, rectangles, hexagons, and octagons, as well as in interlocking curved shapes, such as Moorish and ogee. Floor tiles are available glazed or unglazed. Unglazed tiles tend to be less slippery and to show wear less easily, since the coloration permeates the tile body. Beware, though: these tiles are more porous and can be tougher to keep clean.

- **MOSAICS,** used for both walls and floors, are generally small—typically 1 or 2 inches square. Most mosaics come premounted on a mesh backing, ready to install. In custom mosaic art installations, however, the craftsman creates a whimsical, one-of-a-kind composition from broken tiles, glass shards, fragments of china plates and cups, stones, pebbles, bits of mirror, and even marbles.

- **TRIM AND BORDER TILES** are designed to finish off edges, form coves, and turn inside and outside corners. Use them to break up expanses or serve as transitions between tile patterns or colors, or where the tile meets another surface. You'll also find countertop trim tiles that allow you to tile smoothly around sinks, along counter edges, or below a backsplash.

- **ART TILES** are created in custom shapes, often glazed with interestingly varied colors and adorned with painted or relief-formed designs. Handpainted tiles, created for tile shops by local artists, offer decorative designs such as flowers, trees, and animals. Using even a few of these beautiful (and expensive) pieces can produce great visual impact when you set them as individual accents in a backsplash wall or countertop. On the other hand, entire scenes, such as a basket of flowers or a group of swimming fish, can be painted on a group of tiles, taken to the site, and reassembled there.

- **STONE, GLASS, AND CONCRETE TILES** are other vibrant options that can be used in many of the same ways as ceramic. Full information on all these tile types is provided in "A Shopper's Guide," beginning on page 433.

## Narrowing the field

You can use tile anywhere in the house where you want durability, beauty, water protection, a bit of flash, or a nod to a period style. But it's best to review the following considerations before you visit the showrooms, where you might be overwhelmed by the options.

**MOISTURE RESISTANCE.** One key factor when choosing a tile is how easily it absorbs water. Generally speaking, tiles that are fired at higher temperatures for longer times are denser, making them both watertight and resistant to stains.

The most watertight tiles, usually those made from glass and porcelain, are called "impervious," meaning they absorb less than 0.5% moisture. Tiles classified as "vitreous" are the next in line, absorbing 0.5 to 3%, and "semivitreous" tiles absorb 3 to 7%. Soft-bodied "nonvitreous" tiles, such as glazed wall tiles, art tiles, and terra-cotta, absorb 7% or more, and even when treated with a sealer are only partially water resistant. So why do people choose them? Because they're among the most beautiful tiles of all.

*High-gloss field tiles, art tile accents, borders, and trim combine to form a shower surround that's both water resistant and a real eye-opener in the morning.*

DESIGN: TAYLOR WOODROW

**DURABILITY.** A wall tile's body needn't be super-tough, so most are thinner than tiles intended for floors and counters. Many floor tiles, however, are rated for strength.

The simplest scale divides floor tiles into four use ratings: light duty, medium duty, heavy duty, and commercial. While medium- and even light-duty materials may be adequate for a bathroom floor, you'll probably want heavy-duty tiles for a kitchen or family room.

Some tiles are also rated for glaze hardness—their resistance to scuffing and abrasion. Common systems include the Abrasive Wear Index and the Mohs hardness test. Though you won't need a high rating for wall tiles, you certainly will for an entry floor or kitchen counter. Generally, an Index rating of 3 or a Mohs rating of 7 translates to heavy-duty tile.

**SLIP RESISTANCE.** Tiles destined for interior floors, stair treads, showers, and patios must provide adequate traction for safe walking, whether wet or dry. Generally speaking, unglazed, textured tiles offer better traction than glazed versions, though some glazed floor tiles include enough texture or abrasive additives for safe footing. Unglazed mosaics also work well, since their many grout lines help break up the surface.

Some manufacturers rate tiles with a so-called "coefficient of friction"; your dealer can interpret this for you and make recommendations.

**STAIN RESISTANCE.** Kitchen countertops, kitchen and bathroom floors, tub surrounds, fireplace faces, and patios are areas with high potential for staining. Dense tiles and those with sturdy glazes are best bets here. Sealers (see page 439) help protect porous tiles, but may be unsafe for use on eating and food-preparation surfaces.

**FREEZE-THAW STABILITY.** Tiles used outdoors in cold climates must be able to withstand water absorption and seasonal temperature fluctuations without warping or breaking. In these areas, impervious or vitreous tiles are usually the safest. This is less of an issue in mild climates, where softer, more absorbent tiles like terra-cotta can be acceptable choices.

# WHAT IS TILE, ANYWAY?

Today's ceramic tiles consist of natural clays with additives such as talc or powdered shale to extend the clay and cut down on shrinkage. Most commercial tiles are formed by either the *dust-press method* or by *extrusion*. Dust-pressing entails injecting premixed, nearly dry ingredients into steel dies and subjecting them to enormous pressure. Extruded tiles are squeezed through a set of rollers (picture a giant pasta machine), then cut to size. Compared to precise, crisp dust-press tiles, extruded tiles are mildly irregular—though some manufacturers regrind them to make them more uniform.

In either case, the result—the *green* tile—is fired in a kiln, after which it becomes the *bisque*. Generally, the longer the firing and the hotter the temperature, the tougher and more water resistant the final product. For unglazed tiles, such as terra-cotta, this is the end of the line. But most tiles are then surfaced with one or more thin layers of *glaze* and refired.

Handmade art tiles are often formed in more labor-intensive ways and glazed and painted by hand. And some popular unglazed tiles, such as Mexican saltillos, are still laid out to bake in the sun in the time-honored way; prized tiles bear imprints where dog paws or chicken feet or even leaves have touched damp surfaces.

Most natural stone tiles are first split or gang-cut with diamond saws, then polished and cut into individual units. Not all are polished to a high luster. Increasingly popular are so-called "reverse-polishing" processes, including honing, resawing, and etching. These all furnish rougher, matte finishes—as does "tumbling," which gives an antique-like patina to marble tiles. Some stone tiles, notably slate, are simply split along existing seams, yielding hard, natural-looking, slightly irregular faces.

# designing with tile

**N**OW **YOU** *can begin to fine-tune your decorating plans. As you'll see, tile is an effective medium for evoking both style and mood. The design effects you create result from your conscious manipulation of color, pattern, texture, size, and shape. Beginning on page 373, you'll find scores of room-specific ideas for tile installations. Here, we present some basic design concepts. Remember that these are reliable guidelines, not strict rules.*

## Focus or backdrop?

If you're ready to enter the design process, first ask yourself whether tile should be the focus or the backdrop of your room. More specifically, should it call attention to itself and create its own flashy, charismatic drama, with other furnishings fairly neutral, or should it serve as a supporting background for other decorative elements in the space? Few interior designs, especially brightly colored or heavily patterned ones, can flourish with more than one main focus.

Given the spectrum of colors and array of shapes in which tile comes, it's relatively easy to use it to create visual drama. Part of the fun of today's tile renaissance is seeing the almost limitless stock of vibrant colors and patterns now available.

On the other hand, an understated tile backdrop can handsomely support more attention-getting furnishings, wall coverings, window treatments, and accessories. When deciding, remember that it's simpler to change furniture and fabrics than to redo a relatively permanent tile installation.

## Tile style

A decorating style has physical characteristics that identify it with a particular region, era, or artistic movement—English Victorian, Southwestern, Arts and Crafts, Art Deco, and so on. Because certain tiles are linked to certain historic decorating styles, they can be used to evoke the character of a period—or simply to personalize and give dignity to a bland modern house.

Even so, rarely are styles slavish replicas of historical designs. More typically, designers select among elements that echo the mood of a period or regional look. A mood is the ambience that develops when a style is interpreted in a particular context—cozy, inviting, serene, or precise. What matters is that you choose a style and mood you find sympathetic and comfortable.

On the following three pages, we take a tour of five basic design styles, including period, regional, romantic, country, and contemporary. We also show a sampling of tile types that are linked with each look. Use this information as a starting point for your own explorations.

## PERIOD STYLE

*Old and reproduction homes often are decorated in a style that suits their architecture. Popular tile motifs include quaint Dutch figures (near left) and Arts and Crafts frogs (bottom left). Classic white-trimmed fireplace and hearth (far left) are faced with Dutch delftware.*

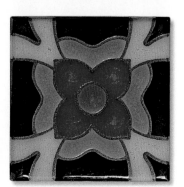

## REGIONAL STYLE

*Responding to climate, indigenous resources, and cultural sensibilities, regional styles frequently include tile. Mexican saltillos and handpainted accents (near left) have a Mediterranean air; Malibu tile (bottom left) is symbolic of sunny Southern California in the early 1900s. The interlocking designs on fireplace and hearth (far left) are hallmarks of Moroccan tile style.*

## ROMANTIC STYLE

*Usually graceful and feminine, "romantic" isn't strictly a style but more an intimate mood. Victorian decors are often romantic, but those of other periods may be as well. Floral tiles in both French faience (above left) and Victorian transfer (above right) versions fill the bill. The romantic master bath (right) is dressed in soft colors and florals, including an elegant handpainted ceramic sink.*

DESIGN: COUNTRY FLOORS

ARCHITECT: REMICK ASSOCIATES ARCHITECTS-BUILDERS, INC.

## COUNTRY STYLE

*To some, country is rustic, distressed, or quaint; to others, it is Shaker-simple, with minimal but distinctive accessories. It can be casual, formal, or eclectic. In tile, country kitchens often employ naturalistic themes like flowers, fruits (both shown above), and vegetables. The formal country kitchen (left) is lavishly dressed with tile, including ornate relief trim and handpainted murals on both vent hood and backsplash.*

ARCHITECT: GGLO/BILL GAYLORD, WILLIAM CASTILLO. INTERIOR DESIGNER: CAROLYNE COBY, DESIGN 5 INTERNATIONAL. LIGHTING: CAROL DePELECYN, CHRISTOPHER THOMPSON

## CONTEMPORARY STYLE

*Contemporary design tends to be sleek, strong, and graphic, with bold colors or shapes set against plain backgrounds. Machine-made ceramic or stone tiles can be highlighted with bright, playful accents (left). Or keep the look monolithic, as shown in the stone-lined kitchen (above).*

## Color

Because color packs such emotional punch, it's of primary importance when decorating. What colors are you most comfortable with? Your current furnishings, clothing, and accessories offer clues. Quickly browse through the gallery of examples in the following chapter, thinking only of color; make note of any strong likes or dislikes.

One familiar rule of color design is that light tones make surroundings seem larger, where as dark colors tend to shrink space.

Whites, creams, and neutrals are traditional favorites and always in style. White reflects and maximizes whatever light is available. A light, neutral background gives you the freedom to use color in furnishings to focus your design.

Warm colors, such as peach, yellow, and terracotta, appear to advance, making a room seem cozier. They're favorites for romantic and country design schemes. They can also help dimly lit or north-facing spaces seem less cool. Warm colors are flattering to skin tones, making them natural choices for powder rooms and entertaining spaces.

Blue, green, and violet, on the other hand, are cool, serene hues. Black adds drama but absorbs light and seems to shrink room size. High contrast has the same impact as a dark color: it adds impact but reduces the perceived space.

■ **MONOCHROMATIC** color schemes, often white-on-white, set up a classic backdrop for furnishings and accents. Using subtle colors throughout a room can unify the space and make

*A monochromatic, white-on-white scheme spreads light and wraps this master bath in quiet, classic style. Tile shapes and sizes are artfully varied for subtle visual interest; matching trim and border tiles help ease transitions.*

awkward details less obvious. But the danger of a monochromatic scheme is that it can be boring. Use shapes, textures, and borders to produce subtle variations. Consider floating a few decorative tiles in a white or neutral field. Remember that all-white or all-dark schemes are the toughest to keep looking clean; texture (see page 366) helps camouflage dirt.

- **ANALOGOUS** color schemes (using closely related colors) may provide more variety than monochromatic plans. They typically employ three to five hues of one primary color.
- **COMPLEMENTARY** color schemes use hues directly opposite each other on the color wheel— for example, yellow and violet. Depending on the hues, the effect can be either startling or satisfying. This way of handling color usually

works best if one of the colors is used more prominently than the other.

Don't forget, fixtures and appliances have color that you may need to consider. Some manufacturers make this process simpler by offering coordinated lines of wall, floor, and trim tiles; other lines match wallpapers, countertop surfaces, and even bathroom fixtures. If you just can't find the color you need, most dealers can special-order a custom color—for a price.

The quality of light greatly affects color. Direct sun, shade, and artificial incandescent, fluorescent, and halogen sources all can render tile hues differently. That's why it's important to examine a sample of the tile you think you want to use under different lighting conditions— preferably in the room where it will be installed.

DESIGN: ANN SACKS TILE & STONE

*This shower design is a textbook example of complementary colors— specifically, the triad of orange, purple, and green. In this case, the hues are gentle and are tempered further by the creamy beige in both center tiles and grout spaces.*

*Two graphic patterns are shown here. Staggered, handmade field tiles* (far left) *are joined by smaller relief dots on a shower wall. The limestone floor* (left) *is jazzed up with bold stripes and accents made from granite and glass tiles.*

## Pattern

The modular nature of tile shapes and sizes provides almost unlimited pattern potential for those wishing to mix and match. High-contrast patterns like checkerboards have obvious drama, but subtler patterns can be created using monochromatic or analogous colors and mixed textures.

The obvious rule about patterns is that small ones are best for small spaces, large ones for large spaces. Complex patterns can feel confining and can disappear in a big room. Simple, open patterns tie together large spaces and lend a sense of freedom and calm.

Patterns can be naturalistic, stylized, geometrical, or abstract. Naturalistic renderings of natural forms, such as flowers, are popular in period, romantic, and country styles (see pages 359–361). On the other hand, geometric, random, and other nonrepresentational patterns fit with most contemporary designs.

Consider the lines formed by the tiles. A repeated floor pattern that runs lengthwise adds depth to a room; running across, it gives a shorter, wider look. Setting tile in a diagonal layout creates a more dynamic rhythm. A busy tile pattern or a mix of several colors makes an area look smaller; using a simple pattern or a single color has the opposite effect.

Airy, quiet patterns allow you to link large areas or a suite of several rooms. Trim and border tiles link patterns and also allow you to define distinct focal points and activity areas. For example, a tiled "area rug" beneath a dining table visually distinguishes this space from the surrounding room.

Don't forget that grout—the cement- or epoxy-base filler between tiles—affects your tile pattern. Unless you wish to play up the gridlike design, pick a grout color that blends with field tiles: light for light installations, dark for dark designs. For decorative tiles, aim to match the grout to the tiles' background color. The width of grout lines also has an effect. Narrow spaces seem to drop away; wider lines create a bolder sense of pattern. See page 371 for more help on choosing and using grout.

*The tiles in this bathroom* (facing page) *are a near-riot of color but artfully laid out. Elements are formed with inexpensive, readily available wall tiles in 1- to 6-inch squares, plus trim and cut triangles.*

LANDSCAPE ARCHITECT: JEFF STONE ASSOCIATES OF LA JOLLA

*The lion-headed wall fountain and spa (above) contrast diagonal checkerboard diamonds in glossy colors with an earthier backdrop of larger backyard brick. Tough, easy-to-clean porcelain relief tiles (facing page) add texture to rangeside backsplash and vent hood.*

## Texture

Less obvious than color and pattern, texture has a major effect on both. Highly polished tiles intensify colors and read as formal. A play of light reflected from glossy surfaces creates brightness, but brings with it a harder, cooler, more high-tech look. Matte finishes and unglazed terra-cotta create a warmer, more casual mood and make spaces feel more intimate. In general, textured tiles are also easier to blend with other elements in the room.

Texture in tile may be perceived either tactilely or visually. Your fingers can feel the sensation of changes in the plane from matte or pebbly glazes, relief patterns, or pockmarks on a tumbled-marble surface. Visual textures are like special effects: the surfaces look varied, but in fact are smooth to the touch.

When considering texture, think about maintenance. Glossy tiles are simple to keep clean but quickly show whatever dirt or grease is present.

Porous tiles with rough textures tend to stain, but mask it better. A good compromise may be a tile with visual texture—one that's smooth but has a shaded or flecked glaze.

## Size and shape

When selecting a size, again the guideline is small tiles for small spaces, large tiles for large rooms. If the tile's scale is too large for a room, the effect will be overpowering. If it's too small, the design will look weak. Squares and rectangles are considered stable shapes; diamonds and triangles add movement.

Because it's difficult to align tiles on adjacent walls and floors, it's best to stagger tile shapes or to work with different sizes. Most installations are intentionally bottom-heavy; that is, they vary from smaller (walls) through medium (countertops) to large (floor) sizes. Another tactic is to organize the floor layout on the diagonal, or set it off from walls with a decorative border.

# gearing up

**INSTALLING** *ceramic tile can be a sizable financial commitment. Be sure to shop around, calculate costs, and order carefully. Remember, it's best to select the tile that's most suitable for the projected use, then consider appearance. Your tile dealer can help with fine points, once you've done the basic research. If you're planning a large installation or are simply overwhelmed by the choices, an architect, designer, or tile contractor can help you winnow down and establish priorities.*

### Showroom savvy

A well-stocked tile center has as many luscious colors and alluring shapes as an old-fashioned candy store; just looking brings on an appetite. But remind yourself, looks aren't enough. The tile you choose must be right for your needs. **DO YOUR HOMEWORK.** Browse through books (like this one), magazines, advertisements, and brochures. Compile a scrapbook of possibilities that appeal to you. You may wish to take a cue from interior designers and create a sample board showing wallpaper and fabric swatches, paint chips, and fixture colors. Also, take rough measurements of your room.

Most tile professionals are knowledgeable and ready to help. They can answer your questions and advise you on tile aesthetics, tile quality, the number of tiles you'll require, and the costs involved in your project. If you've fallen in love with a beautiful but impractical

tile, a good dealer can help you find something similar that holds up better.

Must the tile be waterproof, slip resistant, scuff resistant, easy to maintain, or stable outdoors in freezing weather? Your dealer can verify these properties or refer you to manufacturers' specifications. Be sure the maker's warranty covers the uses you've planned.

Often you can borrow samples to try at home for color, size, and compatibility. Buy a sample of the tile, if necessary. If you own it, you can also test it for scuffing (rub a metal cooking pot against it), smudging, and ease of cleanup.

Most retailers have displays or catalogs of tiles they don't carry in stock. You may have to wait a long time for certain styles, so get reliable information on availability and plan accordingly. **MONEY-SAVING TIPS.** The costs of ceramic tile run from modest to very expensive—from a bargain-basement $1 per square foot for remainders up to $50 and more for one-of-a-kind art tiles, and even more for some stones.

Single-color glazed wall tiles—those commonly used around showers and tubs—are the most economical. The trim pieces for these tiles normally cost more per square foot than do the field tiles. The addition of three-dimensional patterns and multicolored glazes can easily double costs.

If you're on a tight budget, remember these hints:

- **WATCH FOR CLOSEOUTS** that a dealer will sell at a discount. These may be lines that manufacturers have discontinued, colors or patterns that were overstocked, or tiles left over from a large job or cancelled order.
- **SHOP FOR SECONDS;** these tiles are flawed or blemished (usually only slightly), so they cannot be sold with the regular stock at full price. Often, seconds will go undetected if randomly mixed with unblemished tiles.
- **RESERVE COSTLIER ART TILES** as accents in a simpler field of stock wall tile. Space them at regular intervals or sprinkle them randomly. Not only will this kind of plan stretch your budget, it will also help showcase those one-of-a-kind tiles you've fallen in love with.

*A colorful wall's worth of European mural tiles* (facing page) *is sure to get your creative juices flowing. A stone showroom's sample display* (below) *graphically shows part of the amazing range available.*

DESIGN: OSBURN DESIGN/ASN NATURAL STONE

## Making the purchase

Once you're in the final stages, have accurate measurements drawn up for the area to be covered. A plan on graph paper helps you visualize the area and provides clues to the trim pieces you may need. Or use a computer drawing program and a color printer to try out more involved patterns on paper.

When figuring your needs, remember that actual tile sizes may vary from the nominal sizes listed. For example, if your selection is a 6 by 6 glazed wall tile, it may actually be $3/8$ inch smaller or larger. Either measure the tile yourself or verify its dimensions with your dealer.

With your drawing in hand, a tile dealer should be able to help you figure out how many tiles you'll require. Be sure to buy extra tiles—the rule of thumb is 5 percent, though tricky installations may require an extra 10 percent. This allows for breakage during cutting. And if a tile chips after installation, you'll have a replacement on hand—whereas if you wait until damage occurs to search for new tiles, you may not be able to find pieces that match.

*Skilled tile artisans produce many one-of-a-kind designs, like this exuberantly swirled shower mosaic.*

TILE ARTISAN: MARLO BARTELS STUDIO OF LAGUNA BEACH

Before you bring the tiles home, check the cartons to be sure the colors match. Different cartons of the same tile can vary significantly. Check that "shade lot" numbers are the same from box to box. Even so, most installers mix these boxes together before beginning the job.

## Need help?

For a price, you won't need to go it alone when either choosing or installing your new tile. Design help is available from architects, interior designers and decorators, and kitchen and bath professionals. Tile contractors handle the installation process.

Architects specialize in suiting form to function. They can help you analyze your particular needs and find solutions to tricky remodeling problems. Of course, some architects may be more concerned with structural solutions than aesthetics.

Interior designers and decorators may be more attuned to tile style, scale, pattern, and color. Kitchen and bath designers may also know the latest on tile styles and installation glitches. All of these professionals can gain you access to trade-only showrooms and services you might not be able to find for yourself.

Tile contractors can show you samples and advise you on some basic choices, but it's best to already have preferences in mind from your own legwork. The contractor can also advise you on potential structural problems, such as whether your subfloor will support a heavy tile floor without requiring either bolstering or waterproofing.

While today's modern adhesives and grouts have made some tile-setting jobs a snap, the experienced hand of a licensed contractor is still crucial for many projects. For example, installing swimming pool tile is not do-it-yourself work. Applications that require setting tiles in a full mortar bed, such as around a free-form or sunken tub, are best handled by a professional. And a contractor can take on an awkward space that requires a lot of matching of surfaces and/or intricate cuts.

# TILE SETTING: HOW THE PROS DO IT

Should you try tiling it yourself? If you're handy, and if your project is a simple backsplash, countertop, or rectangular floor, you might venture the work yourself. The overview given here provides a basic gloss of the tiling process.

A quality tile installation is an integrated "sandwich," including not just tile but also an appropriate backing material, a setting bed of thin-set mortar or adhesive, and grout to seal and decorate the edges.

You can install new tile over new or existing gypsum wallboard, cement backerboard, exterior-grade plywood, or even wood paneling or existing tile as long as it's in good condition. Don't try to install tile over a springy surface; any movement will cause the grout and tile to crack. If there is a great deal of bounce in a floor, you may need to have a professional install a so-called "floating floor" first.

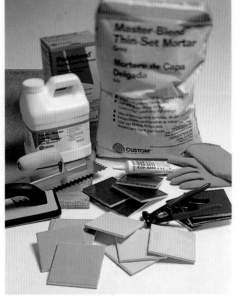

In areas that have to withstand a lot of moisture, such as a shower or tub enclosure, the best choice of backing is cement backerboard, which will not disintegrate when wet. To keep water out of the wall, put a moisture barrier over the backing. Waterproof membrane comes in three basic forms: tar paper, CPE sheets, and a kit consisting of reinforcing fabric and liquid rubber.

Ceramic tile may be set in either a thick bed of mortar or a thinner combed-out bed of mortar or adhesive. Though setting tile in thick traditional mortar gives best results for bathroom tub and shower enclosures, this work is definitely a job for a professional. You can choose from three types of thin-set adhesive—cement-base, organic-base, or epoxy-base. Cement-base thin-set mortars are the pro's choice in most cases, though organic adhesives or *mastics* are suitable in spots that won't see much traffic or be exposed to much moisture. Epoxy products are super-tough but more expensive.

Though grout may seem like a minor player, the time to consider it is early on in your planning. Cement-base grout is the traditional choice, and is adequate for many applications. In bathrooms and kitchens, a mildew-resistant version is in order. Applying a grout sealer can help cement-base grout stand up to both moisture and stains.

Epoxy grouts, while more expensive, are better than cement-base for wet areas and spots where food and chemical stains collect. In most cases you won't need to seal an epoxy grout.

As detailed on page 365, grout color can have a major impact on the overall color and pattern of a tile installation. Grouts now come in a wide selection of colors, in both sanded and non-sanded versions. Choose a non-sanded grout for glazed wall tiles and other machine-made units where grout spacings are 1/8 inch or less. Larger spacings—for example, those between irregular handmade or terra-cotta tiles—call for the extra body and strength of sanded grout.

Where horizontally laid tile meets a perpendicular surface of tile or or another material, use caulking compound—not grout—to fill the joint. This allows the surfaces to flex slightly, minimizing stress cracks in both tile and grout. You'll find that caulking compounds now come in most of the same colors that grout does.

# GREAT TILE IDEAS

**I**N THE FIRST chapter, "A Planning Primer," we explored the principles of choosing tile and creating decorative effects with it. Now we're going for inspiration—this time room by room. **SUBSECTIONS** of this chapter present an exciting array of tile installations, in four zones of the home: kitchen, bathroom, living space, and outdoors. You'll discover a rainbow of colorful ideas for each of these areas, plus space-specific planning pointers. Do you lean toward a traditional sense of repose, a casual country ambience, or a bolder, more modern blast of color? Whatever your taste, you should find sympathetic examples here, as we've aimed to present as broad a spectrum of styles as possible. For specific design guidelines, see pages 358–367. **BROWSE AT YOUR** leisure, perhaps marking your favorite pictures to show a tile supplier or designer. Many of these ideas can be adapted from one room for another, and they can be scaled up or down depending on your needs. For background on the tile types shown here, see "A Shopper's Guide," beginning on page 433.

*great tile ideas*

# kitchens

I**N LIGHT** of the kitchen's central role in household activities, its surfaces must stand up to repeated scrapes and scuffs, spills, steamy pasta pots, and messy school projects. Sturdy, watertight, easy-to-clean tile is the natural choice here, especially since the options are so plentiful.

The two main poles of kitchen style are *country* and *contemporary*. With the right tile (see pages 359–361), you can easily accomplish either look, as well as a full spectrum of period and regional themes. Country kitchens, with earth-tone floors in quarry tile or terra-cotta, often use the backsplash space for tiles with cheerful fruit or floral motifs or for informal decorative murals or for a display of homey handmade or art tiles. High-tech contemporary kitchens are streamlined for efficiency; their sleek, no-nonsense air is often best served by machine-made glazed tiles, typically in white or neutrals, that form a background for gleaming pans, clean-lined cabinets, and perhaps a few accents such as well-placed art tiles. There are always exceptions to these generalities. Some of the most dramatic kitchen designs borrow playfully and shamelessly from the whole range of traditions.

**Backsplash basics.** The backsplash—the wall area between countertop and wall cabinets—is a premier destination for decorative tile, be it a few colorful art tiles in a quiet field, a classic floral mural, or a jazzier art mosaic. This blank "canvas" is typically about 18 inches tall and set about 36 to 54 inches off

*Lively-looking contemporary backsplash features variegated relief art tiles in Paul Klee colors.*

DESIGN: LOU ANN BAUER

the floor. You can match countertop tile (see below), contrast it, echo the countertop's trim, or flaunt another look entirely. Use trim where the backsplash meets countertop tile, or simply run the tile down to another counter material and caulk the joint (see page 371).

**Counter intelligence.** There are pros and cons to tiling countertops. On the positive side, tile is attractive and watertight; on the minus side, it can seem cold, uneven, and hard to clean. If you choose another countertop material, such as stone, wood, laminate, or solid-surface, you can still feature tile on the backsplash—and perhaps use a heatproof tiled counter insert near the cooktop or work area.

If you decide to tile the countertops, machine-made tiles work best because of their greater uniformity. The tiles you choose should be highly stain resistant and, if glazed, resistant to acids and household chemicals. Be sure to ask your dealer if the tiles you like are rated for countertops. Think twice about dark, glossy glazes—they show every stain and smudge. And be careful about sealers: many are inappropriate for eating and food-preparation surfaces.

For a smoother surface that's easier to clean, consider using large uniform floor tiles with narrow grout lines. Choose a mildew-resistant grout.

Of course, you may also decide to tile a kitchen island, eating peninsula, or breakfast table, too.

**Hardworking floors.** Kitchen floors take a pounding. So in most cases, you'll be looking for tough tiles that can stand up to water, spills, and dropped pots while remaining slip resistant and good-looking to boot. Impossible? Porcelain pavers, quarry tiles, glazed floor tiles, and some stones can fill the bill, and you'll find enough color options in all these to build whatever pattern you choose. Terra-cotta creates an appealingly rustic ambience, but should be sealed.

*Diamond-shaped limestone accents march across a kitchen floor of sealed saltillo pavers.*

For a floating, seamless look, consider tiling the spaces below cabinets—called *kickspaces* or *toe spaces*—to match floor or backsplash. If tiling is all you're doing, it's simplest to lay new tiles up to existing cabinet lines (though this can limit later access to pullout appliances). With a major remodel, it's usually best to tile the whole space before adding cabinets and appliances. While you're at it, it's a good time to install a cozy, nonallergenic radiant-heat system below the new floor.

**The stove area.** Think about two other prominent focal points: the vent hood and the range surround. Tiled vent hoods are traditional in country designs, and clearly symbolize the warmth of "hearth and home." Colorful Portuguese, Spanish, or Mexican tiles are popular here; they often sport culinary or floral motifs as well as more stylized patterns. This space is also a good place to display pictorial compositions, such as a tiled fruit bowl, wildflower bouquet, or pastoral mural. Contemporary vent hoods might feature a single trim row of colorful wall or art tiles that repeat backsplash or floor motifs.

The alcove that houses a freestanding range, be it a vintage model or a modern residential/commercial behemoth, is another good location for decorative tile. Even in a streamlined built-in design, you'll still often see a special tiled motif behind the cooktop.

**Details, details.** Wainscoting (a half-wall of tile) or a simple chair rail (a single or double row at "chair height") can help define a breakfast area or office alcove, perhaps echoing a motif in backsplash, vent hood, or floor. Window and door trim can also be tiled to match.

Details can custom-finish the look. You might create tiled wall niches for spices, oils, and utensils. Open shelves and open alcoves for pots and pans look more integrated when tiled. Tiled decks inside greenhouse windows appear more finished and help ward off moisture damage.

*Formal as can be, this floor features 24-by 24-inch polished-marble squares framed by bands of smaller limestone tiles. Countertops are surfaced with solid limestone in the same creamy beige.*

*This Southwest design is organized around a central vent hood, which houses a four-sided mural of handpainted tile. The colors are echoed in countertops, lighted display niche, and backsplashes. Bronze saltillo floor pavers get their warm patina from wax, a traditional sealer for terra-cotta tiles.*

DESIGN: TAYLOR WOODROW

*A rich and playful back-splash mosaic of smashed green tile shards sets off the cherry cabinets, commercial range, and brushed-steel vent hood. Glass accent spheres are scattered through-out the tile, sparkling like colored jewels.*

*French terra-cotta pavers
add a traditional touch to
a thoroughly modern kitchen
that also features a celadon-
and-white tiled island
and granite-topped work
surfaces. Radiant heating
below the pavers keeps the
floor warm, as enjoyed
by the cat.*

TILE ARTISANS: AHMED AGKAMA & JAMAKA HARRIS

DESIGN: BENEDIKT STREBEL CERAMICS

*What if a different orientation were rendered atop the regular grid of a floor tile? You'd get a dynamic, multidirectional design like this one, handpainted in sharp angles, squiggles, swirls, and craggy textures like abstract art.*

*Field tiles and borders with variegated pastel glazes line an under-sink niche recessed in a country kitchen's pickled-pine cabinetry. Patterned encaustic tiles form the floor.*

DESIGN: COUNTRY FLOORS

*This kitchen/great-room is sheathed in intricate Moroccan patterns of glazed tile. Three floor patterns and one wall design repeat the same basic color scheme, divided by dramatic accent bands on stair risers and borders. Tiny individual tiles were shop-fitted to form larger mosaics, then interlocked when laid in place.*

DESIGN: DEWHURST & ASSOCIATES. TILE ARTISAN: F. MICHAEL KING

*This well-aged, cheerfully provincial range surround is covered in classic Mexican blue-and-white stars. Tiles don't stop at the backsplash: they also line both the shelf niche and the face of an old wood-burning oven below.*

*Tough, earth-toned quarry tiles line the hard-working countertops of this Southwest-style kitchen; they're joined by colorful, handmade art tiles in backsplash areas.*

TILE ARTISAN: KAREN KOBLITZ

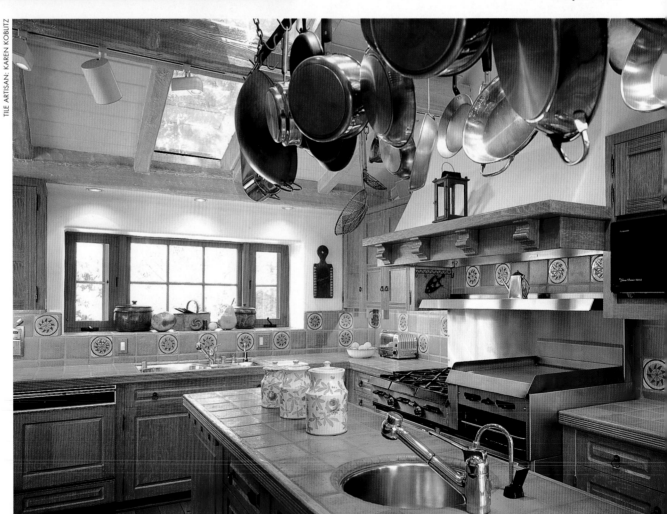

DESIGN: MINOR REVISIONS ARCHITECTURE & DESIGN.
CONTRACTOR: MARK McCARTHY. TILE: BUDDY RHODES STUDIO/AMALFI TILE & MARBLE

*Exuding a quiet
respect for tradition,
this design incorporates
both translucent glazed
field tiles and cast
ceramic pieces. Gleaming
carved ceramic columns
seem to hold the vent
hood aloft; for contrast,
glaze was removed
from the backsplash's
centerpiece wreath.*

*A kitchen island's sturdy
countertop, surfaced with
1- by 1-inch Venetian glass
mosaics, sits a level above
a marble-look floor of
concrete field tiles and
smaller concrete accents.*

TILE ARTISAN: RODGER DUNHAM CERAMIC DESIGN OF PETALUMA

*Honoring the Victorian heritage of the house, the kitchen remodel incorporated antique plates set into diagonally laid field tiles. The plates were "floated" in a thick layer of mortar; then tiles were painstakingly hand-cut to fit around them.*

*Cows amble across a pastoral vista and stare placidly out at the owners of this handpainted back-splash mural. Large tiles with thin grout lines keep the composition unified.*

*Granite tiles sheathe island and countertops in this kitchen. In the cooktop alcove, granite gives way to a diagonally laid slate backsplash panel with glass-mosaic borders and accents.*

*Mustard-color 6- by 6-inch tiles on countertops and walls with hand-painted Mexican borders and diamond-shaped relief accents brighten this Mediterranean-inspired design. Dark-stained wood edgings and cabinets make a rich contrast.*

DESIGN: TAYLOR WOODROW

*Why not tile a table's top? This one has black-and-white checkerboard wall tiles around a painted faux-marble center.*

# bathrooms

**T**HOROUGHLY time-tested since the days of ancient baths, tile is a tried-and-true performer in modern bathrooms as well. Properly installed, it's highly water resistant, easy to clean, and hygienic.

The design possibilities are endless—from elegant repose to romantic Victorian florals, from monochromatic neutrals to riotous color patterns. Both stone and handmade wall tiles add texture, as do the many options in relief borders (often with appropriate marine themes). New terrazzo, glass, and concrete tiles are showing up here, too. Custom art mosaics, handmade art tiles, and murals abound.

But even plain, inexpensive tiles can be combined to bold effect. Just mixing and matching among the many available colors and sizes of commercial wall tile provides almost inexhaustible options.

Design strategies depend in part on how the bathroom is used. Is it a master bath, guest bath, or kids' bath? The master bath, increasingly treated as part of a larger master-suite layout, is private, and design possibilities are wide open. Choose any tile that's stylish and practical and that fits your budget.

Guest baths and powder rooms are at least partially for company. These less-used spaces can be places to enjoy working with less heavy-duty materials. These spaces tend to be smaller than master baths, so a little splurge can go a long way.

Children's baths are in particular need of tile's toughness and water-

*Stone-textured concrete tiles are wrapped in square-within-square fashion by contrasting concrete rectangles and small square accents. The glass baseboard shows just how well mosaics can handle curves.*

DESIGN: MINOR REVISIONS ARCHITECTURE & DESIGN. CONTRACTOR: MARK McCARTHY.
TILE: BUDDY RHODES STUDIO/AMALFI TILE & MARBLE

shedding abilities. Have fun, but remember that tile lasts a long time. The cowboy theme that suited your six-year-old might be viewed with great disdain in later years.

**Waterworks.** Built-in tubs are usually framed by three walls that are tiled to the ceiling or to door or window height. If there's no shower head, you could stop the tile at a lower level. A tiled pedestal or platform helps link the tub to the rest of the room. Tubside tile should ideally be watertight, though with a good backing (see page 371) you can also consider the many glazed wall tiles available. Art tiles, decorative borders, and murals help enliven this area.

Built-in showers are ideal for tiling, too, both inside and out. Frame the opening with borders or handmade art tiles; a clear glass door lets you see the tile display inside, too. Unglazed mosaics make a tough, skid-resistant shower floor. You'll probably want to tile the shower ceiling as well— perhaps diagonally, so it won't fight with wall patterns.

For ease of maintenance, consider gloss or matte-textured wall tiles that are tightly butted with minimal grout lines. Plan to install them with non-staining, mildew-resistant grout. Remember that dark-colored, high-gloss tiles can be difficult to keep looking clean.

*A classic monochromatic scheme blends limestone-like field tiles with a border of handmade relief tiles.*

**Floor options.** Bathroom floors should deliver style, protection against moisture and stains, and secure footing. Porcelain pavers, glazed floor tiles, and mosaics work best, but terracotta and other soft tiles can be adequate if sealed. Slate, limestone, and marble are popular choices for elegant master baths and powder rooms. It's best to choose matte textures for slip-resistance, or add mats or nonslip rugs as needed. A light-use powder room could be floored with wall tiles. To keep the floor design from fighting wall patterns, choose a different tile size or lay tiles on the diagonal.

DESIGN: MINOR REVISIONS ARCHITECTURE & DESIGN. CONTRACTOR: MARK McCARTHY. TILE: AMALFI TILE & MARBLE

Installing a radiant heat system under the floor makes a tiled floor more comfortable on cold mornings.

**On the countertop.** Bathroom countertops and backsplashes are two more surfaces waiting to be tiled. Some wall tiles are adequate here (ask your dealer's advice), but be sure their glaze is tough enough to stand up to scratches, household cleaners, and cosmetic potions like nail polish remover. Ceramic and stone floor tiles are generally tougher, and their larger expanses mean fewer grout joints.

Backsplashes are also a good place to add subtle or not-so-subtle art tiles and mosaics. Mirrors are frequently trimmed in tile. Look for color-coordinated electric outlet and switch plates. With a pedestal sink, consider running a tile backsplash to the floor both for water protection and a flash of style. Pedestal sinks eliminate the bulk of a vanity, but also do away with the cabinet's storage space. To compensate, you might want to have a tiled storage niche between wall studs or a tiled ledge behind the sink to house toothbrushes, soap, and water glasses.

**Eye-catching details.** Accessories are the icing on the cake. Examine what's available in ceramic soap dishes, towel bars and hooks, and cup holders. A handpainted ceramic sink might beautifully tie things together.

Remember that some commercial tiles are color-matched to lines of ceramic sinks, tubs, toilets, and bidets.

Bathrooms are tempting backdrops for intricate tile wainscoting, chair rails, and subtler wall patterns inspired by the explosion of new trim and border tiles. But it's sometimes tricky to blend all these tiled surfaces, angles, and corners smoothly. For best results, test-drive your ideas ahead of time on paper or with the aid of a computer. Most dealers can help you work out the details.

*Tile is, literally, everywhere—even on the ceiling. The tile-setters fitted colorful wall and ceiling patterns around a contrasting chair rail and whimsical crown molding. Then they tiled an antique wall-hung sink to match.*

*A luxurious master bath's carved woodwork is enhanced by dark green marble in 12- by 12-inch floor tiles and solid countertops.*

TILE ARTISANS: AHMED AGRAMA & TAMARA HARRIS

DESIGN: TAYLOR WOODROW

*Glass tiles in blue and iridescent black trim granite stripes on floor, backsplash, and shower (visible in the reflection). Floors and countertops are limestone tiles.*

*A master bathroom's open shower/bath sports an eclectic art mosaic and is framed by extruded tiles that closely mimic bamboo. The random-laid floor makes a neutral backdrop, except for the colored mosaic bits.*

*Intricate North African-derived patterns fill both walls and floor, but look all of one piece. The two dominant patterns, on walls and floors, are separated by contrasting borders.*

TILE ARTISAN: MARLO BARTELS STUDIO OF LAGUNA BEACH

*A nondescript family
bath was given new
life with red-and-white
floor mosaics, a white-
tiled countertop, and
red liner accents that
set off the cabinets'
painted geometrics.*

*Large rectangular tiles
of custom concrete resemble
limestone but are easier
to care for. They line the
tub pedestal and walls,
matching the round tub's
cast-concrete deck.*

*Tiled "area rugs"
mark use areas and
lead the eye through a
narrow corridor bath
between two bedrooms.
Each rug's diagonals
and accents are set
within a field of larger
cream squares.*

DESIGN: GEOFFREY FROST/KITCHEN STUDIO LOS ANGELES. TILE ARTISAN: RICHARD KEIT

DESIGN: MALIBU CERAMIC WORKS

Here's some color for a morning wake-up! Vibrant red and turquoise Malibu tiles form an "area rug" in front of the sink; they're repeated in the backsplash above. The vanity front is painted to match.

Existing tiles elsewhere in the house were the inspiration for this powder-room remodel. New Spanish relief reproductions were mixed into the countertop (note the tricky sink cuts), a single-row backsplash, and the mirror's frame.

This master bath, designed to coexist with existing bath-rooms from the 1920s, is a striking example of balanced tile design. Floor diagonals of earthy quarry tile are echoed by diagonals on the countertops and backsplash; green trim tile fronts the cabinets. Matching Malibu designs are used on floor borders and backsplash, and the tub surround is marked by a complementary pattern.

ARCHITECT: REMICK ASSOCIATES ARCHITECTS-BUILDERS, INC. TILE: STONELIGHT TILE COMPANY

*Ancient mosaic techniques*
*are revived in a modern*
*bathroom and tub platform.*
*The inspiration was tile*
*found in one of the oldest*
*Christian buildings in the*
*Adriatic town of Aquileia.*

DESIGN: PAT KULETO. MOSAIC ARTISTS: DELOS MOSAICS. INSTALLER: THORSON TILE

DESIGN: ANN SACKS TILE & STONE

INTERIOR DESIGNER: OSBURN DESIGN

DESIGN: MINOR REVISIONS ARCHITECTURE & DESIGN. CONTRACTOR: MARK McCARTHY. TILE: AMALFI TILE & MARBLE

*This shower* (above, left) *offers a study in patterns: the intricate dividing rail separates the field above, with accents in a diamond configuration, from the square-and-dot pattern below.*

*A checkerboard marble floor (matching the wainscoting) is studded with clear diamond accents emitting fiber-optic light from below—a nice touch in a guest powder room where users may be unfamiliar with the layout.*

*A new shower surround was the canvas for tumbled-marble rectangles laid as a herringbone-patterned field. Staggered spots are one-of-a-kind handmade art tiles. Color-matched grout becomes an active background element.*

DESIGN: AMY DEVAULT INTERIOR DESIGN

INTERIOR DESIGNER: JANNA LUND RODGERS, BUILDER: PHILLIP BLOIS

*Translucent glass relief
tiles with lively geometrics
are sprinkled along a single
row of white field tiles
to highlight a tile-topped
tub surround.*

A tiled chair rail in a make-up area divides traditional wallpaper above from painted plaster below. The rail includes twin cast-relief borders that bound a single row of limestone tiles with glass-mosaic accents.

DESIGN: TAYLOR WOODROW

A tub surround is wrapped in monochromatic splendor, meshing white diagonals, sink cap, diamond trim accents, and relief border. Tan-colored grout relates the tub to the floor tile.

The space behind a pedestal sink can be awkward. Why not tile it for a bit of flash and extra splash protection? Here, the contrasting grid of dark grout between handmade tiles is definitely part of the pattern.

A *tropical fish* (below) *peers imperturbably from the oceanic backdrop of this bathroom wall. This custom work artfully blends both mural and mosaic techniques, as painted pieces follow natural contours instead of a rigid grid.*

This tub pedestal is clad in variegated handmade tiles adorned with traditional Arts and Crafts thistle-design squares. The field tiles run right up to the windowsill, enhancing the built-in feel.

# living spaces

THOUGH WE'RE all familiar with the use of tile in the kitchen and bathroom, why leave it at that? In Europe, the use of tile throughout the home is traditional, and with good reason: tile is durable, is cool in summer, and provides unlimited decorative opportunities.

Places to ponder include the entry, living room, dining room, and bedroom. Great-room layouts can especially benefit from tile's ability both to tie spaces together and to gracefully distinguish them.

**Elegant entries.** Both ceramic and stone offer abundant style options for entries, whether the style is formal or eclectic. The entry is a public space, offering a first glimpse of the ambience within. Why not greet guests with time-echoing marble, rugged but handsome slate, or pale limestone? Hard-wearing porcelain pavers or colorful glazed tile? Or earthy terra-cotta with spot accents, for a welcoming sense of easygoing individuality?

*A flush-mounted fireplace and wood niche are lined with formal white-and-blue tiles.*

Because it's subject to heavy foot traffic, tracked mud, and moisture, tile for entryways should be hard-working and resistant to both slipping and stains. Unglazed terra-cotta and porous stones should be sealed. Both for safety and for ease of mainte-nance, it's best to choose uniform tiles and set them closely together with minimal grout spaces.

**Living-room options.** Living-room tiles also range from formal to funky. Again, stone choices, such as marble, slate, and limestone, lend a formal air; terra-cotta signals "country comfort." There are many new

INTERIOR DESIGNER: THOMAS BARTLETT INTERIORS

options in both porcelain pavers and glazed floor tiles that convey a variety of design styles. Patterns can be quiet and serene or boldly geometric, or they can flow with subtle variations from room to room to link a great-room layout. Tiled "area rugs" help subdivide a large space, and borders similarly confine the eye.

The fireplace is a traditional destination for decorative tile, be it traditional Dutch or English, handmade Arts and Crafts, or an eclectic modern mosaic. If the tile is sufficiently high-fired, it's easily cleaned, impervious to heat, and can even wrap inside the firebox. Build up the mantel or hearth, or embed decorative tiles flush in surrounding plasterwork. Woodstove surrounds are also good settings for tile. But since fireplaces and stoves are finicky beasts, it's best to check local codes for requirements in your area.

Interior stairs often sport tile, too. Risers, the vertical parts, offer almost unlimited options. Sprinkle varying colors or patterns from riser to riser, if you like, or mix random art tiles with bold patterns, glazes, or relief designs. Treads, the parts you step on, are another matter: uniform nonslip tiles with bullnosed fronts or even wood edgings are advised for these areas.

Sunrooms and sitting rooms can benefit from tiled floors or walls that conserve heat in winter and slow temperature swings in summer. The darker and denser the tile, the better: terra-cotta, quarry tile, and stone—all at least 1/2 inch thick—are good bets.

*This colorful entry joins blue granite stair treads with intricate Moroccan tiles in floor and risers.*

**Fine dining.** Don't forget stylish, easy-to-clean tile for the dining room. Rules for living-room floors apply here, though the dining room probably won't see as much use, and thus its tiles needn't be quite as tough. Subtle changes in shape, scale, or pattern can help define this space as part of a multiroom flow of field tiles. Within a defined dining area, tiled wainscoting or chair rails are two traditional ways to help distinguish subboundaries.

**Bedside aesthetics.** What about bedrooms? In today's master-suite layouts, tile can serve as integrated flooring and also as a major decorative element linking the traditional bedroom area with bathroom, dressing area, spa, exercise room, and/or office You can tile floors, headboards, nightstands, study areas, and makeup centers. Installing radiant heating under a new tile floor can provide warmth underfoot in chilly weather.

**All the trimmings.** Flat planes in living areas—walls and even ceilings—provide ready settings for many other tile effects. Base (floor) and crown (ceiling) moldings come in both ceramic and stone versions in a variety of profiles; you can also choose from myriad trim and border pieces (see pages 446–447).

Window jambs and sills, door casings, built-in window seats, and bay-window aprons can all be tiled. Why not add a decorative tiled arch above a bland tract home's interior passageway?

Tiled wainscoting lends a classic flourish to living rooms, and, especially, dining rooms. Or use a simple row or two of tile at chair-rail height, tied to a pattern in the floor or window trim. Repeat the pattern inside display niches or along built-in shelves. Feature prized antique or art tiles as collectibles, perhaps on a picture rail placed out of harm's way.

In the entry hall, a colorful mural or a tiled mirror might make a fresh and attractive greeting for guests.

**Furnishings with flash.** There's an upswing in the number of tiled accoutrements—coffee tables, end tables, buffets, and so on—that are making their way into living spaces. Why not commission a table from a tile artisan, build one from scratch, or dress up a junkyard find with whimsical hand-set mosaics?

Echo this theme subtly in an adjacent living area or dining room to help direct visitors' eyes to your home's interior.

*An entry foyer combines large honed-marble squares with smaller, tumbled accent grids laid in a gentle arc to direct guests inside.*

*A tile artisan has tiled both easy chair and coffee table with exuberant art mosaics. Unlike most mosaics, these pieces skillfully blend both smooth arcs and disks with random broken pieces.*

TILE ARTISAN: MARLO BARTELS STUDIO OF LAGUNA BEACH

INTERIOR DESIGNER: OSBURN DESIGN

DESIGN: PAT KULETO

INTERIOR DESIGNER: OSBURN DESIGN

*A free-form mosaic wraps around the jambs of an interior door; it's made from factory-assembled stone chips premounted to larger backing strips, then fitted and grouted in place. The mosaic mirrors add a flourish.*

*Classical in feeling, this living room is floored completely in stone, with pale travertine rectangles in the foreground, red travertine steps, and antique Balinese pavers in the space beyond.*

INTERIOR DESIGNER: BAUER INTERIOR DESIGN. TILE: ELLE TERRY LEONARD/ARCHITECTURAL CERAMICS

*This Moorish-looking ceramic fireplace is a dramatic living-room focal point. Cast, handcarved sections and many individual tiles were hard-fired, then carefully fitted on-site. Warm light inside the open grillwork reflects off a copper lining.*

*A sitting-room fireplace just off the kitchen is dramatically framed by colorful, custom relief tiles and quieter, speckled hearth tiles.*

ARCHITECT: ROBERT WYLIE

*The fireplace is a highly visible showplace for period styles and period tiles—in this case, a beautiful rendition of Arts and Crafts repose.*

TILE ARTISAN: F. MICHAEL KING

*A tiled insert enlivens the hardwood floor of this Mission-style design. To avoid cracks, it's best to caulk, not grout, any joints where tile meets another material.*

DESIGN: AMOROSO/HOLMAN DESIGN GROUP

DESIGN: TAYLOR WOODROW

*The shapes and colors of tumbled-marble floor tiles and glass accents are reproduced in paint on the adjacent wall.*

*An "area rug" is precisely*
*formed in this tiled floor mural,*
*which blends motifs from both*
*Oriental rugs and Malibu tiles.*

*A striking tile runner,*
*set in quiltlike fashion,*
*fills the interior hallway*
*and foreground stairs.*

DESIGN: BRIAN & EDITH HEATH

ARCHITECT: REMICK ASSOCIATES ARCHITECTS/BUILDERS, INC. TILE: STONELIGHT TILES

Stair risers make a highly visible accent and, because they're not actually walked upon, can feature glazed or relief tiles unsuitable for treads. These handpainted risers link foreground and staircase areas, with treads and flooring of classic Mediterranean terra-cotta.

Like a fanned-out deck of cards, this circular staircase is painstakingly dressed in a warm, earthy mosaic of old Mexican tiles. Myriad grout joints help furnish slip-resistant footing.

*DESIGN: TAYLOR WOODROW*

*Honed, sealed travertine
squares floor a master-suite
remodel, giving way in
the bedroom area to a
large gridwork of cast,
tinted concrete with
tiled travertine frames.
Channels were cut
for the tile strips after the
concrete was poured.*

*Tile can link the wide
spaces of a great-room
design, but sometimes
a uniform treatment gets
boring. In this case, the
pattern alters subtly and
the dominant stone colors
trade places as dining
room turns to kitchen.*

*A polished-marble and
limestone pattern flows
through the entry foyer
and across the front porch
and walk; the exterior
version has a less-slippery
honed finish.*

DESIGN: MINOR REVISIONS ARCHITECTURE & DESIGN. CONTRACTOR: MARK McCARTHY. TILE: BUDDY RHODES STUDIO/AMALFI TILE & MARBLE

*This dining room's
18-inch concrete tiles and
smaller 4-inch accents
have a marbleized finish.
The pattern repeats in the
adjacent open kitchen.*

# outdoor areas

*In contrast to the predictable path of concrete or brick, this path sports custom-painted, randomly placed striped tile squares.*

**T**ILED PATIOS are already common amenities in mild-weather regions. But the use of ceramic, stone, glass, and other tiles is quickly spreading to other exterior areas as we continue to enjoy extending our living spaces outdoors. Often-overlooked opportunities for tile include outdoor kitchens, barbecues, entertainment areas, and planting beds. Tile cladding also brings walls and exterior trim to colorful new life. And tile is perfect with water features: picture a pool dressed in playful art mosaics or in modern glass tiles that shimmer iridescently in the sunlight.

You may find that just a little outdoor tile is a great way to add style and to personalize a tract landscape, at the same time "stretching" the feel of your home's interior space. It's even better if the tile can be viewed from inside, too.

**Outdoor floors.** First think of the backyard as an outdoor room, an extension of interior space. Why be limited to monotonous poured concrete, or even brick? Given the range of options in ceramic, stone, and concrete tiles, it's easy to create entirely fresh effects with a tiled patio or walk. Envision a winding, tiled path to a quiet, tiled sitting alcove. Or try an integrated patio with handpainted decorative tile on borders, stair risers, and a central fountain. Or plan a tiled interior landing that flows through French doors and out into the garden.

You will need to plan carefully. In cold climates, your tile choice must

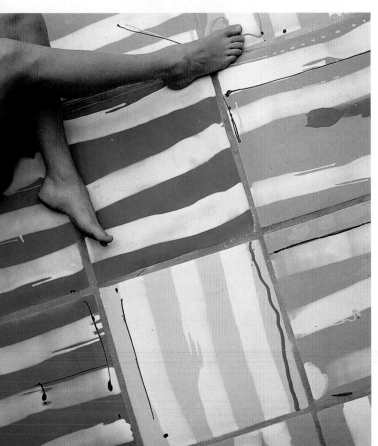

DESIGN: BENEDIKT STREBEL CERAMICS

be freeze-thaw stable. Impervious and vitreous options, including stone, unglazed porcelain, and quarry tiles, are your best choices for cooler outdoor environments. In milder climates, terra-cotta creates an ambience of earthy charm.

Patio tile must also be slip resistant. Matte, sandblasted, and "split" surfaces are workable options. Pavers, glazed tiles, and mosaics now come with abrasive additives for safer footing. Save handpainted or glossy, glazed tiles for small, occasional accents where their lack of traction won't matter. Penetrating sealers can protect soft, porous tiles from moisture and stains.

A tiled patio should be installed over a sturdy base of poured concrete, and in colder climates or unstable soils, over a subbase of crushed gravel. The paving should be sloped slightly away from the house or toward a drain. If you have a boring old backyard slab, you're actually in luck: the base for your new tile is already in place.

**Water features.** Tile makes a great pool surround or deck, provided it's thoroughly slip resistant. Pool steps, in particular, must offer sure footing. Here, unglazed mosaics and glazed tiles with abrasive additives are good choices. The pool edging, or coping, can also be tiled, though poured, tinted concrete is the trouble-free norm. The area just below water level is

*A glistening, glass-tiled spa face works handsomely with both brick and slate in this dramatic poolside setting.*

probably the best place for decorative tile work, such as colorful ceramics, art mosaics, or shimmering glass. Chlorine may react with some glazes, so it's best to consult with an experienced pool contractor before making your choices.

Spa floors, being smaller than pools, are better bets for an overall tile treatment; they're also easier to view. Stone, glass, and ceramic borders are great ways to link a spa and pool, both to each other and to the surrounding landscape.

You'll also see several ideas for decorative tiled wall fountains on the following pages. Go a traditional route with intricate Moorish patterns or formal stone, or get more playful with modern mosaics, glass, or—in mild climates—glazed wall tiles.

**Entertainment areas.** Barbecues, outdoor kitchens, wet bars, fireplaces, and conversation areas all benefit from easy-to-clean decorative tile. Plan here as you would for indoor uses, but be sure to take your climate into account. Don't use soft glazed wall tiles or other nonvitreous types where snow flies.

Tough tiles are especially suitable for countertops on outdoor kitchens and serving tables—they can stand up to both repeated storms and repeated cleanings. And, of course, there's no rule against tiling the top of a patio table or bench.

**Beds and borders.** In landscaping, the use of edgings—the defining trim along garden beds—helps tie together elements of a unified scheme. Why not build them from tile? A tiled garden edging serves the same decorative role as interior borders and moldings, while doing duty as walkway curb, raised-bed edge, or mowing-strip boundary. The tile pattern can restate or play off some tile accent in patio, fountain, or exterior trim. For an even more cohesive look, you can tile a freestanding planter or container to match. Either decorate an existing container or make your own from exterior-grade plywood.

**Wall art.** Walls are traditional garden focal points and offer dramatic expanses for a tile mural, a geometric pattern, or an abstract art mosaic. What about a delicately tiled wall niche? Or a cheery, quaint window box?

Don't overlook the opportunity to work tile into a house façade in the form of window trim, door trim, or random patterns of art tiles along wood siding or embedded in stucco. Tiled street numerals, fence accents, and gate designs individualize the approach from the street to your home.

*Slick tiles can be trouble outdoors, but some new glazed floor tiles are toothy enough for safe footing on the veranda. And while they resemble both stone and terra-cotta, they're easier to maintain than either.*

*This classically casual Southwest patio revolves around a colorful starburst fountain dressed in painted mural tiles.*

*A beautifully crafted stone mosaic forms a decorative "doormat" on a second-story porch; it's surrounded by large squares of limestone tile.*

DESIGN: MONTEGIORDANO MOSAICS

LANDSCAPE ARCHITECT: JEFF STONE ASSOCIATES OF LA JOLLA

*A tiny backyard in a housing-development condo uses saltillo pavers laid atop an old concrete slab. The tiles are grouted with gray mortar and blend with natural flagstones and river rocks.*

*Alternating glazed risers of cobalt blue and playful striped waves are topped with nonslip terra-cotta treads in this outdoor stairway.*

LANDSCAPE DESIGNER: PHIL SNOW

ARCHITECT: ROBERT WYLIE

*A collection of glazed Arts and Crafts-style tiles was the basis for this front-porch remodel. The home-owners laid a commemo-rative tile for each person who worked on the house. These tiles get a bit slick, so slip-resisting mats are added in wet weather.*

*Multihued slate tile wraps an outdoor entertainment space, extending from the huge patio squares over the built-in barbecue and on up the house wall. Note the clean, contrasting borders that trim both serving area and wall corners.*

The pleasing pastels of tiled borders in pool and spa are repeated in intricate mosaic murals behind both fountain and serving counter, pulling this broad outdoor entertainment area together visually.

A water-blue patchwork of glazed tile glows in the playfully winding "creek" that meanders past brushed-concrete spaces to a tiled pond beyond.

TILE ARTISAN: TINA AYERS/GRAPHICS IN TILE. LANDSCAPE DESIGNER: PROSCAPE LANDSCAPE DESIGN. INTERIOR DESIGNER: THOMAS BARTLETT INTERIORS

Iridescent glass tiles dress a classic wall fountain; as twilight falls, fiber-optic strips embedded in glass borders glow and show the tiles' highlights.

TILE ARTISAN: TINA AYERS/GRAPHICS IN TILE

BUILDER: SALVADOR RODRIGUEZ. TILE: OCEANSIDE GLASSTILE

A *tiled water feature*
*doubles as both spa and*
*garden pool. Neutral*
*terra-cotta pavers form*
*a background for intensely*
*colored patterns*
*and borders.*

*More than 20 shades
of blue, purple, and green
tiles, set in concentric circles,
lend new drama to what
was once a worn-out,
white-plastered pool. The
tiles range in size from
1 to 8 inches square.*

*This enclosed front garden's retaining wall features a great view: it's a tiled wall mural. The framed scene is a colorful rendering of a fondly remembered Hawaiian beach.*

TILE ARTISAN: MARLO BARTELS STUDIO OF LAGUNA BEACH

*Tiny ceramic shards add up to form bold, geometric shapes that serve as a dramatic backdrop for this swimming pool. They're weather-tight, too.*

TILE ARTISAN: DEBRA YATES. LANDSCAPE ARCHITECT: RAYMOND JUNGLES

TILE ARTISAN: MARIO BARTELS STUDIO OF LAGUNA BEACH
MEDALLION DESIGN: MATT KENYON

*A collection of antique
Tunisian tiles seems right
at home as a decorative
outdoor wainscot.*

*Iridescent, interlocking
tiles join with cables and
half-round borders to
outline a set of exterior
French doors. Custom
relief-cast ceramic
medallions stud the trim
at regular junctures.*

ARCHITECT: ROB WELLINGTON QUIGLEY. DESIGN: ENVIRONMENTAL DWELLINGS, INC.

# A SHOPPER'S GUIDE

Colorful wall tiles, earthy floor tiles, dazzling art tiles, playful mosaics: with all the choices, it's hard not to feel both exhilarated and a little overwhelmed when stepping into a tile showroom or home center. And ceramic isn't the only game in town. Thanks to current technologies, stone can be a stunning—and newly affordable—tile choice, as can dramatic glass or tinted concrete. This chapter is meant to work in tandem with earlier chapters in the book, serving as a nuts-and-bolts resource to help you implement the ideas discussed in "A Planning Primer." Stimulated by the many colorful installations shown throughout the gallery sections and equipped with this basic technical vocabulary, you should feel comfortable exploring your options and making a final decision. We've said it before but we're saying it again: color, pattern, and texture are only part of the formula for success. The real key is to pick the material that's appropriate for your location. Think water resistance, slip resistance, durability, and ease of maintenance. For information that can help you evaluate different tiles in these respects, see page 356.

# Glazed Wall Tiles

## MIX AND MATCH FOR VIBRANT CONTRASTS AND PATTERNS

ARCHITECT: SUZAN NETTLESHIP. CONTRACTOR: IRIS HARRELL

Smaller, lighter, and thinner than floor tiles, most wall tiles are not meant to withstand either high heels or hot pots. But their lightness is a plus for vertical installation and for cutting, and they come in a dazzling array of colors and textures.

Commercial wall tiles are made by the dust-press method, and the machine-made precision of their shapes works especially well with the clean lines of many contemporary designs. They're usually set closely together, with thin (1/16-inch) grout lines—often calibrated via built-in lug spacers on the tiles' edges.

Although the white, gypsum-based tile bodies are generally nonvitreous (see page 356), the glazing process makes their faces (but not their edges or backs) both water and stain resistant. Water-resistant backing, adhesive, and grout (see page 371) can improve performance, but for vulnerable locations like showers, floors, and exteriors in

*A creative mix of readily available wall tiles and borders echoes kitchen colors elsewhere and neatly ties the sleek hood and cooktop together.*

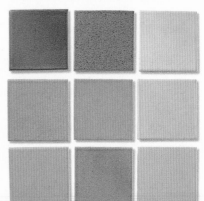

*GLOSS*

*MATTE*

*STONE-TEXTURED*

freezing climates, choose vitreous or impervious tiles.

Increasingly, the distinction between traditional wall tiles and art tiles (see pages 440–443) is blurring, as wall tiles take on both new colors and finishes.

Colors range from quiet whites and creams through soft pastels to glowing reds and deep, intense blues, and if you can't find what you want, your dealer can probably order custom colors. Surface finishes can be glossy, matte, or textured, and glazes can have a metallic, crackled, or brushed look instead of the customary flat color. For a sampling, see the photos below.

Most wall tiles have soft glazes, which are usually not a problem on tub surrounds or backsplashes. A few, with Mohs hardness ratings of 5 or higher, may be suitable for light-duty bathroom or bedroom floors (if they pass the slip-resistance test). In general, the shinier the glaze, the more easily it's scratched.

Some wall tiles are tough enough to be used as countertops. But check with the dealer to be sure the tile's surface can withstand both abrasion and chemicals (the acids in some foods, for example, can etch

*Tile nippers help nibble cutouts and irregular shapes in wall tiles; you'll want them when tiling around sinks or plumbing fixtures.*

through certain glazes, especially those with copper-based green pigment).

Common sizes for glazed wall tiles include 3 by 3, 4 1/4 by 4 1/4, and 6 by 6 inches; larger squares and rectangles

may also be available. These dimensions are nominal and may not be exactly accurate, so be sure to take precise measurements of the tiles you like. Nominal thickness is usually about 1/4 to 5/16 inch.

Prices range from as little as 50 cents per commercial tile to $20 or more per square foot for custom colors or one-of-a-kind creations. Generally, the more tiles of a particular size, glaze, and ornamentation that are manufactured, the less each one will cost.

Remember that you can create complex designs from the most basic of tiles. Commercial wall tiles are easily cut to form variant units that work with basic squares. And because these tiles come in such a variety of colors, they can be mixed and matched to create endless contrasts and custom-look patterns.

Many wall tile lines include coordinated border and trim pieces (for additional details, see pages 446–447). Some integrated lines include matching floor tiles, countertop tiles, and coordinated bathroom fixtures. Some even offer matching ceramic soap dishes, towel bars, and other accessories.

*CRACKLED*

*METALLIC*

*BRUSHED*

# Floor Tiles

GLAZED OR UNGLAZED, THEY'RE TOUGH ENOUGH FOR HEAVY TRAFFIC

Compared to wall tiles, floor tiles are larger, thicker, and more durable. You don't want to use wall tiles on floors, but many floor tiles can also be suitable for countertops and walls.

Floor tiles come glazed or unglazed. Unglazed tiles are generally less slippery and don't show wear as much since their coloration extends throughout the clay body. They are, however, more subject to staining.

Precise terms for floor tiles are hard to corral, as descriptive terms like "paver," "glazed," and "handmade" seem to have different meanings in different locales, and even on opposite sides of the dealer's aisle! With that said, there are basically four types you're likely to encounter: quarry tiles, porcelain pavers, glazed floor tiles, and terra-cotta tiles—each distinguished by its composition and method of manufacture.

*PORCELAIN PAVERS*

## Quarry tiles

These sturdy tiles are made by the extrusion process—you can usually identify them by roller grooves on their backs. Though some quarry tiles are glazed, most come unglazed in natural clay colors of yellow, brown, rust, or red. Some exhibit "flashing," heat-produced shadings that vary from tile to tile. Most quarry tiles are vitreous, making them hardworking and stable outdoors.

Typical sizes are 6 by 6, 8 by 8, and 12 by 12 inches. You'll also find 3 by 6 and 4 by 8 rectangles and a smattering of hexagons. Nominal thickness varies from about $3/8$ to $3/4$ inch.

Though the manufacturing process produces a tough surface that helps ward off stains, unglazed quarry tiles can be sealed to increase stain resistance in heavy-traffic areas.

## Porcelain pavers

The best porcelain is highly refined clay that's dust-pressed and fired at more than 2000°F to form a dense body classified as impervious or vitreous. The waterproof, stain-resistant nature of these tiles makes them great choices for heavy-traffic areas indoors and, if slip resistant, for outdoor patios and walkways.

Porcelain pavers frequently resemble slate, limestone, and other stones, but come in pastel colors, too. While many tiles are polished, more slip-resistant textures include "split" (resembling slate), "sandblasted," and various embossed surfaces with raised grids.

Though 12- by 12-inch pavers are standard, sizes range from 4- by 6-inch rectangles up through 24- by 24-inch Italian *monocottura* (single-fired) squares.

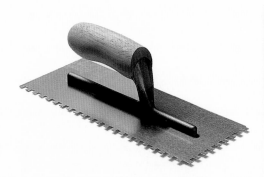

*NOTCHED TROWEL*

*QUARRY TILES*

## Glazed floor tiles

Though they're also called "pavers," the important thing to remember about floor tiles termed "ceramic" or "glazed" is that they're made of high-fired, dust-pressed clay that becomes vitreous or semivitreous. Unlike the extrusion grooves on a quarry tile, raised dots or grids appear on the backs of these.

Of course, there are glazed tiles for walls as well as floors, but floor tiles generally have much tougher glazes. These tiles are often rated for durability: for a heavy-traffic area, choose a tile with an Abrasive Wear Index rating of 3 or higher and a Mohs hardness rating of 7 or 8.

Typical sizes are 8 by 8 and 12 by 12 inches. Nominal thickness is about $5/16$ inch.

Some glazed floor tiles have textured or matte surfaces for better traction and longer wear. They're also increasingly available in stonelike textures and finishes built up from multilayer glazes, some looking remarkably like the real thing. Special nonslip tiles have abrasive additives in their glazes. Still, some experts say, "If it's glazed, don't use it in wet areas."

*GLAZED FLOOR TILES*

## Terra-cotta

Translated from the Italian, *terra-cotta* means "cooked earth." But whether you see terra-cotta in antique French folk tile, hand-formed Mexican slabs, or rustic Italian or Portuguese wares, the charm of this material lies in its very lack of consistency. Unless tiles have been whitewashed or stained, the surface color goes all the way through the clay. Terra-cotta tiles come as squares, rectangles, hexagons, and octagons, as well as in Moorish, ogee, and other interlocking shapes.

Terra-cotta tiles are nonvitreous and highly absorbent, and so are questionable for outdoor use in freezing climates. They also need to be sealed (see facing page) for protection against surface

water and stains. Some quarry tiles mimic the look of terra-cotta (though without its quirky charm) and can substitute for it in high-traffic or wet areas.

Saltillo tiles (named for the area in Mexico where they are made) are especially popular in the Southwest and West, where their rugged, earth-toned honesty seems culturally at home. Here, the clay is hand-packed into wooden or metal frames, set in the sun to dry, then given a low-temperature firing. Lime holes or "pops," dinged corners, variations in size and thickness, color differences from firing—all these variables lend a homey individuality to their look. So-called "super saltillos" have rounded edges that help reduce chipping.

*HEXAGONS WITH GLAZED DOTS*

*TERRA-COTTA TILES*

*ANTIQUE FRENCH PAVERS*

# TO SEAL OR NOT TO SEAL?

In most cases, you needn't seal a floor tile that's glazed. Most impervious and vitreous tiles don't need sealing, either. The prime candidates for sealers are unglazed terra-cotta and some quarry tiles.

In the past, terra-cotta tiles were finished with built-up layers of beeswax or similar coatings which, over time, produced a leatherlike patina. Modern sealers break down into surface and penetrating types.

Surface or top sealers offer more resistance to stains but darken tiles and produce a sheen that may or may not be appealing; they also must be stripped and reapplied periodically.

Penetrating sealers soak into the tile instead of coating its surface. But they're not as protective as top sealers.

Some floor tiles, such as saltillos, are available presealed; others must be sealed on site. Unless you've used an epoxy grout (see page 371), the grout lines may need sealing as well. In this case, grout is often sealed at the same time as the tiles. While it's possible to "paint" sealer onto grout spaces only, this is an extremely tedious process.

Because it's unwise to use toxic sealers around food, most tile experts warn against choosing countertop tiles that require resealing. Some quarry tiles can give you the earthy look of terra-cotta in your kitchen without the sealer danger and maintenance problems. Sealer technology is changing all the time, and some proprietary formulas vary from region to region. What's the lesson? Always explain your installation and ask a knowledgeable dealer for specifics. And be sure to inquire about maintenance requirements.

Whatever sealer you select, it's best to test its appearance on a sample tile before applying it to your floor.

*A stacked pair of saltillo tiles shows the contrast between an unsealed unit* (top) *and the shiny, presealed version* (bottom).

# Art Tiles

TAKE YOUR PICK: FAITHFUL PERIOD PIECES OR BOLD, MODERN DESIGNS

Much of the energy of today's tile renaissance comes from the recent explosion of interest in decorative art tiles, both original designs and recreations of traditional styles.

Aside from its visual and tactile appeal, tile can be a powerful way to allude to period or regional styles, and in this respect a few art tiles or a handpainted mural can go a long way toward setting the decorative tone for an entire room. You can choose handmade tiles with softly irregular shapes to create folk or historical allusions, or

*The tiles shown here and on the facing page give a glimpse of your options, including both hand- and machine-formed tiles decorated in styles from naturalistic to abstract.*

crisp, machine-made patterns to support a high-tech contemporary look. The gamut runs from charmingly pictorial to dynamically abstract designs.

## A rainbow of options

Some art tiles are faithful reproductions of traditional Arts and Crafts, Victorian, or Moorish-inspired designs; others create more exuberant looks that respectfully acknowledge their ancestors but make fresh departures. Still others strike out to create bold, contemporary graphics. A cross section of styles is shown on these pages.

Decorative tiles are generally nonvitreous like glazed wall tiles. Many have glazes that are easily scratched. Traditionally, they've clad fireplace surrounds, stair risers, courtyard fountains, even patio walls in temperate climates. Modern uses include service as kitchen and bath backsplashes, vent hoods, window trim, tub surrounds, and walk-in showers.

Though some art tiles can be used as floor accents, most (with the notable exceptions of encaustic tiles and some decorative terra-cotta) are not meant to handle foot traffic.

Some historic patterns were created from linoleum-block carvings impressed in the clay. Others used wax-based resist lines as barriers between glazes in different colors.

Today, some manufacturers mold their tiles by hand, but others machine-press the clay. Handmade tiles are usually more prized than machined tiles, with "relaxed" shapes and rounded corners, plus variations in size and thickness. These idiosyncrasies,

signs of the individuality of the artisan's hand, are part of such tiles' appeal.

Whether the clay body is formed by hand or machine, the depths and nuances of some art tile glazes are nothing short of magic. Glazing formulas and firing times and temperatures are closely guarded secrets; some art tiles may be glazed and refired eight or nine times.

Handpainted tiles are typically decorated in a labor-intensive fashion,

with small brushes used to apply the color. Other patterns are silk-screened. Some makers use multiple layers and multiple firings to build colors, and others separate them by using wax borders. Less expensive offerings may use applied decals instead.

Art tiles with raised profiles are termed *relief* tiles; those with indentations are called *counter-relief*. Sturdy *encaustic* tiles, used since the days of England's great cathedrals, fill this recess with a contrasting color of liquid clay, called a *slip*.

Most art tile producers are small operations, making their tiles to order. However, larger manufacturers are jumping on the bandwagon, offering a growing variety of art-look machine-made tiles and borders.

*Elegant art tile textures include an etched-copper patina* (below, top), *glossy relief pattern with matching borders* (below, bottom), *and a traditional encaustic design with contrasting clays* (below, right).

## Decorative murals

Tile murals come in two basic types: individual "sheet" murals and large scenes built up from numerous individual tiles. Many murals in showrooms are coordinated with plain field tiles, and some lines also offer border tiles and corner trim.

Most traditional tile murals are built up from numerous individual tiles, handpainted or silk-screened as one, then separated, numbered, and reassembled. Perennial motifs include floral bouquets, fruits and vegetables, animals, and nature scenes. But there's no reason to stop with such subjects: tile showrooms often work with local artisans to custom-design handpainted murals. Treatments can be conservative to whimsical to wild!

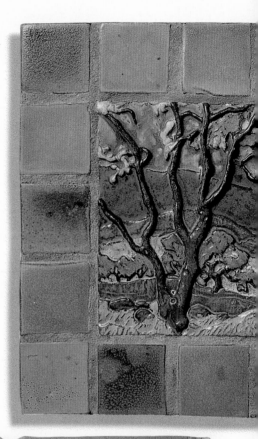

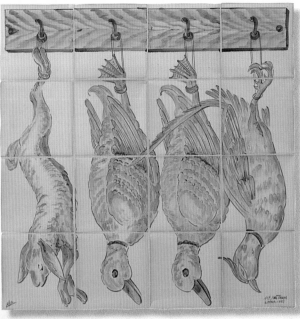

*The decorative Arts and Crafts mural (above, left) is all of a piece. Handpainted Portuguese tiles (above) and sunflowers (left) are assembled from prematched, individual tiles. A photo-mural (below) pairs a light-sensitive emulsion layer with a protective top glaze.*

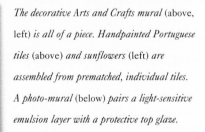

# Ceramic Mosaics

### SHOP FOR PREMOUNTED PATTERNS OR ONE-OF-A-KIND ARTWORKS

Ceramic mosaics are among the most colorful and versatile materials in the tile family. Mosaic tiles look striking on floors and walls, and the smaller ones can wrap around columns or follow the contours of garden walls and swimming pools.

Mosaics come either as premounted, factory-made patterns or as one-of-a-kind, free-form artworks designed and built from scratch.

## Manufactured mosaics

When it comes to commercial products, the term "mosaic" means any very small tile from 3/4 by 3/4 inch up to about 2 by 2 inches. Shapes include squares, rectangles, octagons, hexagons, and special designs.

These small tiles are mounted together on a common backing in larger sections—typically 12 by 12 inches or 12 by 24 inches—and in numerous patterns and grids (grout spacings are included). Backings may be nylon, plastic, or paper; several are shown at right. Most mosaics are meant to be aligned with adjacent panels, then simply pressed into adhesive and grouted when dry. Some, however, are front-mounted: the paper is sponged or peeled away once the adhesive sets.

Mosaics can be of natural clay tile or hard porcelain and are available both glazed and unglazed. Scratch-resistant, unglazed versions are best for floors and countertops; in these,

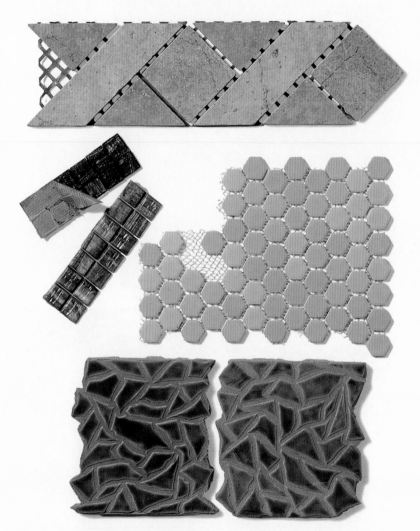

*Premounted products range from tried-and-true squares and octagons to broken shapes that mimic the look of free-form art mosaics. Backings include nylon, plastic, and paper.*

the color is integrated with the wet bisque. Most mosaics are either impervious or vitreous. This, plus the natural slip resistance provided by myriad grout joints, makes them excellent choices for water-susceptible locations in bathrooms and kitchens and outdoors. Some mosaics contain a nonslip

additive for additional safety.

Because of the new-found popularity of free-form or "art" mosaics, you can often order custom designs and decorations premounted at the factory. You may also wish to take a look at mosaics made from stone (see page 451) and glass (page 452).

## Art mosaics

The one-of-a-kind look of free-form design is partly responsible for the current enthusiasm for mosaics and for art tiles in general. Some mosaic works are collages of found materials that might blend bits of smashed tile, shards of pottery or table china, broken glass, pebbles, even marbles. The look can be representational or gleefully abstract.

Most art mosaics are very labor-intensive, so they tend to be expensive. Some are first laid out in factory or studio, mounted on backing sections, moved to the site, and installed. Others are done completely on-site. Dissimilar materials are "floated" to varying depths in a thick layer of "mud" (mortar); the mortar becomes an integral part of the design.

*These two mosaics have the look of one-of-a-kind artworks but can be ordered through a tile showroom. The playful swirls (top) leave plenty of space for contrasting grout, making it an integral part of the pattern. The twin trout (left) are swimming through a mosaic that artfully follows their contours, not those of randomly smashed pieces.*

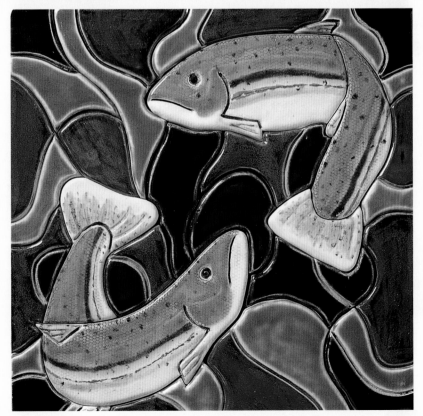

# Borders & Trim

## FINISHING TOUCHES FROM ROPES TO LINERS TO BULLNOSES

Both borders and trim tiles accent and finish off installations of field tiles, particularly on walls and countertops. What's the difference? Borders set off transitions between spaces or between materials and draw the eye to highlighted areas. Offerings include relief tiles, handpainted tiles, and other treatments borrowed from art tiles. Trim tiles, however, are made to blend in with field tiles and finish off the open edges, ends, and corners of those installations.

Many commercial wall tiles come with corresponding trim and coordinated borders. When you're considering a field tile, take a look at these options. Or check borders that match a similar line but work effectively with your selection.

### Borders and more borders

Relief-tile borders can be boldly playful or quietly monochromatic, adding the visual interest of contrasting texture with or without contrasting color.

A selection of shapes and styles is shown on the facing page. Typically, border tiles are more expensive than field tiles.

Most border tiles come in small sections, typically 6 inches long, and are meant to be lined up and grouted like field tiles. Usually, they're staggered so that grout spaces offset field tiles—otherwise, they'd probably be at least a distracting hair off.

Some border tiles double as trim tiles—for example, those used at the top of a wainscot or chair rail. You'll also find ceramic versions of traditional wood moldings, including profiles for base, crown, and chair rail uses.

### Trim tiles

Unlike border tiles, which are primarily decorative, trim tiles are designed to finish off the raw or cut edges of wall or countertop tiles, which are typically unglazed or uncolored.

Trim tiles come in two basic families: surface and radius. Common profiles include bullnose (rounded edge),

*Utilitarian trim tiles* (left) *finish off raw edges, ends, and corners; borders* (facing page) *are unabashedly decorative.*

## TILE ACCESSORIES

Some wall tiles have matching glazed ceramic accessories—soap dishes, towel bars, and glass and toothbrush holders. Accessories are usually laid out in advance and installed and grouted along with field tiles; otherwise, a space is left and they're added after the field tiles set up.

If your tile choice has no accessories—or if you don't like the options—you can either pick a complementary line's accessories or simply downplay their need by building in tiled shelves, niches, and towel hooks as you go.

Remember that numerous lines of commercial tile come in integrated lines that coordinate with bathroom and kitchen fixtures as well as trim and accessories. You can even find beautiful handpainted sinks that match handsome art tiles—though often at a handsome price, too.

down-angle (two rounded edges), cove, quarter-round, half-round, V cap, end cap, and sink corner.

*Surface* trim completes the edges and corners where field tiles were applied directly to a flat wall or countertop surface. It's generally only the thickness of a standard tile. *Radius* trim takes a bigger bend to cover the exposed edge of the substrate below—as when a wainscot of concrete backerboard ends halfway up a wall. Radius trim is also

used at the front edge of a countertop to provide a thicker, more substantial bullnose than surface trim would.

What if the field tile you like doesn't come with trim? Look for a complementary trim in another line; miter (cut) field tiles to turn corners; or opt for unglazed field tiles that have consistent color on their edges and cut surfaces. Tiles with integral color can also be honed or ground to form a bevel or curve.

# Stone Tiles

NEW TECHNIQUES MAKE THEM BEAUTIFUL, PRACTICAL, AND AFFORDABLE

*STONE TILES AND TRIM*

New diamond-saw techniques have made stone tiles, once a luxury, competitive in price with quality ceramic products. Consider stone anywhere you'd use ceramic—for example, on entry floors, patios, kitchen countertops, bathroom wainscots, and backsplashes. Though some natural stone absorbs water and stains readily, new sealers (see pages 450–451) are improving resistance.

Stone tile is installed in a similar manner to ceramic, though variations in size, thickness, and strength can make it a little trickier to work with. When shopping, remember that these tiles are natural, one-of-a-kind products, and be sure to order extra—you can't match them later.

## Stone types

Natural stone falls into one of three general categories: igneous, sedimentary, or metamorphic. *Igneous* rock is hardest, being formed from molten material below the earth's surface under tremendous heat and pressure. *Sedimentary* stones are softest, as they consist of stratified layers of ancient marine or sand deposits. *Metamorphic* rocks are sedimentary in origin, but have undergone changes from heat and pressure that have made them tougher—and sometimes more brittle.

■ **GRANITE** is a hard, close-grained igneous rock that comes in hues from salt-and-pepper gray through rich rust tones to black. Granite is the densest of stone tiles, the equivalent of vitre-

ous ceramic in wear and water resistance. Though costly, it's popular—and appropriate—for tub surrounds, walk-in showers, and countertops.

■ **MARBLE,** an elegant metamorphic rock, offers tremendous variety in color and veining, but is somewhat softer and weaker than granite and more susceptible to stains. It should be sealed when used in wet areas.

■ **LIMESTONE,** usually creamy white to soft gold-beige, is a sedimentary rock that's gaining in popularity as new sealers come on the market. More porous than either granite or marble, limestone must be sealed to prevent unsightly staining.

■ **SLATE** is a traditional, metamorphic choice that tends to split along natural grains and fissures, producing a rustic surface that's appropriate indoors and out. It can also be polished or honed like marble.

■ **TRAVERTINE** is a limestone that's formed near underground springs. Its natural pits may collect grout when installed, and water later; for wet areas, consider a "filled" version.

■ **ONYX** sports rich, swirling amber pockets and quartz veining. Too temperamental and pricey for some applications, it's often reserved for showy but low-maintenance areas.

■ **QUARTZITE** is a pebbly metamorphic rock that's formed from sandstone. Less common than other stone options for tile, quartzite is tough as well as good-looking.

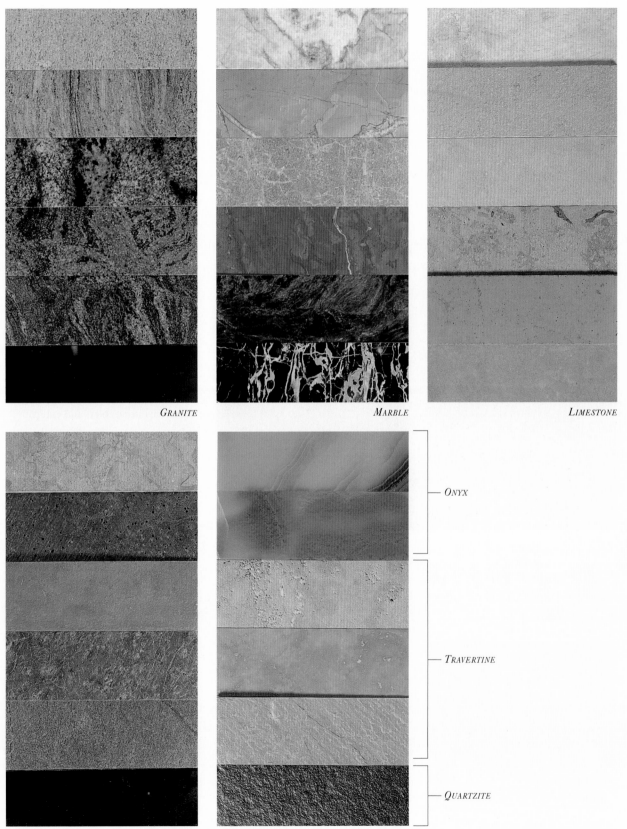

GRANITE

MARBLE

LIMESTONE

ONYX

TRAVERTINE

QUARTZITE

SLATE

*Popular stone textures* (shown above counter-clockwise, from bottom to top) *include polished, honed, tumbled, sandblasted, resplit, and flamed. A striking laser-jet inlay is shown below.*

*Honing* is like reverse polishing—producing a surface that is smooth but less shiny and slippery than that of polished stone.

The popular *tumbled* finish is produced by jostling marble tiles in a machine until they take on a rounded, chalky, antiqued look.

*Resplit* tiles show a cleft, craggy face; *flamed* surfaces are craggy but rounded; and *sandblasted* tiles have a uniform, pebbly surface.

In addition, you'll also find *resawn* faces—a rougher, slip-resistant variation of honed tiles that plainly shows the circular path of the diamond-tipped saw blade.

Chemical treatments include intentional etching (with a muriatic acid solution) which produces dramatic effects, and color enhancing which highlights or darkens stone colors and grains.

Laser-jet technology has made it possible to design and produce striking "inlay" pictures and patterns such as the one shown below left.

## What about sealers?

Like porous ceramic tiles, those made from soft stones, such as marble, need to be sealed against staining and acid damage.

At the very least—and even if you don't mind a little patina—you should apply a stone soap. If you seal with a stone soap, use the same product for routine cleaning.

To better resist surface staining and etching, apply a penetrating sealer and then a hard wax, such as carnauba wax, or a newer natural-synthetic blend. This treatment will buy you some time to clean up spills that could etch through the wax and into the stone.

## New textures, new technologies

Polished marble is the traditional, elegant option for a formal entryway or living room. And although polished surfaces tend to dull and show wear most easily, they can be repolished by professionals.

Other, rougher textures have recently been gaining prominence—partly for their slip resistance, but also for easier maintenance and for the matte, pastel looks they can produce. Several treatments are shown above—including honing, tumbling, flaming, sandblasting, and resplitting.

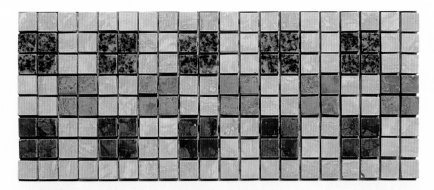

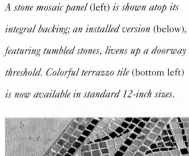

*A stone mosaic panel* (left) *is shown atop its integral backing; an installed version* (below), *featuring tumbled stones, livens up a doorway threshold. Colorful terrazzo tile* (bottom left) *is now available in standard 12-inch sizes.*

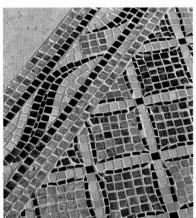

can be installed like stone or ceramic. Usually terrazzos don't have the toughness or color retention of true stone; but they're admirable recycled products, and newer versions are constantly improving in durability.

## Stone mosaics

The tradition of stone mosaics is undergoing a rebirth. Just as with ceramic mosaics (see pages 444–445), stone mosaics come in two types: the premounted composition on backing, and the custom art piece put together from scratch in a studio or on-site.

Stone showrooms can help you select and custom-order a mosaic that's made in a factory or studio, mounted on manageable sections that are numbered in sequence and can be reassembled and grouted on-site.

New surface coatings that will virtually block stains and etching are being developed, but they're expensive and labor-intensive. Since these new products are both locally based and constantly changing, the best approach is to discuss your specific needs with a knowledgeable stone supplier.

## Terrazzo

Known as a manufactured stone or *agglomerate*, terrazzo tile is typically made by setting chips of marble or onyx in concrete and then polishing the surface. Although commonly produced in large slabs, terrazzo is also available in 12- by 12-inch tiles that

# Other Options

TILES OF GLASS AND CONCRETE DANCE NEW STEPS

Glass and concrete are examples of familiar materials that are being used in bold, new ways, including as tile.

Tile dealers and masonry suppliers may have other products as well. When faced with any new tile material, ask the same questions you'd ask of ceramic. Is it durable? Will it stain easily? Will it stand up to moisture or frost?

## Glass

Artistic glass has, of course, been around for centuries, but not in the many tile forms now available. Glass tiles come in many colors, from primaries to pastels—some transparent, some smoked, some opaque. Surfaces may be super-smooth or craggy. Some tiles have graceful relief designs; others have shimmering, iridescent glazes; still others are handpainted. Many offerings are eco-friendly, consisting mainly of recycled materials.

Most glass tiles are impervious to moisture, making them useful inside and out for decorative floors (if slip resistant), backsplashes, tub and shower surrounds, and swimming pools or wall fountains.

Typically, glass tiles are installed much like ceramic tiles, and are trimmed as required with a wet saw and diamond blade. Most installers

*Glass, whether in the form of mosaics* (top left), *wall tiles* (top right), *or art tiles and borders* (right), *offers dramatic decorative possibilities.*

choose special adhesive and grout when working with clear or translucent tiles.

Glass mosaics, like ceramic ones (see pages 444–445), are built up from small pieces (typically 1 by 1 inch) that are premounted on paper sheets. They're sometimes called *Venetian* glass when made from regular shapes.

## Concrete

The news is out: concrete is undergoing a radical transformation. The drab, utilitarian gray stuff is gaining both muted and vivid color palettes and appearing in interesting, surprising textures and bold forms—including tile. This wonderfully tactile material can be made as slick and shiny as a mirror or as rough-textured and non-reflecting as sandpaper.

The new spectrum gives homeowners exciting opportunities for combining textures and patterns, and far more choices when coordinating a concrete surface with other colors and materials in a room.

Concrete tiles make durable floors, walls, and wainscots and, if carefully installed, are suitable for wet areas. The range of shapes and sizes follows that of ceramic tile (including the ubiquitous 12-inch floor tiles). Most new tiles are made to order by custom concrete fabricators.

Concrete contains natural materials—stone, silica-based cement, and water. Like stone (but unlike synthetic products), concrete requires careful maintenance (see pages 450–451) and even when properly sealed can develop a patina from wear over time.

*Concrete takes on new life in the colors and textures of these custom tiles; with proper care, they go anywhere that ceramic or stone can.*

*Sunset*

*ideas for great*

# WINDOW
# TREATMENTS

By Christine Barnes, Susan Lang,
and the Editors of Sunset Books

Sunset Books ■ Menlo Park, California

# contents

# window dressing

**W**HAT WOULD WE DO without windows? They allow welcome light and air into our homes, expand the sense of interior spaciousness, and frame our view of the world beyond. Windows are nothing short of wonderful!

But for all their benefits, windows present more than a few aesthetic and practical challenges. Uncovered, they admit harsh sun, passing glances, and chilling drafts. Bare windows can also appear cold and unfinished unless they're architecturally noteworthy or located where privacy and light control are not concerns. The latter situation is a luxury, however, and for both beauty and function, most windows need window treatments. How to dress your windows, from idea to installation, is what this book is about.

If you think your options are few—a café curtain, a metal miniblind, a pinch-pleated drapery—you are in for a big, and pleasant, surprise. Familiar styles are still available, of course—rod-pocket curtains, tailored Roman shades, plantation shutters, to name a few. And many old favorites are open to fresh interpretations, such as new patterned sheers attached to sleek hardware, or panels that sport innovative pleats. For pared-down decorating schemes, you'll find a wealth of blinds, shades, and shutters in all sorts of colors and finishes.

Settling on a window-treatment style is only part of the process. Once upon a time (in the '50s and before), the only decision was whether to go with beige or ivory antique satin for the living room "drapes." That attitude has evolved, fortunately, and today's

window coverings are an integral part of a decorating plan, not an afterthought.

To give window treatments their due, formulate a few decorating goals: Do you hope to create a high-energy, high-contrast room, where the window treatments take center stage? Or, do you lean toward supporting-role treatments that blend and harmonize with other furnishings? How do you see color and

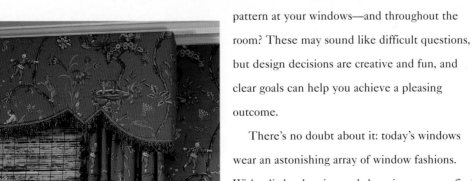

pattern at your windows—and throughout the room? These may sound like difficult questions, but design decisions are creative and fun, and clear goals can help you achieve a pleasing outcome.

There's no doubt about it: today's windows wear an astonishing array of window fashions. With a little planning and shopping, you can find that just-right treatment and add your windows to the best-dressed list.

# A PLANNING PRIMER

Gʀᴀᴄᴇꜰᴜʟ ꜱᴡᴀɢꜱ, relaxed panels, hard-working blinds—behind every winning window treatment is a careful plan, one that suits both the design of your window and the style of your home. If you're not quite sure how to formulate that plan, this chapter will help. Sᴛᴀʀᴛ ᴡɪᴛʜ a style-by-style overview of the possibilities. Then take up color and design considerations, including how to choose coverings that blend into a scheme or command attention. Functional matters count, too; light control, privacy, and safety concerns are just as important as design decisions. Finally, see how different treatment styles look on 11 types of windows. Sᴏᴍᴇ ᴡɪɴᴅᴏᴡꜱ are easy to handle; others are a real challenge. But almost without exception, you have a variety of pleasing and practical choices. Start making plans!

# window wear

**ONE LOOK** *at a decorating magazine will convince you that there's been an explosion in window coverings and their hardware in recent years. To help you make the best choices, look through the following pages to see what today's windows are wearing.*

*Rod-pocket curtains are among the most versatile window-treatment styles, adapting as well to tailored fabrics as to feminine ones.*

## Curtains

The word "curtains" once conjured up images of cheerful cafés or ruffled, crisscross Priscillas. Not anymore. Curtains now come in a wide—and sometimes confusing—range of styles, from sleek and simple to voluminous and structured. Following are the most popular options.

By definition, curtains are panels of fabric gathered onto a rod or attached to it by tabs, ties, clips, or rings. Depending on the width of the panels and the hardware used, curtains can appear full or almost flat. Curtains are sometimes called "draperies," although, strictly speaking, they are not. Draperies are attached to a traverse rod, and you open and close them by means of a cord or wand; if the panels open and close by hand, they are curtains.

**ROD-POCKET CURTAINS.** This well-known curtain style features a stitched pocket that gathers onto a rod; designers sometimes describe rod-pocket curtains as "shirred on a rod." If there's extra fabric above the pocket, a ruffle (called the heading) forms when the panel is gathered. A rod-pocket curtain gathered at both top and bottom is called a sash or hourglass curtain; one that covers the lower half of the window, ending at the sill or below the window frame, is a café.

Rod-pocket curtains are by nature stationary—it's difficult to pull them over the rod—so plan to use them in situations where they will remain in place. The panels may be scooped to the side and held back with tiebacks or holdbacks, or they may hang free.

**FLAT CURTAIN PANELS.** A simple, popular alternative to rod-pocket curtains, "flat" curtains

*Shimmery textured fabrics lend themselves to flat curtain panels. Distinctive hardware is a good choice for simple treatments.*

*Crinkly curtains are clipped to metal rings on wire "rods." Spacing the clips widely allows the panel to droop casually.*

have some fullness, though less than gathered styles. Flat panels are often made of cotton and linen fabrics, but some of the most elegant window treatments consist of silk panels hanging from decorative rings on ornate rods.

**PLEATED CURTAINS.** Is there such a thing as a pleated curtain? Yes, but the difference between a pleated curtain and a pleated drapery is not always obvious. Pleated panels attached to rings or clips are still curtains if they open and close by hand. Confusion arises because pleated draperies on decorative traverse rods (these also have rings) can look just like pleated curtains on rings, and vice versa. You often can't tell until you look up and under the panels to see the hardware. Most of the pleated treatments shown in decorating books and magazines are in fact curtains. (For pleat styles, see pages 462 and 463.)

Linings were once a standard component of curtains, but times have changed, and many curtain panels, especially ready-made ones, are now unlined. That's fine if your room is casual or you prefer a sheer fabric and an airy effect, but review the benefits of linings (page 539) before making a decision.

## KEEPING TABS

Tab curtains—panels with tabs, loops, or ties at the heading—never go out of style, in part because they adapt easily to a wide variety of windows and window-treatment hardware, even whimsical "twig" poles. Fabrics range from nubby cottons to plush velvets.

Most tabs are stitched into the heading of the curtain panel, concealing the ends, or lapped over the heading and topstitched. The latter treatment is often punctuated by a button at the base of each tab. Other variations include tabs that are cinched at the base and tabs made of thin cording or flat braid. Tied tabs form chunky knots if the tabs are short and wide, or drape gracefully over the rod if the tabs are long and slender.

Keep in mind that some curtains with tabs, bows, or knots do not move easily, if at all. Plan to use them primarily as stationary panels, perhaps in combination with a functional shade or blind.

**SLIM TABS**

**TOPSTITCHED TABS**

**SQUARE-BUTTON TABS**

**TIED TABS**

## Draperies

What was once the mainstay of window fashions—the pinch-pleated drapery—has evolved into a collection of designs with imagin-ative and inno-vative pleats. As with curtains, the heading sets the style and mood.

Draperies are pleated panels hanging from hooks that attach to small slides on a standard or decorative traverse rod (see page 543). You open and close the panels by a cord that moves the slides along a track.

Whether you choose a standard traverse rod, which is covered by the top of the pleated panels, or a decorative traverse rod, which is always exposed, depends on the style of your room and the drapery fabric. Standard traverse rods are traditional; decorative models can work in both traditional and contemporary schemes.

Your options in pleats include both classic and current looks.

PINCH PLEAT. This traditional pleat, which has largely been replaced by newer styles, consists of a loop of fabric that's folded into three shallow pleats and tacked at the base; the pleats repeat at intervals across the panel. Crinoline (a 4-inch band of stiffener) stitched inside the heading keeps the pleats crisp. For a more contemporary look, tack the pleats farther up the crinoline. If you like the practicality of draperies but don't care for pinch pleats, consider combining pleated panels with a valance or cornice that conceals the heading.

**FRENCH PLEAT.** Although it's formed much like a pinch pleat, a French pleat features softer, less defined folds.

**REVERSE PINCH PLEAT.** The loop of fabric for a reverse pinch pleat is folded around, to the sides, and tacked at the base for a smooth, rounded heading.

**FAN PLEAT.** Sometimes referred to as a waterfall pleat, this style consists of three folds of fabric, but they are tacked at the top, so that the fullness "fans" down and slightly outward. The absence of crinoline in the heading gives a fan pleat its soft, unstructured look. Extra distance between the pleats creates a free-hanging panel that droops casually at intervals on the floor.

**GOBLET PLEAT.** Perhaps the most formal and sophisticated of the pleat styles, a goblet pleat is formed by tucking or cinching the loop of fabric at the base rather than folding it, forming a cylinder. Crinoline in the heading maintains the shape of the pleats; a newer version, without the crinoline, is less structured. Panels with goblet pleats are not, technically speaking, draperies because they must be stationary—opening them would crush the pleats.

**CARTRIDGE PLEAT.** Smaller than a goblet pleat, a cartridge pleat consists of a loop, usually 1 inch to 1½ inches in diameter, that is neither folded nor cinched. A small piece of crinoline slipped inside each loop helps maintain the shape of the pleats.

**PENCIL PLEAT.** Even smaller than a cartridge pleat, this style is achieved with pleating tape sewn to the back of the panel at the upper edge. Cords inside the tape allow you to gather the heading into narrow, uniform pleats.

**BUTTERFLY PLEAT.** Also known as a two-finger pleat, this style features two folds rather than three. A butterfly pleat uses less fabric and is considered more casual than a pinch pleat.

**BOX PLEAT.** This deep, inverted pleat is another style that's suitable only for stationary panels or valances, not traversing draperies. Because they require firm support, box-pleated panels must be attached to a board.

*Pleats with extra folds of fabric flare at the top. Hooks inserted behind the pleats attach to rings.*

*When tacked at the very base of the crinoline (the stiffener), pinch pleats become long and sleek, an appropriate style for iridescent silk panels.*

*Three small tucks form the characteristic shape of a goblet pleat.*

*Stitched Roman shades (with dowels inserted into the narrow pockets) match painted wood frames. Contrast banding is a traditional trim for Roman shades.*

## Shades

Among the most practical window treatments, shades can be just as decorative as they are hardworking. Options range from soft fabric styles to high-tech versions.

With almost any shade, you can choose an inside or outside mount. A shade mounted inside fits neatly within the window opening, making it ideal for windows with handsome frames. An outside-mounted shade is attached above the window, on the frame or wall, and covers the frame or extends beyond at the sides and bottom when lowered. It's the preferred mount if you want maximum light control and insulation, or if you want to stack the treatment completely off the glass.

When is a shade the best choice?

■ When your window doesn't allow for full, fabric-rich treatments. Corner windows or closely spaced windows are candidates for simple shades, such as inside-mounted roller or cellular models.

■ When you want a crisp, clean look. A contemporary room calls for uncluttered window treatments, such as pleated or Roman shades.

Roman styles include traditional (flat when lowered), soft-fold (forming loops of fabric when lowered), swagged (with tails at the sides), and stitched (often with dowels that keep the folds straight and crisp).

■ When you prefer a natural look. Woven shades bring subtle texture to windows.

■ When you want a fabric treatment, but one that doesn't extend to the floor. Tailored balloon and gathered cloud shades add softness to a room yet almost always stop at the sill or apron (the lower portion of the window frame).

■ When you want to use a minimum of fabric. If the fabric you've chosen is expensive, a flat shade such as a Roman or stagecoach style is a good option.

■ When your fabric features prominent motifs or a large repeat (the lengthwise distance from one motif to the next identical one). Gathered or pleated, such a pattern can look fragmented; shown flat on a shade, the design is clearly seen.

*A woven shade with a self-valance is a handsome treatment for a casement window. Mounting the shade just below crown molding lengthens the look.*

## VISUAL EFFECTS

Are your windows too narrow? Too wide? Do you wish they were set a bit higher in the wall? Designers use a variety of visual tricks to change the apparent size and proportions of windows. You can, too, with a little planning.

The mount, as much as the treatment itself, affects the appearance of a window. Inside-mounted shades and blinds emphasize the actual size of a window (below), or can even make

**INSIDE-MOUNTED ROLLER SHADE**

the window seem smaller—as is the case with sash or café curtains. You may like this effect on a small window in a cozy room.

Mounted outside, most coverings visually lengthen and widen a window (top center). To create an illusion of height, mount the treatment at the ceiling, just below crown molding, or partway between the ceiling (if there's no crown molding) and the window opening. A valance, cornice, or swag

**OUTSIDE-MOUNTED CORNICE AND DRAPERY PANELS**

treatment installed above a window so that the lower edge just covers the top of the glass also lengthens the look. Floor-length panels elongate a window, although puddled panels may make a window appear shorter.

To shorten a tall window, hang a top treatment with its upper edge just above the frame (below), so that the

**OUTSIDE-MOUNTED SWAGGED ROMAN SHADE**

treatment extends well into the glass.

Curtain or drapery panels that almost clear the glass when fully opened can widen a narrow window (below). In the same way, you can make a wide window, such as a picture window, appear narrower by leaving some of the stack-back on the glass. With either approach, it's difficult to tell where the window starts and stops.

Cornices and valances emphasize the horizontal lines of a treatment and can subtly widen and shorten a window. Top treatments with shaped

**OUTSIDE-MOUNTED CURTAIN PANELS**

lower edges, such as a scalloped cornice, lessen this effect.

Where you place tiebacks or holdbacks on curtain or drapery panels is another consideration. When panels are tied or held back high, a window appears narrower; low tiebacks create an illusion of width.

## Blinds

At first glance, blinds appear to be strictly functional. But they can play an important decorating role in both traditional and contemporary schemes. Slat width and material are the defining features.

**HORIZONTAL BLINDS.** Made of metal or vinyl, horizontal blinds come in a wide array of finishes and colors. In metal blinds, you'll find three popular slat sizes. Micro-miniblinds, with $\frac{1}{2}$- or $\frac{5}{8}$-inch slats, are suited to small windows and windows with shallow sills. Standard 1-inch miniblinds are appropriate for most windows and decorating styles. Venetian blinds, with 2-inch slats and optional cloth tapes, can have either a contemporary or a retro feel. Vinyl blinds typically come in a range of sizes.

Wood blinds mimic the look of shutters at much lower cost. Painted, stained, and decorative finishes are available. For an understated look, choose a stain that's compatible with your

*Inside-mounted wood blinds feature a self-valance, made of the same wood as the slats, and decorative cloth tapes.*

*Painted wood blinds make a natty undertreatment for a tab valance on a fabric-covered pole. Mounted outside the window frame, the blinds are concealed when raised.*

walls, for example, a bleached or light pine stain in a creamy white room, golden oak or cherry in a room with richly colored walls. Wood blinds of all kinds can be purchased with cloth tapes, either plain or patterned. Slat sizes range from 1 to 3 inches.

**VERTICAL BLINDS.** Chosen more for their practical features than design attributes, vertical blinds are by nature contemporary. They come in a variety of textures and materials, most often fabric and vinyl. Vertical blinds may be attached to or encased in sheers (see page 557) if you prefer a softer look.

Both horizontal and vertical blinds are fine on their own, especially in minimalist schemes, and many styles have optional self-valances (made of the slat material) that cover the headrail. Often, however, blinds reside under top treatments such as cornices, fabric valances, and swags. Choose a top treatment in keeping with the style of the room—a gathered valance in a young girl's room, for example, or an upholstered cornice in a formal dining room.

## Shutters and shoji screens

In a class by themselves, shutters contribute drama and architectural interest to both traditional and contemporary schemes. Consider your choices carefully; shutters are a big investment, and you'll want to be happy with them for a long time.

Once available only in wood, shutters now come in vinyl as well. The options in vinyl shutters are limited. Solid wood shutters, on the other hand, offer lots of frame styles, louver widths, colors, and finishes.

**TRADITIONAL SHUTTERS.** With 1¼-inch louvers, these shutters are suited to small- and medium-size windows and traditional decorating schemes. Narrow louvers cut down on the light entering the window and block the view more than wider ones, but they provide maximum privacy.

**PLANTATION SHUTTERS.** Wide-louver shutters allow better ventilation and a clearer view

than narrow-louver styles. Types with 2½- and 3½-inch louvers are most popular.

**INNOVATIVE SHUTTERS.** New to the window-treatment scene, these shutters feature materials such as translucent glass, acrylic (mimicking the rice paper of shoji screens), reed, and rattan suspended in wood frames.

Plan to blend shutters with either your walls or, more typically, your window frames for a unified appearance. Play with ways to fold the panels for different looks—open with a slight gap at the center, open but not folded back, or folded back all the way.

**SHOJI SCREENS.** A staple in traditional Japanese homes, shoji screens bathe a room in translucent light. Used over sliding glass doors and windows, shojis either glide in a track or, if hinged, fold back like shutters. The design lines of a shoji screen can affect the apparent proportions of a room: shojis with strong horizontal grids visually widen the window and enlarge the space, while vertical patterns can create an illusion of height.

*An architectural element in their own right, plantation shutters let the sun stream in or tilt for privacy. Fold them back for an unobstructed view.*

*Shoji screens are traditionally used as doors and dividers, as well as window screens. Translucent inserts made of fiberglass diffuse light while ensuring privacy.*

*Soft-fold Roman shades were the inspiration for tailored valances with contrast bands and covered buttons. Adequate wall space in the corner accommodates the folds of fabric.*

## Valances

Once limited to staid, matching top treatments for curtains or draperies, today's valances are among the most imaginative and versatile of window treatments. They are typically paired with no-nonsense pleated or cellular shades or blinds, combining the softness of fabric with the practicality of a hardworking undertreatment.

*Balloon valances with contrast pleats carry out a blue-and-yellow color scheme in a girl's room. Pleated shades hide underneath.*

Many valances are simply shortened versions of curtains, draperies, or fabric shades. Standard valance length is 12 to 18 inches at the center; shaped valances are longer on the sides.

■ Rod-pocket valances are still a classic top treatment for curtain or drapery panels; arched, tapered, and scalloped valances are variations. Contrast banding or piping often punctuates the lower edges of rod-pocket valances.

■ A wide-rod valance is simply a fabric sleeve for a rod up to 4½ inches wide; it may or may not have a ruffle above and below.

■ Box- or kick-pleated valances make tailored top treatments. Box-pleated versions have equally spaced inverted pleats across the valance, with one pleat positioned at each corner. A treatment with a single pleat at the center and at each corner is called a kick-pleated valance. A Kingston (or bell) valance is a softer, more rounded interpretation of a pleated treatment.

■ Balloon and cloud shades in shorter versions are ideally suited to valances. With either of these styles, the poufs or scallops along the lower edge are permanent, and the valance is stationary.

■ Swags (mounted on a board or a pole) and scarves (draped through sconces) are considered valances when they top other treatments. Typically, the lower edge of the swag or scarf covers the headrail of the undertreatment.

■ Stagecoach valances, shortened versions of the shades, can hang from a rod or be mounted on a board.

■ Handkerchief valances, also called pennant valances, consist of flat panels with pointed lower edges. They often combine several colors and fabrics and may be edged with contrast banding and trimmed with tassels.

■ Self-valances, stitched into the heading of a curtain panel rather than hung above the window, look much like a traditional valance when the panels are closed yet leave more of the glass uncovered when the curtains are open.

## Cornices and lambrequins

Used alone or atop other window coverings, cornices and lambrequins are like blank canvases, waiting to be painted, stained, decorated, or upholstered.

**CORNICES.** These structured top treatments serve two practical purposes: they block drafts coming from the window, and they neatly hide the heading and hardware of any undertreatment. They're a natural partner for blinds and shades, which can look unfinished alone.

Mimicking the look of deep crown molding, wood cornices come painted or stained. You can customize some wood cornices with decorative paint finishes. Others are constructed to accommodate standard-width wallpaper borders.

Upholstered cornices give a room a softer look. If your fabric has a noteworthy pattern, a cornice is the ideal treatment for displaying it. You can run the fabric vertically (a necessity if it has a lengthwise design) or horizontally (when there is no direction to the pattern). Running the fabric horizontally, with the selvage parallel to the lower edge, is most economical.

The lower edge of an upholstered cornice may be straight, arched, scalloped, or pointed. Optional embellishments include contrast or same-fabric piping, gimp, braid, and fringe, with

*A straight-edge cornice is a traditional top treatment for traversing draperies on a sliding door. Mounted just to cover the top of the frame, the cornice neatly hides the drapery heading.*

piping the most popular trim.

Plan your cornice carefully; once it's ordered or constructed, you can't change it, even a little. The standard clearance on a ready-made cornice is adequate if it's going over a treatment that fits close to the window, such as inside-mounted blinds. For a cornice over an outside-mounted treatment, such as traversing draperies, calculate the clearance carefully.

**LAMBREQUINS.** Elaborate cornices with "legs" that extend partway down the sides of the window or all the way to the floor, lambrequins are both decorative and functional. Because a lambrequin covers a greater area of the window, it's even more efficient than a cornice at keeping heat in and cold out in winter.

*An upholstered cornice, gently scalloped along the lower edge, is an ideal top treatment for displaying a boldly patterned fabric. A woven shade underneath is both handsome and practical.*

*A black-and-white scarf swag dresses a kitchen window. A casual rosette and jabot trim the treatment at the center; scarf holders support the fabric and form the tails.*

*Silk cutout swags with full-length side panels soften tall windows but do not obscure their beauty.*

## Swags and cascades

These top treatments once graced the windows of only the stateliest homes, but today's versions adapt to both formal and informal decorating schemes. Swags fall into two categories: traditional and scarf.

**TRADITIONAL SWAGS.** Although they appear to spill easily over a board or a pole, traditional swags are in fact highly structured window treatments, each made from a square or rectangle of fabric that's pleated or gathered on the bias. Swags may be solid semicircles of fabric mounted on a board, or they may be open at the upper edge and attached to a pole, forming a "cutout" swag. Use one traditional swag on a window up to 48 inches wide; for a wider window, plan to have swags overlap or just touch. Designers suggest that you use an odd number of swags so that one is centered on the window.

Cascades are gathered or pleated panels that hang at the sides of traditional swags. As a rule of thumb, cascades are at least twice as long as the longest point of the swag.

Shortened versions of cascades, jabots accent swags where they meet.

Most medium and lightweight fabrics that drape well are suitable for traditional swags; avoid stiff fabrics, such as glazed chintz or tapestry, that won't form soft folds. Because the lining shows on cascades, they provide the perfect opportunity to introduce contrasting color and pattern at the window. Accentuate the lines of the treatment with piping or fringe.

**SCARF SWAGS.** These casual cousins of traditional swags consist of one length of fabric draped in sconces or other swag holders (see page 560) or wrapped loosely around a pole. If you decide to make your own scarf swag from a fabric other than a sheer, self-line the treatment so the wrong side doesn't show, or line it with a contrasting fabric as an accent.

## Unusual windows

What if your windows are out of the ordinary? The solutions are varied—and often surprisingly simple.

**DORMER WINDOWS.** These charming windows are nestled into sloping roofs and are typically small, with little space on each side. How much space and how the window operates (most are double-hung or casement) dictate your window-treatment options. In general, stick to uncluttered treatments that require little or no stacking space. Lace or sheer rod-pocket curtains on a tension rod are traditional. For a more tailored look on a window that swings inward, mount a pleated or cellular shade (held down by brackets) on the frame itself; on an outward-swinging window, mount the shade above.

**CLERESTORY WINDOWS.** Also known as ribbon windows, clerestory windows run along the top of a wall near the ceiling. They're effective at admitting light and warmth into a room without sacrificing privacy, and for this reason, they are often left bare. If you must cover clerestory windows, keep the treatment simple—pleated shades, cellular shades, or blinds that stack up compactly, for example. Automated hardware or telescoping poles operate hard-to-reach treatments.

**GEOMETRIC WINDOWS.** When you must cover a geometric window for light control or privacy, choose a treatment that doesn't detract from the window's beauty. Pleated shades, cellular shades, and blinds can be custom cut to fit odd-shaped windows. For an understated look, match the treatment to the window frame or to the wall.

**SKYLIGHTS.** These windows let natural light stream in, bringing warmth deep into a room without loss of privacy. But when there's too much light, glare, or heat gain, skylights require window treatments. Pleated shades, cellular shades, and blinds on tracks can be motorized or operated by a telescoping pole.

**HOPPER WINDOWS.** The opposite of awning windows, hopper windows pivot at the bottom and open inward. Choose a treatment that clears the glass completely when the window is open. Shades or blinds mounted above the frame are practical. Sash curtains attached to the frame allow easy opening and closing of the window.

*Roman shades on guide wires open and close over skylights, allowing full sun or filtered light.*

*Small windows placed high in the wall require no treatment other than painted frames.*

# design decisions

**CHOOSING A** *window treatment sounds easy enough—until you're faced with your own bare windows. Then all sorts of questions come up. As you approach the decision-making process, take a moment to consider the basics of color and design.*

*A pencil-pleated cloud shade (above) made in a traditional floral print is sweet and romantic. Swags and cascades with full-length side panels and tassel fringe (right) are suited to formal schemes.*

## Getting started

You might begin by asking yourself a few questions about your decorating goals.

■ *What's your style?*
Decorating styles, many with exotic and romantic names, fill the pages of home magazines, but for the sake of simplicity, most can be described as either traditional or contemporary. The same is true of window treatments—most can be considered either traditional or contemporary, depending on the interpretation. Swags and cascades, for example, are traditional when they are structured and board-mounted, but casual when wrapped loosely around a pole or draped in scarf holders. Fabric also sets the style: patterned sheers say "contemporary," while their plain, pinch-pleated counterparts serve as modest undertreatments in traditional homes.

Hard window treatments such as miniblinds and pleated shades are generally considered contemporary, yet they work in traditional schemes as well, especially when teamed with traditional top treatments. Shutters and wood blinds adapt to either style; the material, louver width, and finish determine the effect.

To help you select a treatment, turn to the gallery of ideas (pages 486–531) and see what looks appropriate for your windows and your home. The more you analyze decorating styles, the easier it is to make good choices.

■ *What role will your window treatments play?*
Do you envision elaborate swags that take center stage—or plain curtains that barely get noticed? In general, the simpler the treatment and the fabric, the less you will be aware of the windows. Unless yours are noteworthy, stick to treatments that support the room scheme, rather than command attention, and consider your options in the context of other materials in the room. Whenever possible, buy a yard of a fabric you like, attach it to the wall or window, and step back to see its visual impact.

*Unstructured swags with short cascades and long bows top stationary side panels in a mint-green garden room. When window treatments blend with or match the wall color, the effect is harmonious.*

■ *What's the scale of your windows and room?* Scale is one aspect that's easily overlooked when formulating a window-treatment plan. The conventional wisdom is that smaller-scale treatments—shutters with narrow louvers, curtains on slender rods, and flat valances—are best suited to small windows and small rooms. Larger windows and rooms are thought to be the best place for large-scale treatments—plantation shutters, curtains on bold rods, and billowy valances. Although it's a good idea to take into account the scale of your home, also think about the look you hope to achieve. Simple curtains on small hardware will recede in a large room, while bold treatments will advance in a smaller space. Peruse decorating magazines, and you'll see examples of treatments that defy the conventional wisdom, to great effect.

■ *What's your preference—blended or contrasting treatments?* This question is an important one, because how much a window treatment contrasts with the walls dramatically affects a room's ambience. A treatment similar in value

(see page 474) to the walls—pale blue cloud shades against creamy white walls, for example—will quietly blend into the room and put the focus elsewhere.

Another way to blend window treatments with walls is to repeat the wall or trim color—patterned yellow curtains against yellow walls, for example, or ivory-colored Roman shades mounted inside ivory-trimmed double-hung windows. Hard window treatments are often chosen to blend with the walls or trim.

High-contrast window treatments attract more attention and are more difficult to pull off. The treatment may be much lighter or darker in value than the walls, or the colors may come from opposite sides of the color ring (see page 474). Contrasting window treatments will stand out in a room, but keep in mind that your attention may stop at the window. If the view is outstanding, opt for a blending—rather than a contrasting—treatment.

For help in choosing colors, patterns, and textures, see pages 474–477.

*Window treatments that contrast with the walls, such as these ruffled cloud valances, stand out. Be sure to vary the values (lights and darks) of other furnishings and accessories to balance the scheme.*

*A monochromatic scheme works best when you vary the values of the chosen hue, such as the pale green walls and darker green smocked curtains in this sitting room.*

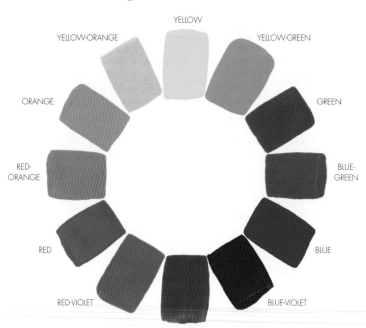

## Color basics

If you think you're not good with color, take heart: a familiarity with some simple color terms and concepts can help you achieve the look you want with window treatments.

**COLOR CHARACTERISTICS.** Window materials offer a wonderful opportunity to pull together a decorating scheme with color. Three key color characteristics—value, temperature, and intensity—determine the impact of a window treatment as much as color itself. If you can learn to recognize and work with these characteristics, you can combine almost any colors in a room.

*Value* is the lightness or darkness of a color. Robin's-egg blue is a light value, and navy blue is a dark value. In between lie medium-value colors, such as chambray blue. When a window treatment is similar in value to the walls—pale curtains in a room with pale walls, for example—the effect is quiet and harmonious. If a treatment contrasts sharply in value, however—dark pleated shades in a white room—the treatment may dominate the room, an effect you may or may not like.

*Visual temperature* has to do with how warm or cool a color feels. Greens, blues, and violets are considered cool, while yellows, reds, and oranges feel warm. For a unified effect, choose window treatments whose visual temperature is similar to that of the walls, such as warm pink-and-yellow balloon shades in a yellow room. The same balloon shades in a minty green room will seem more prominent.

*Intensity* is the brightness or dullness of a color. Apple green is an intense version of yellow-green, while sage is a low-intensity version of the same yellow-green. Almost without exception, your attention will go to an intense color before a low-intensity one. Who pays attention to olive drab—and who can avoid staring at chartreuse? Choosing window treatments that are similar in intensity to the wall color and furnishings is one way to unify a room.

**COLOR COMBINATIONS.** You don't need to know color theory to put together a smashing color scheme, but an acquaintance with the color ring shown on the facing page can get you started. There are three basic kinds of color combination— neutral, related, and contrasting.

*Neutral* combinations consist of black, white, gray, and very low-intensity colors such as taupe and camel. Neutrals are favored for window treatments in subdued schemes, especially when the walls are also neutral.

*Related* schemes are made up of variations of one color (called a *monochromatic* scheme) or colors that lie side by side on the color ring (called an *analogous* scheme). If you plan to use just one color, be sure to use slightly different values and intensities of that color, such as a range of light-to-medium, dull-to-somewhat-brighter versions of peach. Otherwise, a one-color scheme can be monotonous.

For an analogous scheme, such as blue, blue-violet, and violet, consider adding accents of a color opposite on the color ring (yellow-orange, a color you might call "papaya," in this example) to balance the visual temperature.

*Contrasting* color schemes are surprisingly simple to implement. Colors that lie directly opposite on the color ring are known as *complements.* Red and green are complements; so are violet and yellow. Three colors equally spaced on the color ring make up a *triad.* There are other classic color combinations, but in general, if colors are balanced or equally spaced on the color ring, the scheme will be pleasing.

Whether you're working with "givens" or starting from scratch, look to the color ring to help you build a harmonious scheme. If your carpet is a low-intensity green, for example, consider terra-cotta, approximately opposite green on the color ring, for window treatments and, in a lighter version, for walls.

You can also take your color cues from a favorite fabric—many multicolored fabrics are examples of beautifully balanced color combinations. But don't try to match other materials, such as flooring or wall color, to your lead fabric. A little dissonance is more appealing.

Whatever your color scheme, repeat the colors throughout the room. A window treatment whose color doesn't relate to any other element in a room will stand out—or worse yet, look like a mistake.

*Blue and apple green (yellow-green) are not side-by-side on the color ring but are still considered analogous colors. In a two-color scheme, use a mix of patterns, as in this Roman shade.*

*Complementary combinations can be surprisingly soft. Low-intensity red and olive green (a version of yellow-green), near complements on the color ring, are compatible because they are muted.*

## Pattern and texture

Patterned or plain? Smooth or nubby? When to use patterned or textured materials in window treatments is an important decision because both qualities affect our perception of color. A few terms and guidelines can help you combine patterns and textures with confidence.

**PATTERN SCALE.** The relative size of the motifs or designs in a pattern is known as scale. Scale is usually described by designers as small, medium, or large.

*Small-scale patterns* in window treatments tend to read as textured or solid from a distance. Use them with solids or as visual relief among other patterns.

*Medium-scale patterns* are versatile because they maintain their design, even from a distance, yet rarely overpower other patterns. Most patterns are medium in scale.

*Large-scale patterns* may look fragmented if pleated or gathered; be sure to scrunch up or fold a potential fabric before you commit to it.

*One-color schemes like the one below lend themselves to bold patterns. Don't attempt to match the colors in patterned materials— slight differences add interest.*

*Floral and striped patterns on windows and walls combine easily when they share similar or related colors.*

**PATTERN PANACHE.** You'll have the most success with pattern if you follow this advice from designers: choose patterns that are different enough to be interesting yet similar enough to be harmonious. Here's how.

■ Combine various patterns. Naturalistic patterns, such as florals, mingle easily with stripes and plaids.

■ Use a mix of pattern scales—but don't vary them too much. To a medium-scale floral, for example, you might add a smaller-scale plaid. A large-scale pattern and a miniprint may look incompatible.

■ Create places for the eye to rest in the room by introducing solid or textured materials.

■ Distribute pattern throughout a room; if you cluster patterns, the room may look lopsided.

■ Unite different patterns with a common characteristic, such as color. A floral, stripe, and plaid can be pleasing together if each contains a similar—but not necessarily matching—color, such as several versions of pink.

**PATTERN POSSIBILITIES.** Because window treatments and walls touch in a room, it's impor-

*Window treatments
have both actual
texture, which you
can feel, and visual
texture, which you
perceive. A mix of
both kinds of texture
is most effective,
especially in a neutral
color scheme.*

tant to consider the options for patterned and
plain color. Following are the most common
ways to treat windows and walls.

■ Plain walls and plain window treatments are
harmonious and easy to pull off. You see this
approach often in monochromatic (one-color)
schemes. Vary the textures for added visual
interest.

■ Plain walls and patterned window treatments
are popular in both traditional and contemporary
schemes. Choose a window-treatment fabric
or material that repeats or echoes the wall color,
such as a soft blue-and-yellow stripe in a room
with pale yellow walls.

■ Patterned walls and patterned window
treatments work best when one pattern
dominates, such as subtly patterned walls and
more strongly patterned window treatments.
If you use the same pattern at the windows and
on the walls, choose one you'll love to live with.
Used throughout a room, any pattern will appear
bolder.

■ Patterned walls and plain window treatments
work when the colors are similar in intensity,
such as low-intensity celadon (gray-green)
balloon shades juxtaposed with subdued pink-
and-green wallpaper.

**TEXTURE TIPS.** All fabrics possess texture,
from obvious to exquisitely subtle. Hard
window treatments, such as woven-wood shades,
are also textured; even miniblinds have a
"texture," which is smooth. Texture is important
because it influences and modulates color
in powerful ways. On shiny surfaces, a color
appears lighter; on textured surfaces, the same
color appears darker. Yellow silk curtains, for
example, will look lighter than crushed-velvet
panels in the same yellow.

Combining textures, like mixing patterns,
is a balancing act. Here are a few simple
guidelines.

■ Use a variety of textures in a decorating
scheme, just as you would patterns. In a room
with a leather sofa, rattan chair, and handwoven
rug, cotton duck panels are pleasing.

■ If your color scheme is neutral or monochromatic (see page 475), use lots of different
textures, especially if there is little pattern
among your materials.

■ Unite a room by using similar textures. In
a dining room with gleaming wood floors, treat
the windows to shimmering silk curtains. In
a family room with a twill sofa, choose Roman
shades of nubby linen.

*Light streaming
through a split-bamboo
shade casts a pattern
on gingham curtain
panels. Wood beads
visually tie together
the two treatments.*

# practical matters

**W**INDOW **TREATMENTS** *do much more than just adorn windows. For just a moment, set aside questions of style and focus on practicality.*

## Functional considerations

*Gauzy linen panels hanging from square rods and rings are meant to blow in the breeze when the French doors are open. In an indoor/outdoor room, minimal treatments strengthen the visual link between interior and exterior spaces.*

Does light stream through your windows, over-heating your home? Do you need more privacy? Can you childproof window treatments? To best meet your needs, consider the myriad functions of window treatments.

**LIGHT CONTROL.** Allowing natural light into a room is one of the primary functions of windows, and "lots of light" is usually on every-one's wish list for a home. How much light enters depends on the number of windows; their size, shape, and orientation; buildings or plants outdoors; and the window treatments.

If your goal is to admit maximum light, choose treatments that clear the glass when opened or raised. Draperies (with adequate

stack-back on each side) or outside-mounted blinds (with adequate stacking space above) are two options. To filter light and control glare, consider sheer panels, horizontal or vertical blinds, translucent pleated or cellular shades, woven shades, or shoji screens.

The most effective light-controlling treat-ments are outside-mounted curtains, draperies, or fabric shades that are lined, especially those with blackout linings. Blinds of all kinds, when tilted, block most of the light. Some pleated and cellular shades feature two fabrics, one opaque and the other translucent, for maximum flexibil-ity in light control.

**CLIMATE CONTROL.** There's nothing like a breeze through an open window to cool your home. For the best ventilation, choose window treatments that stack back or up completely; stationary panels or deep valances that cover part of the glass will block the flow of air.

You can't consider windows and climate control without taking into account energy effi-ciency (see page 558).

**PRIVACY.** In the daytime, it's difficult to see into a house because the interior is usually darker than the outdoors. Sheer and translucent treatments of all kinds provide some daytime privacy while allowing light to enter.

But at night, when homes are lit, it's easy to see through uncovered windows or windows with translucent treatments. To ensure nighttime privacy, choose a treatment that

*A sheer Roman shade allows privacy and filters light during the day; pleated curtains on rings close easily at night.*

provides maximum coverage, such as lined curtains, draperies, or fabric shades that close or lower completely. Most of the hard window treatments, such as cellular shades, wood blinds, and shutters, also provide excellent nighttime privacy. If you don't like the look of blinds or shades on their own, hide them during the day under a top treatment.

**VIEW.** When the view deserves to be seen, choose a treatment that clears the glass completely; windows with lovely vistas are not the best place for panels tied back low or top treatments that cover much of the glass. A treatment that blends with the walls focuses attention on the outdoors, rather than the window.

If the view is unattractive, choose a white or light-colored treatment that admits light when lowered or closed—and keep it that way. Shutters with narrow louvers and micro-miniblinds are both effective at blocking the view, even to some extent when tilted open.

**SAFETY.** If you have young children or pets, window-treatment safety is a primary concern. Following are some of the safety features you'll find in today's products.

■ Cordless horizontal blinds and cellular shades are available; ask your dealer for product

## MEASURING WINDOWS

To estimate the cost of most window treatments, you'll need to measure your windows. If you order window treatments from a mail-order source, look for detailed instructions in the catalog. For accuracy, use a steel tape measure.

For a treatment mounted inside the window, you need only measure the width of the opening (A) and the length (B). Measure at the top, middle, and bottom of the frame; use the smallest measurement.

For outside-mounted treatments, also measure the area to be covered to the left (C) and right (D) of the opening, called the extensions, and the distance above the opening (E). This distance is typically 4 inches for curtains, draperies, and valances, but it can be less if you want to mount the hardware just above the window frame or on the frame itself.

The distance below the opening (F) varies, depending on the treatment style. Apron-length treatments usually end 4 inches below the opening. Floor-length treatments generally end ¼ to 1 inch from the floor; allow extra length for puddled panels.

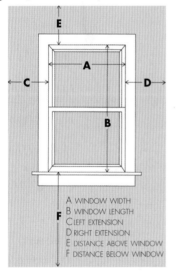

A WINDOW WIDTH
B WINDOW LENGTH
C LEFT EXTENSION
D RIGHT EXTENSION
E DISTANCE ABOVE WINDOW
F DISTANCE BELOW WINDOW

information. With a cordless mechanism, you simply grasp the middle of the bottom rail and lift or pull down.

■ On two-cord shades, cut the cords above the tassel; then add a separate tassel to the end of each cord. Most high-quality blinds and shades come with breakaway tassels, which separate under pressure.

■ For continuous-loop systems, most common on vertical blinds and draperies, install a permanent tie-down device or cleat to the wall or window frame.

■ Replace looped cords with a wand.

# a window-treatment sketchbook

*"WHAT AM I GOING TO DO with these windows?" Whether you're envisioning bare windows in a new home or puzzling over what to do with existing windows, window-treatment decisions do not always come easily. Rather than focusing on the coverings, why not start with your windows? Windows are, after all, the reason for window treatments, and the more thought you give to their attributes (and limitations), the happier you'll be with your choices. Determining which treatments work best on which windows is what this section is about. On the following pages, you'll find 11 window styles, each handled two different ways. Take a look.*

### ARCHED

The arched, or Palladian, window has a long, illustrious history. Semicircular windows, called sunbursts, flourished in the 1700s, and elliptical fanlights appeared later, in the American neoclassical revival. Today's "postmodern" arched windows, popular in new construction, can be integral or have double-hung or casement windows below the fanlight.

Because the arched window is such a noteworthy architectural element, many homeowners choose to leave it untreated if privacy and light control are not issues. Or, leave the arch exposed and treat only the area below with curtains, draperies, shades, or blinds.

Fan-shaped pleated and cellular shades that cover just the arch are available; plan to use a matching shade to cover the rest of the window. Shades and blinds can also be custom-cut to fit an arch, with the slats running horizontally. You can't raise the treatment, of course, but the slats will tilt. Custom wood shutters that cover the entire window are handsome but expensive.

ARCHED

**GOBLET-PLEATED PANELS**

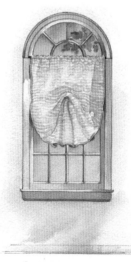

ARCHED

**SHEER LONDON SHADE**

Most fabric treatments that follow the curve of the arch, such as curtains on a custom-bent rod, draperies attached to a wood frame, or simple swags, are stationary and purely decorative.

## AWNING

Like casement windows (see page 482), awning windows are hinged and swing outward. But they're hinged at the top, not on the side, and they're usually rectangular.

AWNING

**WOOD CORNICE AND WOVEN SHADE**

Awning windows come in a number of configurations, all of which provide good ventilation. They typically occur in combination with fixed-glass windows, with the awning portion at the top or bottom of the unit.

Roman, roller, pleated, or cellular shades, along with horizontal blinds, are good choices

AWNING

**ROMAN SHADE**

if your awning window is at the bottom of a fixed unit because you can raise the treatment just enough to allow ventilation, yet keep the upper portion of the window covered for sun control. Avoid treatments that tie back low, such as stationary curtains; they may interfere with the handles. Curtains, draperies, and vertical blinds that stack off the window are other practical options.

An awning window at the top of a fixed window is a good candidate for a top-down/ bottom-up shade, allowing you to bare the awning portion while maintaining privacy below.

## BAY AND BOW

Graceful and romantic, bays and bows are windows everyone loves to have in a home—but few know how to treat. A bay is a recessed window with angled sections; when the sections are set in a gentle curve, the window is called a bow. If the view is outstanding and privacy and light control are not concerns, this is a wonderful window to leave uncovered.

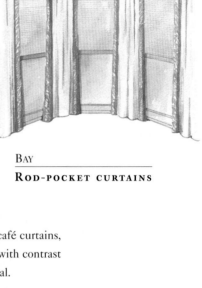

BAY

**ROD-POCKET CURTAINS**

Most bays and bows, however, require window treatments. If your bay features handsome window frames, consider playing them up with individual, inside-mounted café curtains, shades, or blinds. Roman shades with contrast banding are tailored and traditional.

Over simple shades or blinds on closely spaced windows, add a continuous valance or a series of shallow swags. Plan carefully so the top treatment conceals the undertreatments when they're raised.

Rod-pocket curtains and curtains on rings require a hinged, flexible, or custom-bent rod. If there is space, hang a stationary panel between windows and at each outer window. For a bay or bow with little space between windows, flank the entire window area with a pair of panels and top the treatment with a cornice.

BAY

**SWAGS, CASCADES, AND CAFÉ CURTAINS**

## CASEMENT

Hung singly or, more typically, in pairs, casement windows have sashes that are hinged on the side and crank or push outward. In a pair, only one window may be operable while the other is stationary, or both may open. Casement windows often flank fixed-glass windows.

Window treatments that clear the glass completely when stacked back, such as curtains on rings or draperies, flatter the vertical lines of a pair of casement windows and allow maximum light and ventilation. Blinds and shades of all kinds are also appropriate. To soften the look of hard treatments, add a simple valance or a wood cornice.

Traditional swags and cascades are suited to the graceful proportions of casement windows. A scarf swag wrapped around a decorative pole is a casual alternative.

If you prefer to cover some of the window—perhaps the view is not altogether desirable—consider gathered or pleated curtains that meet in the center and tie back low. On a pair of windows where only one operates, hang a single curtain panel and tie or hold it to the fixed side of the window.

CASEMENT
**TAB CURTAINS**

CASEMENT
**WOVEN SHADES**

## CATHEDRAL

Typically angled at the top to follow the slope of the roof, cathedral windows are among the most difficult to treat. If they happen to be placed high, with no possibility of outsiders seeing in, the angled portion is often left bare. Besides, untreated windows allow the most light and reveal the best view.

When cathedral windows top standard-shaped windows, it's easy to cover the lower windows with miniblinds, wood blinds, pleated shades, woven-wood shades, cellular shades, or vertical blinds. Simple curtains on rings and traversing draperies (space permitting) are suitable if you prefer a soft fabric treatment. Because this window is contemporary, stick with a simple window covering and avoid voluminous fabric treatments, such as swags or balloon shades.

Because sun control and heat gain can be major problems with cathedral windows, homeowners often cover the entire window area with individual treatments, such as horizontal blinds, custom-pleated shades, or cellular shades. Although the manufacturers don't recommend raising the shades beyond the point where the angle begins, many homeowners do just that by pulling one of the cords. Be aware, however, that you'll have uneven cords hanging down after the shade is raised.

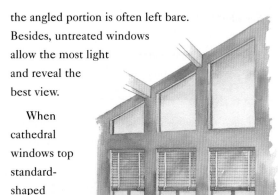

CATHEDRAL (UNCOVERED)
**WOOD BLINDS (BELOW)**

CATHEDRAL
**CELLULAR SHADES**

## CORNER

The two types of corner window are those that meet glass to glass, at a right angle, and those that are separated by window frames or wall space. Choose a treatment based on the way your windows meet and the amount of space, if any, between them. In general, avoid fabric treatments with fullness in the corner, which can make the area look cluttered.

CORNER
**SWAGS AND CASCADES**

Curtains on rings, one-way draperies, or vertical blinds that open from the corner are ideal for a glass-to-glass corner window, whose primary attribute is an unobstructed view. Just be sure the window treatment stacks back completely when opened; otherwise, the window will appear smaller.

CORNER
**SCARF SWAGS WITH MINIBLINDS**

If your corner windows are separated by wall space or window frames, almost any inside-mounted shade or horizontal blind will work—for example, roller shades, pleated shades, woven-wood shades, or wood blinds. Avoid outside-mounted versions unless there is adequate room; when raised, the treatments may collide in the corner.

Top treatments unify corner windows. A continuous valance or scarf swag that turns the corner teams nicely with blinds or shades.

## DOUBLE-HUNG

These are windows everyone likes, as much for their graceful proportions as their hardworking features. Double-hung windows have two sashes—an upper, outside sash that moves down and a lower, inside sash that moves up. Used alone, in pairs, or in groups, double-hung windows allow for almost any window treatment.

Casual curtain options include tab, rod-pocket, and flat or pleated panels on rings. Traversing draperies, topped with a shaped valance or cornice, are dressier. With a curtain or drapery treatment, decide whether you want the panels to stack back completely, revealing the window frame, or to partially cover the glass.

All of the tailored shades suit double-hung windows—Roman, pleated, cellular, and woven-wood. Most shades can be inside- or outside-mounted; with cloud or balloon shades, choose an outside mount to accommodate the volume of fabric.

Traditional swags and cascades are a time-honored treatment for this classic window; scarves are less formal and show off more of the frame.

DOUBLE-HUNG
**PLEATED PANELS**

DOUBLE-HUNG
**SWAGGED SHADE**

## PICTURE

Used alone or in combination with sliding or casement windows, picture windows (also called fixed-glass windows) let in plenty of light and frame the view. Because of the size and shape of picture windows, however, finding the right treatment can be a challenge; choose one in keeping with the proportions of the window.

FIXED GLASS
**FLAT PANELS**

When operable windows flank a fixed window, it's important to select a treatment that stacks back completely. Full-length curtains, draperies, or vertical blinds allow good ventilation when fully opened, and their stack-back helps balance the large window area. On a window without operable side windows, you can leave some of the stack-back on the glass if the view is less than outstanding or if you want to create the illusion of a narrower window.

Consider top treatments for picture windows carefully. A deep valance can accentuate the

FIXED GLASS
**SCALLOPED VALANCE AND PANELS**

window's width; a gently scalloped valance or a shaped cornice that just skims the top of the glass can soften the lines and create the illusion of a slightly taller window.

If you opt for blinds, pleated shades, or cellular shades, check with the manufacturer to make sure the treatment comes in the width you need. For very wide windows, plan to mount multiple treatments on a single headrail.

## FRENCH DOORS

Elegant and graceful, French doors are at the top of the list of desirable windows. They usually consist of a pair of matching glass-paneled doors,

one or both of which open. With outward-swinging French doors, almost any treatment is appropriate. On doors that open inward, however, the treatment must clear the door frame or be attached to the doors themselves.

Sash and hourglass curtains made of lace or sheers were once the standard treatment for French doors. Blinds are a more up-to-date option, but keep in mind that they will move with the doors; attach clips at the bottom to hold the treatment in place. Avoid heavy fabric shades, such as soft-fold Roman shades.

Formal French-door treatments include draperies that stack completely, topped by a matching valance or cornice. Pleated curtains on rings can be formal or casual, depending on the

fabric and the hardware. Swags and cascades require adequate space above so that the lower edge of the treatment doesn't dip into the doors.

French doors often have transoms (windows above) or side-

FRENCH DOORS
**CRINKLY SHEERS**

lights (vertical windows flanking the doors). You can treat the entire area as one or cover each section separately.

FRENCH DOORS
WITH TRANSOM
**SCALLOPED VALANCE AND PANELS**

## SLIDERS

Composed of two or more panels, sliding glass windows and doors are among the most utilitarian of windows. Easy operation should be a primary consideration when you're choosing a treatment for a sliding door.

SLIDING DOORS
**VERTICAL BLINDS**

Draperies on one-way traverse rods allow for convenient opening of sliding doors but require a large stacking area; you may decide to keep some of the stack-back on the fixed portion of the door. Vertical blinds stack back compactly, making them a good choice where space is tight. Like draperies, they have the added benefit of allowing passage without uncovering all of the glass. Another option is a vertical pleated or cellular shade.

If you opt for horizontal blinds, pleated shades, or cellular shades for a sliding door, choose a style that stacks up compactly. It's best to mount two blinds or shades on one headrail, permitting you to raise just the one over the operable part of the door.

On sliding windows, top any of the hard treatments with a shaped valance or simple cornice. Pennant valances, with

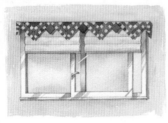

SLIDING WINDOWS
**PENNANT VALANCE**

their irregular points, break up the strong horizontal lines of sliding windows. Shutters on sliders add architectural interest to a room.

## TALL WINDOWS

Windows of grand proportions lend themselves to equally elegant treatments and trimmings in a formal scheme. If the room is large, consider voluminous fabric treatments, such as goblet-pleated draperies or traditional swags and cascades. Even a treatment as simple as rod-pocket curtains looks luxurious on a tall window if the fabric is sumptuous silk.

Tall windows are ideally suited to top treatments over traversing or stationary panels. An upholstered cornice with a shaped lower edge, used in combination with draperies, constitutes a formal, traditional treatment.

TALL WINDOWS
**SWAG VALANCE AND PANELS**

Arched or scalloped valances, sometimes too fussy for windows of lesser proportions, are graceful in combination with curtains. One advantage of tall windows is that a top treatment may extend well into the glass area and the effect will still be pleasing. For sun control and privacy, add sheer draperies or a woven shade.

In starker set-

TALL WINDOWS
**GATHERED VALANCE, PANELS, AND CLOUD SHADE**

tings, tall windows can accommodate contemporary treatments, such as sheer curtain panels or pleated shades. Choose blending—rather than contrasting—treatments to minimize the window's proportions. Use a telescoping pole to operate a hard treatment, or automate it.

# GREAT WINDOW TREATMENTS

It's time to get inspired! And as you'll quickly discover in this photo-filled chapter, ideas for great window treatments are both plentiful and varied, sometimes to the point of pleasant confusion. You can approach your search for a suitable window treatment in one of several ways: You might look carefully at the examples of a particular style, such as a cloud valance or curtains on rings. Does the treatment seem appropriate for your windows? Is it practical for your life-style? Will it fit in with the style of your home? Or simply peruse the pages and see what strikes your fancy among this collection of window fashions. Perhaps you like the softness of lace panels, the elegance of silk swags, or the simplicity of pleated shades. The ideas are here; take them all in and consider them carefully. The perfect window treatment for your windows and your home may be one you're about to see.

great window treatments

# curtain call

These casual curtains appear to fold forward at the top, but each "valance" is actually a separate piece of fabric stitched to the top of the panel. (To achieve a similar effect without piecing, you must line each panel with the same fabric.) Contrast banding emphasizes the edges.

Pleats tacked at the top of the heading fan out for a relaxed look. These unlined linen panels, like the other treatments on these pages, are technically curtains because they are sewn to wood rings and are moved by hand.

A layered treatment
in an attic hideaway
consists of semisheer
and sheer panels, both
pleated and attached
to small rings.

Pleated curtains are
relaxed yet crisp,
thanks to crinoline
(a stiffener) stitched
into the heading of
each panel. Curtains
that match the window
trim blend into the
room for a quiet effect.

# sheer simplicity

*great window treatments*

*An ivory lace valance, drawn up at the center and each corner, bears a slight resemblance to a swagged Roman shade; a smaller, one-scallop version is just right for a tiny corner window. Mocha-colored trim unites the window treatments and walls.*

*Lace panels with pointelle edging hang from tension rods. Flat, rather than gathered, curtains are ideal for showing off delicate patterns.*

*A lace curtain tied to one side covers a plain sheer in an elegant white-and-silver powder room. Subtle patterns and textures, at the window and on the walls, play an important role in a minimal color scheme.*

Rod-pocket sheers are scooped back by the arms of
a wicker love seat. A woven shade underneath is both
practical and decorative.

Gauzy tab curtains
create the perfect
backdrop in a
dramatic dining
room. Short, wide
tabs hang from metal
poles with birdcage
finials.

Fan-pleated sheers
feature a wide band of
brown silk near the
lower edge; a narrow
band placed high
repeats the color and
accentuates the lines of
the clerestory window.

*Loosely woven linen panels, casually pleated at the heading,*

*hang softly from wood pegs. The upper-edge trim and graceful*

*bows are sewn from an iridescent, copper-colored semisheer.*

*Both fabrics marry well with decorative paint finishes and*

*architectural elements throughout the room.*

*A length of fabric, "swagged" and attached to a custom-cut board, follows the elegant curve of a wide arched window. (This treatment is sometimes referred to as a "portiere drapery.") Patterned sheers diffuse light.*

*Striped sheers crisscross at the top of arched windows, then puddle gracefully on the floor. Metal holdbacks gather the panels to each side.*

*Contemporary sheers, slit in a fashion reminiscent of cutwork embroidery, reveal the exquisite lines of French doors and an arched transom.*

# versatile shades

*Copper mesh Roman shades with brass grommets and exposed cords filter light and create horizontal bands of color as they are raised.*

*Fringed Roman shades mounted below elliptical windows are a slight departure from tradition. Trim of any kind can visually unify window treatments and other elements in a room.*

Striped Roman shades keep their crisp pleats by means of narrow dowels slipped into stitched pockets. Repeating the wall color in the window treatments unifies the room and highlights French doors and sidelights.

Stitched Roman shades, with the tiny tucks toward the window, are a classic treatment for tailored schemes. Mounting the shades above the window opening lengthens the look.

*An unlined linen shade filters light and softens a pair of*

*casement windows in a cloakroom; inverted pleats, embellished*

*with sisal buttons, are the only details. A scalloped wood valance*

*complements the simple shade.*

Mounted at the soffit of a bay, swagged shades visually elongate a trio of windows. A single pleat on both sides of each shade helps shape the scallops.

Plain and simple, a burlap shade adds neutral color and nubby texture to a pantry window.

A striped sheer forms its own "trim" at the sides, where the hems turn under.

*Natural shades in a window seat control sun when*

*lowered yet do not block the view. Woven shades work well*

*in a scheme that includes other patterns and textures.*

*Outside-mounted woven shades with self-valances visually unify different, yet closely spaced, corner windows.*

*An antique Japanese shade rolls forward, held up by cording attached to bronze hooks. Silk brocade binds the edges; black tassels embellish the treatment.*

# billowy clouds

*The same floral fabric looks different gathered into cloud*

*shades than it does spread across the bed. Gingham ruffles*

*in compatible colors trim the shades and the bolster.*

Silk celadon shades dress a recessed window and
nearby windows in quiet, elegant color. Thick
welt, knotted at the ends, finishes the upper edges.
Pink-and-green tassel fringe links the window
treatments to walls and furnishings.

A blue-and-white cloud valance, shirred at the
heading and ruffled at the lower edge, is a
romantic top treatment for a little girl's room.
Miniblinds underneath control light and
maintain privacy.

# shutters and shojis

*Shoji screens offer the best of both worlds: when closed, they bathe a room in translucent light, yet they still provide daytime privacy. These screens glide in tracks for easy opening and closing.*

More than just a window treatment, traditional shutters are an important architectural feature in a room. In this tailored scheme, stained wood shutters unify large and small windows.

*Custom-painted plantation shutters display their own color scheme, echoed in the room's furnishings. Painting the frames, slats, and tilt bars different colors emphasizes their structure.*

*Reeded-glass panels diffuse and distort light for privacy during the day. They are appropriate in both contemporary and traditional schemes.*

# top treatments

*Tab-top valances
with short, shallow
box pleats and
pennant points team
with plantation
shutters in a bay.
Tassels punctuate
the lower edges.*

*A bright cloud valance on a
wide rod sports a contrasting
rod pocket and ruffle; narrow
gold welt and puffy stars trim
the treatment.*

*Matching fabric ties hold up an
outside-mounted stagecoach
valance. (Notice that the pattern
aligns on the ties and the face of
the shade.) Stained wood blinds
with cloth tapes echo colors in
the botanical fabric.*

*Tall windows and high ceilings accommodate fabrics with large-scale patterns, such as this multicolored cornucopia print. (Careful centering of motifs is a must with large-scale patterns.) Woven shades underneath the balloon valances and on the door do the real work.*

*A balloon valance made of crinkly silk frames the view in a stunning bow window. Sumptuous fabrics and trims turn simple styles into elaborate treatments.*

*Pleated bells add classic detailing to a tapered Kingston valance (also called a bell valance). The lower edge just skims the top of the window, allowing the most light and the best view.*

*Cascades and stationary side panels turn a tapered Kingston valance into an elaborate, formal treatment. Italian tapestry trims the edges.*

*his "green room" is dressed in a Kingston valance and lacy shades, all trimmed in green gingham. Individual shades are ideal in a bay; the continuous valance ties together the treatment.*

*Gently gathered and
scalloped silk valances
top matching side
panels in a grand
dining room.
Mounting the top
treatments just below
the crown molding
allows the handsome—
and different—
transom windows to
show. Woven shades
make practical
undertreatments.*

*A box-pleated
valance, ever so
slightly gathered, and
matching side panels
cover a pair of
casement windows.
The spacing of the
embroidered motifs
determined the size of
the pleats.*

*An upholstered cornice doubles as a shelf and a
top treatment for a banded Roman shade.
Textured, tone-on-tone fabrics add visual interest
to a neutral scheme.*

*A marbleized wood
cornice with gold
highlights is the focal
point of this sleek
curtain treatment. The
rod-pocket panels are
made of antique satin,
trimmed with a
contrast fabric and
tied back with cord
and tassels.*

*A shaped cornice finished with self-welt
follows the line of a noteworthy transom window.
Matching Roman shades mounted on French doors
control light and ensure privacy.*

Casually gathered, these traditional swags and cascades are nevertheless formal. A small center swag balances the outer ones in the starring treatment; stationary side panels are held back low. Single swags are in scale with smaller windows.

A "country" fabric goes formal when made into traditional cutout swags. The treatment appears to be continuous, but it's just an illusion—each swag is constructed and attached separately. Stationary side panels frame the window.

A straight cornice
edged with welt
provides the backdrop
for a series of
overlapping swags.
Because the French
doors open inward,
the entire top
treatment must clear
the frame. Stationary
side panels feature
bishop's sleeves.

# pattern play

*A blue-and-yellow toile pattern has a different look on walls, windows, and beds. Swagged valances trimmed in tassel fringe team with sheer white shades with slats that tilt like blinds.*

*Dressing the walls, windows, and bed in the same quiet fabric is a recipe for tranquility. Stripes accentuate the graceful lines of traditional swags and cascades. Shutters are appropriate companions for soft fabric treatments.*

*Nearly identical patterns (one is checked, the other not) adorn the windows and walls in a bedroom hideaway. Fan-pleated curtains on rings are trimmed with tassel fringe and tied back low.*

*great window treatments*

# yellow is primary

*Gathered "pleats" give curtains on rings their fullness
and shape. Gingham welt and lining complement
the floral pattern; a Roman shade is a practical and
decorative undertreatment.*

*Cloud shades made of silk taffeta contrast quietly with
green walls and white trim in a formal sitting room.
Lace sheers dress the French doors.*

*Bright, bold scalloped
valances, mounted just
below the crown molding,
are paired with matching
side panels in a sunny
bedroom. Tassel fringe
repeats the color scheme;
plaid lining peeks out
from under the valances
and leading edges.*

# window seats

*Shallow single pleats accommodate the bulk of embroidered and interlined cotton panels in a window-seat bay.*

*A contemporary window seat gets treated to a fresh cloud shade. (The narrow ruffle is cut from the blue-green stripe in the fabric.) Companion fabrics and a wallpaper border complete the look.*

*A pencil-pleated valance and pleated side panels make up a simple treatment for a wide window seat. Miniblinds underneath allow room darkening.*

*Stitched Roman shades dress a window seat in crisp blue and white. A medley of patterns gives this two-color scheme variety.*

# special effects

*Tab curtains take on a whole new look when the fabrics are luxurious silks and velvet. Chenille caterpillar fringe trims the side and lower edges; a chenille rosette decorates the base of each tab.*

*An unlined silk curtain ties to one side for a look that is nonchalant but elegant.*

*Voluminous, one-of-a-kind silk swags frame outward-swinging French doors. The color scheme is analogous (page 475), ranging from peach through pink, with values (page 474) that vary from light to medium. French wire ribbon is the only embellishment.*

*Stripes and a curvilinear design are pleasing in combination when they share colors and textures. Silk welt separates the banding from the panel.*

*Pinch-pleated panels make the most of a striped silk fabric. By spacing the pleats so that they fall only in the ivory stripes, the taupe sections dominate the heading. As the panels open toward the bottom, the stripes are revealed.*

*A simple treatment, rod-pocket curtains, goes formal when*
*the windows are beautifully proportioned and the fabric is*
*silk. The panels are interlined for body; they hang from*
*oversize gold- and silver-leaf rods.*

# not just for windows

*Sheer bed curtains (below) consist of flat linen panels hanging from tiny colored rings. Details make a difference (bottom), no matter how simple the treatment or the hardware.*

*A box-pleated valance and stationary panels look just as appropriate dressing a bed as a window. Companion fabrics unify the treatment.*

*Satin ribbons threaded through grommets and tied into*

*bows (above) are a variation on tabs. Ceramic holdback*

*(left) made of tile shards and offbeat embellishments*

*dresses up the plain panels.*

# A SHOPPER'S GUIDE

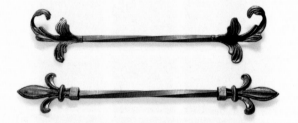

Whether you start out with a few notions about the best way to handle your windows or glean some concepts from this book, you still must put those ideas into action. If you're set on shades or shutters, what are your choices? If blinds are the ticket, what are the various styles you're likely to find? How do you choose curtain or drapery fabric? What's new in decorative hardware? This chapter will help you find the perfect off-the-shelf solution or custom window treatment. You'll discover what's available in the marketplace, where to shop, and what features to look for. You'll also find practical tips on installing and caring for window treatments. There's even advice on new windows, in case ugly or rickety ones are inhibiting your choice of window coverings. The world of window treatments awaits you—and it's full of more products and possibilities than ever before.

# Windows

## THE FRAME FOR YOUR DISPLAY

There are good reasons to consider your windows themselves when you're making decisions about window treatments. After all, the new treatments will draw attention to the openings on which they are placed.

Are your windows suitable companions for the coverings you favor? Perhaps your interior decor—including your taste in window coverings—is traditional or country, while your aluminum sliders typify the 1950s ranch-style house. Or maybe you'd like luxurious, high-quality coverings but don't want to waste them on unattractive or dilapidated windows.

If your inclination is to disguise problem windows, you may end up with different coverings—and a completely different look—than you desire. Hiding such windows may conflict with your need to keep them uncovered for at least part of the day, to maximize sunlight, let in fresh air, or enjoy a view. Should you conclude that your windows need replacing, you can console yourself with the fact that good-looking, well-built, energy-efficient windows are an investment that adds to a property's value. Plus, they help show off beautiful window treatments.

## Choosing windows

The range of windows available today is staggering. Manufacturers produce literally thousands of standard variations, from arched casements, old-fashioned bays, and fixed windows in semicircles, ovals, trapezoids, and other shapes to hinged or sliding French doors, all with an assortment of framing and glazing options, many designed for energy efficiency. If the window you want isn't standard, most manufacturers will make one to your specifications. As an alternative, you can group standard windows in unusual configurations to achieve a unique custom look.

Windows are sold through many sources, including manufacturers, name-brand dealer networks, window stores, home centers, and building-supply yards. Often, the window you order is built at the factory and then shipped to the dealer, where it's prepared for installation before being delivered to you. If you prefer, you can probably find a company that manufactures windows closer to home; there's less risk of damage to the product in transit, and you can work with a local supplier.

A good-quality window should be solidly constructed with strong, tight joints and smooth operation. Sashes should open easily and close flush all around, and window locks should shut securely without undue force. Each pane should be fully sealed in the sash, and weather stripping should provide a continuous seal around the window.

**FRAMES.** The most common window-frame materials are wood, clad wood (the wood is covered with a thin

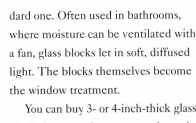

layer of vinyl or aluminum), vinyl, and fiberglass (a relative newcomer). A less familiar option is steel. Neither steel nor aluminum frames are nearly as insulating as the other types. Of the more energy-efficient frames, clad wood and fiberglass tend to be costlier than wood or all-vinyl. Wood units require regular refinishing and can rot if not properly maintained. Vinyl frames require the least maintenance; clad wood and fiberglass demand little upkeep if you don't paint their factory finishes.

**GLAZING.** Many of the greatest strides in window technology are taking place in glazing. Most quality windows sold to homeowners today include insulating glass, which is made of two or more panes of glass sealed together, with a space between panes to trap air. Low-e (low-emissivity) glass usually consists of two sealed panes separated by an air space and a transparent coating to reflect heat and screen out the sun's ultraviolet rays. Some window manufacturers use argon gas between panes of low-e glass to add extra insulation.

Warm-edge technology is another feature offered. Instead of an aluminum spacer between panes of insulating glass, warm-edge windows have a less conductive spacer that won't transfer heat as easily. The result is less condensation buildup around the edge of the window, often a problem in cold climates.

## Glass blocks

Where privacy is important but opening the window isn't, you may opt for a glass-block window instead of a standard one. Often used in bathrooms, where moisture can be ventilated with a fan, glass blocks let in soft, diffused light. The blocks themselves become the window treatment.

You can buy 3- or 4-inch-thick glass blocks in many sizes; rectangular and curved corner blocks are also available in a more limited selection. Textures can be smooth, wavy, rippled, bubbly, or crosshatched. Most block is clear, though Italian block also comes in blue, rose, and green tones, and German block in a gold tone.

Glass blocks are usually sold individually and are mortared together on the job. Prefabricated panels are sometimes available, but they're very heavy. Installation of any type of glass block is best left to a professional.

To locate glass block, look in the yellow pages under Glass—Block.

You may be able to special-order blocks through a regular glass or tile dealer.

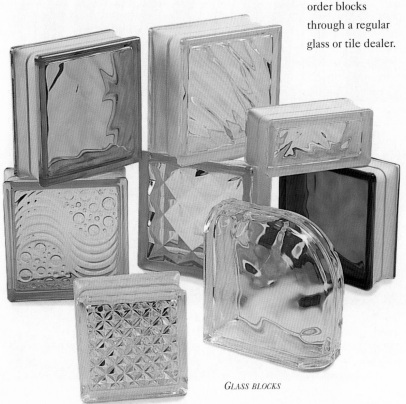

*GLASS BLOCKS*

# Fabric

LET'S GET MATERIALISTIC

To anyone browsing through bolts of fabric or stacks of swatches, it's obvious that fabrics come in an astonishing range of choices, many of them suitable for any given window treatment. Some basic facts about fabric and a few shopping tips will help you select with confidence.

## Understanding fabric

Fabric is a material made up of a fiber, such as cotton or rayon, or a blend of fibers. (For details on the most common fibers, see the chart on page 539.) But shopping for fabric isn't as simple as asking to see a cotton or rayon curtain material. That's because the same fiber can be made into diverse fabrics; for example, cotton can be woven into filmy scrim, crisp chintz, plush velvet, lustrous damask, or stiff canvas.

Usually, the heavier the fabric, the tighter the weave should be if the treatment is to hang properly. The looser the weave, the more a fabric is affected by heat and moisture. In humid climates, the hemline in loosely woven draperies can rise and drop noticeably.

A pattern can be woven into or printed onto a fabric. In woven patterns, which are durable and generally costly, the colors show in a reverse design on the wrong side. In printed patterns, dye is applied to the surface, though it often seeps through to form blurry images on the opposite side. Modern fabric mills use machinery that can print dozens of colors, making more intricately hued, richer fabrics possible. For example, you can buy affordable printed versions of such expensive woven fabrics as damask.

Although some fabrics hold their colors better than others, an absolutely colorfast material doesn't exist. Bright colors appear to fade more than subdued colors, and solids more than prints. Sun rot can be another problem. If the window treatment will be exposed to strong sunlight, choose a rot-resistant fiber such as linen, polyester, or acetate.

## Choosing fabric

An interior designer can show you material suitable for your situation. But if you're shopping on your own and fabric stores are unfamiliar territory,

*Fabric stores often group patterned fabrics by dominant colors.*

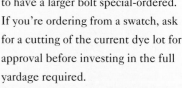

here are some guidelines. You'll be looking at the store's decorator fabrics, which are often grouped apart from garment fabrics.

Most decorator fabrics are 54 inches wide and are wound on cardboard tubes rather than flat cardboard. They usually have a higher thread count (they're more tightly woven) and stand up better over time than garment fabrics. Because they're not preshrunk, they shouldn't be washed. Another reason to avoid laundering them is that they're treated with finishes to make them resistant to stains, mildew, and wrinkles and to add more sheen or stability.

Consider a fabric's suitability for the window treatment you're planning—for instance, fabric for a swag should be supple, and one that will be drawn up in folds should have body without being too heavy or stiff. Check on fiber content and special finishes, information usually printed on the selvage (finished edge) or on the label. When choosing more than one fabric for a single window treatment, such as a curtain panel with contrast banding, look for similar weights and cleaning compatibility.

A knowledgeable salesperson can help you choose, as well as figure out how much fabric to buy. Take along paint chips, carpet scraps, and upholstery samples from the room that will contain the new window covering. Also bring accurate measurements of the window (see page 479 for measuring instructions) and your plans for its treatment.

Don't just look at a serious contender on the bolt. Unroll several yards and gather one end in your hand. Does it drape well? Does a pattern hold its own, without getting lost in the folds? Stand back several feet to see how it looks from afar. Ask for samples so you can examine them at home in daylight and under artificial light. If a sample is too small, consider buying ¼ yard.

Once you've decided on a fabric, buy all you need at one time—and, if possible, from one bolt. Before cutting, though, unfurl the bolt and inspect the fabric for flaws. Slight color differences among bolts may be noticeable in the finished window treatment. If not enough fabric is available on a bolt, ask to have a larger bolt special-ordered. If you're ordering from a swatch, ask for a cutting of the current dye lot for approval before investing in the full yardage required.

---

## CHOICES, CHOICES

Many fabrics are suitable for window treatments. If you're overwhelmed by the possibilities, check out these tried-and-true choices.

- Plain, patterned, or crinkled sheers for diaphanous curtain or drapery panels
- Semisheers, such as lightweight linen or lace panels, for a bit more privacy
- Chintz, a type of polished cotton print, for curtains, draperies, fabric shades, or valances
- Cotton/linen prints, including tea-dyed or old-world look-alikes, for all types of treatments

- Toile, which depicts country scenes in one color on a light background, for a variety of treatments
- Soft, drapable sateen, antique satin, or shantung for swags or draperies
- Lightweight velvet for curtains or draperies
- Cotton duck or ticking for Roman shades or tab curtains
- Canvas for simple panels and flat valances
- Jacquards—heavy tone-on-tone fabrics including damask, brocade, and tapestry—for formal draperies and cornices

## Comparing costs

Fabrics sold through interior designers usually cost the most. Retail outlets that rely on sample books generally sell at higher prices than stores that stock fabrics by the bolt.

You can save money by buying "seconds"—fabrics that have minor defects, though sometimes they're simply over-runs. Some outlets sell seconds clearly marked as such; others mix seconds with first-quality fabrics and offer them at the same price. If you see flaws on a fabric and it's not marked as a second, ask about it.

*Sheers come plain, patterned, or crinkled and in classic white or colors.*

When comparing the cost of two fabrics that look the same, make sure they really are the same. Fabric houses often "down-print" a pattern on a less expensive or flimsier fabric—one that may not hold up as well as you wish.

## What next?

If you've chosen material on your own and don't sew, who will fabricate the window treatment that you have in mind? A designer or decorating service may agree to work with your fabric—or you can go directly to a drapery workroom, the place where designers go to have window coverings made for their clients.

Some workrooms will just fabricate the treatment you want based on measurements you give them; others offer a turnkey operation including measuring, fabric selection, and installation.

Because selling fabric is a source of profit for most workrooms, they may charge an extra fee for using fabric you've purchased elsewhere.

To find a drapery workroom, look in the yellow pages under Draperies, or ask at a fabric store. Get references and check them; also find out if the workroom guarantees its work in writing.

# COMPARING FIBERS

## NATURAL FIBERS

### Cotton

**Advantages.** Stable and durable; myriad weights, textures, and patterns.

**Disadvantages.** Fades and rots in direct sun; mildews; shrinks with washing; burns unless treated.

### Linen

**Advantages.** Strong and durable; resists sun rot.

**Disadvantages.** Fades in direct sun; wrinkles unless blended with a more stable fiber, such as cotton or polyester; can stretch or shrink in humid climates unless blended with a nonabsorbent synthetic fiber, most commonly polyester; burns unless treated.

### Silk

**Advantages.** Long-lasting if lined and kept out of direct sun; versatile (can be made into fabrics as different as chiffon and velvet).

**Disadvantages.** Fades and rots in direct sun; wrinkles; mildews; shrinks with washing or in humid climates; picks up static electricity; burns unless treated.

### Wool

**Advantages.** Durable; more stable if blended with a synthetic fiber.

**Disadvantages.** Fades and rots in direct sun; reacts to humidity and temperature changes; picks up static electricity; burns unless treated.

## SYNTHETIC FIBERS

### Acetate

**Advantages.** Stable; colorfast when solution-dyed; resists sun rot; melts rather than burns.

**Disadvantages.** Wrinkles; picks up static electricity.

### Nylon

**Advantages.** Stable and durable; washable; wrinkleproof; melts rather than burns.

**Disadvantages.** Fades and rots in direct sun; picks up static electricity; has a synthetic appearance unless blended with other fibers.

### Polyester

**Advantages.** Stable and durable; colorfast and resistant to sun rot; washable; wrinkleproof; often made into fabrics that look like silk; blends well with other fibers.

**Disadvantages.** Picks up static electricity.

### Rayon

**Advantages.** Drapes well; dyes well, making it available in beautiful, sophisticated colors; blends well with other fibers.

**Disadvantages.** Rots in direct sun; mildews; shrinks when washed; wrinkles unless blended with a more stable fabric; burns unless treated.

# LININGS: THE INSIDE STORY

A lining acts as a buffer between the decorative face fabric and the sun, the window glass, and any dust or dirt drifting in. It improves the way the window covering hangs and gives the window a finished look from outdoors.

With swags, cascades, and other treatments where the lining shows from the front, line with the same or a coordinating fabric. Where the lining is hidden, use a special fabric sold as "lining."

Some linings resist water stains or ultraviolet rays. Others are designed for energy conservation. Still others completely block light.

Most window-treatment linings are made of cotton or a cotton-polyester blend. They're usually sateen, a strong, tightly woven fabric. Insulating and blackout linings are laminated with vinyl or layered with foam acrylic.

White, off-white, and ecru are the standard colors sold; fade-resistant colored linings are also available. Interlining is a soft, loosely woven fabric used between the lining and the face fabric to provide extra insulation and body. Soft cotton flannel is a common choice, as is "bump," an English felt.

# Trims

## FABULOUS FINISHING TOUCHES

Trims are an easy and clever way to give an ordinary window treatment a custom look or fancy finish. They are useful in accenting a window treatment and in emphasizing its shape and form. The embellishments range from thick, corded tiebacks and tasseled fringes to ruffled lace trim and velvet ribbons. These trimmings are known collectively as *passementerie*.

Tassels are sold by the piece, other trims by the yard. Look for a wide assortment in fabric stores and shops specializing in drapery and upholstery supplies, or order them through an interior designer. Of the items described here, tassels are

commonly found in mail-order catalogs and retail stores that sell decorative window hardware and ready-made curtain and drapery panels. You can also make your own tassels from kits.

High-quality trimmings from a decorator or designer showroom are beautifully constructed (sometimes by hand), luxurious-looking, and expensive—you can easily pay hundreds of dollars for a single tassel. Trims from retail sources, including fabric and drapery supply stores, aren't as lavish, but the cost is much less.

Trims are available in natural or synthetic fibers. High-end items are often made of silk, linen, cotton, or wool, with rayon or viscose sometimes added for sheen. Many mass-marketed products are made of polyester, rayon, or acetate. Popular chenille trims are made from various fibers. Some of the more exclusive or innovative trims incorporate materials such as crystals or wood or ceramic beads. Additionally, some manufacturers offer metallic jewelry ornaments in various motifs, such as butterflies or dragonflies, that you can pin onto window treatments.

Choose trimmings that are compatible with the weight of the fabric or other material used

*Tassel fringe and jumbo tassels on tiebacks are color-coordinated with multihued silk curtains.*

in the window treatment. Also consider care and cleaning of trims that will be attached permanently. Use washable trims (and prewash them) on curtains or other window treatments that will be laundered, and dry-cleanable ones on treatments that will be sent to the dry cleaners. When shopping for trims, bring along a sample of the window-treatment material so you can see how the colors and textures blend. And take home a piece of the trim to see how it looks in the room.

Here are definitions of some trims commonly used as flourishes on window treatments.

**BRAID.** A flat border, usually 1 to 3 inches wide, with two finished edges.

**CORD.** A rope made up of twisted strands or fibers, often used as a tieback for curtains or draperies. Lipped cord has a narrow flange that allows the cord to be sewn into a seam.

**EYELET.** A flat or ruffled fabric trim with small holes. Eyelet beading has slits through which ribbon can be threaded.

**FRINGE.** A border with short strands of yarn or cord on one edge. Types with densely packed, often multicolored cut threads are called brush fringe. Those with twisted strands are called rope fringe or bullion. In loop fringe, the strands are looped instead of hanging free. Other variations include caterpillar fringe (tubed yarn), ball fringe

(little balls), tassel fringe (tassels), and tasseled bullion (a combination of yarn strands and tassels).

**GIMP.** A narrow braid, up to about ½ inch wide, with looped or scalloped borders.

**TASSEL.** A dangling ornament made by binding strands of yarn or cord at one end. The most common type is a tassel tieback, which consists of one or two tassels attached to a looped cord or rope and is used for holding back curtains or draperies. Specialty trims include the swag tassel, which is designed to be suspended from a top treatment.

**WELT.** A fabric-covered cord, available in various diameters from about ¼ to 1 inch, with a narrow flange that can be stitched into a seam.

*The various types of fringe, cord, and braid shown here can add flair to draperies, soft fabric shades, swags, and other window coverings.*

# Hardware

## A NEW ACCENT ON STYLE

Until recently, most of the window-treatment hardware readily available to consumers was manufactured by just a few companies and consisted of a limited selection of rods, rings, and finials. For more interesting—and much costlier—hardware, you had to order through a decorator or find a shop specializing in brass or other metalwork.

Now choices abound, thanks to an explosion of interest in home decorating. You'll find all kinds of appealing, useful, and affordable items in fabric stores, linen and bedding shops, home furnishing stores, mass-merchandise outlets, and mail-order catalogs. Where you might once have seen a preponderance of strictly functional hardware that was meant to be concealed, today decorative items rule the racks.

The following are the main types of rods and accessories you'll encounter.

## Stationary rods

These include decorative models for hand-pulled curtains attached by tabs, ties, rings, hooks, or clips, as well as concealed types for fixed panels, such as sash curtains, rod-pocket curtains, and valances.

**DECORATIVE RODS.** In the past, most of the widely sold metal rods were café models: narrow-diameter, round or fluted brass rods with understated finials. The café rods are still around, but in colorful painted finishes as well as brass. The metal-rod category has grown to include rods of assorted diameters and finishes, including bright or antiqued brass, wrought iron, verdigris, brushed nickel, and pewter.

*These decorative metal curtain rods and finials of metal, glass, and ceramic are just a few of the scores of readily available hardware possibilities.*

Some rods adjust to various lengths, while others come in fixed lengths to accommodate a number of window widths.

Rather than resting immobile in brackets, some decorative metal rods are hinged so you can swing the rod with its curtain away from the open window or door. You move the swing rod back toward the window when you want the glass covered.

Wooden poles are sold plain or fluted in a choice of diameters (typically $1^3/_8$ and 2 inches) and various lengths (most commonly 4, 6, or 8 feet), which can be cut to fit. You can get poles unfinished, stained, or painted in solid colors as well as distressed, crackled, or otherwise "antiqued."

The many types of metal rods and wood poles are supported by brackets that you attach to the wall or window frame. If a rod is longer than about 5 feet, you'll need a center support, which is usually in a loop shape. Though some rods and poles incorporate finials, many accept screw-in finials of your choice. These end pieces can give your window treatment a lot of extra appeal. (See the section on Accessories on pages 544–545 for more about these items.)

Pole sets, which have a wood or metal finish but are actually constructed of rolled steel, usually come complete with pole, finials, and decorative brackets. The poles are adjustable in length.

Wire rods are newcomers to the decorative-rod category. The rod is sold with a length of wire, special brackets, and a center support. You attach the curtain (lightweight fabrics are recommended) to the wire with decorative clips.

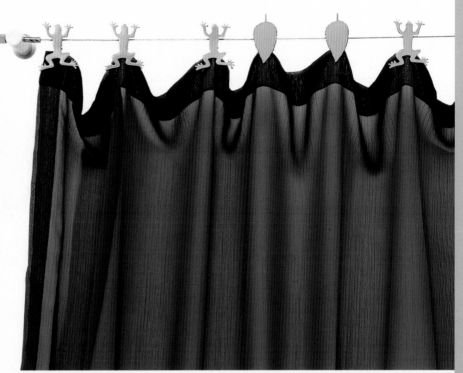

*Whimsical clips attach a lightweight curtain to a wire curtain rod.*

**CONCEALED RODS.** The most familiar type is the adjustable white metal lock-seam rod, though other, more stylish choices in various metallic finishes are available—and with those, you won't mind if some of the hardware is visible. With a standard lock-seam rod, you insert one piece into another, then snap the ends onto brackets that you affix to the wall or window frame. Single flat rods are made with projections (the distance they stick out from the bracket) ranging from about $1^1/_4$ to 6 inches. Those with deeper projections, allowing them to clear other treatments beneath them, are sometimes called valance rods. Double and triple rods accommodate layered treatments.

Other common concealed options are the sash rod, which holds sash or hourglass curtains neatly against French doors and casement windows, and the tension rod, which has a spring mechanism to keep the plastic- or rubber-tipped ends snugly within the window frame.

Yet another type is the wide-pocket rod, available in widths up to $4^1/_2$ inches. Inserting the rod into a heading on an abbreviated panel is a quick, easy way to make a shirred valance. An optional foam fascia that snaps onto the rod can be covered with fabric for an instant cornice. Special corner brackets allow you to use wide-pocket rods in bay windows.

Other concealed rods include flat types hinged to fit corner and bay windows, and custom-bent and flexible rods to follow curves on arched windows. Purely functional swing rods are also available.

## Traverse rods

These adjustable rods are used for draperies that open and close with a cord or a wand. The rod contains sliding holders, called carriers, into which you slip the drapery hooks. When the draperies are closed, the rod is hidden; when they are open, the rod is visible unless cloaked by a top treatment.

A two-way traverse rod, which moves the panels from the center to the ends and back, is standard. A one-way traverse rod, which moves only one panel in one direction, is used over sliding patio doors or where two windows meet at a corner. Custom traverse rods for bay or other odd-shaped windows can be special-ordered from drapery suppliers. On all types, you need a center support, which fits over the rod and screws into the wall, for rods wider than about 4½ feet.

Decorative traverse rods work the same way as conventional types, but

they're designed to be seen whether the treatment is open or closed. The draperies are attached to rings that slide on a concealed track. Many people prefer a decorative stationary rod and rings to which they attach curtain hooks or clips. The greater choices in stationary rods makes up for having to move the fabric panels by hand.

## Accessories

The strictly functional accessories stocked by stores carrying curtain rods include items such as weights for drapery hems, extension plates for mounting brackets beyond the window frame without putting holes in the wall, and stackable shims to build out blind and

*Decorative brackets and holdbacks come in many materials and winsome motifs. Some are meant to be attached to the tops of window frames, while others are designed to sit at the sides of windows.*

shade brackets to clear window trim or handles. Various gizmos designed to help you create no-sew top treatments, such as plastic valance pleaters, are also sold.

Additionally, you'll find lots of useful but highly decorative items, including finials, ornamental brackets, holders for swags and scarves, and holdbacks. All offer many opportunities to be creative with window treatments.

**FINIALS.** These end pieces add a lot of character and charm to a window treatment. You'll find an intriguing selection in a wide range of sizes, motifs, and finishes including various metals, wood, glass, ceramic, rattan, and molded resin. Finials come in innumerable shapes, including spears, arrows, balls, leaves, pineapples, moons, stars, suns, scrolls, birdcages, flowers, and seashells.

**BRACKETS.** Once strictly utilitarian or unimaginative in design, these supports, which you affix to the top outer edges of the window frame or to the wall, now come in an extensive array of motifs.

Types sold for supporting a rod or pole range from subtly decorative to highly ornate, and they come in the same materials as rods and finials. With some, you set the rod or pole in a depression in the bracket; others have a loop that you place the rod through. A center bracket, typically in a loop shape, is usually recommended for rods longer than 5 feet.

Many products labeled as "sconces" or "scarf holders" are ornate brackets with a hole in the middle (it is visible

*Once plain and unadorned, rings, clips, and hooks now come in many stylish designs.*

only from the side) that you can use to support a rod or thread a swag or scarf through—or you can use the same brackets to serve both functions. Generally quite large and sculptural, these brackets are often made of resin molded into shapes such as animal and human figures, grape clusters, flowers, and leaves.

**HOLDBACKS.** These include various types of decorative hardware for holding draperies and curtains, or even tailed swags and scarves, to the sides of a window. Some styles can be mounted at the tops of windows and used in the same way as brackets to anchor swags and scarves; others are inappropriate for that use.

Holdbacks come in various sizes,

designs, and finishes, just as brackets do. Most consist of a plate that you attach to the wall or window frame, a stem that juts out several inches, and a decorative front piece. If the decorative piece is hooked, you tuck the fabric into the hook; otherwise, you secure it behind the front piece. You can also attach tassels and other tiebacks to this type of hardware.

**RINGS, CLIPS, AND HOOKS.** These once-simple items for attaching curtains and draperies to rods have acquired some flair over the years. Today's options include wrought-iron rings in various finishes, sleekly twisted hooks, and clips hidden behind decorative faces shaped like leaves, stars, and other objects.

# Ready-made Panels

QUICK MAKE-OVERS FROM THE SHELF

**B**uying stylish ready-to-hang panels is a good alternative to having curtains or draperies made to order, if you lack the desire or budget for a custom job. Or time may dictate an off-the-shelf purchase—perhaps overnight guests are due shortly and the windows in your spare room are still bare.

Look for ready-made curtain and drapery panels in retail outlets such as linen and bedding shops, home furnishers, department stores, and mail-order catalogs. In addition to stocking panels for standard windows, many suppliers carry panels for doors and sidelights (glass on either side of a door). Most also carry decorative rods and other hardware for hanging the panels, as well as matching valances, scarves, and other top treatments.

## Appealing choices

You'll encounter styles ranging from casual to dressy. Some incorporate trimmings: you'll find panels embellished with lace, fringe, ruffles, and ribbons. Lengths range from short café curtains to long panels that are meant to puddle luxuriously on the floor. Drapery panels are generally pleated. Curtain panels, when mounted, may be tightly gathered, slightly gathered, rippled, or nearly flat; attachment options include rod-pocket sleeves and decorative loops, ties, bows, tabs, grommets, rings, and clips. You'll also find novelties, such as sheer panels with pockets at intervals along the surface for displaying small items (see opposite page, bottom right photo).

Among the many fabric choices are gauze, scrim, lace, ticking, toile, velvet, denim, canvas, sailcloth, and damask. Some fabrics consist entirely

*The ready-made panels shown here and on the facing page demonstrate a few of the many style, fabric, and color possibilities. Tab tops, rod-pocket sleeves, and rings are common methods of attachment.*

of a single fiber type (for example, cotton, polyester, or silk), while others are blends (for instance, jute and cotton creating a linen look). Most ready-made panels are unlined and require dry cleaning to prevent shrinkage and to preserve their look, feel, and finish.

Formerly available in a limited range of solid colors and prints, today's ready-made panels come in an enticing array of colors, plaids, florals, geometrics, and playful prints. Even sheers, once largely restricted to plain white and ecru, include colorful as well as patterned and crinkled choices.

Matching scarves are optional with some panels. They are often sold in a set width and in a choice of yardage, such as 4, 6, or 8 yards.

## Select carefully

Before shopping, ascertain the dimensions of your windows (see page 479 for instructions on measuring) and any adjacent areas you want to cover. The total panel width you need depends on the type of panel you choose. With nearly flat panels, you'll need little more than the actual width you measured. With gathered panels, figure on getting twice the measured width. For door panels, add just a few inches. If you don't intend to close curtain panels but rather want them to frame the window, get a width adequate for your purpose. In most cases, you'll want just two panels for each window: divide the required width by 2 to find the ideal panel width.

Also consider how long the panels should be. For floor-length panels, figure on stopping from ¼ inch (many professionals use this figure for traditional draperies on traverse rods) to about 1 inch above the floor. Long curtain panels in soft fabrics can puddle on the floor. The length of shorter curtains depends on how far above the window frame you intend to hang them and how far below you want them to extend—some suppliers suggest 4 inches above and 4 inches below the window.

Ready-made panels may be sold individually or in pairs. The width is listed first, then the length. Most panels are available in a single width and several lengths, although some come in a choice of widths as well. Some curtain styles lend themselves to doubling up panels on each side for wide windows. If you're in doubt, consult the supplier.

Be sure to deal with a reputable company. Many firms will accept returns if you don't like the way the treatment looks when you hang it, but check on the return policy first. When dealing with a catalog company, be aware that colors may not reproduce faithfully; to be safe, request swatches before ordering the panels.

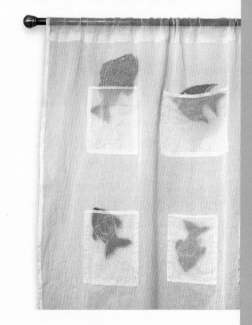

# INSTALLING CURTAIN AND DRAPERY RODS

For a complicated or heavy window treatment, it's best to have professionals handle installation. But some setups are so simple that you can easily install them yourself.

## Choosing a fastener

For a sturdy installation, use a fastener suited to the surface and strong enough to bear the hardware and the fabric. For the most secure attachment, plan to screw into the window casing or into wall studs.

Use wood screws (not the nails that come with some hardware), substituting longer screws for the ones that the manufacturer provides if they look inadequate or you feel extra strength is needed. When drilling into the window casing, positiion your drill bit at least ¼ inch from the edge of the molding to avoid splitting the wood. If you're drilling into the wall around the window, you have a good chance of going into solid wood—the window is framed with doubled studs at either side and a header on top.

If you must attach brackets to plaster or wallboard, use plastic anchors or toggle bolts—but limit this to only the lightest treatments.

To fasten hardware to aluminum, vinyl, fiberglass, or steel window frames, use self-tapping or sheet-metal screws. On a brick or concrete surface, use masonry bolts with expanding plugs.

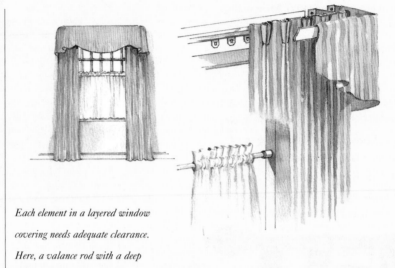

*Each element in a layered window covering needs adequate clearance. Here, a valance rod with a deep return provides ample room for the traverse rod beneath to operate smoothly. Likewise, the traverse rod's return permits a comfortable gap between the back of the draperies and the front of the stationary curtain panel on the tension rod.*

## Installing the rod

The first order of business is to decide where the rod will go and to mark the brackets. Positioning conventional draperies on a traverse rod is easy if you imitate the professionals who leave ¼ inch between the bottom of the draperies and the floor. Since a little fabric is taken up by the rod itself, you'll automatically achieve that spacing by setting the top of the brackets at a height equal to the finished length of the draperies.

With a decorative rod, placement depends on the curtains' method of attachment to the rod—for example, tab-top panels will hang lower than rod-pocket panels—and on the design of the brackets. Place the panel on the rod and have someone hold it up for you to see.

Once the rod is properly positioned, hold up the brackets in the appropriate locations and mark them with a pencil. Before drilling, use a carpenter's level to be sure the rod will be level. Don't just follow the lines of the window frame: if the frame isn't square, the rod will be crooked and the fabric won't hang properly.

Drill holes for the screws or bolts and fasten the brackets securely in place. For a heavy or wide panel, add support brackets every 4 or 5 feet to keep the rod from bowing. You can open adjustable rods to the maximum recommended length if you use an extra support.

# Shades

TRADITIONAL TO HIGH-TECH LOOKS

There's no shortage of choices in window shades! They run the gamut from no-frills, ready-made vinyl roller shades that sell for only a few dollars to handwoven, motorized Roman shades costing thousands of dollars. Although traditional shades that draw up or roll up in tidy or billowing folds are still very popular, high-tech styles continue to make inroads. These newer shades include types with an insulating honeycomb design, and ones made of sheers with fabric slats between that tilt like horizontal blinds.

Function is important in choosing a shade. Consider whether the shade is suitable for the window type and size. Decide whether you want filtered sun, a clear view, privacy, or room darkening, then test the fabric (ask for swatches) to see if it serves your purpose. For energy conservation, pick a shade that covers the entire window surface snugly with no gaps. If you need a shade that's wider than standard for that particular product and the supplier suggests overlapping or seaming, ask to see a sample before you purchase.

A shade should be neatly finished, with no frayed edges. If the shade is unlined, consider how it will look from the street. Be sure the operating mechanism works smoothly: the shade should remain level when you raise and lower it, and it should stay where you stop it. Various mechanisms include standard cords, continuous or looped cords, beaded chains, and battery-operated remote controls. For a shade positioned over a stairwell or other hard-to-reach area, a telescoping pole will allow you to hook onto the cord or onto a ring attached to the end of the cord and pull; automated operation is a costlier alternative.

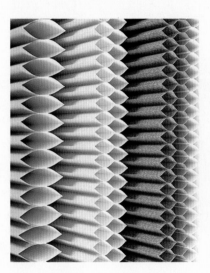

*Cellular shades are available with single, double, or—for maximum energy efficiency— triple honeycombs.*

Inquire about the warranty for a quality shade. Some professionally in-stalled shades are guaranteed to be free from defects for as long as you own them. If you plan to install a shade yourself, see page 554 for some tips.

**PLEATED SHADES.** Most draw up in 1-inch pleats, though larger and smaller sizes are also sold. Typically all-polyester, the shades come in many colors, textures, and fabric styles, including lace, antique satin, and faux marble. Some designs cater to kids.

Light options range from sheer to opaque. Some shades have two separate fabrics, one translucent and one opaque, with separate pull cords on the same shade so you can switch between the two. Other shades have a thin metallic backing to reflect damaging sunlight.

Attached to a metal headrail, pleated shades are usually pulled by a cord into a compact stack at the top of the window. For special situations, you can get shades that stack at the bottom or unfold from both the top and the bottom to meet in the middle. For side-by-side windows or sliding patio doors, more than one shade can be attached to the headrail and operated independently. Shades can also be custom-fitted to odd-shaped windows such as semicircles and angle-tops as well as skylights; for the latter, the shade runs on tracks and is crank-operated or motorized.

**CELLULAR SHADES.** These single-, double-, and triple-celled shades, with their honeycomb design, evolved from the plain pleated shade and are used in much the same way. Their main advantage is energy efficiency, since the pockets trap air. But don't expect a cellular shade to solve your energy problems if your window is drafty and

*A colorful cloud shade provides just the right playful touch in a young child's room.*

**ROLLER SHADES.** Used alone or in conjunction with other window treatments that are sheer or don't cover the entire window, roller shades provide privacy and block light when pulled down, but they are unobtrusive when rolled up.

If you want a reverse roll (the shade pulls down from the front of the roller), you must specify it. A reverse roll hides the roller and allows an inside-mount shade to sit flush with the window casing.

The operating mechanism is either a standard spring roller or a bead chain, which stops the shade in any position. A bead chain keeps the shade cleaner since you touch only the chain and not the fabric. The chain also makes it easy to raise and lower heavy or hard-to-reach shades.

Custom roller shades are usually made from cotton, linen, or other tightly woven fabrics. Much of their appeal rests in the choice of a decorative hem and shade pull.

Most stock shades are vinyl. Several companies offer inexpensive shades that you can easily size yourself to fit a window. Just slide the adjustable roller to your window's width, strip off excess shade material (tear along scoring in the vinyl), and press the material to the roller. Some brands are plain white, while others offer some choice in color and pattern.

**SOFT FABRIC SHADES.** This category includes diverse shade styles. One type is the stagecoach, a custom shade that you roll up by hand and secure with ties. More common are ones that draw up with the aid of cords strung through rings on the back of the shade. With some, the pull cord locks the shade at the desired height;

you keep the shade raised or allow light gaps.

Pleat sizes range from ⅜ to 2 inches, and color and texture options are constantly increasing. Light choices range from sheer to opaque. Like plain pleated shades, some cellular ones have a dual-light option, switching from a translucent to an opaque material on the same shade. Also like pleateds, you can get ones that stack at the bottom or meet in the middle. Some cellular shades that stack at the top are cordless: you just push up or pull down on the bottom bar to move the shade.

In addition to being used in standard windows, cellular shades are often custom-fitted to angle-top, arched, and other odd-shaped windows. They can also be used in the same way as pleated shades in skylights. Though cellular shades are almost always set horizontally, they can be positioned vertically, as they sometimes are on sliding glass doors.

*All the various kinds of Roman shades draw up, like these two, in folds.*

with others, you stop the shade by winding the cord around a cleat. These familiar kinds include Roman shades, which draw up into neat horizontal folds; Austrian shades (scalloped folds); and balloon and cloud shades (billows).

Many suppliers offer variations of these classic shade types—for example, shades with deep overlapping folds, with a single scallop at the bottom instead of several, or with a flat top and a poufed bottom.

Fabric shades from the companies that make pleated and cellular shades are another possibility. They work like Roman shades, with folds available in several sizes. Be aware that the headrail into which the shade dis-

appears may be bulky and protrude from the window frame.

**WOVEN SHADES.** These shades consist of strips of wood (matchstick shades have very thin strips), natural fibers, reeds, or grasses. You can usually order an optional lining as well as a fabric edging.

Most shades in this category are Roman shades, though some roll up with a cord-and-pulley system. Many of the Roman types require lots of stacking space, so be sure that there's enough room and that the stacked shade can clear the window glass.

When buying woven woods, look for straight-grained, smoothly cut strips; wood that was kiln-dried is warp resistant.

*Popular woven shades are available lined or with fabric banding.*

# Shutters and Shoji Screens

GREAT FRAME-UPS

Both louvered shutters and shoji screens are elegant, time-honored ways to cover windows. Hybrids consisting of standard fold-back shutter frames with translucent decorative glass or woven cane inserts are newcomers to the market.

## Shutters

Quality interior shutters with movable louvers for light control can be costly, but they're one window treatment that adds to a home's value.

Traditional shutters have 1¼-inch louvers. Plantation shutters have wider louvers—choices range from about 2½ to 4½ inches wide—for more ventilation and a clearer view. Since slats can become floppy with age, consider a model with an adjustable tension system. Most shutters have tilt bars, but types that work by moving the louvers directly (you flip one to move all the louvers on a panel) are also sold.

Shutters can be custom-fitted for arched and other odd-shaped windows; they're also available for French doors and sliding patio doors. Horizontal louvers are traditional, but louvers can also be set vertically.

Make sure there's room to swing open or fold back the shutter panels. Shutters can be mounted inside or outside the window frame, though some windows may not allow for an inside mount or may have insufficient clearance for the louvers to open. Stock-shutter dealers typically recommend an outside mount because installation is easier and the panels don't have to fit so precisely.

Quality custom shutters are almost always professionally installed; some dealers won't sell the shutters otherwise, as they don't want to be responsible for the consequences of poor installation. For help in installing stock shutters yourself, see page 554.

Custom and stock shutters are available in three materials—solid wood, vinyl laminated on a foam or wood core, and extruded vinyl.

**WOOD SHUTTERS.** These offer more options than their synthetic counterparts. In addition to a greater selection of louver widths and frame styles, you can get wood shutters in standard or custom-matched stains or paint colors. Quality wood shutters can be refinished and are worth repairing.

*Plantation shutters hung in front of sliding patio doors create a graceful transition between garden room and garden.*

*Four shoji panels consist of rice paper inserts in cedar frames. When slid to either side, the screens clear the glass on a pair of double-hung windows.*

Custom shutters are commonly made from incense cedar (often labeled as cedar) or alder, flexible woods that won't warp or split. Manufacturers also use other hardwoods, including poplar. Basswood makes a satisfactory shutter, though it's best suited to long, thin elements, such as narrow louvers. Stock shutters, sold by the panel in lumberyards and home centers, are typically made from soft, cheap grades of pine.

Don't count on price to distinguish premium from lesser-quality custom shutters. Look for doweled rather than glued joints (two or three dowels per joint signify a solidly constructed shutter). The louvers should be securely fastened to the tilt bar; they should stay open in a breeze but also close tightly. The finish should be smooth, with no paint or stain buildup.

**VINYL LAMINATED SHUTTERS.** Vinyl is laminated onto a foam or wood core. The durable finish is unaffected by ultraviolet light, is easy to clean, and never needs refinishing.

Just like solid wood shutters, custom-laminated shutters can be made to fit odd-shaped windows. The laminates are limited in color selection (typically white and ivory), louver widths (most commonly $2\frac{1}{2}$ and $3\frac{1}{2}$ inches), and frame styles. A quality product should have tight joints and louvers that hold steady when tilted. Some look more realistic than others, so shop carefully.

**EXTRUDED VINYL SHUTTERS.** These shutters have a cellular or honeycombed interior. They're as durable and maintenance-free as the laminated types, but because they consist of vinyl throughout, there won't be any color change if you nick or cut the surface. Because current technology does not allow panels to be extruded into odd shapes, these shutters are limited to rectangles.

They share the same limitations as the laminates in color, louver width, and frame style. As you would with

the laminated models, check for tight joints, steady louvers, and a realistic appearance.

## Shoji screens

These custom-made decorative screens consist of translucent inserts in a wood frame. Although often found in place of windows in traditional Japanese homes, where deep overhangs protect the screens, elsewhere shojis are used as a window treatment.

Rice paper is the traditional insert material, but because it tears easily, it has been largely supplanted by fiberglass treated to look similar to rice paper. Eventually, the fiberglass deteriorates in sunlight and must be replaced. Other synthetic materials, many of them from Japan, are also commonly used.

Shoji screens can be made to slide along a wood track or fold over a window like shutters. Several panels can be hinged together and stacked to one side of the window.

# PUTTING UP SHADES, BLINDS, AND SHUTTERS

The supplier of custom shades, blinds, and shutters will usually mount them, but you may want to install inexpensive types yourself—especially if professional installation will cost more than the window covering itself.

First, make sure the window treatment fits in the spot you planned for it. Hold it in place, positioning the headrail or mounting board at the correct height. The treatment shouldn't interfere with any window hardware, such as handles, and shouldn't impede the smooth operation of the window. If it does, try adjusting its position just enough to avoid the problem.

Window treatments, especially heavy ones, must be securely fastened to the window or wall. To choose the right fastener, see page 548.

If you have different brackets for inside and outside mounts, be sure to use the appropriate ones. Since your window frames may not be perfectly square, use a carpenter's level to position the brackets or hinges; then mark the screw holes with a pencil. Drill holes to accommodate the screws or bolts, and securely fasten the brackets or hinges to the mounting surface.

## Shades and blinds

Most shades and blinds come with a pair of brackets, and very wide or heavy ones come with additional support brackets. Once you've attached the brackets, the usual next step is to slide the shade or blind onto the bracket or snap it into place.

If you need extra clearance, use shims or projection brackets to hold the treatment away from the wall or window casing. Some blinds and shades, especially those to be mounted on a door or hinged window, also come with hold-down brackets to keep the bottom stationary. Don't use brackets to keep pleated or cellular shades from being windblown, since doing so can twist the shade.

## Shutters

Installing inside-mount shutters is tricky if the window isn't perfectly square (use a carpenter's square, as shown at left, to check). To make the panels fit, you'll have to trim or shim them. You'll also need to nail stops (strips of wood) to the inside top and bottom of the window frame to keep the panels from swinging into the glazing and breaking the hinges. If your window is severely out of square, use an outside mount.

With an outside mount, you can either screw the shutter hinges directly to the window casing or attach them to a frame that you build and screw into the casing.

Another way to install shutters is to use a hanging strip; screw it to the jamb for an inside mount, as shown at left, or to the casing for an outside mount. Some companies that market shutter panels sell kits containing hanging strips, hinges, and screws. Or you can buy preassembled shutters that incorporate hanging strips.

*Before installing shutters, check window jambs with a carpenter's square. If they're fairly square, you can use an inside mount: attach each shutter to a hanging strip screwed to the jamb.*

# Blinds

SIMPLE, SLEEK WAYS TO CONTROL LIGHT

With most window coverings, it's all or nothing. When the treatment is drawn over a window, you can't adjust the amount of light that enters. But with both horizontal and vertical blinds, you can tilt the slats to let in the desired amount of light, or you can darken the room completely. The slats stack out of the way when you want the window uncovered.

Stock blinds are fine if you find ones that fit your window opening perfectly. Otherwise, opt for made-to-measure blinds, especially if you want them for an inside mount. Even at custom prices, most blinds are very affordable, especially for standard, rectangular windows. High-quality wood blinds are at the high end of the price range for blinds, but they're still about half the cost of wood shutters. Vertical blinds with fabric vanes can cost as much as wood blinds, depending on the fabric selection.

Some suppliers offer limited warranties; others promise to repair or replace defective blinds for as long as you own them. Warranties don't usually cover normal wear and tear, though. With horizontal blinds, getting a new blind may cost less than replacing a broken slat.

## Horizontal blinds

These traditional blinds are suitable for most windows, including arches and other odd shapes. They're also suitable for skylights and for doors (hold-down clips will keep the blind steady when the door swings open or shut). Most blinds are made of metal, vinyl, or wood—types described on page 556. Also available are blinds with tinted polycarbonate plastic slats that are transparent when closed; on some models, the slats become opaque when they're tilted a certain way.

Any horizontal blind is only as good as its operating mechanism. If you have access to display models, give them a workout before deciding on a

*Richly grained wood blinds feature 2-inch slats and decorative cloth tapes.*

particular product. Make sure the blind opens and closes smoothly and quietly. The slats should tilt uniformly. As you draw the blind, it should remain level and hold in place where you stop it. The hardware should be sturdy and well constructed, with no rough edges.

For room darkening, choose a blind with opaque, reasonably thick slats. Be sure the slats close tightly and there is no gap between the headrail and the top slat. Light will seep through cord holes that are exposed when the slats are closed. Some blind makers get around this problem by making the holes small, or even by eliminating them and looping cords around the slats instead. Other solutions include covering the holes with decorative cloth tapes, positioning small holes near the back of slats so that they're overlapped when the blind is closed, and placing the holes at the far ends of the slats so that they're positioned against the window frame or wall.

The area that you can cover with one blind varies according to the type of blind. To span the desired distance, you may have to put more than one blind on a single headrail. To protect small children, consider blinds without conventional pull cords. Options include automated systems as well as cordless blinds that you operate by lifting up or pulling down the bottom rail. To cut down on blind cleaning, consider a dust-repellent model.

**METAL BLINDS.** Typically, metal blinds are made of aluminum alloy with a baked enamel finish; matte finishes are also available. Most makers offer a wide range of colors. Metal blinds come in a variety of slat widths, most commonly 2 inches (Venetian

*These sleek vinyl miniblinds are inexpensive but sturdy enough to withstand rough handling.*

blinds), 1 inch (miniblinds), and $1/2$ or $5/8$ inch (micro-miniblinds). In-between slat sizes, such as $1^3/8$ inches, are also sold. Contrasting cloth tapes are optional with most 2-inch metal blinds.

**VINYL BLINDS.** Like their metal counterparts, these come in a range of slat sizes. Moisture-resistant vinyl blinds are a good choice for bathrooms and kitchens. Low price makes them a favorite window treatment in kids' rooms (most vinyl blinds are now lead-free, but check before buying). Two-inch vinyl blinds have grown in popularity—and price—because of the fashionable textured finishes available; you can coordinate them with cloth tapes.

**WOOD BLINDS.** In addition to all-wood blinds, this category now includes blinds made of synthetic materials: vinyl laminated onto a wood core and extruded vinyl. Because these blinds can be heavy to raise (the synthetics actually weigh more than real wood slats), keep a single blind to less

than about 6 feet wide. Also note that the wider the slat, the fewer the slats there are and the less stacking room is required. Even wide-slat wood blinds need considerable stacking space, so ask before buying.

Solid wood blinds feature slats from 1 inch to about 3 inches wide, in your choice of stain or paint finish (options include washes and faux finishes); coordinating cloth tapes are optional. Manufacturers warn customers to expect some variation in wood grain and color. Look for quality, kiln-dried wood, because it will resist warping.

Makers of synthetic wood blinds usually offer two or three slat widths, and a variety of colors and textured finishes. These blinds are moisture and warp resistant, making them suitable for humid climates and for use in kitchens and bathrooms. They also wear better in extreme temperatures and direct sunlight than blinds made of solid wood.

## Vertical blinds

These blinds, which stack compactly to the side, are practical for sliding patio doors and picture windows. They can be used on other types of windows, even bays and odd shapes such as arches. They require less cleaning than horizontal blinds since gravity keeps dust from piling up.

The vertical slats, called vanes, are usually 3½ inches wide, though wider and narrower versions are also sold. The vanes are most commonly made of fabric or vinyl. You can also get vanes of wood, metal, or tinted poly-carbonate plastic—the same materials used in many horizontal blinds.

For fabric vanes, choose either free-hanging fabric panels with weighted hems or fabric strips inserted into a grooved backing. Manufacturers have taken fabric vertical blinds a step farther, attaching white fabric vanes to a sheer panel-like face fabric, creating the effect of a curtain when the vanes are open; when you rotate the vanes to a shut position, the sheer curtain becomes opaque. As an alternative, you can "slipcover" existing verticals in sheer panels sold for that purpose;

*When closed, these vertical blinds with fabric vanes provide complete privacy.*

*Vertical vanes made from vinyl can be extruded in many shapes.*

you simply remove the cover to wash the sheers.

In addition to plain vinyl vanes in solid colors, you'll find versions that have been extruded in various printed designs and in curves, ridges, and other shapes. You can also get vanes perforated with tiny holes that will filter light without blocking the view.

Operating options include standard cords or a single wand that allows you to rotate the vanes as well as open and close the blind. Motorized vane rotation is also available. Sturdiness is important with vertical blinds: tug on the vanes to make sure the attachment to the headrail is secure. Because hangers holding the vanes can break, find out if they're replaceable.

# A Word to the (Energy) Wise

Most window treatments have an insulating effect, but some do a better job than others at keeping the sun's heat outside in summer and heated air inside in winter. Depending on your situation, you may want window coverings that are efficient during hot weather or cold weather, or in both situations.

Remember, there's no point in having energy-wise treatments unless they're shielding your windows at the critical times. During hot months, close the treatments early in the day before the temperature soars; in cold weather, draw them at sunset.

## Cool in summer

You may find that some rooms, especially those facing south or west, become uncomfortably hot in summer. Shutters and blinds (both horizontal and vertical) do a good job of barring heat, as do cellular shades (double- and triple-celled shades trap more heat than single-celled types).

Choose white or metallic backings on treatments to reflect sunlight away from the windows. The materials used in some window coverings will also protect against ultraviolet rays, which can fade the contents of a room.

## Toasty in winter

The following are some treatment types as well as strategies to help prevent heat from escaping your home's

*Insulating, snug-fitting shades bar the sun's rays in summer and keep heated air from escaping in winter.*

interior during the cold season.

Among the most energy-efficient treatments are cellular shades (double- and triple-celled types do a better job than those with single cells), shutters, and quilted Roman shades. Remember, inside-mount shades must fit snugly within the frame if they are to be effective.

Layered treatments—for example, heavy draperies with sheers next to the glass or curtains with a pleated shade underneath and topped by a cornice or valance—also inhibit heat loss. Curtains and draperies that extend well beyond the window, perhaps from the ceiling to the floor and at least several inches on either side of

the window, do a considerably better job of shielding against heat loss than ones that cover more skimpily.

Linings can greatly increase the energy efficiency of draperies and other fabric window treatments. In addition to linings made of standard cotton and cotton-polyester blends, you can order energy-efficient insulating and/or blackout linings. Interlinings provide even more insulation. (For more about the various types of linings, see page 539.)

If you have older windows that leak a little, try sealing the edges of the window treatment with hook-and-loop fastening tape, commonly available at fabric stores.

# Top Treatments

CROWNING GLORIES FOR YOUR WINDOWS

Top treatments are providing much of the excitement in today's window fashions. The treatment can sit above the window, or it can frame the top and sides. You can use it alone as an accent on an uncovered window or, where privacy is an issue, combine it with curtains, shades, or other window coverings.

The most common toppers are cornices, valances, swags, and scarves, described below. Other types of embellishment can consist of simple wood poles that you cover in fabric, or elaborate molded architectural accent pieces available through decorators.

*This painted wood cornice conceals the tops of undertreatments, while adding panache.*

*An easy way to hang a swag or scarf is to thread it through decorative brackets positioned at the upper corners of a window.*

## Cornices

This is a shallow, boxlike frame installed across the top of a window. (If the frame has legs that extend to the floor, it is called a lambrequin.) The frame projects out from the window, hiding a curtain or drapery heading or the tops of any other undertreatments.

Cornices are traditionally built of wood, then padded and upholstered in fabric. Modern ready-made versions are often constructed of molded polystyrene or other lightweight materials, usually with facades that resemble oversized crown molding. The frame is closed at the top to keep dust away from any undertreatments. Manufacturers typically offer these frames in a couple of colors and in several widths and heights, to about 9 inches high. They suggest customizing the cornice by adding paint, wallpaper, fabric, or rubber-stamp impressions, or by gluing on decorative objects for a three-dimensional look.

As an alternative to the standard frame, you can make your own shallow cornice (to about $4\frac{1}{2}$ inches high) from a wide-pocket rod. Just snap on the manufacturer's optional foam fascia, then cover with fabric.

## Valances

This type of fabric top treatment may be flat, pleated, or gathered and hung from a rod, pole, or board. A simple valance that you can make yourself is a short fabric panel with a heading that you shirr onto a wide-pocket rod (minus the fascia) or one with tab tops that you thread onto a pole.

You can find ready-made valances in many styles, including ones with bottoms that are arched, scalloped, pointed, pleated, or poufed, as well as types with tails that drape down the sides of the window. Some valances consist of a single panel, while others have two panels; for the latter, an insert valance (a middle piece) is sometimes sold for wider windows.

## Scarves and swags

These are pieces of fabric that you drape artfully over the top of the win-

dow and down the sides—you may decide to stop partway down the window or go all the way to the floor.

Though the terms are sometimes used interchangeably, a scarf consists of a single piece of fabric and a swag of several pieces joined together. The reason for forming a swag from more than one piece is so that it will drape in a characteristic curved shape. Rather than have swags sewn, decorators often just pin pieces of fabric until they find a shape that works, then staple them neatly together. The same suppliers who offer curtain and drapery panels also sell scarves and swags that are ready for draping.

Draping scarves and swags attractively takes some time and expertise, though various tools and techniques will help you. Assorted decorative brackets, including those labeled "scarf holder," "swag holder," or

"sconce," are popular for securing the fabric at the top corners of the window; use an extra holder in the middle for wide windows. Just thread the fabric through the holders, or drape it over their tops. You can use the holders with or without a pole or rod. Holdbacks are another type of hardware that you can use to secure long scarves or cascades at the sides of windows. In addition to serving an important function, the various hardware pieces add beautiful decorative accents to the window. (For more about these, see pages 544–545.)

Another simple approach is to install a pole or rod, then loosely wrap a scarf around it or anchor a swag to it. You can staple fabric to a wooden pole to keep it in place. Some manufacturers of window-treatment hardware produce special rubber pads for pinning fabric to metal rods.

The hardware makers also turn out plastic templates, some of them labeled "design rings," to help you form poufs or rosettes, or arrange fabric artistically in other ways. With valance pleaters (notched plastic that you install at the top corners of the window), you can drape fabric in addition to forming valances.

*Gathered valances trimmed with oversize contrasting welt are color-coordinated with window-seat cushions and pillows.*

# CARE AND CLEANING

Your window coverings will look better and last longer if they're cared for properly. Follow the manufacturer's instructions for care and cleaning; also refer to the tips below.

■ Some draperies and Roman or Austrian shades need "dressing" to train them into pleats or folds. Smooth the fabric into place by hand as you draw the draperies or raise the shades. Eventually, the treatment will form precise pleats or folds on its own. For an easy way to train draperies, see the illustration at right.

■ Most curtains and draperies should be dry-cleaned rather than washed, but do so infrequently as harsh chemicals can harm some fabrics. Even if the decorative face fabric withstands chemical cleaning, a lining weakened by exposure to the sun may come back in shreds.

To lengthen the intervals between dry cleanings, vacuum often to remove dirt that might otherwise be absorbed over time. Once or twice a year, tumble the panels in the clothes dryer. To avoid removing drapery hooks, secure the hem over the hooks with safety pins. Add a dry, all-cotton terry-cloth towel to absorb dirt and, unless the fabric contains polyester, a fabric softener sheet. Set the dryer on "no heat" or "air fluff" and run it for about 30 minutes. Remove and hang the curtains or draperies immediately;

*To train draperies, open the panels completely. With your fingers, smooth the fabric into pleats or folds, and then tie them in place with soft fabric strips. After a few days, remove the ties.*

you may have to iron or steam them to get wrinkles out. Panels cared for in this manner should look good for years without dry cleaning.

For washable curtains (if the fabric has been preshrunk), hand-wash one panel at a time in sudsy water that is comfortably hot to the touch. Drain the water as soon as it turns dirty, then rinse. Wash and rinse again. Hang to dry; touch up with an iron if needed.

■ Keep shades clean by vacuuming them often. To remove a stain from a pleated or cellular shade, lightly sponge the area with mild detergent and lukewarm water. When the shades begin to look soiled or dowdy, ultrasonic cleaning is a good way to spruce them up (see at right). Check

the manufacturer's instructions for the proper way to clean other types of shades.

■ Keep horizontal or vertical blinds looking fresh by dusting them with a clean, soft cloth or vacuuming with a soft brush attachment. To clean both surfaces, go over the blinds with the slats tilted one way and then the other, but not completely closed. To avoid scratching polycarbonate plastic blinds, use a very soft cloth and an extremely diluted, mild detergent or a cleaner recommended for computer screens. To keep stained wooden blinds in good condition, dab furniture oil on the cloth when you dust.

For do-it-yourself cleaning of metal or vinyl blinds, use a damp cloth and mild detergent, then wipe dry immediately to prevent spotting. You can immerse vinyl blinds in the bathtub, but dunking metal blinds can cause rusting. For professional cleaning of blinds, consider ultrasonic cleaning.

■ Many window treatments can be ultrasonically cleaned, the same kind of process used for cleaning jewelry. The solution in which the treatment is immersed contains tiny soundwave-generated bubbles that knock dirt loose. Pleated and cellular shades—as well as horizontal and vertical blinds made of metal, vinyl, plastic, fabric, or wood—can be cleaned in this fashion.

*Sunset*

*ideas for great*

# PATIOS AND DECKS

By Scott Atkinson
and the Editors of Sunset Books

Sunset Books ■ Menlo Park, California

# contents

# deck, patio, or both?

**I**N THE QUEST for more living space, there's one spot we often overlook: outside. What better way to take the heat off interior traffic, bring the outdoors in, and frame dramatic views than to build or expand an outdoor hardscape?

Your outdoor room might be classic and formal or fluid and naturalistic. You may be yearning for an inviting entertainment space, a remote private refuge, a restorative spa, or simply for a flat spot for sunbathing and stargazing. Or maybe you want it all. You needn't settle for that boring patio slab. Interior design ideas are migrating outdoors and new shapes, colors, textures, and amenities abound.

First things first: would you prefer a patio or a deck? Sometimes it's simply a matter of site or style. Deck lumber is durable and resilient underfoot, and it won't store heat the way other materials can. Decks can tame sloping, bumpy, or poorly draining ground. Designs and materials are dancing new steps. Hardwoods add a furniture-like elegance; man-made and recycled products are also on the rise.

Patios, on the other hand, lend an unmatched sense of permanence and tradition to a formal garden or house design. You might choose unit masonry such as traditional brick, ceramic tile, or elegant stone. Concrete pavers are rising stars, and they're easy for the do-it-yourselfer to install. And don't rule out concrete; you'll discover there are lots of jazzy techniques for coloring, texturing, and softening the familiar slab. Loose materials are yet another option.

Or why not combine both patio and deck in one multifaceted design?
A blend of masonry and wood allows great flexibility in space, texture, and
finished height.

On the following pages you'll find solutions for large lots, tiny lots, and
hilly lots. The first chapter, "A Planning Primer," will walk you through the
evaluation of your present site and help you refine your thoughts. For a tour
of patio styles and solutions, take a good look at the photos in the next chapter, "Great Patios and Decks." For shopping tips and pointers, see the third
chapter, "A Shopper's Guide."

And since summer's always just around the corner, isn't now the time to
get started?

# A PLANNING PRIMER

**A**S FUN AS IT IS to daydream about the new outdoor living space you are going to create, careful planning is what will make the dream become reality. **TO CHOOSE THE BEST SITE,** you'll first need to study your property's orientation, its topography, and its weather patterns and produce a base map. That's where this chapter begins. **COMPARING VARIOUS OPTIONS** in design and materials will help you visualize what you want; browse through the photos in Chapter Two, "Great Patios and Decks," for ideas. For help evaluating materials, see pages 651–669. **RETURN TO THIS CHAPTER** for both solid design guidelines and a guided walk through the planning process. When you've finished, you should have working drawings in hand. Use these to communicate with professionals or, if you're so inclined, to build the project yourself.

# taking stock

**THE PATH** *to a comfortable new patio or deck begins right outside your door. In the following pages we take a look at basic site strategies and consider some important weather factors. Then we show you how to make a detailed base map of your property.*

## What are your options?

Many people regard a patio or deck as a simple rectangle off the back door. But why not consider a succession of patios and level changes connected by steps, or a secluded "getaway" deck to make use of an attractive corner of your property? Perhaps you could even reclaim a forsaken side yard. Some of the possibilities are discussed below.

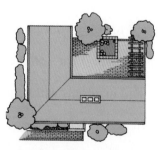

PATIO FOR L-SHAPED HOUSE

WRAPAROUND

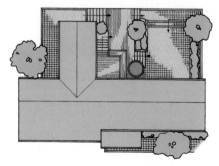

MULTILEVEL LAYOUT

DETACHED PATIO

**L- AND U-SHAPED SPACES.** A house with an L or U shape almost cries out for a patio or deck. Surrounding house walls already form an enclosure; a privacy screen and a decorative structure overhead (such as an arbor, pergola, or even a simple roof) complete the "outdoor room." Often such a site can be gracefully accessed from several different parts of the house.

**WRAPAROUNDS.** A flat lot is a natural candidate for a wraparound patio, which enlarges the apparent size of the house while allowing access from any room along its course. If there's a gentle grade, rise above it with a slightly elevated wraparound deck, which the Japanese call an engawa.

**DETACHED SITES.** Perfect for serving as a quiet retreat, a detached patio or deck can be built on either a flat or a sloping lot and looks very much at home in a casual cottage-garden landscape. Create access to it with a direct walkway or a meandering garden path. A patio roof, privacy screen, or small fountain can make such a space even more enjoyable.

**MULTILEVEL DECKS AND PATIOS.** A large lot, especially one with changes in elevation, can often accommodate decks and patios on different levels, linked by steps or pathways. Such a scheme works well when your outdoor space must serve many purposes.

**ROOFTOP AND BALCONY SITES.** No open space in the yard? Look up. A garage rooftop adjacent to a second-story living area might be ideal for a sunny outdoor lounging space. Or consider a small balcony patio with a built-in bench and planter box. Just be sure your existing structure can take the weight of additional wood or masonry (consult an architect or structural engineer), and plan for adequate drainage.

**ENTRY PATIOS.** Pavings, plantings, and perhaps a trickling fountain enclosed by a privacy wall can transform an ordinary entry path or front lawn into a private oasis. If local codes prohibit building high solid walls, try using a hedge, arbor, or trellis to let in light and air while screening off the street.

**SIDE-YARD SPACES.** A neglected side yard may be just the spot for a sheltered outdoor sitting area to brighten and expand a small bedroom or master bath. And what about a container-grown herb garden or sunny breakfast deck off a cramped kitchen, accessed by way of French or sliding doors? If you're subject to fence height restrictions, use an arbor or overhead structure to protect privacy.

**INTERIOR COURTYARDS.** If you're designing a new home, consider incorporating a private interior courtyard, or atrium. If you're remodeling, perhaps your new living space could enclose an existing patio area.

**PORCHES.** Where summers swelter, the classic porch still evokes a traditional kind of indoor-outdoor living. In bug country, however, screened porches or sunrooms make sense. Some porches can be opened up when the sun shines and battened down when hard winds blow.

**RECLAIMED DRIVEWAYS.** Your driveway can double as a masonry patio. Concrete turf blocks can support car traffic but yield a softer appearance than plain asphalt or concrete; planting small spaces between pavers achieves the same result. Enclosed by a gate, the front drive becomes an entry courtyard.

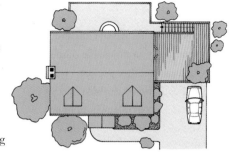

GARAGE ROOFTOP

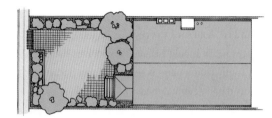

ENTRY PATIO

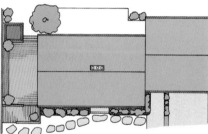

SIDE-YARD SPACE

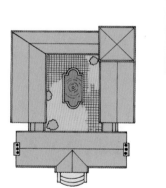

INTERIOR COURTYARD

BACK PORCH

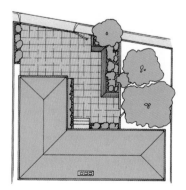

RECLAIMED DRIVEWAY

## How's your weather?

Your site's exposure to sun, wind, rain, and snow can limit its potential as an enjoyable outdoor room. Microclimates (weather pockets created by very localized conditions) can also make a big difference. Studying these might prompt you to adjust the site of your proposed deck or patio, extend its dimensions, or change its design. You may be able to moderate the impact of the weather with the addition of an overhead structure, walls, screens, or plantings.

**BASIC ORIENTATION.** In general, a site that faces north is cold because it receives little sun. A south-facing patio is usually warm because it gets daylong sun. An east-facing patio is likely to be cool, receiving only morning sun. A west-facing patio can be unbearably hot because it gets the full force of the afternoon sun; in late afternoon, it may also fill with harsh glare.

But there are exceptions. For example, since mid-July temperatures in Phoenix often climb

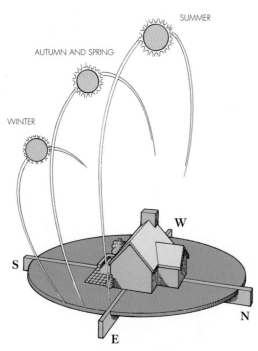

*The sun's rays strike your property at predictable angles, depending on the time of year and where you live. A south-facing patio gets maximum sun and heat; a northern site is coldest.*

above 100°F, a north-facing patio there could hardly be called "cold." In San Francisco, on the other hand, a patio with a southern or western exposure would not feel overly warm in July because stiff ocean breezes and chilly fogs are common then.

**SEASONAL PATHS OF THE SUN.** Another factor to consider is the sun's path during the year. As the sun passes over your house, it makes an arc that changes slightly every day, becoming higher in summer and lower in winter. Changes in the sun's path not only give us long days in summer and short ones in winter, but also alter shade patterns in your yard.

**UNDERSTANDING WIND.** Having too much wind blowing across your patio on a cool day can be just as unpleasant as having no breeze at all on a hot day. Check your lot in relation to three types of air movement: annual prevailing winds, localized seasonal breezes (daily, late-afternoon, or summer), and high-velocity blasts generated by stormy weather.

Chances are that air currents around your house are slightly different from those generally prevailing in your neighborhood. Wind flows like water—after blowing through the trees, it may spill over the house and drop onto your patio. Post small flags or ribbons where you want wind protection and note their movements during windy periods. You'll soon see where you need shelter. If you decide to build a screen or fence to block wind, remember that a solid barrier may not necessarily be the best choice. Sometimes angled baffles, lattice-type fencing, or appropriate plantings disperse wind better.

**DEALING WITH RAIN OR SNOW.** If, in assessing your climate, you learn that winter storms generally blow out of the northeast, you may want to locate your patio or deck where it will take less of a beating from the weather— perhaps on the south side of the house, where it will be partially protected by trees or a roof overhang.

If you live in an area where brief summer cloudbursts frequently occur, you can extend

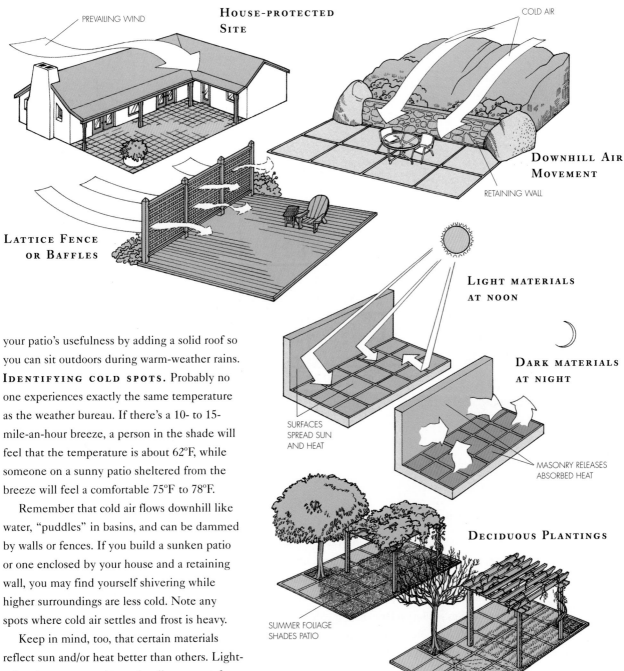

**HOUSE-PROTECTED SITE**

PREVAILING WIND

COLD AIR

**DOWNHILL AIR MOVEMENT**

RETAINING WALL

**LATTICE FENCE OR BAFFLES**

**LIGHT MATERIALS AT NOON**

**DARK MATERIALS AT NIGHT**

SURFACES SPREAD SUN AND HEAT

MASONRY RELEASES ABSORBED HEAT

**DECIDUOUS PLANTINGS**

SUMMER FOLIAGE SHADES PATIO

WINTER SUN WARMS PATIO

your patio's usefulness by adding a solid roof so you can sit outdoors during warm-weather rains.

**IDENTIFYING COLD SPOTS.** Probably no one experiences exactly the same temperature as the weather bureau. If there's a 10- to 15-mile-an-hour breeze, a person in the shade will feel that the temperature is about 62°F, while someone on a sunny patio sheltered from the breeze will feel a comfortable 75°F to 78°F.

Remember that cold air flows downhill like water, "puddles" in basins, and can be dammed by walls or fences. If you build a sunken patio or one enclosed by your house and a retaining wall, you may find yourself shivering while higher surroundings are less cold. Note any spots where cold air settles and frost is heavy.

Keep in mind, too, that certain materials reflect sun and/or heat better than others. Light-colored masonry paving and walls are great for spreading sun and heat (though they can be uncomfortably bright) and dark masonry materials retain heat longer, making evenings on the patio a little warmer. Strategically placed barrier plantings can help block wind, while allowing some breezes through. Deciduous trees can shelter a patio from hot sun in summer, yet admit welcome rays on crisp winter days, when their leaves are gone.

*Microclimates affect patio comfort, as shown. Cold air flows downhill and may be dammed by a house or wall (at top); light-colored materials reflect light and heat, dark colors absorb it (center); deciduous plantings provide shade in summer, allow sun to penetrate in winter (at bottom).*

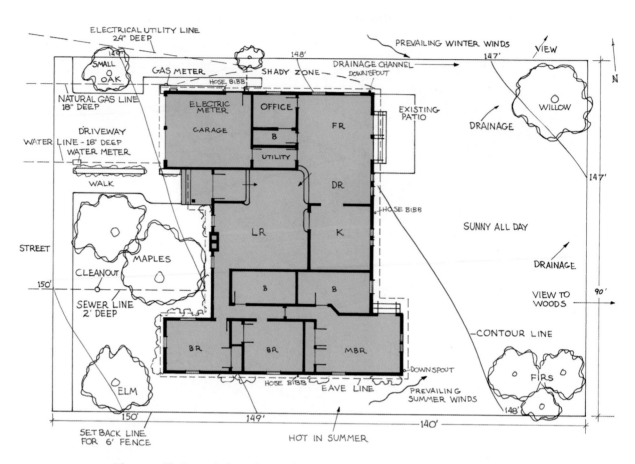

*A base map, like the sample shown above, can be one of your most effective planning tools.*

## Making a base map

Even if you've lived with a landscape for years, mapping it can be a way to make some interesting discoveries about what you thought was familiar territory. Use your observations about your site to produce a base map like the one shown above. Later, slip the base map under tracing paper to sketch designs to your heart's content.

You can save yourself hours of measuring and data-gathering by obtaining dimensions, gradients, and relevant structural details from your deed map, house plans, or a contour map of your lot. If you don't have these, see if they're available through your city hall, county office, title company, bank, or mortgage company.

The following information should appear in one form or another on the base map.

■ **BOUNDARY LINES AND DIMENSIONS.** Outline your property accurately and to scale, and mark its dimensions on the base map. Indicate any required setback allowances from your lot lines. Also note the relation of the street to your house.

■ **THE HOUSE.** Show your house to scale within the property. Note all exterior doors (and the way each one opens), the height of all lower-story windows, and all overhangs. Mark the locations of all downspouts and any drainage tiles, drainpipes, or catch basins.

■ **EXPOSURE.** Draw a north arrow, using a compass; then note on your base map the shaded and sunlit areas of your landscape. Indicate the direction of the prevailing wind and mark any spots that are windy enough to require shielding. Also note any microclimates.

■ **UTILITIES AND EASEMENTS.** Map the placement of hose bibbs and show the locations of all underground lines, including the sewage line or septic tank. If you're contemplating a patio roof or elevated deck, identify any overhead lines.

■ **GRADIENT AND DRAINAGE.** Draw contour lines on your base map, noting high and low points (here's where the official contour map is helpful). If drainage crosses boundaries, you may need to indicate the gradient of adjacent properties as well, to be sure you're not channeling runoff onto your neighbor's property.

Where does the water from paved surfaces drain? Note any point where drainage is impeded (leaving soggy soil) and any place where runoff from a steep hillside could cause erosion.

■ **EXISTING PLANTINGS.** If you're remodeling an old landscape, note any established plantings that you want to retain or that would require a major effort or expense to remove or replace.

■ **VIEWS.** Note all views, attractive or unattractive—the outlook will affect your enjoyment of your patio. If appropriate, you can use a ladder to check views from different elevations. Consider whether a patio, deck, or similar structure might block a favorite view from inside the house. Also take into account views into your yard from nearby houses or streets.

## Code concerns

Before you launch into the design phase, check with your local building department to find out whether you need a building permit and learn what codes affect a potential structure's design and placement. Local codes and ordinances can govern the height of an outdoor structure, its maximum footprint, the materials from which it is built, its setback from lot lines, and even the nailing pattern its construction requires.

Also check your property deed for possible building easements or restrictions that might affect your project's location or design. Note any relevant code concerns on your base map.

### TOOLS OF THE TRADE

To draw your base map (and, later, your final plan), you'll need 24- by 36-inch graph paper (¼-inch scale, unless the size of your property requires ⅛-inch scale), an art gum eraser, a straightedge, several pencils, and a pad of tracing paper. Optional are a drafting board, a T-square, one or more triangles, a compass, a circle template, and an architect's scale. For taking measurements in the existing landscape, choose either a 50- or 100-foot tape measure; anything shorter is exasperating to use and can lead to inaccurate measurements.

You can draw your base map directly on graph paper or on tracing paper placed over graph paper. (If you plan to have a blueprinting company make copies of your base map, you will have to use tracing paper; a blueprint machine will not accept regular graph paper.)

If you can use a personal computer, don't overlook the growing collection of drawing and landscape-planning software programs. Unlike earlier CAD programs aimed at professionals, some of the newer offerings are designed for the more limited skill levels and budgets of homeowners.

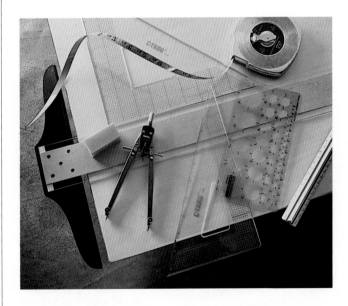

*Simple drawing and measuring tools can help produce a clear, easy-to-read base map and final plan. Shown are T-square, 45° and 60° triangles, compass, circle template, eraser, architect's scale, and 50-foot tape measure.*

# experimenting with your ideas

**WITH YOUR** *base map complete, you can begin trying out your ideas and determining the style of your patio or deck. As you brainstorm, you'll begin to work out use areas and circulation patterns and make general decisions about what kinds of structures and amenities you'll need and where to place them. You may also wish to review some design basics (see page 576).*

### What's your style?

*A Moroccan-tiled water feature sits in a patio of Saltillo pavers; it doubles as both soothing spa and garden pool.*

One early design decision you must make is whether you want a formal or informal outdoor environment. The style you choose should be compatible with the architecture of your house and appropriate to your climate.

Formal landscapes are symmetrical, with straight lines, geometric patterns, and clearly established balance; they often include sheared hedges, topiaries, and fountains, pools, or outdoor sculpture. Paving might be of mortared brick, cut stone, tile, or poured concrete.

Informal styles, on the other hand, tend to favor curves, asymmetry, and apparent randomness; adjacent plantings are usually more naturalistic, too. Masonry units, if used, are set in more casual sand beds (see page 581). Flagstones, river rocks, and gravel can give a native, nature-oriented look. Wooden decks seem at home in just about any informal setting.

You can learn a lot about style by studying gardens that you visit or see in magazines, as well as those illustrated throughout this book. Here are some stylistic themes that are part of a wide range you may encounter:

- Period (as in Georgian, Victorian)
- Mediterranean
- Tropical
- Asian
- Avant-garde
- Rustic
- Naturalistic
- Eclectic

Patio styles traverse a spectrum from rustic through eclectic. The one above features spaced stepping-stones and mortared twin "islands" of Arizona flagstone that fit with a nearly natural background of gravel, ground covers, border plantings, and mature oaks. The patio at left uses diagonally laid slate tiles to set off sculptural palms, a planting of tall horsetails, and whimsically colorful furniture.

# GUIDES TO GOOD DESIGN

Experienced landscape professionals employ several criteria to ensure that a deck or patio is useful and comfortable and that it also complements its surroundings visually. In well-designed landscapes no one plant, structure, or feature stands out too much, but rather all the parts work together to establish a sense of unity. Note how construction materials or plants are used with repetition or placed for dramatic emphasis. All the elements should be in proportion to the rest of the garden and in scale with the size of the house, the property, and the people who live there. Also, note how harmony is achieved by balancing simplicity (in form, texture, and color) and variety (in materials and plants).

When planning, you may also wish to review the following specifics.

■ **Meet your needs.** Your design should be able to accommodate your family's favorite activities, from relaxation and casual gatherings to children's games, barbecues, and entertaining.

■ **Protect privacy.** As an extension of your indoor living space, your patio should offer the same feeling of privacy as interior rooms do, but with no sense of confinement. Building an elevated deck, for example, can open as many unpleasant views as attractive ones—and expose you to view as well. Do you need to add screens, arbors, or plantings to remedy the problem? Could an ivy-draped wall and a trickling fountain help buffer unwanted noise?

*This private side-yard sitting area, paved with widely spaced flagstones, marks a gentle transition between a formal brick landing and the nearby rose garden.*

■ **Be aware of safety.** Patio paving materials have different properties. For example, some become slippery when wet; others are too sharp or uneven for children's games. Passage from house to patio and from deck to garden must be safe and unobstructed. Adequate lighting should be provided at steps and along garden paths.

■ **Use color.** As in a beautiful indoor room, colors should be placed in a coordinated relationship to one another. Brick, adobe, wood, and stone have distinctive, generally earthy colors. Concrete has more industrial overtones, but can be softened with aggregate, stamping and staining, or integral color.

Even plants on or around your patio or deck should contribute harmonious tones. Use complementary colors sparingly, as accents. Remember that all foliage is not simply "green"; the range of shades is really very large.

■ **Think transitions.** A patio or deck should entice people outdoors. So be sure to consider the transition from the inside of your house to the outside. Wide French or sliding glass doors make the outdoors look inviting and also make the interior space expand psychologically.

Try to create attractive transitions between different areas of the deck or patio and between these and the rest of the garden. The use of edgings, borders, steps, and railings can make or break your design.

## Define use areas

Focus on your family's needs and activities. Think about the way you live, making a list of what's most important to you (if you have children, get their input, too); then, if you need to compromise, you can compromise on the less important things.

Next, review your yard's assets. Can your plan capitalize on a fine view? Perhaps your design can take advantage of a sunny southern exposure or an impressive garden tree.

Consider also your yard's handicaps. Is your lot on a steep slope? How much of the lot is exposed to street noise or a neighbor's view? If you're rethinking an existing patio or deck, ask yourself whether it opens off the wrong room, gets too much sun or shade, or lacks sufficient space.

Now get ready to try out your ideas. For each design attempt, use a separate sheet of tracing paper placed over your base map, sketching rough circular or oval shapes ("balloons") to represent the location and approximate size of each use area. For an example, see the drawing at right.

As you sketch, concentrate on logical placement and juxtaposition. Are you locating a children's play area in full view of your living area? Is the small, private sunning spot you envision easily accessible from the master bedroom? Do you really want a patio designed for entertaining guests to be located next to the recycling bins? If you have doubts about the lay of the land, consult the information on grading and drainage on page 582.

## Design with shapes

When your experiments with diagrams have resulted in a rough sketch, lay a clean sheet of tracing paper on top of it. On this sheet, and on as many more as you need, begin drawing in the various building blocks of the design—paving, enclosing walls or hedges, arbors, benches, and perhaps a pool or spa.

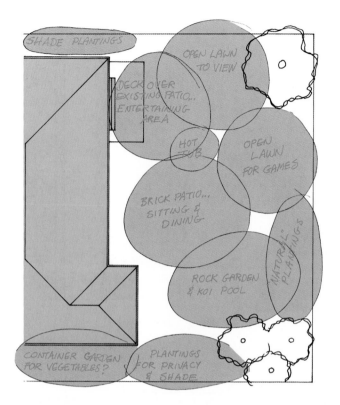

*To make a balloon sketch, place tracing paper over your base map; then sketch circles to indicate use areas and other features. Keep circulation patterns in mind. Consider your design as a whole, balancing design elements and relating the patio to both garden and house. Draw as many designs as you can—early mistakes cost nothing.*

At this point, keep in mind two tricks of the landscape designer. First, work with clear, simple shapes; second, relate those shapes to the lines of your house. A design that is made up of familiar shapes such as squares, rectangles, triangles, and circles is easier to understand than one filled with abstract lines. Repeating a familiar shape brings simplicity and order to the design, unifying paving, paths, walls, arbors, and other features.

To add interest, vary the sizes of the shapes you work with, but don't use too many little shapes or you will end up with a very busy design. Add a curve, perhaps, to connect two rectangular spaces, or use a diagonal line to emphasize the longest dimension in a small

### CLEARANCE FOR TABLE WITH CHAIRS

RISING SPACE 32"

SIDE PASSAGE 22"
(32" FOR HANDICAPPED)

### PATHWAY CLEARANCE

### BENCH CLEARANCE

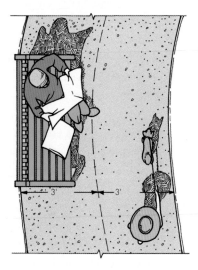

2' TO 3'

4' TO 5'

3'   3'

SERVICE PATHWAY     MAIN PATHWAY     SITTING     WALKING

---

## A PLANNING CHECKLIST

Look closely at the successful deck and patio designs shown in "Great Patios and Decks," pages 586–649. What components do you need to include to create your own ideal outdoor environment? Which materials would work best in your situation? (For practical guidance, also look through the information in "A Shopper's Guide," pages 651–669.)

As you begin to firm up your design, account for the following structural elements:

- Decking or paving materials
- Retaining wall for hilly or sloping areas
- Walls, fences, or screens for privacy or noise control
- Overhead structures
- Steps or formal stairs for changes in level
- Walks and footpaths linking use areas
- Edgings where appropriate
- French or sliding door for access from the house

Although some finishing touches, such as outdoor benches and planters, can be added later, now is the best time to think about the amenities you want and to sketch them on your design. If you might want to add lighting or perhaps a sink or wet bar to your outdoor living area later, plan now for the necessary wire or pipe runs.

- Arbor or trellis
- Gazebo
- Garden pool, fountain, waterfall, or stream
- Spa or hot tub
- Barbecue area or kitchen facilities
- Storage cabinets or shelves
- Built-in benches or other furniture
- Outdoor lighting (120-volt or low-voltage)
- GFCI-protected electrical outlets
- Outdoor heater or fireplace
- Hose bibb
- Raised beds for plants or built-in planter, perhaps with built-in drip irrigation

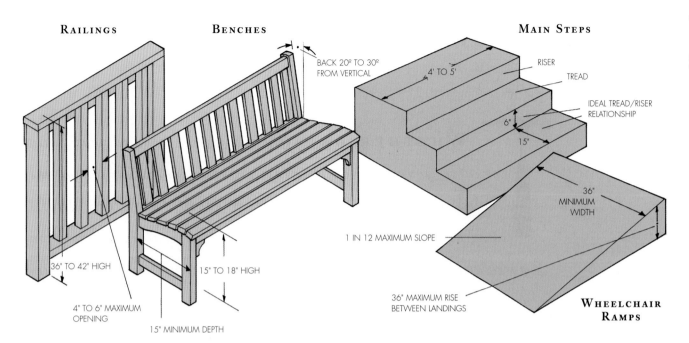

**RAILINGS**

36" TO 42" HIGH

4" TO 6" MAXIMUM OPENING

**BENCHES**

BACK 20° TO 30° FROM VERTICAL

15" TO 18" HIGH

15" MINIMUM DEPTH

**MAIN STEPS**

RISER

TREAD

IDEAL TREAD/RISER RELATIONSHIP

6"

15"

4' TO 5'

1 IN 12 MAXIMUM SLOPE

36" MAXIMUM RISE BETWEEN LANDINGS

36" MINIMUM WIDTH

**WHEELCHAIR RAMPS**

garden. Some structures will work themselves very naturally into your plan and others won't fit at all. Use the checklist on the facing page to help select the features that will serve your situation best.

## Examine circulation patterns

Also consider foot-traffic connections between use areas, as well as from individual areas to the house and yard. Will too much traffic be channeled through areas meant for relaxation? Can guests move easily from the entertainment area to the garden? Can the lawn mower or garden cart be moved from the toolshed to the lawn without disturbing someone's repose?

One way to improve access to and from the house is to add a door. But if you have to open up a wall to improve circulation, be sure you won't end up producing a traffic pattern that runs through the middle of a room.

When planning pathways, steps, and other parts of the route, you'll need to allow at least the established minimum clearances; for guidelines, see the illustrations above and on the facing page.

## MAKING A MOCK-UP

If you are having difficulty visualizing the finished landscape or can't quite decide on the specifics of certain elements, you may wish to mock up the design on your actual property. Seeing an approximation of the layout in the form of stakes, strings, and other markings can help you determine the exact dimensions necessary for features such as decks, terraces, and walks.

To outline paving areas, patio or deck construction, pathways, and planting beds with straight or gently curved lines, mark each corner with a short stake and connect the stakes with string. Use taller stakes to mark fences and walls. Tall stakes can also represent trees or elements like fountains, sculptures, or posts for overhead construction.

If your design is mostly curves and free-form shapes, snake a garden hose to lay out the lines to your liking. Limestone or gypsum, common soil amendments, can be used to lay out freeform designs such as the outlines of planting beds and borders. Powdered chalk in different colors is useful if you have overlapping elements. To revise your plan, simply turn the powder over into the soil and start again.

# nuts and bolts

**W**HETHER OR NOT *you intend to build your patio or deck yourself, you'll want a basic understanding of the materials and methods involved. A knowledge of these details can help you evaluate your do-it-yourself zeal and zero in on material costs; you'll also be able to communicate more easily with dealers and professionals.*

### Patio profiles

Most patios are constructed in one of two ways—with a poured concrete slab or base or atop a bed of clean, packed sand.

A concrete slab suits heavy-use areas and for-mal designs. The slab should be at least 4 inches thick (see drawing on facing page, top) and, for better drainage, underlaid with 2 to 8 inches of gravel. Welded wire mesh helps reinforce the structure. Wooden forms define the slab's shape; they're usually removed once the concrete has set. Wet concrete is poured into the forms like batter into a cake pan. While still plastic, the concrete is leveled and the surface is smoothed. Colored aggregates (small stones) or stamped patterns can customize and soften the concrete's appearance.

A thinner concrete pad, typically about 3 inches thick, can serve as the base for masonry units such as ceramic tile or flagstones set in mortar (see drawing on facing page, bottom).

A sand bed (see drawing on facing page, center) is popular for casual brick, paver, and cobblestone patios and walks, and some con-tractors use this method for formal work, too. A layer of gravel provides drainage and stability;

damp sand is then carefully leveled—or "screeded"—on top. Paving units, either spaced or tightly butted, go atop the screeded bed, and then additional sand is cast over the surface and worked into joints to lock units in place. Edgings help define the patio and keep units from shifting.

Whatever surface you choose, you should slope it a minimum of 1 inch per 8 feet for drainage. Walkways can be angled slightly so that water is channeled away.

### Deck details

If grade or drainage presents insurmountable problems, or if you simply prefer the look and feel of a wooden surface, a deck may be your choice.

A deck can be freestanding or, as shown on page 583, attached to the house via a horizontal ledger. The structure is designed with a stacking principle in mind, with each new layer perpendicular to the one below. Concrete footings secure precast piers or poured, tubular pads, which in turn support vertical wooden posts. Horizontal beams span the posts; joists run perpendicular to ledger and beams. The

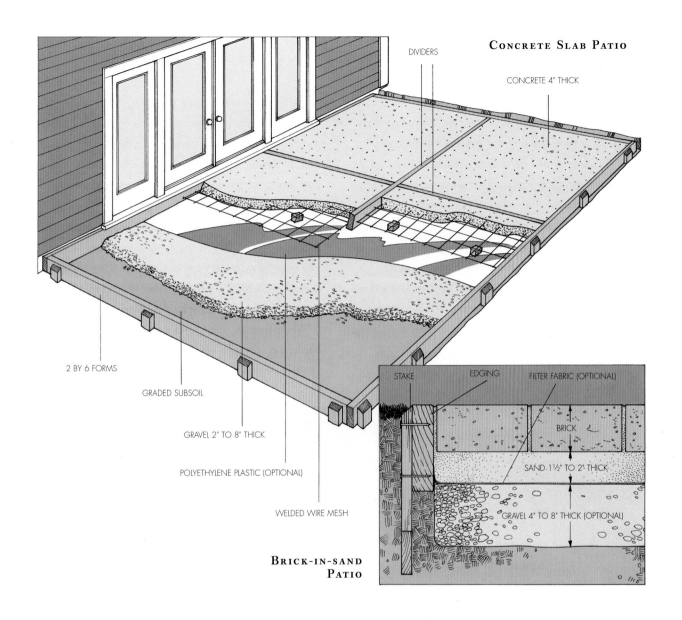

## Concrete Slab Patio

DIVIDERS

CONCRETE 4" THICK

2 BY 6 FORMS

GRADED SUBSOIL

GRAVEL 2" TO 8" THICK

POLYETHYLENE PLASTIC (OPTIONAL)

WELDED WIRE MESH

STAKE

EDGING

FILTER FABRIC (OPTIONAL)

BRICK

SAND 1½" TO 2" THICK

GRAVEL 4" TO 8" THICK (OPTIONAL)

### Brick-in-sand Patio

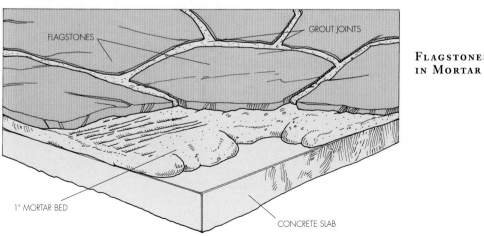

FLAGSTONES

GROUT JOINTS

### Flagstones in Mortar

1" MORTAR BED

CONCRETE SLAB

# OBSERVING THE LAY OF THE LAND

Whenever you can fit any landscape element into the existing topography with little or no disturbance of the soil, you save time, effort, and expense.

However, that isn't always possible. Sometimes the existing topography has inherent problems, or you realize you must alter it in order to accommodate your ideal design. Then you must grade the site—reshape it by removing soil, adding soil, or both. In most cases, it's best to consult a landscape architect or soils engineer.

If your property lies on a slope so steep that without skillful grading and terracing it would remain unstable and useless, consider constructing one or a series of retaining

walls. The safest way to build a retaining wall is to place it at the bottom of a gentle slope, if space permits, and fill in behind it. That way you won't disturb the stability of the soil. Otherwise, the hill can be held either with a single high wall or with a series of low walls forming graceful terraces.

Always route water away from the house. If your landscape is nearly flat, it must have adequate surface drainage—a minimum slope of 1 inch per 8 feet of paved surface, or nearly 3 inches per 10 feet of unpaved ground. Steeper gradients are better for slow-draining, heavy soils.

Where property slopes toward the house, you may need to shore it up with a retaining wall and slope surfaces to direct runoff to a central drain, like a "bathtub."

Poor subsurface drainage can be a problem where the water table is close to the surface. Plastic drainpipes or dry wells can be the answer in many situations. But a major problem calls for a sump pump. To plan and install a drainage system for a problem hillside, get professional help.

## STANDARD SLOPED RUNOFF

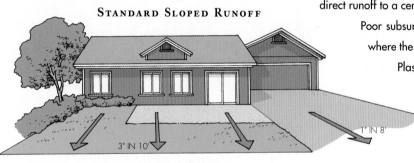

3" IN 10'        1" IN 8'

*A uniform slope, as shown above, directs water away from the house; hilly yards and retaining walls may call for a central catch basin, as shown below.*

## "BATHTUB" PATIO

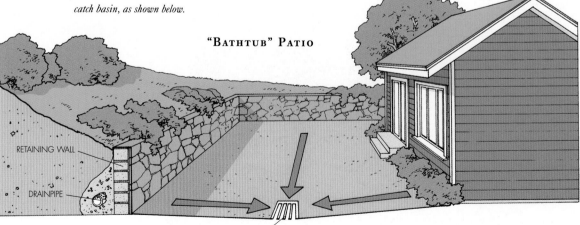

RETAINING WALL

DRAINPIPE

CATCH BASIN

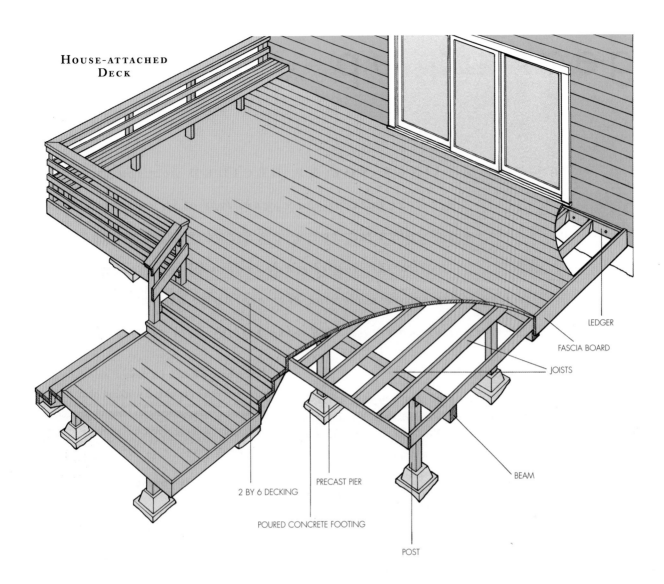

**HOUSE-ATTACHED DECK**

LEDGER

FASCIA BOARD

JOISTS

BEAM

PRECAST PIER

2 BY 6 DECKING

POURED CONCRETE FOOTING

POST

decking itself, typically 2 by 4 or 2 by 6 lumber, is nailed or screwed to the joists. Be sure that your decking is at least 1 inch below any door sill and that there are ⅛- to 3/16-inch drainage gaps between boards.

Overhead structures, benches, railings, and steps are often integral to a deck's framing. While it may be feasible to add these later, it's simplest to design and build the whole project at once.

In a deck's structure, the size and spacing of each component affect the members above and below. Minimum and maximum sizes are stipulated by your building code. Posts taller than about 3 feet may require bracing, especially in areas prone to earthquakes or high winds. Elevated decks require railings (again, specified by local code).

Fascia boards, skirts, and other trim details help add a custom touch to the basic structure. For a closer look at decking lumber, hardware, and finishes, see "A Shopper's Guide," pages 651–669.

Are you planning a rooftop deck? It must be sloped above an impermeable membrane—a job for a roofing contractor.

# gearing up

ONCE YOU'VE DECIDED *how you want to use your outdoor space, what type of structure will accomplish this best, and what alterations of gradient are called for, you're ready to firm up your plan. This rendering is the end result of the design process; use it for fine-tuning, for estimating materials, and when talking with professionals.*

### The final plan

To create your plan, place a sheet of tracing paper over your base map. Draw carefully and label all features clearly. Most designers create a "plan" view and one or more "elevations." (A plan view is the classic bird's-eye view of the layout as if seen from above; an elevation, or straight-on view, shows how the scene would look to a person standing in one spot nearby.)

*What's your choice— earthy and muted, or sleekly smooth? Classic masonry units, like the terra-cotta tiles and green-glazed accents shown at right, fit well in many regional and traditional settings. But the cast-concrete veranda on the facing page makes a sophisticated, modern statement, spreading down past concentric steps from a sheltered entertainment patio with built-in barbecue and fireplace.*

If you have a knack for design, there's no reason why you can't develop a working plan, though it's wise to have at least an hour's consultation with a professional landscape architect or designer (see facing page).

### Can you do it yourself?

If you are a skilled weekend carpenter, you should have no serious problem building a simple deck or overhead structure, such as an arbor. However, certain conditions may require professional help.

A deck on unstable soil, sand, mud, or water needs special foundations for support—and perhaps the advice of an engineer as well as of a builder. A high-level deck or one on a steep hillside also involves special design methods and may be too difficult for an amateur to build.

Concrete work, while straightforward, can present a logistical and physical challenge. If your job is complex or requires a large, continuous pour, leave it to pros. Patios assembled from smaller units such as bricks or stones can be built at a more leisurely pace. But be advised that, for the average weekend mason, the constant lifting, mixing, and shoveling may take their toll.

## Working with professionals

Who is the right advisor to help you adapt, develop, or build your patio or deck? Here are some of the people who can offer assistance, along with a brief look at what they do.

**ARCHITECTS AND LANDSCAPE ARCHITECTS.** These state-licensed professionals have a bachelor's or master's degree in architecture or landscape architecture. They're trained to create designs that are structurally sound, functional, and esthetically pleasing. They know construction materials, can negotiate bids from contractors, and can supervise the actual work. Many are willing to give a simple consultation, either in their offices or at your home, for a modest fee.

**LANDSCAPE AND BUILDING DESIGNERS.** Landscape designers usually have a landscape architect's education and training but not a state license. Building designers, whether licensed (by the American Institute of Building Designers) or unlicensed, may offer design help along with construction services.

**DRAFTSPERSONS.** Drafters may be members of a skilled trade or unlicensed architects' apprentices. They can make the working drawings (from which you or your contractor can work) needed for building permits.

**STRUCTURAL AND SOILS ENGINEERS.** If you're planning to build a structure on an unstable or steep lot or where heavy wind or loads come into play, you should consult an engineer.

A soils engineer evaluates soil conditions and establishes design specifications for foundations. A structural engineer, often working with the calculations a soils engineer provides, designs foundation piers and footings to suit the site. Engineers also provide wind- and load-stress calculations as required.

**GENERAL AND LANDSCAPE CONTRACTORS.** Licensed general and landscape contractors specialize in construction (landscape contractors specialize in garden construction), though some have design

experience as well. They usually charge less for design work than landscape architects do, but their skills may be limited by a construction point of view.

Contractors may do the work themselves or assume responsibility for ordering materials, hiring qualified subcontractors, and seeing that the job is completed according to contract.

**SUBCONTRACTORS.** If you prefer to act as your own general contractor, it's up to you to hire, coordinate, and supervise whatever subcontractors the job requires—specialists in carpentry, grading, and the like. Aside from doing the work according to your drawings, subcontractors can often supply you with product information and procure materials. Of course, you can hire other workers on your own; but in that case, you'll be responsible for permits, insurance, and any payroll taxes.

# GREAT PATIOS AND DECKS

**I**F YOU'RE LOOKING for inspiration, you've come to the right place. The following pages are crammed with photos that showcase both patios and decks in action. You'll find a wide range of materials, formal and informal styles, landscapes large and small. **WE BEGIN** with two large sections that traverse a range of successful patio and deck designs. Then come sections with outstanding solutions to some common—and not so common—site problems. **AS YOU BROWSE,** note the custom touches that turn a basic platform into a distinctive outdoor room. Pay particular attention to edgings and borders; as pros know, these transitions can make or break your design. Feel free to borrow a deck detail here, a patio accent there. Many of these ideas are appropriate for either wood or masonry, or for a mix of both. **IF AVAILABILITY** is a question, you'll find plenty of information on specific materials in "A Shopper's Guide," beginning on page 651.

# patio profiles

**MANY PATIO STYLES** are established, at least in part, by the materials you choose for them. Brick is one of the most adaptable and frequently used surfaces available. Set in mortar or, more casually, in sand, brick can blend with nearly any architectural or landscaping style. Precast concrete pavers, available in many shapes and sizes, can be used in much the same way as brick—in fact, in some areas, "brick-style" pavers are more popular than the real thing.

Though often typecast as cold and forbidding, poured concrete is perhaps even more adaptable than brick. Used with the proper forms and reinforcement, it can conform to almost any shape. It can be lightly smoothed or heavily brushed, surfaced with colorful pebbles, swirled, scored, tinted, patterned, or molded to resemble another material.

Ceramic tile works well in both formal and informal situations. From the earthy tones of terra-cotta to the bright primaries of hand-painted accents, tile can support just about any landscaping style. Flat flagstones and cut stone tiles are ideal for formal paving. For a more informal look, you can use more irregularly shaped rocks and pebbles, setting them in soil or embedding them in concrete.

For economy, good drainage, and a more casual look, consider including loose materials such as pea gravel, bark, or wood chips in your patio plan. Gravel can be raked into patterns or used as a decorative filler with other materials. You might employ dividers to set off different colors and textures.

*Seeded aggregate creates a classic, nonskid concrete surface. An octagonal brick border defines the dining area; matching brickwork is used in other parts of the patio.*

*Tile leftovers, colored stones, and a set of concrete footprints form a whorled and whimsical courtyard mosaic.*

*An outdoor room with a crackling fire makes the day's warmth linger longer. The brick patio, set in a classic running-bond pattern, surrounds a small pond and gentle waterfall. Low walls with flagstone caps corral plantings and provide extra seating.*

*This rear patio's for-
mal brickwork is set
on concrete with neat-
ly tooled mortar
joints, continuing the
orderly look of the
stucco-clad two-story
house behind.*

*A geometric pattern of concrete
pavers tops an easy-draining
base of filter fabric and
packed gravel. Pressure-treated
wooden edgings help lock the
patio in place.*

*A blue concrete river meanders through a side-yard patio, past fragmented islands in a gray field. A band of dark blue ceramic tile halts the flow of curves. Some areas of concrete are smooth, others scored and brushed.*

*The outdoor sitting area above features alternating patches of Korean grass and spaced concrete paver blocks that support the casual furniture. Young crab apple trees follow the curving boundary between patio and garden.*

*A sunny wraparound veranda is clothed in nonslip, light-toned concrete that stays cool in direct sun. Note how the concrete's color and texture complement the house's exterior walls.*

*Patinaed by time, this Mediterranean-style courtyard blends terra-cotta tile squares and diagonally set blue-glazed accents. The design centers on a vibrant tiled fountain.*

*There's no law against having fun with tile. Colorful Malibu tiles, shown above, make lively porch accents. The playful path shown at right sports custom-painted, randomly placed striped tile squares.*

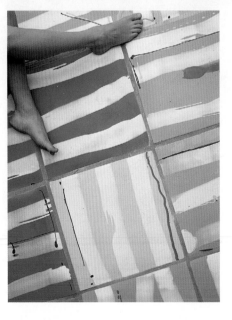

*Slick tiles can be trouble outdoors, but some new glazed floor tiles are toothy enough for safe footing on the veranda. And while they resemble both stone and terra-cotta, they're easier to maintain than either.*

*At once formal and earthy, these Indian slate tiles, with*

*matching accent courses, help wrap an outdoor pavilion*

*and adjacent pool in warm, variegated tones.*

*A colorful mosaic compass stands out against background pavement of randomly shaped broken flagstones.*

*Arizona flagstone slabs are laid with tight joints; some are grouted, but many cracks remain, allowing lemon thyme and woolly thyme to gain a footing.*

*A front-yard clearing, lined with gray gravel and ringed*

*by old stone walls and colorful flower beds, forms a*

*casual and comfortable backdrop for dining, gardening,*

*or—in the orange cat's case—some serious snoozing.*

Gravel's casual appeal makes an effective transition from formal patio to the garden proper. Here, graveled areas are bounded by curved rubber edgings for a striking contrast in color and texture.

This highly sculptured study in dark pea gravel and vanilla-colored concrete is broken by a poured concrete bench and curb and by planting beds strewn with red-wood chips.

# decked out

**F**EW MATERIALS can match the natural, informal quality of wood. Its warm color and soft texture bring something of the forest into your landscape, and if stained or painted, wood can hold its own in even the most formal company.

A wooden deck—either freestanding or house-attached—provides a solid, relatively durable surface requiring little or no grading and a minimum of maintenance. Because decking is raised above the ground and can dry quickly, it's a natural wherever drainage is a problem.

For even less maintenance and a lower environmental impact, consider surface decking that's made from recycled materials; a graphic example is shown on the facing page. (Note, however, that you'll still need wood or another material for structural members; this decking is not rated for strength.)

Whether it's new or old, natural or man-made, decking at ground level feels right in almost any outdoor setting. A low-lying deck can link house and garden at flower-head height, smoothing out bumps and riding over drainage problems that might preclude masonry pavings. A wrap-around extends living space into the landscape, offering an unbeatable way to expand cramped living quarters.

Any deck more than 30 inches above the ground requires a railing or similar barrier. Beyond safety, railings contribute an important design element, too. What's the view? Use railings to frame it or block it. Fill gaps with vertical slats, safety glass, or screening.

*Sunlight glows on a cedar-surfaced waterfront deck; stone slab steps link it to a concrete patio above. Note how the deck's edge is cut to accommodate the big boulders.*

*This broad backyard structure is at home with the surrounding forest, but its decking "boards" aren't wood—they're splinterless, composite products made largely from recycled plastic. Built-in wooden bench seating surrounds a fire pit that, when covered, becomes a coffee table.*

*Natural wood decking extends the old concrete slab at house level; openings make way for mature oaks, which double as hammock supports. The deck is shored up by a stone-capped retaining wall; steps lead down to the paver patio.*

*A low-level cedar deck seemingly floats above a rock-lined garden pool; 2 by 3 decking boards are finished with semi-transparent stain.*

Designed and built by the homeowners and a contractor friend, this house-attached structure features dark-stained 2 by 4 cedar decking with a penetrating finish on top. Built-in benches, planters, and a ground-level "bridge" over river rocks add a note of permanence and help tie the deck to the landscape. So does the deck's skirt, which repeats the house's siding style and color.

A soothing hot tub holds center stage on this detached garden platform. Note the crafted patterns and accents on the deck surface.

This low entry deck establishes a transition between the house and the landscape while providing a smooth surface and efficient drainage. Leisurely curves lead the eye toward the front archway beyond.

*Cantilevered above a steep hillside and accessed via a winding "mountain path," this austere perch hovers above a seemingly wild landscape. The deck is sparingly dressed with a space-frame arbor and built-in bench.*

*A cascade of stairs and landings pinwheels around a rocky outcrop and two venerable trees. The stairs leading from the upper-level deck are freestanding. They're supported by cross-stacked redwood 4 by 4s that allow the curving form to be developed.*

*Built for entertaining large crowds and guarded by a
copper pipe railing, the star of this elegantly planned two-
level redwood deck is the built-in sofa in the center. The edge
of the upper deck forms the seat; the planter provides
back support.*

*These three decks rail against convention. Child-safe netting, shown above, snaps into place, and can be removed for views or when entertaining. Armed with a saber saw, the owner of the deck shown at top right gave each 1¹/4 by 4-inch cedar rail a whimsical shape. Custom baked-enamel steel railings at right combine with steel cable and turnbuckles for a clean, uncluttered look.*

*Some views can take your
breath away. To keep this one
unobstructed while adding wind
protection, the owner placed
panels of safety glass in the deck
railing's straight sections.*

# coping with slopes

**IF YOU'RE FACED** with a hilly, hard-to-drain site, you can either learn to live with it or, depending on your soil and your budget, you can start over. Sites that require extensive grading—via excavation and backfilling—can get both complicated and expensive. Drainage can also present a daunting challenge. (For a look at the logistics, see page 582.)

A simpler solution could be either a step-down, multiplatform arrangement or a cantilevered deck that can float over steep spots. Both ideas allow for exciting effects. Consider the view from inside—you may wish to drop the top platform below sight.

In plans for either patios or decks, you may need to include a retaining wall to hold back the earth and prevent erosion. You have a choice among three basic wall-building materials—wood, stone, and concrete—and among a number of new modular masonry systems developed with the owner-builder in mind. As always, planning for drainage is essential.

Garden steps bridge slopes and shuttle traffic. They can also offer design opportunities. Think of them as transition zones between patio levels; extensions might double as benches, planters, or display perches. Regardless of the material you use, put safety first: treads should give safe footing in wet weather, and adequate lighting must be provided. Be sure that step dimensions are comfortable—not too long and not too steep.

*How do you integrate a flight of aggregate stairs into the garden? First widen them to form a landing. Then soften them with ground covers and border plantings. The result is a graceful set of landscaped terraces.*

*A cramped, steep lot presented a design challenge, but this multilevel, multiuse structure was a creative response. Sitting areas top retaining walls; luxurious plantings and earthy paving materials soften hard lines. Here, as with any hillscape, establishing proper drainage was crucial.*

*A striking multilevel redwood deck glows with warm sunset light. Its layout transforms a steep hillside into a spacious, flexible outdoor room. Built-in benches, wide steps, and matching railings add finishing touches.*

*What can you do with a steep slope on a small urban lot? This designer built up the slope to make space for a front-yard patio with great views. A new concrete-block retaining wall (right) atop the old one raised its level. The resulting back-filled platform is dressed with concrete pavers, trellised railings, built-in benches, and a sunny garden bed (below).*

# small miracles

**W**HEN SPACE IS SHORT, your landscape must work harder. Vertical stacking is one way to handle sloped or multistory layouts; intensify the available space by creating small, separate areas. For example, let a small elevated deck feed down to a ground-level container-plant patio and onward to a separate sitting area along the back fence. Flat lots also benefit from changes in level—even a few inches.

Small-space designs often employ a deliberate sense of "misdirection." Use diagonal lines and offset patterns to lead the eye outward. Use winding paths, grouped containers, screens, arbors, and plantings to slow traffic, to frame tiny views, and to create hidden spots that blur boundaries. Even the smallest pond or pool can make a space seem larger by creating an illusion of depth and by reflecting the sky and surrounding surfaces.

Invest in quality materials. Pay particular attention to your use of paving and amenities. Because the space is small, it must stand up to close scrutiny.

Consider the inside-outside connection (for ideas, see pages 622–625). A set of glazed doors or a window wall can link the house and garden, stretching space in both directions.

To protect privacy, grow a screen of green. Tall plants or vine-covered arbors block out views of neighboring houses. A trickling waterfall or fountain masks noise.

*A hilly, narrow side yard now accommodates a waterfall, a spa, and several sitting areas (one is shown)—all artfully integrated as a series of descending tiers.*

*A tract lot that was formerly bare dirt now sports whitewashed, low-level decking that's angled to enhance the sense of space. Wood gives way to Saltillo tiles beyond, also laid diagonally. A trickling wall fountain makes a tranquil focal point off the living room. Tall plantings and a house-attached arbor offer a sense of enclosure and screen off the neighbors' houses.*

*On a steep lot along a busy street, a slender, 12- by 35-foot courtyard leads to this house's*

*entry. French doors connect the living room directly to the stamped-concrete patio, making*

*it possible for interior and exterior rooms to borrow space from each other.*

*A waterfall masks street noise.*

A small mixed-gravel patio tucks into the U shape formed by the house and the neighbors' wall at right (not shown). The casual hardscape incorporates both patio and garden, trimming down the more usual space-consuming borders between them. Banks of French doors and windows open to the area, extending interior space, too.

Water makes this narrow urban yard into a small oasis. The waterfall makes a peaceful background sound, while a set of "floating" stepping stones involves inhabitants directly with the landscape.

# up-front ideas

**W**ITH LOT SIZES shrinking and land values soaring, you want to make every inch of your outdoor space count. And though we tend to picture the patio area as being behind the house, why not look out front?

In place of lawn and landscaping designed for public view (and not much else), enclose the space with garden walls to create a private front courtyard—a very old Moorish and Spanish tradition. With garden walls in place, you can open up street-facing rooms with a glass door or curtainless windows, bringing in more daylight and playing up the courtyard connection. An arbor overhead adds shade and shelter. You can also move the indoors out, adding amenities such as a fireplace, soft lighting, and a dining area.

Of course, on lots blessed with privacy out in front, you can choose just about any scheme—perhaps adding a knee wall, a screen, or an arbor to help define the space.

*A patio might as well start right at the front steps. This set combines flagstone treads and glazed-tile risers. The way leads through a rustic gate to a raised front patio of spaced flagstones with grass growing between them.*

*Twin arched arbors frame the brick path from the street to a front-yard patio just beyond the swinging teak privacy doors. The house entry is to the left past the doors.*

Driveways can do double duty. Soften harsh paving with planting pockets or replace it with concrete turf blocks. Relegate the car to its allotted corner and reclaim the remainder as a courtyard. Good-looking interlocking pavers say "patio," but can stand up to car traffic.

A front-yard room may be simpler to build than an indoor room of comparable size, but it is still subject to building codes. Of primary concern are the wall height and the setback from the street.

An inviting private courtyard (right) has a pitch-roofed arbor overhead, rising above the curve of the arched entry-way. The space enjoys morning sunlight, but thanks to the fireplace, it's also suitable for evening entertaining. The new front wall (above) recaptures part of the driveway.

Cantilevered over the edge of a steep street-front slope, this limestone-lined entertainment patio enjoys great views and—due to its height—privacy as well. Double sets of wide French doors give access from the kitchen.

# inside out

I<small>N</small> TEMPERATE CLIMATES, you can relax the line between indoors and outdoors, creating a leisurely transition between the two. The effect begins with your choice of patio doors. French and sliding models are time-honored options, but consider other types, too: folding, pivoting, pocket, and overhead. You can also group glazed doors with operable or fixed window units to make a window wall that seems to merge directly into the landscape.

*With the flick of a wrist, the segmented roof above this outdoor dining room silently changes from an open trellis to partially angled louvers for sun control, then becomes a closed, watertight surface.*

To further the effect, consider using the same paving inside and out. Because tile and stone both look great indoors, they're popular flooring choices for an indoor room that's related to a patio as well as for the patio itself. Poured concrete is showing up, too, especially in modernistic design schemes.

Enclosed patios form effective bridges between indoor and outdoor living spaces. Use arbors, trellises, and screens to define a transition zone. In harsh climates, the sun-room is an option as an indoor-outdoor space. Some sun-rooms can be opened up when the sun shines and battened down when hard winds blow.

If you're planning a new home or an extensive remodel, you may wish to incorporate an interior courtyard, or atrium, into your plans, perhaps one accessed from several interior rooms. And don't rule out the classic porch, currently enjoying a deserved comeback.

*Two sets of multifold doors open the side and end of this living room to a jasmine-shrouded patio. To further blur the distinction between inside and outside, a fossilized flagstone floor runs throughout.*

*Homeowners in a temperate climate stretched their indoor living space by fashioning an outdoor living room complete with couches, spa, and a lighting scheme that's also an echo of the indoor lighting.*

*When the owners of this home are feeling cooped up but it's too damp or windy to go out in the yard, they retreat to the indoor-outdoor garden room off the rear bedroom of their house. The brick-floored addition is open to the air at the top of both ends and in the arched doorway, but the side walls and glazed roof panels provide protection from the weather.*

The classic porch is, of course, a time-tested way to bridge
house and garden. This one fronts a turn-of-the-century
historical dwelling faced with massive chunks of local
granite. Rustic tiles pave the elevated floor; traditional
furnishings add period ambience.

# remote retreats

*Blue chairs and a white arbor are tinged with yellow sunrise light. The owner-built structure, floored with flagstone and soft star creeper, perches atop an east-facing hillside garden and makes a great vantage point for morning or evening views.*

GETTING AWAY FROM IT ALL gets tougher and tougher, but a detached patio or deck can offer restful privacy while utilizing an otherwise undeveloped garden area. It can be tiny. A small paved clearing, borrowed from the garden, might contain just enough solid brick to anchor a bench or chairs, drinks, and a thick novel or two.

Or it can be more substantial. A freestanding deck or a bower (a rustic shelter with arbor roof, built-in bench, and perhaps a trickling fountain) might perch above a distant view or face inward to a quiet reflecting pond.

Gazebos are being rediscovered. Evocative of country bandstands on summer evenings, they become poetic-looking retreats and romantic garden destinations. The traditional gazebo has either six or eight sides and sloping rafters joined in a central hub at the roof peak. Newer, looser interpretations can be husky—with hefty corner columns and stacked beams—or quite airy, consisting of little more than four posts connected by pairs of 2 by 6s.

Remote retreats take beautifully to amenities: decorative path lights or downlights, hammocks or swings, fountains or spas. Make the route to your hideaway direct or circuitous; mark the spot with a clearly visible overhead structure or use subtle screening and tall plantings as camouflage.

*A symbol of repose, this secluded teahouse sits atop a low-level platform deck that rests on sturdy boulders amidst lush plantings, waterfalls, and a pond that's home to flickering orange koi.*

Some gardens just cry out for a meandering path and a

remote sitting area or two. This small clearing is sparely

floored with square concrete paver blocks; the winding

path moves onward to several other hidden spots.

*This quiet clearing, seemingly returning to the elements, blends an engulfing carpet of beach grasses with just enough weathered railroad ties to support two chairs and a few container plants.*

*An aggregate path leads toward the wooden bridge and onward to a traditional gazebo, sited in a quiet corner away from the bustle of house and patio. Waterfall and stream add a sound track to simple daydreaming or moon-watching.*

# going vertical

**A**N ARBOR OR TRELLIS launches your landscape into another dimension—the vertical—while doubling as an accent, shelter, plant support, or privacy screen.

A trellis is typically a simple, flat framework of vertical supports and horizontal crosspieces. An arbor takes flanking trellis walls and adds a trellis-like roof; classic arch arbors curve this roof. A beefier, longer arbor, laid out in colonnade fashion, becomes a pergola, traditionally shored up with stout timber posts or cast columns.

You can make your own trellis or buy a commercial model at a garden center or through a mail-order supplier. Some types are made of sturdy dimension lumber, some of wooden strips or lattice, and others of sturdier wrought iron. Whatever the material, the trellis must be strong enough to support the weight of mature plants and durable enough to stand up to the rigors of your climate.

*A classical poolside loggia is ready for a quiet summer evening's repose. Besides shade and style, overhead structures like this furnish hidden anchors for outdoor light fixtures.*

*A green-painted, garage-attached arbor harbors a cooling crop of shady grape leaves and shelters a gravel-lined pocket patio. It also supports an old-fashioned porch swing.*

Whether freestanding or attached to a building, an arbor is held up by a series of posts or columns. These support horizontal beams, which usually support rafters. In a house-attached structure, a ledger takes the place of a beam, and the rafters are laid directly on the ledger. The rafters can be either left uncovered or covered with lath, lattice, poles, grape stakes, or solid panels.

*Morning sun angles across an aggregate patio that's backed*

*by a long, open pergola. An informal garden path flows*

*through this tunnel which, besides dividing garden spaces*

*and supporting a thick growth of vines, also forms a handy*

*support for hanging plants and garden ornaments.*

*An evenly spaced grid of traditional painted lath forms a stylish privacy screen and, with the peaked framework overhead, helps create a rather formal outdoor room.*

*A lazy-making hammock is one of the great pleasures of summer, but trees sturdy enough to support one are not always handy. Here the solution is a slender arbor with two hefty 6-by-6 posts spaced 13 feet apart.*

*great patios and decks*

# the outdoor kitchen

**FAMILY COOKOUTS** and entertaining are often centered around the barbecue. But although the familiar kettle shape may still preside over the proceedings, you can go a step further—and bring the comfort and convenience of an indoor kitchen to poolside or patio.

*Built of rustic brick, an outdoor kitchen houses a gas-fired barbecue and griddle, metal-doored storage cabinets, and a tiled countertop. The arbor above provides shade and some shelter, and helps define the space.*

The layout of your outdoor kitchen and your choice of cooking elements will depend on your favorite cooking technique, whether it's grilling, stir-frying, or griddle cooking. Commercial barbecues and cooktops abound. More sophisticated masonry units incorporate built-in smokers, commercial-quality woks, or pizza ovens that accompany a traditional grill.

Facilities around the barbecue may include preparation and serving areas, storage cabinets, a vent hood, an under-counter refrigerator, a sink with disposal, a dishwasher, a wet bar, and a dining area. Built-in entertainment centers with TV or audio/intercom systems are other possible additions.

*This wood-fired outdoor oven sees plenty of pizza-baking and chicken-roasting action. The carefully crafted granite structure houses a prefabricated oven insert, a chimney, a wood bin, and even a digital timer. Nearby are handy built-in stone countertops and a gas-fired barbecue.*

Maintaining and cleaning outdoor cooking facilities can be a challenge. If you use protective grill covers and rugged materials such as concrete or tile, you can clean the kitchen area simply by hosing it down.

Many outdoor kitchens are at least partially sheltered overhead or housed in a gazebo. Depending on the site's exposure and microclimate, you may need to add screens, trellises, or even heavy-duty bifold or sliding doors to help screen wind and hot sun or provide temporary enclosure during winter months.

*A granite-tiled eating counter (right) backs a curved entertaining area that's fully integrated into a poolside patio design. The well-equipped kitchen area (above) is set two steps below general patio level, making serving and conversing more comfortable. The lowered floor also encourages swimmers to join in, using the tile-topped "tables" along the pool's edge.*

*Though canopied by lush foliage, this outdoor dining area contains everything necessary for a casual meal: gas barbecue, sink, refrigerator, ice-maker, cabinets, teak dining table, and folding rattan chairs.*

# a splash of water

**IN RECENT YEARS** swimming pools have been slimmed to fit home landscapes rather than overpower them. Some can be shoehorned into tight sites and integrated more easily into relatively modest schemes. The lap pool is a case in point.

If you're planning a pool, also provide a paved area or deck adjoining it. As a general rule, the poolside area should be at least equal to the area of the pool itself, and should drain away from the pool. Nonslip masonry is safest, but wood stays cooler underfoot. The surround sets the mood: with the addition of boulders, flagstones, bridges, and other free-form edgings, naturalistic pools and spas can double as garden ponds.

Spas come in a rainbow of colors, shapes, and textures; materials range from sleek acrylic to formal concrete. Wooden hot tubs, a cousin from California, resemble large, usually straight-sided barrels. Place your spa or hot tub poolside or sequester it in a private nook. Be sure to plan shelter from wind, rain, and the neighbors.

Whether trickling as a wall fountain, meandering as a stream, or collected as a full-scale garden pond complete with lilies and fish, a decorative water feature brings a sense of magic and repose to the outdoor environment. Your pond may be formal or informal, edged with angular brick, or rimmed with native boulders. And it needn't be built in; even the tiniest layout can make way for a tub garden or a small spill fountain.

*The house tucks in beside the lap pool and opens to it through a sliding glass wall from the living room. The pool was there first: the rebuilt house was designed to incorporate it.*

*A foreground spa, two garden ponds, and a swimming pool (not shown) all nest efficiently in this back-yard scene. Wood decking ties all the elements together and provides a platform for a leisurely stroll.*

*Flagstone paving reflects warm evening colors in a*
*dramatic "vanishing-edge" pool, seemingly cantilevered*
*beyond the canyon rim (the secret is a retaining wall*
*hidden from sight, plus a recirculating pump). Boulders*
*form massive accents, setting off both waterfall and spa. A*
*poolside oak grows inside a circular well.*

*The pleasing pastels of tiled borders in pool and spa are repeated in intricate mosaic murals behind both fountain and serving counter, pulling this broad poolside entertainment area together visually.*

*Formal as can be, the view through this classical masonry arch highlights a wall fountain, a marble-lined spa, and the enclosed courtyard patio beyond.*

*A detached patio surrounds a formal water garden. The
concrete pavers are rigidly rectangular, but softened by
abundant border plantings. The pond is home to thick-
growing water lilies; spray fountains add sound and
movement to the colorful spectacle.*

*This built-in spa, adjacent to a master bedroom, features a retractable teak cover that slides on steel tracks recessed in the concrete-and-terrazzo patio. When the cover is closed, it doubles as a small low-level deck.*

*Three water features in one, this combination wall fountain/spa/garden pond contrasts diagonal tile diamonds in glossy colors with an earthier backdrop of conventional brick.*

# finishing touches

**DON'T FORGET** the custom touches that can turn a hardscape into a comfortable outdoor room.

Safety, security, and decor can all be improved with a good outdoor lighting scheme. The only restriction is to keep both glare and wattage at a low level. Because the contrast between darkness and a light source is so great, glare can be a problem at night. Three rules of thumb: choose shielded fixtures; place fixtures out of sight lines; and lower overall light levels. A little light goes a long way at night. You can choose a standard 120-volt system or use a low-voltage scheme. For additional details, see pages 666–667.

When it comes to seating, opt for freestanding, portable patio furniture or built-ins or both. Architectural built-ins supplement portable patio furniture and free up floor space for other uses. Build benches into wide steps or transitions between levels. Make them from nonslip masonry, wood, or metal, and plan carefully for drainage. For fun, add overhead support for a porch swing or hammock.

Portable containers can bring annuals and perennials, shrubs, and even vegetables to any favorable location. On the other hand, built-in planting spaces lend a custom look to your structure. Add formal masonry beds or leave planting pockets between paving units (run drip tubing below the surface). Incorporate planters into steps or level changes.

*This front-yard fireplace helps turn a gentle slope into an entertainment area. Courtyard paving is level with the house's floor for easier indoor-outdoor passage. A heavy-beamed trellis scales down the tall chimney.*

*A slatted wood porch swing complements the warm tones of variegated sandstone paving.*

*An entry patio's vividly colored
bench-wall conceals seated
guests from the street beyond.
The same acrylic house paint
was used for house walls and
the bench; flagstones top the
table and form footrests along
the curve of the bench's base.*

*A simple but graceful patio planter bed doubles as a
bench; the stuccoed knee wall is capped with bent wood.
The pocket cactus garden keeps patio loungers alert.*

*A multilayered forest of oaks and madrones gains almost magical drama through carefully placed deck lighting that picks up tree shapes and depth. The 150-watt uplights are mounted to a deck fascia; softer downlights (to guide foot traffic), mounted to the house siding, are fitted with glare-reducing louvers.*

*Subtle night lighting highlights plantings and helps turn an arbor-topped patio into an around-the-clock extension of interior space. Discreet downlights provide ambient and accent light; strip lights along horizontal beams are almost purely for fun.*

*Plant containers offer seasonal flexibility and help blur the borders between hardscape and garden. Containers can be portable, like the stone iguana pot shown above; they can be built-in, like the (bottomless) steel culvert pipes at top right; or they can leave the ground entirely, like the hanging pot at right.*

*What can you do with a narrow patioside planting bed that's backed by boring stucco walls? This twiggy trellis, shaped like a four-paneled screen, has horizontal grids built from birch branches fastened to 1½-inch spacers screwed into the house wall. The arching tops are formed by bundles of whiplike birch twigs bound together with copper wire.*

*Morning sun casts tulip shadows across tightly fitted*

*flagstone paving. The elliptic shape of this planting pocket*

*gives it an informal, unpredictable quality.*

# A SHOPPER'S GUIDE

**W**HETHER YOUR PREFERENCE is for wood or masonry, this chapter can help you sort out your options. Here we focus on flooring materials for your new outdoor recreation space. We'll try to demystify some of the ritual and jargon surrounding lumberyards and garden centers. Special features along the way help you understand the intricacies of lumber specifications, concrete make-overs, and outdoor heating and lighting. **L**OCAL INFORMATION can be a big help. Ask your building department or garden supplier about the best deck stain, tile type, or base treatment for use in your area. Be sure to survey current local offerings before buying; new products appear constantly. **I**F YOU'RE BUILDING the project yourself, you may wish to consult the Sunset titles *The Complete Deck Book* and *The Complete Patio Book* for detailed help.

# Lumberyard Primer

A CRASH COURSE IN DECKING LINGO

Because wood comes in so many sizes, species, and grades, a visit to a lumberyard can be a daunting experience for the uninitiated. Busy salespeople may not be adequately responsive if you're completely unfamiliar with deck-building terminology. But once you know a few basics, it's easier to get help with the fine points.

Basic deck components are shown on page 583.

## Lumber terms

Your choice in lumber, which will take the biggest bite out of your project budget, strongly influences the appearance of your deck. It pays to explore the options carefully before you make a final plan.

**SOFTWOOD OR HARDWOOD?** All woods are one or the other. The terms don't refer to a wood's relative hardness, but to the kind of tree from which it comes. Softwoods come from evergreens (conifers), hardwoods from broad-leafed (deciduous) trees.

Decks are generally built from softwoods. However, more economical offerings of hardwoods such as mahogany, angico, and plantation-grown teak (the boat builder's favorite) have recently entered the market.

**HEARTWOOD AND SAPWOOD.** A wood's properties are determined by the part of the tree from which it came. The inactive wood nearest the center of a living tree is called heartwood. Sapwood, next to the bark, contains the growth cells. Heartwood is more resistant to decay; sapwood is more porous and absorbs preservatives and other chemicals more efficiently.

Among heartwoods, the most decay-resistant and termite-proof species you can buy are redwood and cedar. This durability, combined with their natural beauty, makes them favorites for decking. On the other

hand, they are softer, weaker, and more expensive than ordinary structural woods such as Douglas fir and Southern pine. To get the best of both worlds, most professional designers use fir or another structural wood for a deck's substructure, but redwood or cedar for decking, benches, and railings. For any wood nearer than 6 inches to the ground or to concrete foundations, though, choose decay-resistant heartwood or pressure-treated wood (see facing page).

**GRADES.** Lumber is sorted and graded at the mill. Generally, lumber grades represent several factors: natural growth characteristics (such as knots); defects resulting from milling errors; and commercial drying and preserving treatments that affect strength, durability, and appearance.

The higher the grade, the better

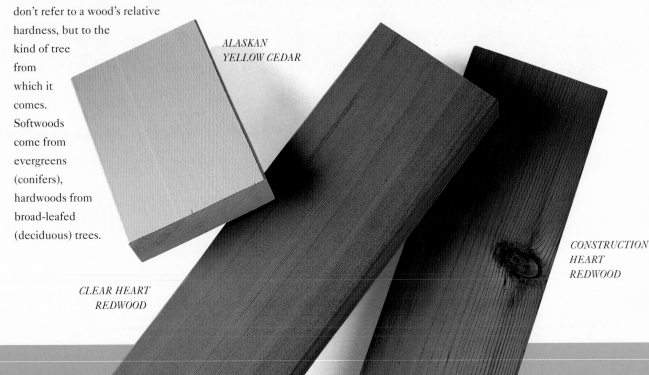

*ALASKAN YELLOW CEDAR*

*CLEAR HEART REDWOOD*

*CONSTRUCTION HEART REDWOOD*

the wood—and the more you will have to pay. One way to save money on your project is to choose the most appropriate grade (not necessarily the highest grade) for each element.

Redwood is usually graded for its appearance and for the percentage of heartwood versus sapwood it contains. Among pure heartwoods, Clear All Heart is the best grade, then B Heart, Construction Heart, and Merchantable Heart, in descending order.

Cedar grades, starting with the highest quality, are Architect Clear, Architect Knotty, and Custom Knotty. These grades don't indicate whether the lumber is heartwood or sapwood.

### ROUGH AND SURFACED LUMBER.

Most lumberyards handle both rough and surfaced lumber. Rough lumber tends to be available only in lower grades, with a correspondingly greater number of defects and a higher moisture content. Surfaced lumber, the standard for most construction and a must for formal decking, comes in nearly all grades.

### NOMINAL AND SURFACED SIZES.

Be aware that a finished "2 by 4" is not 2 inches thick by 4 inches wide. The nominal size of lumber is designated before the piece is dried and surfaced, so the finished size is smaller. Here are some examples:

> 2 by 3 = $1\frac{1}{2}$" by $2\frac{1}{2}$"
> 2 by 4 = $1\frac{1}{2}$" by $3\frac{1}{2}$"
> 2 by 6 = $1\frac{1}{2}$" by $5\frac{1}{2}$"
> 4 by 4 = $3\frac{1}{2}$" by $3\frac{1}{2}$"

You may also run across decking boards with thickness designated in fractions—for example, "$\frac{5}{4}$." This traditional hardwood term means "five-quarter" or a nominal $1\frac{1}{4}$ inches ($\frac{4}{4}$ would indicate a 1-inch thickness). The actual thickness of these surfaced boards is usually about $\frac{1}{4}$ inch less than the nominal measurement.

## Treated lumber

Though redwood and cedar heartwoods resist decay and termites, other woods that contact the ground or trap water may quickly rot and lose their strength. For this reason, less durable types such as Southern pine and Western hem/fir are often factory-treated with preservatives to protect them from rot, insects, and other sources of decay. These woods are generally less expensive and in many areas more readily available than redwood or cedar. They can be used for surface decking as well as for structural members such as posts, beams, and joists.

Working with treated lumber isn't always a pleasure. Compared with redwood and cedar, which are easy to cut and nail or screw, treated wood is often hard and brittle and more likely to warp or twist. Moreover, some people object to its typically greenish brown color (applying a stain can conceal it) and the staplelike incisions that usually cover it (some types come without these marks).

Because the primary preservative used contains chromium, a toxic metal, you should wear safety glasses and a dust mask when cutting treated lumber, and you should never burn it.

*MAHOGANY*

*ANGICO*

*PRESSURE-TREATED HEM/FIR*

## Deck hardware

Nails, screws, and deck clips secure your decking to the framing below. The fasteners you choose help create the strength of your finished deck and also affect its appearance.

**NAILS.** Box or common nails are used for most outdoor deck construction. Buy hot-dipped galvanized, aluminum, or stainless steel nails; other types will rust. In fact, even

*GALVANIZED BOX NAILS*

the best hot-dipped nail will rust in time, particularly at the exposed head, where its coating has been battered by a hammer.

A nail's length is indicated by a "penny" designation ("penny" is abbreviated as "d," from the Latin *denarius*). Most decking jobs are done with 8d (2½") and 16d (3½") nails.

*DECK SCREWS*

**DECK SCREWS.** Though more expensive than nails, coated or galvanized deck screws provide several advantages: they don't pop up as readily, their coating is less likely to be damaged during installation, and their use eliminates the possibility of hammer dents in the decking.

Choose screws that are long enough to penetrate joists at least as deep as

---

### NEW LUMBER ALTERNATIVES

Shrinking forests and dwindling supplies of quality lumber have encouraged the timely development of both environmentally sensitive wood products and engineered materials suitable for decks and other garden structures.

When it comes to lumber, you might consider woods other than the best grades of redwood and cedar, which generally come from the oldest trees. Instead, seek out plantation-grown woods or those from certified forests; or look for suppliers of salvaged lumber from orchards or demolished buildings.

Some manufacturers are also combining landfill-bound wood with waste plastic to produce so-called "wood-polymer composites." Though

not meant for structural purposes, these weatherproof products can be used for decking and railings. Available in several colors, they can also be painted or stained and cut,

drilled, and shaped like standard lumber. For families with young children, these synthetic boards have the additional advantage of being splinter-free.

*Made from recycled wood and plastics, new synthetic decking "boards" can stand in for traditional lumber.*

*DECK CLIPS*

the decking is thick (for 2 by 4 or 2 by 6 decking, buy 2½- or 3-inch screws).

**DECK CLIPS.** To keep fasteners from showing, you can use special deck-fastening clips. Nailed to the sides of decking lumber and secured to joists, these fasteners hide between deck boards. Deck clips also elevate boards off the joists a hair, discouraging the rot that wood-to-wood contact may foster. On the down side, clips are more expensive to buy and install than nails or screws.

## Deck finishes

There's no substitute for using decay-resistant wood like heart redwood or pressure-treated lumber in places where deck members come in contact with soil or are embedded in concrete. Applying a water repellent, a semi-transparent stain, or a solid-color stain can, however, protect other parts of a deck and preserve the wood's beauty.

Whatever product you choose, it's best to try it on a sample board before committing your entire deck to it. Always read labels: some products should not be applied over new wood; others may require the application of a sealer first.

**WATER REPELLENTS.** Also known as water sealers, these products protect

decking wood. Clear sealers won't color wood, but they darken it slightly. These products allow the wood to gradually fade to a neutral gray. You can buy them in either oil- or water-base versions. Many formulations include both UV-blockers and mildewcides. Some brands come in slightly tinted, dye-color versions.

Don't use clear surface finishes such as spar varnish or polyurethane on decks. They wear quickly and are very hard to renew. They're also expensive.

**SEMITRANSPARENT STAINS.** These contain enough pigment to tint the wood's surface but not enough to mask the natural grain completely. You can find both water- and oil-base versions. Usually one coat is sufficient. Besides stains in traditional gray and wood tones, you'll find products for "reviving" a deck's color or for dressing up pressure-treated wood.

**SOLID-COLOR STAINS.** These are essentially paints; their heavy pigments cover the wood's grain completely. You can usually get any available paint color mixed into a solid deck-stain base. But even though these products are formulated to withstand foot traffic, you'll probably have to renew them frequently.

*Deck finishes offer plentiful choices in color and protection. Shown at right, from top to bottom: unfinished redwood board; clear water sealer; tinted oil-base repellent; semitransparent gray stain; and red solid-color stain.*

# Brick

SET IN SAND OR IN MORTAR—EITHER WAY, IT'S A CLASSIC

Brick's use dates back at least 6,000 years. To make bricks, clay is mixed with water, then hand-molded or machine-extruded into traditional forms, then fired in a kiln. A rich palette of colors and a broad range of styles make brick a perennial favorite for garden paving.

Countless patterns can be created when designing with brick, and each one elicits a slightly different response. Six of the most popular are shown on the facing page.

## Brick types

Of the bewildering variety of bricks available, only two basic kinds are

*Brick samples range from machine-extruded common type (far left) to brand-new "used" bricks to hand-molded ones (far right). Color comes from the chemical composition of the clay and the firing method and temperature.*

used for garden construction: rough-textured common brick and smoother-surfaced face brick.

Most garden paving is done with common brick. People like its familiar, warm color and texture, and it's less expensive than face brick. Common brick is more porous than face brick and less uniform in size and color (common bricks may vary up to ¼ inch in length).

Face brick, with its sand-finished, glazed surface, is not as widely available as common brick. More often used for facing buildings than for paving, this brick is best reserved for elegant raised beds, attractive edgings, and other accents where its smoothness won't present a safety hazard.

In addition to the familiar orange-red, some manufacturers offer bricks in colors created by the addition of chemicals to the clay. Manganese can give a metallic blue tone. Iron pro-

duces a dark speckling. "Flashed" brick is fired unevenly to darken either its face (large surface) or edge.

Used brick has uneven surfaces land streaks of old mortar that can look very attractive in an informal pavement. Manufactured "used" or "rustic" bricks cost about the same as the genuine article and are easier to find. Firebricks, blond-colored and porous, provide interesting accents but don't wear well as general paving.

The typical brick is about 8 by 4 by 2⅜ inches thick. "Paver" bricks, which are made to use atop a concrete base, are roughly half the thickness of standard bricks. "True" (or "mortar-less") pavers are a uniform 4 by 8 inches (plus or minus ⅛ inch) and can be invaluable for laying a complex pattern with tightly butted joints. To calculate the exact amount of brick you'll need for a project, visit a building supplier first, measuring tape in hand.

All outdoor bricks are graded according to their ability to withstand weathering. If you live in a region where it regularly freezes and thaws, buy only bricks graded SW, which indicates they can withstand changing weather conditions.

## Sand or mortar?

Brick set in sand or rock fines (a mix of grain sizes) is casual-looking and less uniform than mortared brick, with more textural variation (for a construction detail, see page 581). This method allows percolation, which is important when installing a patio over tree roots. Bricks in sand can move around and may eventually have to be reset, but repairs are easier than with grouted bricks.

When set in mortar and grouted, brick has cleaner lines, which can give a design a more formal or contemporary look. The surface is easier to maintain and safer for walking in high heels, as long as joints are wider than ¼ inch. The grout becomes an important part of the design. Browns soften or blend with the pattern, whereas lighter colors, providing contrast, may emphasize it.

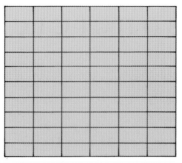

*JACK ON JACK*

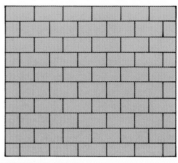

*RUNNING BOND*

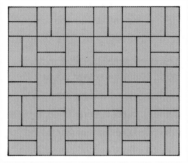

*BASKET WEAVE*

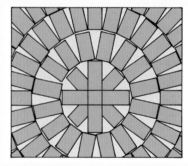

*HERRINGBONE*

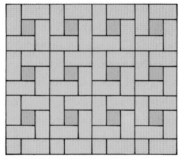

*PINWHEEL*

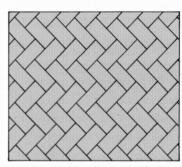

*WHORLED*

# Concrete

FLUID NEW SHAPES, EARTHY COLORS, AND SOFT TEXTURES

Though often unfairly dismissed as cold and forbidding, poured—or more accurately, cast—concrete is even more adaptable than brick. Used with the proper forms and reinforcement (see page 581), concrete can conform to almost any shape. It can be lightly smoothed or heavily brushed, surfaced with colorful pebbles, swirled, scored, tinted or painted, patterned, or molded to resemble another material. And if you get tired of the concrete surface later on, you can use it as a foundation for a new pavement of brick, stone, or tile set in mortar.

## Shopping for concrete

Strictly speaking, concrete is a mixture of portland cement, sand, aggregate, and water. Cement is what binds everything together and gives the fin-

ished product its hardness. The sand and aggregate (usually gravel) act as fillers and control shrinkage.

Buying bagged, dry, ready-mixed concrete is expensive but convenient, especially for small jobs. The standard 90-pound bag makes ⅔ cubic foot of concrete, enough to cover about a 16-inch-square area 4 inches deep.

If your project is fairly large, it pays to order portland cement, sand, and aggregate in bulk and mix them by hand or with a power mixer. Some dealers also supply trailers containing about 1 cubic yard of wet, ready-mixed concrete (about enough for an 8- by 10-foot patio). For larger-scale work, a commercial transit-mix truck can deliver enough concrete to fill large patio forms in a single pour.

Exact formulas of concrete vary from area to area, depending on local

climate, season, and materials. In areas with severe freeze-thaw cycles, you'll need to add an air-entraining agent to prevent cracking. Be sure to ask your supplier about the best formula for your needs. If you're using ready-mixed, figure about .37 cubic yards of concrete for every 10 cubic feet.

## Jazzing it up

Concrete pavings are typically given some type of surface treatment, both for appearance's sake and to provide traction.

You can wash or sandblast concrete to uncover the aggregate. Or embed colorful pebbles and stones in it (this finish, generally known as seeded aggregate, is probably the most popular contemporary paving surface). The addition of larger river rocks and fieldstones can also give new interest to a dull slab.

Other ways to modify standard steel-troweled concrete surfaces include color-dusting, staining, masking, sandblasting, acid-washing, and salt-finishing. A professional can also stamp and tint concrete to resemble stone, tile, or brick. Stamped patterns simulate either butted joints or open ones, which can then be grouted to look like unit masonry.

*A basic concrete recipe includes portland cement, sand, aggregate, and water.*

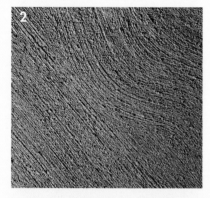

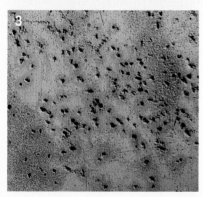

## Creating a softer look

Several techniques can allow concrete to be used pleasingly in a more casual environment. You can also leave planting pockets in a freshly poured slab, then fill them with soil and plants.

Or dig holes or shape curved forms and fill them with concrete. The resulting pads—with planting spaces in between—can be smoothed, textured, or seeded with aggregate.

*Shown above are six basic concrete finishes. Semismooth texture (1) is achieved with a wooden float. Broomed surface (2) is best where maximum traction is needed. Rock salt (3), exposed aggregate (4), and travertine (5) are three popular decorative finishes. Stone-tile pattern (6) is one of many stamping possibilities.*

## CONCRETE MAKE-OVERS

If you have a deteriorating concrete patio or driveway, you can either demolish it and build anew or, in some cases, give it a face-lift. Asphalt is usually best removed, but an existing concrete slab, unless heavily damaged, can serve admirably as a base for brick, pavers, tile, or stone. Another possibility is to construct a low-level deck over the slab.

Professionally applied solutions include the treatment of concrete with one of three methods: bonding, staining, or top-coating.

In bonding, a mixture of colored cement and a binder is sprayed over the entire surface. Then a design is created by the use of incised patterns or imitation grout lines.

Several companies offer chemical stains in a variety of colors that can be applied directly to the surface of an existing slab to give it a camouflaging patina.

One innovative top coat is made of ground-up bits of colored recycled rubber bonded together with a clear epoxy. Or you can cover the concrete with seeded aggregate. Or float on a new colored mix, which can then be stamped or textured.

# Concrete Pavers

NEWLY STYLISH, BUT STILL TOUGH ENOUGH FOR TRAFFIC

Available in many sizes, colors, and textures, concrete pavers are no longer limited to the ubiquitous 12-inch squares you've seen for years. Paver shapes now include circles, rectangles, triangles, and contours that interlock. Easily installed atop a packed sand bed (see page 581), pavers are an ideal choice for do-it-yourselfers.

## Paver possibilities

A simple square can be part of a grid or even a gentle arc. Squares or rectangles can butt together to create broad unbroken surfaces, or they can be spaced apart and surrounded with grass, a ground cover, or gravel for textural interest.

Interlocking pavers fit together like jigsaw puzzle pieces. Made of extremely dense concrete that is pressure-formed in special machines and laid in sand with closed (butted) joints, they form a surface more rigid than brick. No paver can tip out of alignment without taking several of its neighbors with it; thus, the surface remains intact even under very substantial loads. Interlocking pavers are available in tan, brown, red, and natural gray, plus blends of these colors.

Modern cobblestone blocks are very popular for casual gardens. Butt them tightly together and then sweep sand or soil between the irregular edges.

Turf blocks, a special paver variant, are designed to carry light traffic while retaining and protecting ground-cover

plants. These suggest the possibility of grassy patios and driveways, and can create side-yard access routes that stand up to wear.

Concrete "bricks," available in classic red as well as imitation used or antique styles, are increasingly popular as substitutes for the real thing, and in many areas cost significantly less.

## Shopping for pavers

Circles, squares, and rectangles can be found at most building and garden supply centers. Some interlocking shapes are proprietary, available only at a few outlets or directly from distributors. To locate these, check the yellow pages under "Concrete Products."

Some professionals cast their own pavers in custom shapes, textures, and colors—mimicking adobe, stone, or tile, for example.

Be cautious when choosing colored concrete pavers. The pigment in some is very shallow, and bare concrete may show through deep scratches or chips.

# HEATING IT UP

You may want to consider adding some type of heating device to your new patio or deck to take the edge off the weather and increase the hours and days you can spend outdoors.

A fireplace is one way to go. But using a patio heater is a quicker way to turn your outdoor room into a pleasant place to spend a brisk evening. You can buy a freestanding heater or install a more permanent gas or electric unit, which may prove more effective and less visible.

*A stainless steel mushroom heater (right), also known as an umbrella, radiates its warming rays from the top cylinder. A gas-fired directional heater (left) mounts to a house's eaves, allowing it to throw heat efficiently without being obtrusive.*

For a heating unit to perform well, you must place it in the right location. Shelter it from the wind. Pick a spot to heat that's intimate and comfortable. For extra warmth, place your heater near a wall or other solid structure so the heat can radiate back into your seating area.

Be sure to block any breeze at ground level so your feet won't get cold while you're sitting outside.

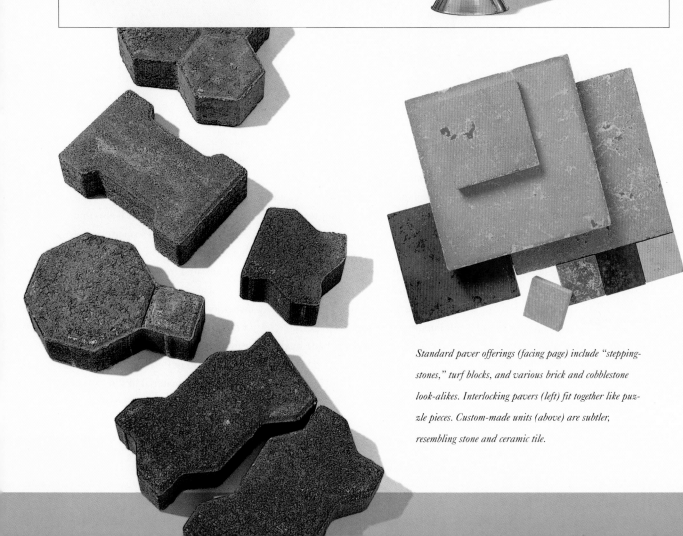

*Standard paver offerings (facing page) include "stepping-stones," turf blocks, and various brick and cobblestone look-alikes. Interlocking pavers (left) fit together like puzzle pieces. Custom-made units (above) are subtler, resembling stone and ceramic tile.*

# Ceramic Tile

TILE TURNS BLAND LANDSCAPES INTO LIVELY OUTDOOR ROOMS

Tile works well in both formal and informal garden situations. Its typically earthy tones blend with natural colors outdoors, and the hand-fired pigments are permanent and nonfading. Because tile looks great indoors, too, it's a good flooring choice for an indoor room that relates to a patio as well as for the patio itself.

Heavy tiles that are at least ¾ inch thick can be laid in a sand bed. However, the most stable bed for any tile is a 1-inch mortar bed over an existing concrete slab or a newly poured one (for details, see page 581).

## Glazed or unglazed?

Glaze is a hard finish, usually colored, applied to the clay surface before final baking. Most bright, flashy tiles you see in tile displays are glazed.

Unless a special grit is added to glazed tiles, they can make treacherous footing when wet. For paving, it's best to use unglazed tiles, reserving their shiny counterparts for occasional accents or for edgings or raised planting beds.

## Outdoor types

In cold climates, your tile choice must be freeze-thaw stable. So-called impervious and vitreous tiles, including quarry tiles and unglazed porcelain, are the best choices here. In milder climates, terra-cotta can hold its own.

*PORCELAIN PAVERS*

Porcelain pavers can be made to resemble slate, limestone, and other stones, but come in straightforward pastel colors, too. While many tiles are polished, more slip-resistant textures include split (resembling slate) and sandblasted surfaces and surfaces embossed with raised grids. Though 12-inch square pavers are standard, sizes range from 4- by 6-inch rectangles up through 24-inch squares.

Tough quarry tiles are made by the extrusion process (picture a giant pasta machine)—you can usually identify them by roller grooves on their backs. Though some quarry tiles are glazed, most come unglazed in natural clay colors of yellow, brown, rust, or red. Some exhibit "flashing," heat-produced shadings that vary from tile to tile. Typical sizes are 6 by 6, 8 by 8, and 12 by 12 inches. You'll also find some rectangles and a smattering of hexagons.

Translated from the Italian, terra-cotta means "cooked earth." But whether you see terra-cotta in antique French folk tiles, hand-formed Mexican slabs (known as Saltillo tiles), or rustic Italian or Portuguese wares, the charm of this material lies in its very lack of consistency. Terra-cotta tiles come as squares, rectangles, hexagons, and octagons, as well as in Moorish, ogee, and other interlocking shapes. These tiles are generally nonvitreous and highly absorbent, and so are questionable for outdoor use in cold climates.

## To seal or not to seal?

Some unglazed tiles are sealed at the factory. Unsealed, unglazed units such as terra-cotta and some quarry tiles need to be sealed for protection against surface water and stains.

Surface or top sealers offer the most resistance to stains but darken tiles and produce a sheen that you may or may not find appealing. These coatings must also be stripped and reapplied periodically.

Penetrating sealers soak into the tile instead of sitting on its surface. But they're not as protective as top sealers.

Sealer technology is changing all the time, and some proprietary formulas vary from region to region. Explain your intended use to a knowledgeable

local dealer and ask for a specific recommendation. Be sure to inquire about maintenance requirements.

Whatever sealer you select, it's best to test its appearance on a sample tile before you apply it to your entire patio.

*QUARRY TILES*

*TERRA-COTTA TILES*

# Stone

Stone pavings have the appeal of a thoroughly natural material, and most are very durable. Flat flagstones and cut stone tiles are both ideal for formal patios. For a more informal look, try setting irregularly shaped rocks and pebbles in mortar or directly in the soil.

## Flagstone

Technically, flagstone is any flat stone that's either naturally thin or split from rock that cleaves easily. The selection pictured below gives you an idea of the range of colors and textures available at masonry and building supply yards. Costs depend on where you live in relation to where the stone originates: the farther from the quarry, the higher the price. Expect to find natural color variations within each type of stone.

When selecting flagstone for outdoor paving, think of how it will be used. Formal entry and entertaining areas should be smooth surfaces, safely accommodating high heels. Patios that serve as sitting and dining areas also need a level surface for chairs and tables; select a stone with a fairly smooth surface. Also, some types of flagstones (notably sandstones) are porous and may be difficult to maintain under dining areas or near messy fruit trees. Some kinds can be slippery when wet.

Flagstones come in various thicknesses. The thinnest (also called

veneer) range from ¼ to ¾ inch thick, and should be laid on a stout, 4-inch-thick concrete slab. Thicker stones are typically laid in mortar atop a thinner concrete base (see page 581). Or, for a more casual look, consider setting stones in sand and adding plants between the joints.

## Stone tiles

Many stone types are available precut in rectangular shapes. Popular tiles include those made from slate, sandstone, granite, quartzite, limestone, travertine (a pitted limestone that may be "filled"), and adoquin (a dense volcanic stone).

Outdoor tiles must be slip resistant. Naturally textured stones, including split slates and sandstones, are traditional choices. Other attractive slip-resistant textures are achieved by tumbling, sandblasting, flaming, or resplitting stone tiles.

Like porous ceramic tiles, those made from soft stones, such as limestone, may need to be sealed to protect against staining and acid damage. Since sealant products are constantly changing, the best approach is to discuss your specific needs with a knowledgeable stone supplier.

Stone tiles are usually laid in mortar with very thin grout lines, which gives them a stylish, formal look. However, beefier tiles—those about 1 inch thick and thicker—can be set in sand.

## Other stones

Fieldstones, river rocks, and pebbles are less expensive than flagstone and

*You'll find a good selection of random-size flagstones at most masonry yards. We show some most often used, but offerings vary by region—and by supplier.*

*A sampler of stone tiles includes (clockwise from top): bluestone slate, flamed limestone, tumbled travertine, sandblasted quartzite, and Arizona sandstone.*

# Lighting Up the Night

Safety, security, and decoration—all three are functions of outdoor lighting, and all can be achieved with a good lighting scheme. The only restriction is the need to keep both glare and wattage at a low level.

## Low-voltage or standard current?

When it's time to light up your landscape, you can choose either a standard 120-volt system or a low-voltage scheme.

Because low-voltage lights are safer, more energy efficient, and easier to install than 120-volt systems, they have become increasingly popular outdoors. Such systems use a transformer to step down household current to 12 volts. Although low-voltage fixtures lack the "punch" of line-current fixtures, their output is sufficient for many outdoor applications.

The standard 120-volt system still has some advantages outdoors. The buried cable and metallic fixtures give the installation a look of permanence; light can be projected a greater distance; and 120-volt outlets accept power tools and patio heaters.

## Fixtures and bulbs

Outdoor fixtures range from well lights and other portable uplights to spread lights that illuminate paths or bridges to downlights designed to be anchored to the house wall, eaves, or trees.

Most outdoor fixtures are made of

*Low-voltage systems consist of transformer, timer, and easy connections to small cables run on or just below the surface. Compact, innovative fixtures include uplights, downlights, and step lights in many styles.*

bronze, cast or extruded aluminum, copper, or plastic. But you can also find decorative stone, concrete, porcelain, and wood fixtures (redwood, cedar, and teak weather best). Sizes vary. When evaluating fixtures, look for gaskets, high-quality components at joints and pivot points, and locking devices for aiming the fixtures.

Choose the bulb you want first and then the appropriate fixtures. Low-voltage halogen MR-16 bulbs are popular for accenting; PAR spotlights, available in both low and standard voltage, are best to light trees or wide areas.

## Less is best

Because the contrast between darkness and a light source is so great, glare can be a big problem at night. Three rules of thumb are: choose shielded fixtures; place fixtures out of sight lines; and lower overall light levels.

With a shielded light fixture, the bulb area is protected by an opaque covering that directs light away from the viewer's eyes. Instead of a hot spot of light, the eye sees the warm glow of the lighted object.

Place fixtures either very low (as along a walk) or very high. By doing

*COBBLESTONE*

*RIVER ROCKS*

that, you can direct them in such a way that only a play of light in the tree branches is noticed—rather than a bright glare. Use several softer lights strategically placed around the patio and yard rather than one harsh bulb.

A little light goes a long way at night. Twenty watts is strong, and even 12 watts can be very bright. If you're using line current, choose bulbs with a maximum of 50 watts.

On patios, low light levels are usually enough for conversation or dining areas. Add stronger lights for serving or barbecuing areas. Downlights are popular, but indirect lighting, diffused through plastic or another translucent material, is also useful.

Illuminating foliage can be an effective way to combine functional and decorative lighting. Decorative mini-lights help outline trees and lend sparkle to your landscape.

Strings of mini-lights are also useful for lighting steps, railings, and walkways. If your house has deep eaves or an overhang, consider placing weatherproof downlights there to conceal the fixtures while illuminating use areas.

Don't forget the view from inside. To avoid a black hole effect, try to balance light levels on both sides of a window or French doors. Use soft light in the foreground, build up the middle ground, and save the highest wattage for the background.

*120-volt lighting packs a bigger punch but requires beefier components and extra safety measures. Boxes and fixtures must be sealed from weather, and wires run via buried cable or in metal conduit.*

tile. These water-worn or glacier-ground stones form rustic pavings that make up in charm for what they lack in smoothness underfoot.

Smaller stones and pebbles can be either set in mortar or seeded into concrete. Large stones may be laid directly on the soil as raised stepping-stones. An entire surface can be paved solid with cobblestones set in concrete or tamped earth. Or use mosaic panels to break up an expanse of concrete, brick, or larger flagstones.

Some natural stones can become dangerously slick in wet weather. Because their shapes are irregular, they may be uncomfortable to walk on. It's best to confine such surfacing to a limited area.

# Loose Materials

TINY PIECES CAN ADD UP TO ONE BIG PATIO

*WOOD CHIPS*

*QUARTZ PEBBLES*

*RIVER ROCKS*

For economy, good drainage, and a more casual look, consider including materials such as pea gravel, wood chips, or even cocoa hulls in your patio plan.

You needn't opt for the large, boring expanses that give some aggregates a bad name. Gravel can be raked into patterns or employed as a decorative element with other paving materials. You might use dividers to set off different colors and textures. Buy loose materials by the bag (small jobs only), by the ton (gravel and other rocks), or by the cubic yard.

## Rock

Gravel is collected or mined from natural deposits. Crushed rock is mechanically fractured and then graded to a uniform size. If the surface of the rock has been naturally worn smooth by water, it's called river rock. Frequently, gravels are named after the regions where they were quarried.

When making a choice, consider color, sheen, texture, and size. Take home samples as you would paint chips. Keep in mind that gravel color, like paint color, looks more intense when spread over a large area.

Crushed rock compacts firmly to give stable footing on paths and walkways, but its sharp edges may hurt bare feet. Smooth river rock feels better, but tends to roll underfoot. Small river rock, also called pea gravel, is easiest to rake.

What about a glassier look? Paths or spaces between pavers may be filled with sparkling glass cullet, a gravel-like material that resembles fine beach pebbles. The glass, collected from recycled bottles, is crushed mechanically, then tumbled to smooth any sharp edges. The cullet comes in assorted colors—greens, deep amber, and clear.

## Bark and by-products

Leftovers from lumber mills, wood chips and bark are springy and soft underfoot, generally inexpensive, and easy to apply. You'll probably find a wide variety of colors and textures. To work successfully as patio surfaces (rather than as mulch, for which they are also sold), they must be confined inside headers.

Shredded bark, sometimes called gorilla hair, compacts well and is especially useful as a transitional covering between patio and plantings.

Other specialized commercial by-products appear in garden centers and nurseries according to regional availability. Fresh cocoa hulls, a current favorite among West Coast landscapers, smell so pungent that chocolate fiends may want to go back to brick or concrete just to get some peace.

*GORILLA HAIR*

*DECOMPOSED GRANITE*

*LAVA ROCK*

*COCOA HULLS*

# IDEAS FOR GREAT KITCHENS
## design credits

**FRONT MATTER**

4. Design: Brad Polvorosa. 6. Interior designer: Susan Christman. Cabinets: Phil Garcia Elements. 7. Interior designer: Lou Ann Bauer. Contractor: Robert Rosselli. Cabinets: Euro-Art Cabinet/Doug Lucchelli.

**CHAPTER ONE/
A PLANNING PRIMER**

8. Interior designer: Janice Stone Thomas/Stone•Wood Design, Inc. Architect: Forrar Williams Architects. 18. The Kitchen Source/ The Bath & Beyond. 19. Architect: Backen, Arrigoni & Ross. Cabinetmaker: Werner Schneider Construction. 20. Interior designer: Lou Ann Bauer. 21. Interior designer: Macfee & Associates Interior Design. 26: Interior designer: Marilyn Riding Design.

**CHAPTER TWO/
GREAT KITCHEN IDEAS**

28. Architect: Charles Rose. Interior designer: John Schneider. Kitchen designer: Sheron Bailey.

**High Style**

30. Interior Design: Miller/Stein. 31. Interior designer: Agnes Bourne, Inc. 32 (both). Design: J. Allen Sayles Architecture/Rutt of Lafayette and Tina Chapot. 33 (both). Architect: Remick Associates Architects-Builders, Inc. Interior designer: Donna White Interior Design. 34–35 (all). Design/contractor: City Building, Inc. 36 (both). Interior designer: Kremer Design Group. 37. Architect: Ellen Roche, Mojo Stumer Associates. 38. Architect: Jane Mah. Contractor: Steven Donaldson. 39. Architect: Colleen Mahoney/Mahoney Architects.

General contractor: Cove Contruction. 40. Janice Stone Thomas/Stone•Wood Design, Inc. 41. Janice Stone Thomas/Stone•Wood Design, Inc. 42. Interior designer: Judith Kenyon Burness. Tile artisan: Marlo Bartels Studio of Laguna Beach. 43. Architectural and interior designer: Lynn Hollyn. 44. Stove surround, countertops, fireplace: Euro-Stone. Wood island countertop: T.S. Milani. 45. Interior designer: Osburn Design. Architect: David Williams.

**On the Surface**

46. Design: Taylor Woodrow. 47. Design: Adele Crawford Painted Finishes. 48. Architect: Miller/Hull. 49. Architects: Hsin-Ming Fung and Craig Hodgetts. 50 top. Design: Joan Fulton. 50 bottom. Architect: Dennis DeBiase. 51. Interior designer: Steven W.

Sanborn. 52 top. Tile artisan: Rodger Dunham Ceramic Design of Petaluma. 53 bottom. Architect: Lindy Small. Concrete: Concreteworks Studio. 53. Interior designer: Macfee & Associates Interior Design.

**Storage Solutions**

54. Architect: Alison Wright Architects. 55. Architect: Robert Nebolon. 56. Interior designer: Lou Ann Bauer. Contractor: Robert Rosselli. Cabinets: Euro-Art Cabinet/Doug Lucchelli. 57 top. Stove surround: Euro-Stone. 57 bottom. Interior designer: Kremer Design Group. 58 top. Interior designer: Susan Christman. Cabinets: Phil Garcia Elements. 58 bottom. Design/contractor: City Building, Inc. 59. Interior designer: Steven W. Sanborn. 60 top: Janice Stone Thomas/Stone•Wood Design, Inc. 60 bottom (both). Architect: Heidi Richardson. 61. Architect: William E. Cullen.

**Bright Ideas**

62. Architect: Colleen Mahoney/Mahoney Architects. General contractor: Cove Contruction. 63. Architect: Robert Nebolon. 64. Architect: Mark Horton. 65. Architect: Marcy Li Wong. 66. Interior designer: Osburn Design. 67. Lighting designer: Melinda Morrison. Lighting design architects: Byron Kuth, Liz Ranieri, Doug Thornley (Kuth/Ranieri). 68. Architect: Marc Randall Robinson. Design: Epifanio Juarez/Juarez Design. Interior Architecture and Design: Scott Design. 69. Interior design and lighting: Margaret M. Wimmer. Architect: Carrasco & Associates.

**Elegant Options**

70. Architect: Steven Ehrlich. 71. Interior designer: Lou Ann Bauer. Contractor: Robert Rosselli.

Cabinets: Euro-Art Cabinet/Doug Lucchelli. 72 (both). Architect: Mulder/Katkov Architecture. 73. Interior designer: Osburn Design. 74–75 (all). Design: Nancy Cowall Cutler. 76 top. Interior designer: Steven W. Sanborn. 76 bottom, 77. Architect: J. Allen Sayles Architecture/Rutt of Lafayette. Interior designer: Sue Kahn.

## CHAPTER THREE/
## A SHOPPER'S GUIDE

78. Interior designer: Rick Sambol.

### Cabinets
81 (all). The Kitchen Source/The Bath & Beyond. 83 (4 drawers). The Kitchen Source/The Bath & Beyond. 86 (bottom). KitchenWorks.

### Countertops
87. The Plumbery. 86 (tile). Design: Esther H. Reilly. 89 (wood). The Kitchen Source/The Bath & Beyond. 89 (stainless). Designer: Osburn Design.

### Waterworks
90. Country Floors. 91 (stainless). The Plumbery. 91 (cast iron). Kohler Co. 91 (composite). The Plumbery. 91 (solid-surface). The Kitchen Source/The Bath & Beyond. 91 (vitreous). Kohler Co. 91 (copper). The Plumbery. 92 (top left, bottom). The Plumbery. 92 (top right). Delta Faucet Co. 93 (left, far right). The Kitchen Source/The Bath & Beyond. 93 (center). General Electric Co.

### Ranges, Cooktops, and Ovens
94. Architect: Remick Associates Architects-Builders, Inc. 95 (left). General Electric Co. 95 (right). Interior designer: Osburn Design. 96 (top). The Kitchen Source/The Bath & Beyond. 96 (induction). Designer: Barry Rowley/Carmel Kitchens & Baths.

97 (gas). The Plumbery. 97 (commercial). The Kitchen Source/The Bath & Beyond. 98 (top). Jenn-Air Co. 98 (bottom). The Kitchen Source/The Bath & Beyond. 99 (top). Miele Appliances, Inc. 99 (bottom). Architect: Morimoto Architects.

### Ventilation
100. Architect: Morimoto Architects. 99 (all). The Plumbery.

### Refrigerators
102 (both). Sub-Zero Freezer Co. 103 (left). KitchenAid, Inc. 103 (right). Interior designer: Lou Ann Bauer. Contractor: Robert Rosselli. Cabinets: Euro-Art Cabinet/Doug Lucchelli.

### Trash Talk
104. Rev-a-Shelf, Inc. 105 (top left). Miele Appliances, Inc. 105 (top right). Iron-A-Way, Inc. 105 (bottom). Design: Scott Strumwasser and Mahtash Rahbar/ Enclosures Architects.

### Flooring
106. Janice Stone Thomas/ Stone•Wood Design, Inc. 107 (resilient). Designer: Gary Hutton Design. 107 (ceramic). Architect: Remick Associates Architects-Builders, Inc. 107 (wood). Designer: Plus Kitchens. 107 (stone). Designer: Julie Atwood Design.

### Light Fixtures
110 (sconces, downlight, track). Architect: House + House of San Francisco. Interior designer: Osburn Design. 110 (strip). Interior designer: Rick Sambol.

### Design Credits
670. Interior designer: Claudia Bordin. 671. Architect: Remick Associates Architects-Builders, Inc.

## PHOTOGRAPHERS

Unless noted, all photographs are by Philip Harvey. Patrick Barta: 50 top. Glenn Christiansen: 89 (stainless). Grey Crawford: 50 bottom, 70 bottom, 105 bottom. Mark Darley: 65, 86 bottom. Delta Faucet Co.: 92 top right. Doug Dun: 19. Chris Eden: 48. General Electric Co.: 93 center, 95 left. Jamie Hadley: 55, 63, 64. Paul Harris: 54 bottom. Iron-A-Way, Inc.: 105 top right. Ken Jenkins: 86 top. Jenn-Air Co.: 98 top. KitchenAid, Inc.: 103 left. Kohler Co.: 91 (cast iron), 91 (vitreous). David Duncan Livingston: 21, 30, 53. Andrew McKinney: 38, 74–75. Miele Appliances, Inc.: 99 top, 105 top left. Norman A. Plate: 52 bottom, 60 bottom left, 60 bottom right, 110 bottom left. Rev-a-Shelf, Inc.: 104. Mark Samu: 37. Tim Street-Porter: 49. Sub-Zero Freezer Co.: 102 (both). John Vaughan: 95 right. Russ Widstrand: 89 bottom. Tom Wyatt: 47, 61, 88 bottom, 89 top, 94, 96 bottom left, 96 bottom center, 97 left, 107 (ceramic), 107 (wood).

# IDEAS FOR GREAT BATHROOMS
# design credits

## Tubs & Showers

200 (top). Jacuzzi Whirlpool Bath. 200 (bottom). The Bath & Beyond. 201 (top). Design: Harrison Design. Contractor: Lucas Construction. Marble fabricator: Boris Cobra. 201 (bottom). Interior designer: Lequita Vance-Watkins/adVance Design of Carmel. 202 (top). Architect: Remick Associates Architects-Builders, Inc. Interior designer: Gary Hutton Design Inc. 202 (bottom). Jacuzzi Whirlpool Bath. 203. Architect: Raymond L. Lloyd. Design: Michael Assum/Mark Twisselman. 204 (top). Architect: Remick Associates Architects-Builders, Inc. 204 (bottom). The Bath & Beyond. 205. The Bath & Beyond. 205 (spray-bar). Architect: Buff, Smith & Hensman. Designer: Schlesinger Associates.

## Toilets and Bidets

206. American-Standard, Inc. 207 (top). The Plumbery. 207 (bottom). The Bath & Beyond.

## Ventilation

208. Architect: Remick Associates Architects-Builders, Inc. 99 (top left and right). Architect: Remick Associates Architects-Builders, Inc. 209 (bottom). The Bath & Beyond.

## Flooring

210 (resilient). Designer: Gary Hutton Design. 100 (ceramic). Architect: Remick Associates Architects-Builders, Inc. 211(wood).Architect: Peter C. Rodi/Designbank. 211 (stone). Interior designer: Osburn Design. 211 (carpet). Designer: Diane Johnson Design.

## Wall Coverings

212. Ann Sacks Tile & Stone. 213 (top). Laura Ashley Inc. 213 (bottom). Architect: Remick Associates Architects-Builders, Inc

## Light Fixtures

216 (sconces). Architect: J. Allen Sayles. 216 (under-counter).

Interior designer: Marilyn Riding Design. 216 (downlight). Architect: House + House of San Francisco. Interior designer: Osburn Design. 216 (mirror lights). Interior designer: Osburn Design.

## Finishing Touches

218 (brab bars). Hewi, Inc. 218 (showroom). The Plumbery. 219. Architect: Carson Bowler/Bowler & Cook Architects. Design: Rainer Concepts Ltd.

## Design Credits

672. Interior designer: Susan Christman. Cabinetmaker: Phil Garcia Elements. 673. Architect: Morimoto Architects.

## PHOTOGRAPHERS

# IDEAS FOR GREAT GREAT ROOMS
# design and photography credits

# photography

Unless otherwise credited, all photographs are by **E. Andrew McKinney**.

# IDEAS FOR GREAT WINDOW TREATMENTS design credits

Interior designer: Dominique Sanchot Stenzel—La Belle France. Builder: Godby Construction, Inc. 497. Interior designer: Agnes Bourne, Inc.

**Versatile Shades**

498 (top). Interior designer: Richard Witzel & Associates. 498 (bottom). Interior designer: Tres McKinney of Laura Ashley. 499 (top). Interior designer: Dominique Sanchot Stenzel—La Belle France. Builder: Godby Construction, Inc. 499 (bottom). Interior designer: Richard Witzel/Richard Witzel & Associates. 500. Interior designer: Dianna V. 501 (middle right). Interior designer: Monty Collins Interior Design and Willem Racké Studio. 501 (bottom). Design: Layne Gray. 502–503. Interior designer: Richard Witzel & Associates. 503 (top). Interior designer: Amy Weaver of Weaver Design Group. Decorative painter: Page Kelleher. 503 (bottom). Interior designer: J. van Doorn Design.

**Billowy Clouds**

504. Interior designer: Lisa DeLong/DeLong Designs & Interiors. 505 (top). Interior designer: George Davis Interiors. 505 (bottom). Interior designer: Elizabeth Hill of Selby House Ltd. Window treatment: Rossetti & Corriea Draperies.

**Shutters and Shojis**

506. Design: Japan Woodworking & Design. 507 (top). Design: Summer House at One Ford Road, Newport Beach, by Pacific Bay Homes. 507 (bottom). Design: smith +noble windowware.

**Top Treatments**

508 (top). Interior designer: Claire L. Sommers/McCabe & Sommers Interiors. 508 (bottom). Window treatment: Sharon Williams. Furniture: Bellini for Babies & Children. Muralist: Janet White. 509. Interior designer: Colienne Brennan. 510. Interior designer: Leavitt/Weaver, Inc. 511. Interior designer: Richard Witzel & Associates. 512 (both). Interior designer: Janice L. McCabe/ McCabe & Sommers Interiors. 513. Interior designer: Tres McKinney of Laura Ashley. 514–515. Interior designer: Monty Collins Interior Design. 515. Interior designer: Geoffrey De Sousa/de sousa hughes. 516. Interior designer: Janice L. McCabe/McCabe & Sommers Interiors. 517 (top). Window treatment: Cindy Lorensen. 518. Window treatment: Rossetti & Corriea Draperies. 519 (top). Window treatment: Rossetti & Corriea Draperies. 519 (bottom). Interior designer: Elizabeth Hill of Selby House Ltd. Window treatment: Rossetti & Corriea Draperies.

**Pattern Play**

520 (top). Interior designer: Richard Witzel & Associates. 520 (bottom). Interior designer: Joan Neville Designs. 521: Interior designer: Lindsay Steenblock/ County Clare Design.

**Yellow Is Primary**

522 (left). Interior designer: Diane Kremer/Kremer Design Group. 523. Interior designer: Suzanne Tucker/Tucker & Marks. Architects: Hunt, Hale & Associates.

**Window Seats**

524 (top). Interior designer: Geoffrey De Sousa/de sousa hugh-es. 524 (left). Interior designer: Lindsay Steenblock/County Clare Design. 524 (bottom). Interior designer: Ann Davies Interiors. 525. Interior designer: Elizabeth Hill of Selby House Ltd. Window treatment: Rossetti & Corriea Draperies.

**Special Effects**

526–527 (all). Interior designer: Osburn Design. 528 (top). Interior designer: City Studios. 528 (bottom). Interior designer: J. van Doorn Design. 528–529. Interior designer: Paulette Trainor.

**Not Just for Windows**

530. Interior designer: Mel Lowrance. 530 (right and bottom). Interior designer: Ann Welch Design Group. 531 (both). Decorative painter: Peggy Del Rosario.

**A SHOPPER'S GUIDE**

532. Interior designer: Norm Claybaugh/Juvenile Lifestyles, Inc. Decorative artist: Rebecca. 533. Calico Corners.

**Windows**

534. Home Depot. 535 (top and middle). Dolan's.

**Fabric**

536–537. Calico Corners.

**Trims**

540–541 (bottom). Calico Corners. 541 (top). Design: Mary Cason.

**Hardware**

542. Conso Products Co., Rue de France (www.ruefrance@efortress. com), smith+noble windoware (www.smithandnoble.com). 543. Conso Products Co. 544 (top). Calico Corners. 544 (bottom). Rue de France, smith+noble windoware. 545. Conso Products Co., Ikea, Restoration Hardware (www.restorationhardware.com), smith+noble windoware.

**Ready-made Panels**

546. smith+noble windoware. 547 (top panel). Restoration Hardware.

**Shades**

550. Interior Designer: Elizabeth Hill/Selby House. 551 (top). The Roman Shade Co. 551 (bottom). smith+noble windoware, Maxwell Window Shades, San Francisco, The Roman Shade Co.

**Shutters and Shoji Screens**

552 (top). San Francisco Shutter Co. 553. Interior designer: Jan Higgins. Window treatment: Hana Shoji & Interiors.

**Blinds**

555, 556, 557 (bottom). smith+noble windoware. 557 (top). Beauti-Vue Products.

**A Word to the (Energy) Wise**

558. Window treatment: Muffy Hook.

**Top Treatments**

559 (top). Interior designer: Janice L. McCabe/McCabe & Sommers Interiors. 559 (bottom). Bracket: smith+noble windoware. Swag design and fabrication: Lynne Tremble. 560. Window treatment: Muffy Hook.

**DESIGN CREDITS**

676. Interior designer: Elizabeth Benefield. 677. Window treatment: Mara Rigel.

**PHOTOGRAPHERS**

Unless noted, all photographs are by E. Andrew McKinney.

Philip Harvey: 460, 490 (bottom), 491, 492, 494–495, 497, 509, 510, 522 (left), 526–527, 530 (all), 535 (bottom), 552 (bottom), 558, 560. Colin McRae: 549. John O'Hagan: 457 (left). Tom Wyatt: 471 (bottom).

# IDEAS FOR GREAT PATIOS & DECKS design credits

Landscape architect: Jeffrey B. Glander & Associates.

**The Outdoor Kitchen**

634. Landscape architect: Ransohoff, Blanchfield, Jones, Inc. 635. Landscape architect: The Berger Partnership. Pizza oven: Authentic Stone & Brickwork. 636 (top) and 637. Hardscape: Southwinds Landscaping & Pools. Softscape: Roger's Gardens. 636 (bottom). Design: David Squires.

**A Splash of Water**

638. Architect: Steven Ehrlich Architects. 639. Landscape architect: Michael Kobayashi/MHK Group. Additional design: American Landscape, Inc. 640. Architect: Churchill & Hambelton Architects. 641 (top). Tile artisan: Tina Ayers/Graphics in Tile. Landscape designer: Proscape Landscape Design. Interior designer: Thomas Bartlett Interiors. 641 (bottom). Landscape designer: Roger's Gardens. 642. Designers: Roger Fiske and Margo Partridge 643 (top). Architect: Olson Sundberg Architects. 643 (bottom). Landscape architect: Jeff Stone Associates of La Jolla.

**Finishing Touches**

644. Landscape designer: Schlegel Landscapes of Carmel. 645. Design: Steve Adams/Adams Design Associates. 646 (bottom). Architect: Morimoto Architects. 647 (top). Lighting designer: Randall Whitehead/Light Source. 647 (bottom). Architect: Backen, Arragoni & Ross. 88 (top left). Design: Jean Manocchio/Belli Fiori. 648 (top right). Landscape architect: Richard William Wogisch. 648 (center right). Design: Bud Stuckey. 648 (bottom left). Design: Kent Gordon England. Construction: Whitehill Landscape. 649. Landscape architect: Mary Gordon.

**A SHOPPER'S GUIDE**

650. Landscape architect: The Berger Partnership. 655 (top center). Deck clips: Deckmaster. 659 (bottom right). Landscape architect: Neil Buchanan/Glen Hurst & Associates. 661 (bottom right). Buddy Rhodes Studio. 662 and 663 (top). Galleria Tile. 663 (bottom). Fireclay Tile. 665 (top). ASN Natural Stone of San Francisco. 666 and 667 (bottom left). City Lights, Illumination Sales Corporation.

**DESIGN CREDITS**

678. Design: Artistic Botanical Creations. 679. Landscape designer: Scott Cohen/The Green Scene.

**PHOTOGRAPHERS**

Unless noted, all photographs are by Philip Harvey.

Scott Atkinson: 564, 575 (top), 590, 598, 632, 644, 649, 654 (bottom), 95 (right). Peter Christiansen: 664–665 (bottom). Glenn Cormier: 606 (bottom). Art Gray: 636 (bottom). Ken Gutmaker: 62 (bottom). Lynne Harrison: 633 (top). David Hewitt/Anne Garrison: 586, 620 (top), 621. James Frederick Housel: 609. Mark Luthringer: 646 (top). Allan Mandell: 633 (bottom). David McDonald: 597 (top). Jack McDowell: 659 (1–5). Owen McGoldrick: 645. Richard Nicol: 589, 591 (bottom), 603, 610. Gary W. Parker: 623, 624 (bottom). Norman A. Plate: 648 (all), 661 (top left and top right). Richard Ross: 594 (bottom right). Phil Schofield: 608 (top right). Tim Street-Porter: 594 (top). Dominique Vorillon: 616. Darrow M. Watt: 656–657 (bottom). Alan Weintraub/Arcaid: 638 (bottom). Tom Wyatt: 639, 668–669.

# IDEAS FOR GREAT TILE
## design credits

**PPhotographers:**
Unless noted, all photographs are by **Philip Harvey**.

**Alexis Andrews:** 403 bottom. **Peter Christiansen:** 414. **Saxon Holt:** 420. **Christopher Irion:** 429. **Muffy Kibby:** 381 top. **David Duncan Livingston:** 374 bottom; 386 bottom; 403 top. **Norman Plate:** 423. **Tim Street-Porter:** 372; 382 top. **Lanny Provo:** 430 bottom. **Richard Ross:** 418 bottom. **Alan Weintraub:** 364. **Russ Widstrand:** 375 **Tom Wyatt:** 351 top; 434 top.

**Photo credits/product shots:**
**ASN Natural Stone:** 448–449 all; 450 top and bottom; 451 top. **Country Floors:** 359 top right; 360 top left; 368 right; 374 top; 438 top right; 439 top left; 443 top right; 447 right. **Rodger Dunham Ceramic Design of Petaluma:** 373. **Fireclay Tile:** 349; 355 358; 359 lower right; 360 top center and bottom right; 404 top; 437 bottom; 438–439 bottom right; 439 far right; 440–441 all; 444 bottom. **Fireclay Tile/ Galleria Tile:** 345; 446; 447 left. **Galleria Tile:** 436; 437 top right; 438 bottom left; 444 top and center. **Galleria Tile/Tile Visions:** 451 bottom left; 452 top left. **Oceanside Glasstile:** 388 top; 110 bottom. **Osburn Design/ASN Natural Stone:** 369; 451 right. **Laird Plumleigh/ Alchemie Ceramic Studio:** 357 top; 359 center right; 418 top; 442–443 center top. **Buddy Rhodes Studio:** 453. **ANN SACKS Tile & Stone:** 346 top; 351 bottom; 357 bottom; 359 bottom right; 360 bottom center; 361 bottom left and bottom right; 434 bottom; 435 bottom; 442 top left and bottom right; 445 top left and bottom left; 452 top right. **Diane Swift:** 350 top left; 368 top left; 442 bottom left; 443 bottom right. **Tile Visions:** 443 bottom left..

# cover and front matter credits

**Front cover:**
Top: Photography: Emily Minton; Interior design: Karen Graul; Kitchen design: Kirk Craig; Architect: Kurt Archer
Bottom from left: (A) Photography: Courtesy of Ann Sacks Tile & Stone. (B) Photography: Ralph Bogertman; Interior design: Linda Lee Design Associates; Stylist: Susan Piatt. (C) Photography: Delta Faucet Co. (D) Photography: Courtesy of Smith + Noble Windoware

**Back cover:**
Top left: Photography: John Granen; Architect: SkB Architects, Seattle
Top right: Photography: Courtesy of Smith + Noble Windoware
Bottom left: Photography: John Granen; Design: John Kenyon, Sundance Landscaping
Bottom right: Photography: Courtesy of Ann Sacks Tile & Stone

**Page 1:**
Photography: George Ross; Stylist: Susan Piatt

**Page 2:**
Photography: George Ross; Stylist: Karin Strom

**Page 3:**
Photography: Sylvia Martin; Design: Mary McWilliams

# index

Page numbers in **boldface** refer to photographs